The Basic College Writer

PETER CARINO

Indiana State University

SCOTT, FORESMAN/LITTLE, BROWN HIGHER EDUCATION

A Division of Scott, Foresman and Company

Glenview, Illinois   London, England

Acknowledgments for copyrighted materials not credited on the page where they appear are listed in the Acknowledgments section beginning on page 345. This section is to be considered a legal extension of the copyright page.

A separate *Instructor's Edition: The Basic College Writer* is available through a Scott, Foresman sales representative or by writing the Scott, Foresman English Editor.

Library of Congress Cataloging-in-Publication Data

Carino, Peter.
    The basic college writer / Peter Carino.
       p. cm.
    Includes index.
    ISBN 0-673-38078-5
    1. English language—Rhetoric. I. Title.
PE1408.C29565   1990
808′.042—dc20   89-10294
ISBN 0-673-47381-3, Instructor's Edition   CIP

1 2 3 4 5 6-MVN-94 93 92 91 90 89

Preface

Instruction in *The Basic College Writer* rests on two premises. First, writing is best taught as a process leading to a definite goal—a letter, a paragraph, an essay, and so on. The book presents the writing process to students, showing them in the first chapter the way experienced writers write and asking them to begin developing processes of their own. While the writing process is divided into parts—invention, drafting, revising, and editing—the text recognizes that the process is also recursive, that the parts overlap. In addition, the coverage of the process is flexible, recognizing from the start the idiosyncracies of individual writers and encouraging students to develop their own best methods for writing from those presented in the text. Second, this book strongly endorses, implicitly and explicitly, the notion that reading and writing are interrelated processes of making meaning, that learning to write well requires learning to read well.

These two premises govern the organization of the text, which can be divided into three major units. Chapters 1–5 teach students to write personal experience essays using the readings as prompts and models. Chapters 6–9 provide instruction in reading and academic writing. Chapter 10, on editing, serves as a handbook to which students can refer throughout the course. Chapter 1 spotlights writing as process, and other chapters maintain this emphasis as students move from personal writing to more academic writing. Thus, students learn to apply what they know from writing about their own experiences to writing about the ideas, arguments, and experiences of others in progressively more challenging topics.

In introducing students to writing as a process, Chapter 1 examines the way considerations, such as role, purpose, and audience affect the writing process. Chapter 2 discusses the purposes of and provides practice in choosing between general and specific language. Chapters 3 and

4 highlight essays and prargraphs, grounding both in the writing process. Chapter 5 focuses on revision, reinforcing and previewing the references to revision throughout the text. Chapter 6 offers strategies and exercises to increase reading comprehension and speed. Chapter 7 provides students with the instruction and practice in paraphrasing, summarizing, and using quotations they will need to write the source essays covered in Chapters 8 and 9. Chapter 10 concentrates on standard English in its proper context among other forms of English. This chapter helps reduce students' fear of error, eschewing grammatical jargon as much as possible for simple explanations and practical exercises.

The *Basic College Writer* contains the following special features:

1. The language is purposely accessible and the tone friendly, offering analogies from common areas of experience to explain difficult concepts and presenting instruction in a style that is conversational but not condescending.
2. Key terms are in bold type, followed by definitions and a handy glossary in the margins, affords students easy references to the terms.
3. Though student writing should be central to any skills course, numerous exercises make the various aspects of the writing process more manageable and familiar. Many of these exercises function in sequence, leading students through the process to write particular essay types. Others require students to apply principles of good writing in their drafts and revisions.

To trace the many lines of influence that have shaped my thinking as a teacher and textbook writer would be impossible, so I will offer thanks to those who must remain unnamed. There are many, however, who can and should be recognized for their contributions. First and foremost, I would like to thank Anne Smith and Patricia Rossi of Scott, Foresman—Anne for her confidence and encouragement in the book's initial stages and throughout the project; Tisha, for her careful reading and astute suggestions; both for their pleasantness and good humor. I am also indebted to the following reviewers: Audrey Elwood, Merritt College; Sallyanne Fitzgerald, University of Missouri–St. Louis; Chris Fracas, Central Piedmont Community College; Maxine Hairston, University of Texas at Austin; Martin McKoski, University of Akron; Renata Schmitt, Merritt College; and Ted Schoenbeck, Cleveland State University. Their careful reading and commentary at various stages of the manuscript helped me to think and rethink my purpose and approach in response to the perspectives of experienced and talented teachers. Of course, it would be impossible to overestimate my debt to the many students whose writings appear throughout the text and the many more whose comments and suggestions on earlier drafts helped make it better than it ever could have been. Finally, I would like to thank friends and family members whose patience, sympathy, and encouragement were much appreciated at times when I was more consumed with the project than reason should allow.

P. C.

To the Student

Each day, millions of people across the country write. Businesspeople write letters and memos, scientists write reports, teachers write lesson plans and learning aids, police officers write arrest reports, doctors and nurses write progress reports on patients, students of all ages write papers for school, and many other people write letters and diaries. Although these people may not be famous writers, they are still writers—they put words on paper with the purpose of communicating to other people.

More than likely you too are already a writer, though you may not feel you are an experienced and skillful one. If you have just finished high school, you can probably remember doing some writing there. If you are entering college after having been out of high school for a while, you may have difficulty remembering what you wrote back then, but you probably wrote. Since high school, you may have occasionally composed a letter, either to a friend or for personal business. If you have been working, perhaps your job required some writing, and you may have kept a diary at some time in your life. Take a rest from reading for a minute, and try to remember anything you have written, in or out of school. How did you feel about organizing your words to express your ideas? Was it difficult? Did you like what you wrote?

Writing is difficult. There's no way around that. The prospect of writing may make you anxious or even downright scared, but the readings, exercises, and assignments in *The Basic College Writer* can help make writing easier and more enjoyable. You will learn to develop a process for writing that can lead to successful products in your English classes and other classes you take. In addition, you can increase your confidence as a writer and your control over what you write. In short, you can gain power over your writing. When you do, writing assignments will no longer provoke the anxiety and fear they once did. Good luck!

P. C.

Contents

■ CHAPTER 2

General Versus Specific Writing   32

■ CHAPTER 3

Writing Essays   48

■ CHAPTER 4   **Writing Paragraphs**   **86**

■ CHAPTER 5   **Revision**   **117**

■   ## Acknowledgments   345

■   ## Index   347

CHAPTER 1

Writing as Process

Writing can range from short notes stuck on a refrigerator to encyclopedias written in many volumes. But we can think of most writing in two ways: as a *product* and as a *process*. When students say their writing is good or their writing is bad, often they are talking about their written products — completed pieces of writing. To know whether their writing is good or bad, they must have finished it and received comments and responses on it from friends, classmates, relatives, or teachers.

The completed piece of writing — the product — is important because it is all the reader has. It must communicate clearly to the reader the writer's purpose and message. The writer is not usually available to answer any questions the reader might ask. The product will also make an impression — good or bad — on the reader.

In contrast to the written product, the **writing process** is the activity writers go through, from start to finish, that results in the product. Students who say their writing is good or bad rarely are referring to the process of writing; instead, they usually are judging their products. But what these students do not realize is that the quality of the **product** depends a great deal on the quality of the process. If the product is bad, probably the writer's process was bad too. Most likely, the process is bad because the writer does not know much about the process.

Inexperienced writers usually ignore the process of writing and think only of the product. As a result, they think that they cannot learn to write well. Inexperienced writers often think that good writers just sit down, write their ideas, and when they are finished, by some miracle of talent, their written work is clear, organized, and free of error. When inexperienced writers sit down to write, they try to write the same way they think good writers do — by just sitting down and writing. Inexperienced

Writing process: The writing process includes all the activities that produce a piece of writing, a product. The parts of the process are invention, drafting, revision, and editing, and they occur sometimes step by step and sometimes simultaneously.

Product: The completed piece of writing that results from the writing process.

writers begin by staring at a blank page and thinking. Then they write a sentence or two, crumple up the paper, and start over again. They do this three, four, five, or ten times, and begin to break out in a sweat. Then they try again. By this time they are so frustrated and angry that they don't care how the writing sounds or whether they are getting their ideas down clearly; they just want to get finished. So they keep writing, maybe crossing out a word or sentence here and there. Then they neatly copy over their papers, and that's what they call the final products.

I know about this approach to the writing process because I used it in high school and in my early writing in college. I called it the "crumple and sweat" method of writing. Many freshmen writers have told me that they have used the same method. Fortunately, these students learned better ways to go about the writing process and have saved a lot of sweat and paper.

■ How Do Writers Write?

Experienced writers write well for these reasons: First, they have mastered a process for planning, drafting, revising, and editing their writing. Second, experienced writers are aware of the writing situation; that is, they have an aim or purpose in writing, and they know for whom they are writing.

Process

Every writer has his or her own process; there are different ways to make the product. Some processes are good, and some — like the crumple and sweat approach — are bad. Though the processes of experienced writers may differ somewhat, if the process is effective, it usually contains four elements: invention, drafting, revision, and editing.

Invention Simply defined, *invention* is the part of the process during which the writer comes up with ideas to write about. Because a lot of invention takes place before the writer begins writing, invention is sometimes called prewriting. Invention involves everything from thinking about the topic to be written while waiting for a bus; to writing down lists of ideas; and to coming up with ideas that occur in writing a first draft. Later sections of this chapter present a number of strategies for invention.

Drafting *Drafting* is the part of the process in which writers begin to write the sentences and paragraphs that make up the paper. Inexperienced writers usually begin with drafting. That's why writing can be difficult for them. Experienced writers, however, having come up with many ideas in the invention part of the process, have an easier time in the drafting stage.

Revision   You have probably heard the word *revision* before, but you probably have not thought much about it. Notice that it contains the word *vision*. In its most exact sense, the word *revision* means "re-seeing." When writers revise, they re-see their drafts and make changes. These changes are often major ones: adding paragraphs, taking out paragraphs, changing the order of the paragraphs, adding or taking out whole sentences, rewriting sentences to make them smoother, changing words, and so on. Writers revise, in other words, to improve the content (what they are saying) and the style (how they are saying it) of their writing.

Editing   *Editing* is the part of the process in which the writer checks for correctness. As editor, the writer makes sure that words are spelled correctly and that errors in grammar are corrected. Beginning writers often confuse editing with revision, but revision can involve major changes of content and style, while editing involves only small changes for correcting errors.

Sometimes these parts of the process are discussed as steps or stages that a writer goes through. In a way they are steps. You should start with invention to come up with ideas to write about. Once you have completed a first draft, you usually need to do some revision. Before you write or type a final copy, you go over it to correct any errors you find. In this way, the process does go along step by step.

However, often the parts of the process overlap and occur at the same time. Let's look at some examples. Suppose you are drafting a paper, and you realize that you have misspelled a word or made a punctuation error. When you stop to correct this error, you are editing. Or suppose you have made a lot of notes before writing, and you think you have all your ideas in order. But as you are drafting your paper, you come up with other ideas even though coming up with ideas is usually part of invention. Similarly, although you revise after completing a draft, you might make some major changes in sentences and paragraphs as you are drafting. As you can see, the writing process does not always proceed step by step. In fact, it can get quite messy.

It is important to understand how the parts of the writing process fit together. First, if you lack writing experience, you may not realize that writing is a process. Second, you may have heard about the parts of the process in high school, but you may think they should always work step by step. Some students believe that they are not following a process because once they start writing, all the parts run together. That's OK. Other students write well but believe that they are not good writers because they have to go through so many messy steps. If an instructor asks to see their notes or drafts, they may become embarrassed because the notes and drafts contain scratched-out words and sentences or words and sentences added between the lines. However, these students are writing as they should. Yet, they see themselves as poor writers because they do not know that, except for a few extremely talented people, most good writers have to go through these messy steps too. The writing process may be messy, but, in the end, it makes you a better writer. And the best thing about the process is that it can be learned.

In most writing, the reader never sees the process. The writer writes alone, and the reader reads the finished product. In many writing classes, however, you can get help during the process. You can discuss notes for invention with your instructor or have the instructor go over your rough draft with you without worrying about how messy the draft looks. Or perhaps your instructor will have you and your classmates read one another's drafts and comment on them.

There will be more about the parts of the writing process later in this chapter. Let us turn now to another element of writing that good writers are aware of: the writing situation.

The Writing Situation

Writing is produced as the result of situations. A doctor, for instance, refers a patient to a specialist and writes a brief report of the patient's illness so that the specialist knows how to deal with the patient. A high school teacher writes a letter of recommendation for a student to a college admissions director. A college student writes a term paper for a history course. In each case, writing is produced as the result of a situation that requires writing. Also, the writer has a particular role, a purpose for writing, and a specific audience (a reader or readers) in mind. Whether you are a beginner or a professional, when you write, your role, your purpose, and your audience make up the parts of the **writing situation.** Before we examine these parts of the writing situation, we will look at how they affect the language of your writing.

Writing situation: The circumstances in which something is written and in which the writer determines a purpose for communicating with an audience and a role in relation to the audience.

Formal Versus Informal Language   All the elements of the writing situation — your role, purpose, and audience — determine how formal or informal your language will be. Formal language shows a serious attitude toward all three elements. For example, a psychiatrist reporting on a patient to another psychiatrist might write: "Philip North, a seventy-year-old male, suffering manic depression and chronic delusions, was institutionalized." In contrast, the patient's unsympathetic neighbor might say to another: "I hear that crazy Phil was carted off to the booby hatch." Unlike the psychiatrist, who is communicating seriously about something considered serious by his or her audience, the neighbor's language is informal to the point of sarcasm.

Of course, language cannot always be classified as either formal or informal because there are degrees of formality and informality depending on the situation. In a job interview, for example, you would not speak so formally as to make yourself sound stuffy, but neither would you speak as informally as you do in a casual and familiar situation with a friend. The same is true of writing. As we discuss the elements of the writing situation, notice how the situation helps determine the language.

Who Are You? The Writer's Role   You play many roles in your life. You are a student, perhaps a wife or husband, perhaps a boyfriend or girlfriend, perhaps a worker, perhaps a son or daughter. In using the term

Role: The writer's relation to his or her readers. The writer's role can be friend, teacher, student, citizen, consumer, and others, depending on the purpose.

role this way, we are not talking about anything phony. An actor *plays* a role in a movie, but you cannot have a role that you are not. For instance, if you are not in school, you do not have the role of student. If you are not married, you do not have the role of wife or husband.

Whatever roles you have, you use them as you write, and they affect the way you write. If you write a paper for a science class, you do not use slang words because in your role as student you know that using slang will not get you a good grade. If you write a letter to a friend, you write casually, much as you speak; and you avoid formal language because in your role as friend, you know that your reader expects you to be casual and familiar. If you write a letter to your mayor about the terrible potholes in your neighborhood, you will probably be forceful in your role as dissatisfied citizen. You probably will not curse because as a citizen you know that civic matters are not discussed in curse words even when people are angry.

In any writing situation, it is wise to define your role. Sometimes this can be difficult if you are not used to the role. For instance, as a beginning college student, you may wonder how you should sound in that role. Sometimes students think they should use all the big words they know and write long, fancy-sounding sentences. It is fine to draw on your vocabulary, but don't use big words if you are unsure what they mean and if a less fancy word would get the point across more clearly. Don't go out of your way to make your sentences long, but combine them when you find they are so short that the writing sounds choppy or childish. And, of course, try to correct as many grammar problems as you can, because in the role of college student, you will be expected to write correctly.

Why Are You Writing? The Writer's Purpose When asked why they are writing, students often say they write because their instructor asked them to and because they need to do well in the course. Whether the person is an instructor or a boss, satisfying someone who asks you to write can certainly be part of your purpose. However, that's not the most important **purpose** in writing.

Purpose: The reason a writer writes: to provide information, to display knowledge, to entertain, to instruct or persuade an audience, to ask for something.

As a writer, you should know what effect you want your writing to have on your reader. Do you want to tell a story to entertain someone? Do you want the reader to solve a problem for you? Do you want to persuade the reader that he or she should do something you want? Do you want to tell someone how to do something? Do you want to explain how something works? Do you want to show someone what you know about a subject?

You should keep the question of your purpose clearly in mind throughout the writing process, since your purpose, like your role, will influence the way you write. In writing to the mayor about potholes in your neighborhood, your purpose would probably be to persuade the mayor to have the street fixed. Keeping this purpose in mind, you would give examples of how bad the potholes are and what kinds of problems they have caused you and your neighbors. Your purpose would also determine your language, much as your role does. Though you might be very angry about the potholes, you would not curse or be sarcastic because that would anger the mayor, and you know that people who are angry with you usually will not do things for you.

Who Is Reading Your Writing? The Writer's Audience   Simply defined, your **audience** is the reader or readers of your paper. In a writing class, this is not always true. Sometimes your instructor may ask you to write a paper for an audience of fellow students. Though your instructor will read the paper, he or she may evaluate it in terms of how well it would communicate to other students.

You need to ask yourself three questions about your audience: (1) Who are the members of the audience? (2) What are the audience's attitudes toward what you are writing? (3) How is the audience going to use your writing? These questions seem simple enough, but they raise other questions. Let's take each question one at a time and see what other questions it leads us to.

Who is your audience? In all writing situations, you know something about the members of your audience, and in some situations you will know your audience better than in others. In a letter to a friend or relative, you know the audience intimately. In a paper for psychology class, you know the professor, but not in the same way you know a friend or relative. If you write a paper in a writing class and you are assigned to write for fellow students, you know some things about students as a group, though what you know may not be true of every student. Even if you write a letter to a company or government agency and begin it with "To Whom It May Concern," you know that someone who reads it will take care of the matter covered in the letter.

When writers forget about their audience, they usually write as if they are writing to someone *exactly* like themselves. Because no two people are exactly alike, the writer can fail to communicate. Indiana State University, for instance, which is located in the central part of the state, attracts students from both northern and southern Indiana. In their writing, students from the north refer to Indiana State as "down here," and students from the south are likely to write, "up here." In both cases, the students are writing as if everyone is like them. The lesson to be learned is that the writing won't communicate if you don't say something in a way that means the same thing to your reader as it does to you. For these students, a simple remedy would be to write "Indiana State" because all of them know what that means.

For many writers, even experienced ones, it is a common problem to write as if readers are just like them. In addition to using terms the audience might not know, writers often assume wrongly that the audience knows as much as they do about their topic. Some student athletes, for example, write about their sport as if any reader knew as much about it as they do. Some students write about their hometowns as if the reader knows the town as well as they did. Students will write about something they have learned in another course as if the reader took the course too

Audience: The readers of a piece of writing. Audiences have values and needs that the writer must consider if the audience is to be able to use the writing in the way the writer intends.

and knows all that the writers do. If you know that your reader does not know as much about a subject as you do, then you need to explain your subject in more detail and in simpler terms. For instance, an essay written for Americans about high schools in England would have to explain how students are divided into college-bound and non-college-bound groups because these groups are chosen differently from the way they are in America. However, if the essay were written for people in England, this explanation would not be necessary.

What are your audience's attitudes toward what you are writing? A relationship always exists between writer and audience. Part of this relationship comes from the reader's attitudes toward what the writer is saying. Because these attitudes can vary, you, as writer, need to raise questions about them. Will the audience be friendly and receptive toward what you are saying, inclined to agree? Will the audience be hostile, inclined to disagree? Will the audience be neutral? Given your purpose, these can be important questions. For example, in writing to the mayor to get the potholes fixed, you may know that the mayor does not like to spend money unless a situation absolutely requires it. Therefore, you will have to show clearly that the potholes are a danger to public safety. If you know that the mayor will gladly spend money to keep the city in good shape, your letter may not have to be as convincing.

You already are familiar with this feature of audience from your daily encounters with others. If you needed to borrow some money and you had one friend who was generous with money and another who was stingy, you probably would use two different approaches in asking each friend for the money. With the stingy friend, you might go into more detail about how, and how soon, you would repay the loan.

How is your audience going to use your writing? Just as writers write for a purpose, readers read for a purpose. The reader's purpose may be general, as is the case when someone reads the newspaper to be informed. Or the reader's purpose may be very specific, as is the case when someone reads a recipe for baking a cake or directions for building a doghouse. Readers *use* writing. If you read a book of jokes, you are using the book to entertain yourself. The mayor will use the letter about potholes to make a decision. A history professor reading an examination will use the writing to evaluate a student's knowledge of history.

As a writer, you need to consider what the audience needs to know to use the writing the way you want it used. In the letter about the potholes, before deciding to spend city funds, the mayor needs to know exactly where the holes are, how many there are, and how people have been endangered or inconvenienced by them. To see that a student knows about a particular period in history, the professor needs names, dates, and details of events, causes and effects of the events, and the relationship of the events to other events.

The way you want your audience to use your writing is directly related to your purpose. Let's say the editor of your college newspaper is planning to write an editorial on problems with campus parking. Her purpose is to point out to the administration that since there are not enough spaces, students are inconvenienced daily. She has no solution to the problem, but she hopes the administration will use what she has written to study the problem and perhaps come up with a solution. She wants her audience to use the writing to see that there is a problem. In this case, the editor will have to show what problems students face when trying to park, when these problems occur, how many students are affected, and what the consequences of the problems are for students (being late for classes, becoming ill from walking far to class in bad weather, getting tickets from parking illegally to get to class on time).

Six months later, nothing has been done. This time the editor has an idea: build a multitiered parking garage. Now her purpose is different; she wants her audience to use her writing differently. Instead of just informing the administration of a problem, now she wants to persuade the administration to consider building a garage. To get her audience to use the writing this way, in addition to showing that parking is a problem, she will have to show where a garage could be built, how many cars it will have to hold to solve the problem, and how it will be paid for. Because she wants the administration to use the writing to take some action, she must show that there are available solutions.

The following questions can help you analyze your audience when you write. This list can get you started, but you may think of others as well.

1. Who is your audience?
   a. What do members of your audience know about the topic?
   b. What references can you assume they will know?
   c. What references must you explain?
2. What are your audience's attitudes toward what you are writing?
   a. Are members of the audience most likely to agree?
   b. Are they most likely to disagree?
   c. Are they neutral?
3. How is your audience going to use your writing?
   a. To inform themselves?
   b. To entertain themselves?
   c. To make a decision?
   d. To examine or solve a problem?
   e. To change their behavior?

As you can see, the writing situation can affect what you write and how you write it. As you approach a writing situation, always consider your *role, purpose,* and *audience* because they affect what you say and how you say it.

EXERCISE 1.1 The following are some writing situations. Identify the writer's role, purpose, and audience. Then briefly analyze how the writing situation will affect what the writer writes. Study the example before completing the exercise.

Example A stockbroker's report to a client about some new bonds

Role An expert counseling someone who is not an expert

Purpose To inform the client so that he or she can decide whether the bonds are worth buying

Audience A client who is uninformed about the bonds and also not a financial expert

Analysis The writer would have to be sure to include an explanation of the type of bonds as well as their cost, interest rates, and time of maturity. Since the writer is trying to help the client, not just sell the bonds, he or she will have to explain the risks as well as the benefits of buying the bonds. Not being an expert, the client, as audience, would want careful explanations and complete information. But the writer could assume that the client knows some basic terms such as interest rate.

1. A recipe for cheesecake written for inexperienced cooks
2. A recipe for lasagna written for experienced cooks
3. A newspaper editorial, written in a newspaper read by the general public, arguing that smoking should not be allowed in public
4. A pamphlet on baseball written for visiting Russian dignitaries who will be attending a major league game
5. A paper on child abuse written as a requirement for a psychology class
6. A letter asking a company to refund your money for a defective product
7. A two-page essay introducing you to your writing teacher
8. A letter to a friend telling about your first experiences as a college student

■■■■■■■■■■■■■■

E X E R C I S E 1.2 This exercise provides you with writing situations followed by information that you can use in writing. Given the situation, determine whether the information is appropriate or inappropriate for the situation and tell why. Consider both what the information says and the way it is written. If the information is inappropriate, tell what should be done to make it appropriate.

Example

Situation Term paper on Adolf Hitler written for a professor in a class on World War II

Information   Hitler was a cruel dude.

Answer   Inappropriate. Slang should not be used in a term paper. Substitute the word *man,* or *dictator,* for *dude.*

1. *Situation:* Letter to a friend about your first day of college
   Information: I am pleased to inform you that having completed my first day at an institution of higher education, all my faculties remain intact.
2. *Situation:* Lasagna recipe for experienced cooks
   Information: Mozzarella is a white cheese available in most supermarkets.
3. *Situation:* College handbook for new freshmen
   Information: If you are unsure about your course of study, you can designate yourself "nonpreference." Nonpreference simply means that you have not yet chosen your major. You may remain nonpreference for two semesters; then you will have to decide on a major.
4. *Situation:* An economics textbook for beginning students
   Information: Increases in the GNP often result in fiscal drag and a reduction of aggregate expenditures.
5. *Situation:* A letter asking a company to repair a defective stereo
   Information: I purchased a TechMaster stereo, model xj 1130-1, on March 19 at Victor Electronics in Phoenix, Arizona. While still under warranty, the stereo began to lose volume on low settings.

We have looked at the ways experienced writers write — by analyzing the writing situation and by using the writing process. As a beginning college writer, you will need to learn to use the writing process, too.

■ Using Invention Strategies

Invention strategies:
Invention strategies are methods for coming up with ideas and for developing details to support the ideas.

Invention strategies are not formulas that always work the same way and lead to the same idea, but they are more efficient than trial and error. Invention strategies are used before you write a first draft and sometimes as you draft. As you gain practice using the different types of invention strategies discussed in this section, you can decide which one is the best for you.

Brainstorming

Brainstorming: An invention strategy in which a writer lists everything about a writing topic that comes to mind.

In **brainstorming,** a writer thinks of the topic to be written about and then lists in single words or phrases all ideas or details that come to mind. Suppose you are assigned to write an essay on smoking. Whether you are a professional writing for a magazine or a student writing for a class, a brainstorming list can help. Thinking of smoking, you may come up with a list such as this one:

expensive	smokers are a minority
prohibited in certain places	heart attacks
cancer	ways to quit
lung disease	good to quit
once considered sexy	dirty ashtrays
secondhand smoke is harmful	smells bad
hard habit to break	can't advertise on TV
some nonsmokers militant	cigarettes heavily taxed
rights of smokers	warning on pack
big part of economy in tobacco states	

By making this list, you get down many points about smoking that you can begin thinking about. The list saves you from staring at the blank page and helps you develop a sense of purpose, if you do not already have a purpose. As you look over the list, you can ask questions about what you want to say about smoking. Do you want your paper to encourage smokers to quit? Do you want to help them quit? Do you want to encourage young people not to start smoking? Do you want to show the effects of smoking on the body? Do you want lawmakers to ban smoking in public places? Do you want to defend the rights of smokers?

Assuming your purpose is to help smokers quit, you can sort through the list crossing out anything that is not a reason or a way to quit. The fact that tobacco is a large part of the economy has nothing to do with quitting. The fact that smokers are a minority does not fit in, and most smokers are aware of that. You may also cut the points about the militancy of nonsmokers and the effects of smoke on them because smokers have to quit for themselves, not for others. The rights of smokers would not fit in because you are trying to encourage your audience to become nonsmokers. What else would you cut? The part about TV ads being banned? Probably. After you cross these things out, your list will look like this:

expensive	ways to quit
cancer	good to quit
lung disease	heart attacks
dirty ashtrays	warning on pack
smells bad	cigarettes heavily taxed
hard habit to break	

With this smaller list, you can begin to group related points together — everything about health in one group, everything about cost in another, everything about quitting in another. Your list might then look like this:

warning on pack	lung disease
cancer	hearts attacks

expensive
cigarettes heavily taxed

dirty ashtrays
smells bad

hard habit to break
ways to quit
good to quit

Once you have broken down your list into groups, examine it again, asking yourself if you want to cut or add anything else. You might consider not telling your audience that smoking is a hard habit to break, but you think that if you make it seem easy to quit, your audience won't believe you because they know it is hard. So you keep this point. You then think that smokers often like the smell of smoke, although it is unpleasant to nonsmokers. So you cut the point about the smell. What do you do with the point about dirty ashtrays? Perhaps group it with "good to quit" because not having to look at and clean dirty ashtrays is one of the benefits of quitting.

By this point, your list should be fairly well organized. Now you can decide the order in which you want to present your information. Since your purpose is to help your audience with a problem, you might begin by defining the problem, then providing the solution, and finally showing the benefits. In this case, you would put the health problems caused by smoking first, followed by the expense, followed by the ways to quit, and ending with the benefits. But as you look over the list, you discover that starting with the effects on health might put the smokers off. Most of them know the health effects and might not read further. You decide to start by talking about the difficulties of quitting, so that your opening shows that you understand smokers. Once you have decided on the order in which you will make your points, you put your list in that order:

hard habit to break

warning on pack
cancer
lung disease
heart attacks

expensive
cigarettes heavily taxed

ways to quit
good to quit

If you had ideas about each point, you could now begin writing. But even with this list you could get stuck. If you begin writing and you can't think of reasons why it is hard to quit or you can't think of ways to quit, then it is wise to brainstorm again, this time focusing on each point of the list in turn. You might end up with a detailed list like this one for each different point:

hard habit to break
    smokers enjoy taste
    smokers enjoy having cigarette in hands and mouth
    people used to smoking at particular times
        after meals
        in the car
        on the phone
        when drinking
        in social gatherings
    nicotine is physically and mentally addictive

With a list as detailed as this one, you will have a lot to write about in the opening section of your paper. And if you make similar lists for each section of the paper, they would provide an outline to follow, and you would be on your way to getting the job done.

Making and sorting out all these lists may seem very time-consuming, but actually you can make them fairly quickly. The alternative of staring at the blank page and writing by trial and error takes even more time and is not likely to result in a good product.

Of course, the more you know about a topic, the easier it is to brainstorm. If you know nothing about smoking, you could not come up with the lists we did unless you first do some research. However, sometimes when you think you know nothing about a topic, brainstorming helps you recall what you do know, and often you discover that you know a lot more than you think. Brainstorming is also helpful when the topic is broad and general. The lists can help you narrow the topic down, decide on your purpose, and put your information in an order that your reader can follow and use.

E X E R C I S E   1.3 Below are some broad topics for writing. Pick *one* and make brainstorming lists leading to a final list that could serve as an outline for a paper. Remember that during or after your brainstorming to make the first list, you need to decide your purpose and audience.

1. women's softball teams
2. teenage drinking
3. raising children
4. clothing
5. a political issue
6. TV game shows
7. working at a particular job (fast food, office, retail store)
8. senior citizens
9. high school education
10. managing money

Clustering

Clustering: An invention strategy in which the writer draws a diagram with the main topic circled in the center with lines leading out to related ideas and details.

In some ways, the strategy known as **clustering** is similar to brainstorming. As in brainstorming, you begin with a broad topic and put down whatever you think of regarding that topic. Clustering differs from brainstorming in that you create a diagram, which can be helpful for writers who like to see things in images. You write the topic in the middle of a page and draw a circle around it. You then draw lines coming out from the circle, and at the end of each line you put one of the ideas that come to mind as you are thinking about the topic. Here is an example of a cluster for the topic of smoking:

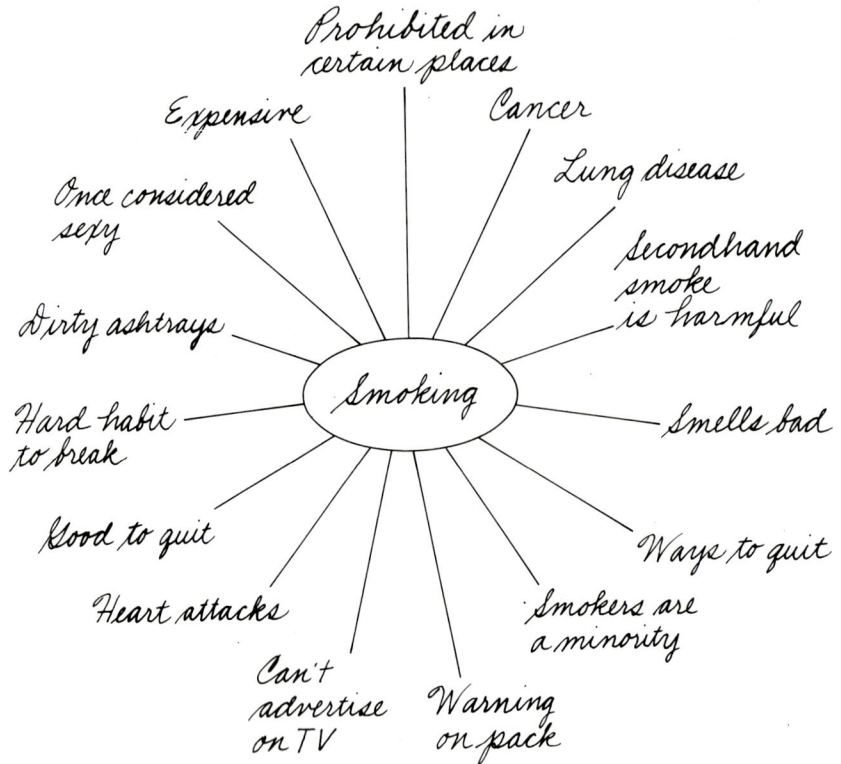

A few points did not fit into this cluster. Some writers do not like clustering diagrams because they think the diagrams cannot hold as much information as brainstorming lists. But writers who prefer diagrams to lists just use bigger sheets of paper. The advantage of clustering is that you can usually see and sort out your points more easily than you can with a list. Depending on your purpose, you can then take a point and expand on it again using another cluster.

If you are using clustering to write the paper to convince smokers to quit, you can use a diagram to expand on each point from the first cluster:

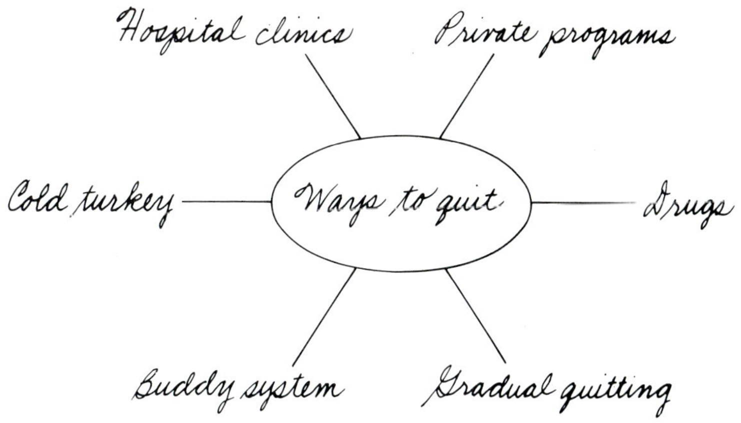
Hospital clinics
Private programs
Cold turkey
Ways to quit
Drugs
Buddy system
Gradual quitting

You can then cluster even further to get to the details about each way to quit:

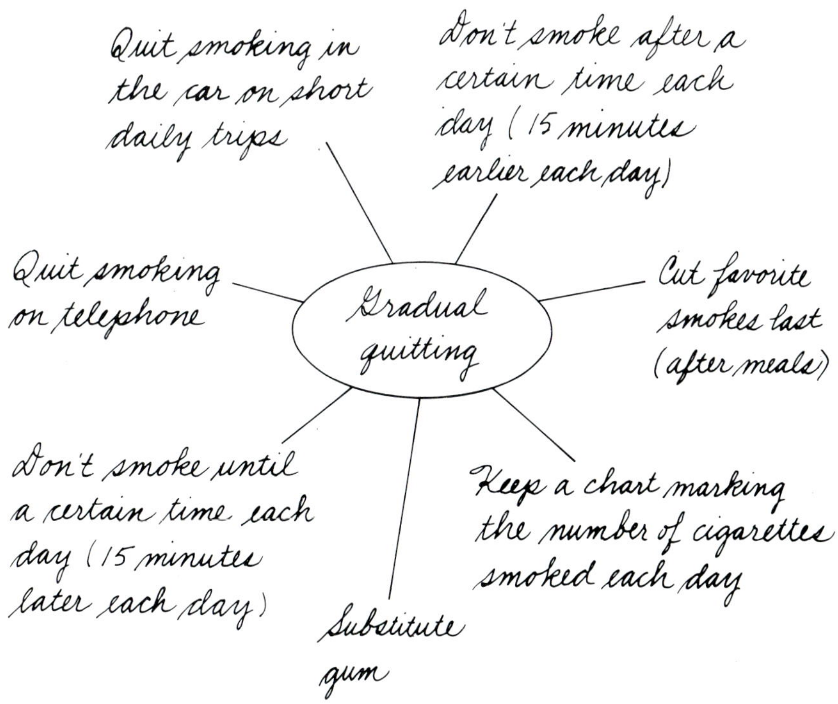
Quit smoking in the car on short daily trips
Don't smoke after a certain time each day (15 minutes earlier each day)
Quit smoking on telephone
Gradual quitting
Cut favorite smokes last (after meals)
Don't smoke until a certain time each day (15 minutes later each day)
Substitute gum
Keep a chart marking the number of cigarettes smoked each day

If you make a cluster diagram like this one for each section of your paper, you will have much of your work done before facing that blank page. Clustering works well if you like to think in images rather than in straight lines. Whether clustering or brainstorming is the better invention strategy depends on what you as a writer find easier and more effective.

From the list of topics in Exercise 1.3, choose a topic different from the one you used for brainstorming lists and this time explore the topic by clustering.

Freewriting

Freewriting: An invention strategy in which the writer writes quickly, putting down any ideas on the topic without worrying about spelling, grammar, or the order of the ideas.

Freewriting is an invention strategy in which you write. When you freewrite, you take the broad topic and begin writing whatever comes into your head as quickly as you can, preferably without stopping. You don't worry about spelling, grammar, sentence structure, or the order of your ideas; you just get the ink flowing and the ideas down. Also, you don't ignore any idea that comes into your head. A piece of freewriting on the topic of smoking might look like this:

> I really don't like smoking. It smells bad and it's bad for people too. It causes cancer. Lung disease. It's also very expensive. It bugs me in restaurants that the no smoking sections are so small. Heck, there's less smokers. Why do they get the most tables. They might have a heart attack while they are eating. Smokers like to smoke after eating, they say. They say smokers can't taste food as much as nonsmokers. My father always does. I am not rude to smokers, though, like some people. I just try to move away. I guess there is money to be made from smoking. The government and the tobacco companies. Even if they can't advertise on TV. The taxes make the cigarettes even more expensive. Smokers ought to quit. There's always ways advertised. Gum and pills or just cut down slow or go cold turkey. They would be healthier, live longer lives, be able to breathe better. Be worth it.

This paragraph contains some spelling and grammar errors, and the ideas are not in any logical order. You just put them down as they come to you. That's fine. Although you need to figure out your purpose and audience and then sort out the ideas, at least you have ideas to start with. You can read through the paragraph and underline the ideas that you think are most interesting and important and then pick out a few and work them into a main idea for your paper.

If you pick out the idea that people should quit smoking, you can search through the freewriting to find reasons why, and you can organize those reasons as points to be developed in a paper:

Smoking causes many health problems.
People have many ways to quit.
Quitting results in better health and a better life.

Details for each of these points are scattered throughout the freewriting. With additional organization, you can group the details from the freewriting under points they are related to and begin to develop a sense of what the paper will say and in what order the ideas will be placed.

Or you can take any one of the ideas in the new list and begin to freewrite on it:

> Quitting results in better health and a better life. Nonsmokers tend to live longer on the average. They don't tire as easily and can be more active. They are free to take up a recreational sport and more likely to exercise. They don't miss as many days of work because they do not get sick as much. In not having to worry about their health as much, they might not be under as much stress. And they won't ever again have to clean dirty ashtrays or be forced to sit in the back of an airplane.

At this point, you have nearly completed a section of the paper. Even though you need to revise this paragraph somewhat, you have a section of the paper moving toward completion.

Freewriting has advantages and disadvantages over brainstorming and clustering. Some of the advantages are that the act of writing tends to generate more ideas than listing. Freewriting occasionally results in details that develop ideas more fully than a list does. Among the disadvantages, some writers feel that writing sentences slows down their thoughts, whereas listing speeds them up.

You can combine strategies. You might freewrite on a topic, pick out an important idea from the freewriting, and then make a brainstorming list or cluster diagram for that idea. Or you might start with a cluster diagram or brainstorming list and then freewrite on one of the items from the diagram or list. As you gain experience, you will find the best strategy to fit your personality and habits.

E X E R C I S E   1.5   From the list in Exercise 1.3, pick a topic different from the ones you used for Exercises 1.3 and 1.4 and freewrite about it. Try to write for at least ten minutes without stopping. When you are finished, pick out an idea that you think could be developed as the main idea of an essay.

Asking the Journalist's Questions

Used for years by newspaper reporters, **the journalist's questions** — five Ws + H — are another invention strategy that can help you explore a topic to come up with ideas and details needed for writing. To use this strategy, simply ask the following questions:

The journalist's questions: An invention strategy consisting of the Five Ws + H: Who? What? When? Where? Why? How?

Who?
What?
When?
Where?
Why?
How?

The following opening paragraphs from an article about a forest fire show the results of asking these questions, some more than once.

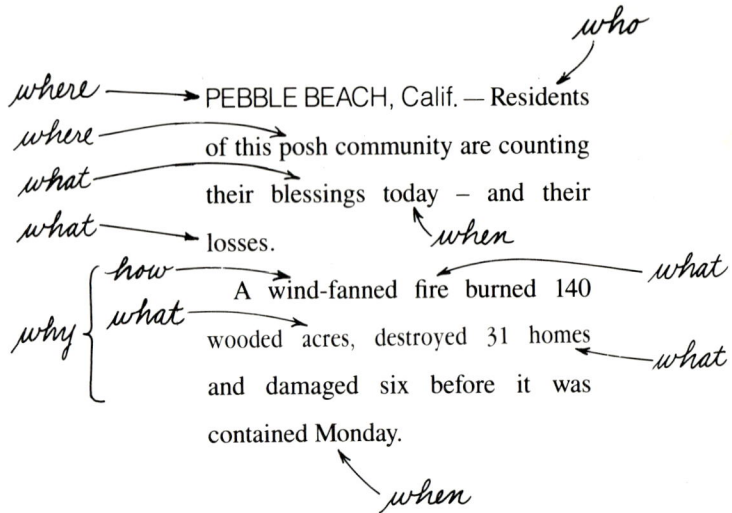

who

where → PEBBLE BEACH, Calif. — Residents
where of this posh community are counting
what their blessings today – and their
what losses.   *when*
how A wind-fanned fire burned 140   *what*
why { *what* wooded acres, destroyed 31 homes   *what*
and damaged six before it was
contained Monday.
when

Linda Green and Nels Johnson,
USA Today, June 2, 1987

The rest of the article goes on to discuss details of the fire, giving dollar estimates of the damage, quoting people whose property was destroyed, and telling how the government planned to help these people. Even if you are not going to become a reporter, the journalist's questions can help you generate and organize ideas for almost any kind of writing.

You can use the journalist's questions to explore broad topics, but you have to narrow down your answers to the questions. Suppose you are writing an essay about adult high school dropouts earning general equivalency diplomas (GEDs). You might get the following answers to the journalist's questions:

Who?   adult high school dropouts of any age
What?   GED
When?   as soon as they wish
Where?   in any local program that offers GED classes
Why?   so they can go to college
How?   by attending GED classes in the evenings

If you put these notes together, you might come up with a pretty good main idea for an essay: Adult dropouts, no matter what their age, can go to college if they first earn a GED by attending evening classes offered by local programs. This sentence will give you a good start. Your purpose would be clear: informing people that adult dropouts can get a GED and go to college.

Using the journalist's questions on this topic entailed less thinking and sorting out than did the other strategies because you started with a limited topic. The questions did not lead you to the topic, but they did help you put an idea down clearly and completely. Next you must generate details that explain the process of getting a GED and applying to college. You could pose the journalist's questions again, either as a group or one at a time. For details about how to begin GED classes, you might try the "how" question:

How? Call the local school board, which will have a GED office or can put you in touch with the one nearest your home.

How? Have the GED office send you the papers you need to fill out and a schedule of classes. Complete and return your papers.

How? Attend the evening classes you need to fulfill your GED requirements and pass the GED examination on completion of the classes.

By posing the question most important to each section of your essay, you can continue to come up with the details you need to make your explanations clear.

The journalist's questions are a more structured method of ordering ideas. Their disadvantage is that usually you must limit the topic somewhat before the questions can help you. Their advantage is that, unlike clustering, brainstorming, or freewriting, they help you see relationships between ideas. For instance, if you need to keep asking "why" questions to develop an idea in a paper, you are more likely to dig into the causes of *what* you are writing about. Also, the questions are the same questions readers ask. If you write the paper on the GED and do not include how a person can get one, you will leave your readers wondering. As with the other invention strategies, you can use the journalist's questions in combination with other strategies. You might freewrite or cluster to narrow down a topic and then use the journalist's questions to explore it.

■■■■■■■■■■

E X E R C I S E   1.6 Use the journalist's questions to explore one of the topics you have not worked with in the list of topics in Exercise 1.3.

■ Drafting

Drafting: The writing of a paper in rough form.

Once you have gone through the invention process, you are ready to write a rough draft. In some ways, **drafting** is the least teachable part of the writing process. You can learn strategies for invention. You can learn guidelines for revising. And you can learn grammar rules for editing. But when it comes time to draft the paper, you sit down by yourself. Even so, several elements can contribute to a successful drafting stage.

Creating a Comfortable Writing Environment

Writing is difficult enough without doing it in an uncomfortable place and atmosphere. In his later years Marcel Proust, French novelist subject to ill health, wrote in bed. Thomas Wolfe, an American writer, was so tall that he could not sit comfortably at a desk, so he often wrote standing up, leaning over his mantelpiece or his refrigerator. These writers may be extreme cases, but the point is to try to find or create a comfortable environment that suits you. If you cannot write when it is noisy, and your home or dorm room is noisy, try the library.

Consider at what level of noise you are most comfortable writing. Some people need absolute quiet. Other people like some noise. Jerzy Kosinski, a skilled novelist, writes with the television on in the background, though he does not watch it. Other writers prefer a certain kind of music. But if you do like some noise, make sure the noise does not distract you. If you write with your favorite TV show on, you may be unable to attend to the writing. If you listen to music that is so loud you are dancing in your chair or singing along, chances are you will not get much done. While a writing environment has room for noise, if the noise distracts you, the environment is no longer comfortable. Otherwise, there is nothing wrong with wanting some background noise as you write. It does not make you a better or worse writer than someone who writes in quiet. On the other hand, if you need a quiet place, find one.

Choosing Your Tools

Decide what tools you like best for writing. Do you prefer to draft in pen, in pencil, on a typewriter, on a computer? If in pen, what kind? Ballpoint? Felt-tip? What color? One student drafts her papers with a green felt-tip pen because she likes the way the pen moves across the paper, and the color is easy on her eyes. Consider the kind of paper you like best. Do you feel more comfortable with lined paper or unlined? Does the paper have to be white, or do you like yellow or a pale shade of another color? Do you like a pad or loose pages?

Some writers get very serious about their tools. A friend who has published three books will not write unless he has a number 2 pencil and a yellow legal pad. Now he writes on a computer, but he always makes a draft first with pencil and pad. Other writers are not such fanatics about tools. But those who choose certain tools are not just being silly. Aside from feeling comfortable with their tools, these writers make writing a ritual. Thus, they take it more seriously. Also using the same tools makes the task of writing seem routine and familiar each time. As a result, writing may seem easier.

Your instructor may specify the kind of paper, ink, or type for the final copy of a paper or for writing done in class. But when you draft, use whatever tools make you most comfortable.

Managing Your Time

Some students can write a short paper an hour before class or can stay up all night writing a long one due the next day. Perhaps you are one of them. Unless these students are extremely talented, their papers produced this way are probably not very good. And unless their instructors have easy standards, their papers probably do not receive very good grades. Some things can be written quickly — letters or short writings in class on a limited topic. In grading such work, your instructor considers the amount of time you have. For papers written out of class, you need to plan your time.

Planning your time requires that you become familiar with your writing habits. Given a paper that would require two hours of drafting, some people could work on the draft for half an hour a day over four days. Another person might lose his or her train of thought on this schedule and do better if he or she set two hours aside to work continuously. Some people write faster than others so they might set aside less time. As you gain experience in writing, you will begin to know how much time you need to complete a particular piece of writing. Always plan on a little more time than you think you need.

When you plan your time, consider that you will probably take breaks. These breaks may include pacing around the room trying to think of ideas or words or having a cup of coffee and forgetting about the paper so that you can come back to it fresh. If you use breaks wisely, they can help make the writing easier. But since it is normal to seek pleasure and comfort, you have to be careful that you don't take so many breaks that the writing never progresses.

Drafting and the Writing Process

The parts of the writing process often overlap, and they tend to overlap most when you are drafting. So be prepared. If you write a sentence and then think of a better way to make the point, don't be afraid to cross out the first sentence. Remember that good drafts are often very messy, and messiness can be the sign of a good writing process. In drafting, you might also catch a grammar or spelling error and edit it on the spot. It is probably a good idea to do some revising and editing as you go along, but don't get bogged down editing and revising every sentence and paragraph. You will revise and edit the whole draft when it is complete. While you are drafting, your goal is to get your ideas and details down in an orderly way so that you can see how and if they fit together to fulfill your purpose.

Along with doing a little revising and editing as you draft, you will probably still be involved in the invention stage. Sometimes you may come up with only a few new ideas or a few additional details about the idea you started with. But sometimes you may change your paper completely. As you begin writing the paper on ways to quit smoking, you may decide that none of your notes are very good because they are unreasonably difficult, have side effects, or do not work in the long run. This discovery may change the whole purpose and audience of your paper. Instead of showing smokers why and how they should quit, your paper now might call for health professionals to conduct research into new and more effective methods for quitting.

If your main idea changes as you are drafting, don't feel that you have made a big mistake. Sometimes, no matter how many invention strategies you use, you will not discover what you think and want to say until you write. In this sense, your first draft becomes a means of discovery.

Leave yourself plenty of room to make changes as you draft and later when you revise and edit the draft. Some writers like to write on every other line so they can make changes on the clean lines. Other writers leave wide margins where they can make notes and changes. Whatever you do, avoid crowding the page to the point where you have no room for changes. A crowded page is also much more difficult to read when you revise and edit.

Reading and Drafting

One study comparing experienced and inexperienced writers found that the experienced writers read and reread their drafts more often as they wrote. The experienced writers also asked others to read their drafts much more than inexperienced writers did. The message is clear: read your draft and have others read it.

You as Reader   As you write your draft, stop to reread it occasionally. You need not read every sentence before writing another, but stop to read at least every page. Also stop at times and read the draft over from the beginning. Rereading will keep you aware of what you have said and what you still have left to say. In addition, you can check to see if your paper is fitting together or if you have gone off track. Often it is good to read the whole draft each time you return from a break. Your mind is fresh, and you can see the draft clearly. When you are stuck, reading the whole draft can help get you going again. As you draft, remember that reading helps writing.

Others as Readers   If you are shy about having others read your writing, you will need to overcome your shyness. If experienced writers read a draft that needs work, they won't look down on you because they know that writing requires revision. If inexperienced writers read a draft with problems, chances are they have the same problems.

When you have a draft completed or even partially completed, ask a friend or family member to read it. Even if this person is not a writing expert, his or her reaction as a reader can help you see if your draft needs to be clearer or better organized. In a writing class, some instructors may collect and comment on all the students' drafts before the students write their final copies. If this is not your instructor's practice, you can ask him or her to read and discuss your draft with you in conference. Some writing teachers also set aside class time in which students read and comment on one another's drafts. If yours does not, you can meet with other students for coffee and reading. The idea is to get as many readers and as much feedback as you can before you revise your draft.

■ Revision

Chapter 5 gives many suggestions and strategies for revising. Here we briefly consider some questions that affect revision.

When Do You Revise?

Some revision will take place as you are drafting. But once a draft is finished, you should set aside time for **revision.** Unless you are absolutely pressed for time, you should not revise your draft right after you finish it. If you revise right after drafting, all the ideas that should be in the paper are still fresh in your mind. When you begin to read the draft, you might read into it ideas that you have not really made clear in the paper. Because of the ideas fresh in your mind, you may not see the paper clearly. Remember that *revision* means "re-seeing."

Revision: The stage of the writing process in which the writer makes changes in the content, arrangement, and style of the writing. Revision occurs during drafting and after a draft is complete.

Instead of revising immediately, wait awhile. If you have enough time, let the draft sit until the next day. Waiting before revising will clear your mind and allow you to see the paper as it is, not as you think it is. If you don't have time to wait until the next day, try to wait at least two hours. During that two hours, do something else. Study another subject, watch TV, but do not think about your paper. Get it out of your head so that when you come back to it, you will revise with clear vision.

How Do You Revise?

Sometimes students want to revise, but they do not know what to look for. The following points will help you consider ways in which your paper can be revised.

Remember Your Purpose   As you revise, keep your purpose clearly in mind. If you find that you have changed the purpose of the paper in the process of drafting, rethink what you want your purpose to be. If you want to keep the original purpose of your paper, then you may have to add or cut material to keep the paper on track.

Suppose that in a paper for a political science class your professor has asked you to discuss the forces that can influence the way congressional representatives vote on laws. Some of these forces are party loyalty, special interest groups, and the effect of the law on people in a representative's district. As you reread your paper, you find that you have spent more than half of it explaining how bills become laws. Maybe you started out wanting to *briefly* give this explanation to show how the forces of the representatives fit in with the lawmaking process, but you spent too much time on the process and not enough on the forces that influence voting. Since the professor assigned you the topic of discussing the forces, you have to stick to that original purpose. As a result, you need to cut a lot of the discussion about how a bill becomes a law and then add more information on the forces that affect congressional votes.

Consider Your Audience   When you revise, always consider your audience. Three questions can help. First, are you giving your readers all they need to know to use the writing the way they want to? Your political science paper will be used to evaluate your knowledge. If you are writing about the forces that influence the way representatives vote on laws, have you included all that you know about the forces? Remember that a piece of writing must stand on its own. You can't say to the professor later, "I knew that, but I thought you could see that I did."

Second, are you using language appropriate to the audience? Remember that you should use language that best fits the writing situation. In a letter to a friend, you write in casual and familiar language because you want to be seen as a friend. In a political science paper, you want to be seen as an informed student of political science, not as the professor's friend, so you use the kind of terms that you find in your political science readings. If you read through either the letter or the political science paper and find language that does not fit, you will have to make some changes.

Third, if your audience is a group, have you accounted for the differences among individuals in the group? For example, in writing the first draft of this book, I often forgot that my audience, college freshmen, is a wide and varied group. I assumed at times that all college freshmen are nineteen-year-olds living on campus at a four-year school because that is the situation I am used to. I geared many of the examples in my draft to students at such a school. However, I realized that many students who use this book could be older, could live off campus, or could be attending two-year colleges. So I added many examples that would appeal to a more diverse group.

Reshape Your Writing   Reshaping your writing includes finding ways to express ideas more clearly and finding the best order in which to present ideas and examples.

As you revise, read your sentences aloud. Ask yourself if each sentence is clearly making your point. If not, you may be trying to put too much into one sentence. Ask yourself if you can make the sentence sound better so that it reads more smoothly. If your sentences seem short and choppy, see if combining two or more sentences helps.

Just as you can reshape sentences, you can reshape the whole paper by moving sentences and paragraphs. To do so, you need to figure out the best arrangement in terms of your purpose and audience. Remember that in ordering points for the paper on smoking, you moved the points around on your list so that you would not put off smokers by beginning with the ill effects of smoking on health. Just as you reorganize a brainstorming list before you draft, you can reorganize a draft once it is written.

You can move material around in a number of ways that do not require you to recopy the whole draft. If you want to change the order of sentences in a paragraph, you can draw arrows indicating where you want the sentences to go. For whole paragraphs, you can write notes or numbers in the margin to indicate the order you want to use when you write the second draft. Some writers use the "cut-and-paste" method. They cut up parts of the paper, put them in the order they want, and then tape or paste them on new sheets of paper. This method may sound silly or drastic, but it can be very helpful.

As you gain experience in writing, you will develop your ability to revise your papers. Writing experts say that "good writing is rewriting." Revision is so important a part of the writing process that we cover it in a separate chapter later in the book.

■ Editing

Editing: The stage in which the writer corrects errors in grammar, punctuation, and spelling. Some editing is done during drafting, but it also must be done after a draft is completed and revised.

Some students confuse editing with revision or lump the two together. If you think of revision as focusing on content, style, and organization, and you think of **editing** as focusing on grammar and correctness, you will be more successful in each activity, and you will write better papers. It may come as a surprise to you, but good grammar is not the most important thing in writing. A piece of writing that contains no grammatical errors may still be poorly organized, unclear, and lacking in ideas and examples. Another paper with four or five grammar errors but with good organization and clear, thoughtful, and fully developed examples may be better than the paper with no errors. Still it is important to edit out as many errors as you can, not because errors are sins against your English teacher but because errors distract readers. When readers read your writing, they want to understand your message. If they keep getting distracted by errors, they will have a hard time concentrating on what you are saying.

You will do some editing as you draft and revise. If you catch an error, correct it. But it is necessary to edit your final draft again when you have finished your revisions. You should also edit the final copy that you present to your instructor. Most instructors will not object to a few corrections made neatly on a final copy.

If you have done some writing and have had trouble with editing, you know that one difficulty is that there are many possible errors you can make. Chapter 10 covers those errors and shows ways to correct them. You should refer to that chapter whenever you have trouble with a point of grammar. You might not become a grammar expert, but by using Chapter 10 and developing some editing strategies, you can reduce distracting errors.

Editing by Sound

To catch some errors, you may find it helpful to read your paper aloud. Suppose you wrote, "Most people thinks that going to college will improve their lives." In reading this sentence aloud, you would probably catch the error because in speech you say, or hear others say, "Most people think."

Editing by Sight

Though editing by sound is helpful, you cannot hear many errors. Read this sentence aloud: The presidents cabinet met yesterday to discuss the budget. If you realized that an apostrophe is missing before the *s* in *pres-*

idents, you caught that error by sight because there is no difference in the way you read the plural form *presidents* and the possessive form *president's.* Another common error that cannot be heard is the confusion of words that sound the same but have a different spelling and meaning; for example, bare/bear, do/due, for/fore/four, here/hear, know/no, to/too/ two, their/there/they're. When you edit, read your paper two or three times *looking* for errors that need to be seen.

Keeping an Error Log

An **error log** is a notebook in which you keep a record of your writing errors so that you can avoid them in future writing. When your instructor returns a graded essay, after you have read and thought about his or her comments on the content, form, and style of the paper, reread the paper. Then write in your error log the kinds of errors you made. Next to each error you record, rewrite the sentence correctly with the help of the discussion of the error in Chapter 10. Before you edit your next paper, review your error log and make sure you look carefully for the errors it contains. After you have written a few papers and recorded your errors in the error log, you will begin to see which points of grammar you need to study.

Error log: A notebook in which the writer keeps track of errors and corrections to avoid repeating the same errors in future writing.

Eliminating all errors takes time and experience, but if you use the error log, you will reduce the number of errors you make. You will also develop a knowledge of grammar that will help you avoid making the same errors over and over again. In short, you will become a better editor of your writing.

■ Computers and the Writing Process

Just as computers have affected almost everything in our society, they have influenced the way many people write. Writing on computers is commonly called *word processing.* If your school has computers available for writing, your instructor may require you to use them and provide instruction for doing so. Even if you are not required to use computers to write, you should learn how to use them if you can. Many different word processing programs exist as well as programs that help students directly through the writing process. Your school may have one or more of these that you can use.

When you write on a computer, the words you type on the keyboard appear on the screen of a monitor. When you are finished with a draft, you can instruct the computer to print out the draft in typed copy. You can read through the typed copy and think about what you would like to change. You can then call the writing back onto the screen and make changes. Using the computer, you can add, cut, and move words, sentences, and even full paragraphs — all with a few strokes on the keyboard. You can then print out your writing a second time with all the changes.

Some words of warning: As you write a draft on a computer, you will do some editing and revision as you go along, just as when you write a draft by hand. However, when you do the final revision and editing of your paper, always make changes on a printed copy before you make the changes on the screen. If you try to edit your paper by reading only what is on the screen, you will miss many errors because the glare of the screen can play tricks with even the best eyes. Also when working on the printed copy, be very careful in revising and editing. Because the printout of your draft is neat and clean, it has a finished look, not the messiness of a handwritten draft. As a result, you may think you are finished when you are only getting started. Though computers cannot do your writing for you, they can make writing easier.

Essay for Reading

Writing: The Agony and the Ecstasy

Pamala Gasway

Pamala Gasway entered Indiana State University five years after graduating from high school. Originally majoring in political science, she eventually became an English major because of her love-hate relationship with writing. She wrote this essay when she was a junior.

Vocabulary Cues

idiosyncrasies: habits of behavior particular to one person
obsession: a constant thought about something
Flaubert: a French writer of the nineteenth century
procrastinate: put off until later
stereotypical: having to do with common assumptions a person or
    group makes about other people
ritual: a set method followed faithfully each time it is repeated

Questions to Guide Your Reading

1. How does Gasway react when she receives a writing assignment?
2. Where does Gasway write and why?
3. How does Gasway reward herself for writing?

I guess I am a good writer. At least I've been told (on occasion) that I write well. However, few people see my many revisions. They don't suspect the state of frenzied irritation I work myself into while writing. They see the "finished" product. I say "finished" because I don't believe anything I write is ever completely done — just put aside for a while or usually handed in to meet a deadline. I don't know if I have become a product of too much composition study, or if I have a high need to conquer chaos. I think my obsession with organization makes conquering chaos the more likely of the two. Believe it or not, I love writing; I just hate doing it. I feel akin to Flaubert who stated, "I am a violinist whose ear is true, but whose fingers refuse to reproduce precisely the sounds he hears." When I write I can hear the sounds, but it sure is hard work getting the score down. When I am given a writing assignment, my first reaction is pure panic. I nearly break out into a cold sweat, and I feel nauseated. Because I have such high anxiety about writing, I have developed my own writing process which combines my own idiosyncrasies with methods I learned in writing class.

To begin with, I do not procrastinate. Sure, you say, if you dread writing so much — just don't think about it. Surely if it brings so much anxiety with it, procrastinating would also suspend the tension. Ha! No thank you. I've spent too many "night-befores" in a nervous state that resulted in an outbreak of hives and desperation typing. It has taken me a while, but I have finally learned that putting off the task will not reduce — but increase — the anxiety. Therefore, when I first receive the assignment, I start mentally brainstorming. The topic plays around in my head for hours, days, sometimes weeks, depending on the amount of time I have. I think of ideas while I'm driving to school, doing laundry, cutting the grass.

When I've fine tuned an idea, I start writing. At first my writing is very simple — lists, phrases, a few sentences. I could write up a formal outline; however, I know I must get my ideas on paper — visualize them so I can see what I think — and the lists let me do that quickly. I carefully look over my notes, write down a possible thesis statement, decide on an arrangement for my ideas, and prepare my favorite work area to begin drafting.

Friends of mine have told me they can write in the school library. I have tried it, but I have no luck there. The library was just too confining — I'm a very territorial and noisy writer. To begin by declaring ''my space'' minimizes my being uncomfortable. So, after clearing the kitchen table, I lay out plenty of looseleaf notebook paper and black pens — my favorite writing instruments. I place them directly in front of me along with my list of ideas. I then set my *Webster's* and my grammar handbook on the corner of the table within easy reach.

Having listed my ideas and staked out my territory, I'm now almost ready to start a draft — ''almost,'' because first I need to warn everyone in the house. No one should disturb a ''genius'' at work. I've found that people can come up with endless reasons to interrupt. I guess someone hard at work organizing words and communicating with an invisible audience is just too tempting for most people. They immediately want to add their input, ''What are you working on?'' or ''Hum (while looking over your shoulder), that sounds pretty good.'' Don't get me wrong. Verbally discussing my writing with someone is extremely beneficial, but not at this stage. I must get my rough draft completed first; then I talk to others about it as much as I can. But if I start talking when drafting, I might never get the rough draft done to talk about later.

Speaking of talking, I talk while I'm writing. What is written with my pen has usually been spoken from my mouth. I guess my speech classes make me yearn to hear myself, so I read out loud while I'm composing. I do this often to help my sentences flow and to keep my thoughts consistent. However, my thoughts aren't all I verbalize. It is not unusual to hear me making strange and wacky noises while sitting in the kitchen scribbling away. I'll often start out with boisterous ''Bum bum boom ba boom,'' then screechy ''Ta ta da do do dee dee day,'' and run through a whole range of ''noises'' (I envision myself as various instruments — tuba, oboe, flute, etc.). Unfortunately I have had no formal musical training, but I've discovered that by making these noises I verbally release the frustrations I feel. After all, writing is no easy task.

Because I get so involved with my writing, I make sure I have at least two hours. There's no need starting and getting all tuned up if I'm going to have to quit in fifteen or twenty minutes and go to class or work. Depending on the length of the paper, two hours gives me a good start and sometimes a complete rough draft if the essay is short. Boy, what a rough, rough draft it is too!

While I am writing a draft, I try not to stop, but just as people create interruptions, so does my stomach. Yes, hunger is one of the easiest interruptions to give in to, but the stereotypical "starving writer" is not what I am talking about here. I am referring to one hour after I've finished lunch. I can just have had a complete meal, but when I sit down to start writing, I'm suddenly hungry! Aha! Clever body, but I'm wise to my own tricks now. I know I'm not *really* hungry; I just want an excuse to quit writing. So you see, hunger is a created interruption.

Believe it or not, I force my created hunger off by reserving food as a reward for completing the draft. Often I make treats or buy specialties; they are in the kitchen while I'm writing but are kept out of reach. My favorites are chips and dip, piecrust cookies, chocolate cake, brownies, and for really difficult writing projects — créme horns. Another reward is the TV. I will allow myself to watch television only when I have completed a rough draft. This works especially well when I want to see a special or one of my favorite shows — *St. Elsewhere* or *The Tracey Ullman Show*. So you see, when I finish my first writing session, I am doubly rewarded. I have a rough draft, and I get a treat.

Now wait a minute. You're thinking, "This woman is an adult. She doesn't *really* do this." Well, I most certainly do. Like I've told you, I love to complete a piece of writing; it is just the process I find so frustrating and thus difficult. But by sticking to my process of writing for rewards, I reduce the anxiety associated with the writing task, making it less difficult. Picture yourself indulging in a créme horn while watching your favorite television show.

Of course, once the show is over, I have to revise, either that night or the next day, but then there are more treats and TV after each revision. I am sure other people have their own processes for writing, but mine works well for me. My only fear is that if I ever become a professional writer, I'll be spending my summers at a fat farm.

Questions for Study and Discussion
1. What does Gasway say that people who call her a good writer do not know?
2. What does Gasway mean when she says she loves writing but hates doing it? Can you think of any activity you feel the same way about?
3. What kind of invention strategy does Gasway use and why does she use it?
4. Gasway's imitations of musical instruments may seem a little weird, but what purpose do they serve?
5. Why does Gasway first speak what she writes, and why does she reread her drafts out loud?
6. Why does Gasway set aside at least two hours for writing?
7. What does Gasway say about talking to others about her writing?

8. Explain Gasway's system of rewards. Do you use such a system in any activity besides writing?
9. What are Gasway's role, purpose, and main idea in this essay?
10. Who is her audience?
11. Assuming that her audience is other students, what do you think of her use of informal language and humor?

Writing Assignments

1. The exercises in this chapter asked you to explore some topics with invention strategies. Choose one of those topics and write a short essay (300–400 words) on it. Make sure you have a purpose, a main idea, and a sense of audience.

2. Write a short essay (300–400 words) on your experience as a writer. Include your past experience and what you expect to learn in taking this course.

3. If you have done much writing, write a short essay (300–400 words) describing your writing process.

CHAPTER 2

General Versus Specific Writing

Have you ever read advertisements in the newspaper for used cars? They don't tell you much. Consider this one, for instance:

> '76 Honda Civic, runs good, body and interior in fair shape, great gas mileage, 46,000 on speedometer, $600

This car doesn't sound like a bad deal, especially if you want a low-priced car that won't break down or cost much to run. You figure that "fair shape" means that the body has a few minor dents and scrapes and maybe a little rust. But when you go to look at the car, you find that the ad did not describe it accurately. The car you see sitting in the driveway is painted a faded orange, has a crumpled fender, and is rusting heavily around the wheel wells and lights. Inside you see a rip in the driver's seat patched with tape.

Though you are disappointed, you think that if the car runs well, you might offer the owner four hundred dollars for it. You meet him, take the keys, and break into a smile when the car starts up right away and purrs smoothly. But when you take the car for a test drive, you feel the steering wheel shaking slightly in your hands, notice that the speedometer is stuck at 46,000 miles, and nearly run a stop sign when the brakes are slow to work. By this time, you don't care how good the gas mileage is; you wouldn't offer the owner one hundred dollars for the junk. You go home disappointed, feeling that the ad lied to you and that the owner wasted your time.

You might think that the ad contained false statements, but actually the problem with the ad was that it described the car poorly — so poorly that you were misled. While the words "runs good" do describe the engine, they fail to state the condition of the steering wheel and brakes. The problem is that the words "runs good" are general — they could refer either to the engine or to the whole car. If the ad had said that the car was "mechanically sound," then you could say that the owner lied, since the word "mechanically" applies to all mechanical parts of the car, including the brakes and steering wheel.

■ Defining General and Specific Language

General language:
Refers to a whole class of things, people, or activities. The general word *school* could refer to a small neighborhood preschool or a large university.

The terms *general* and *specific* are used to describe language. **General language** refers to a whole category of things, people, or activities. For example, the word *student* is general. It covers a large group of people that could include anyone from a five-year-old boy in kindergarten to a forty-year-old woman studying for a doctoral degree. Similarly, the word *fun* is a general reference to a positive activity. It can refer to anything from square dancing to fishing to going to a party or to any other activity that some people find pleasurable.

Specific language refers to a particular thing, person, or activity that belongs to a larger category. For example, a high school freshman is a specific member of the general category students.

General and specific language has degrees of generality and specificity. Some words are general, some are less general, some are specific, and some are more specific. The linguist S. I. Hayakawa showed the degrees of generality and specificity as steps on a ladder. If you think of these degrees as steps on a ladder, you will understand them more easily. Note how each step leads down from the more general word to the more specific word, or up from the more specific word to the more general word.

Specific language:
Refers to a particular thing or person in a group.

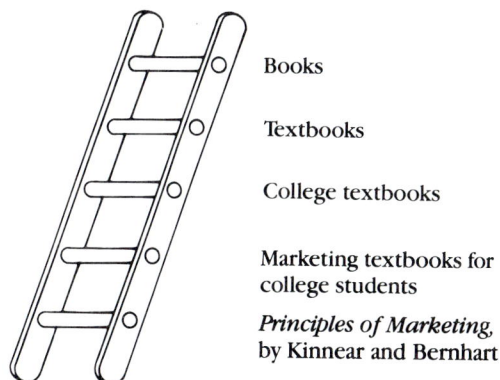

Books

Textbooks

College textbooks

Marketing textbooks for college students

Principles of Marketing, by Kinnear and Bernhart

E X E R C I S E   2.1 Following the example, arrange each of the groups of words into a ladder diagram. Put the most general word at the top rung and the most specific at the bottom.

Example college English courses, courses, freshman English courses, college courses, your English class, education

education
courses
college courses
college English courses
freshman English courses
your English class

1. potatoes, food, french fries, vegetables
2. wars, problems, fighting, World War II
3. Saturday night at the drive-in with —————, male-female relationships, dating
4. Hondas, compacts, cars, Japanese compacts, a friend's new Civic
5. *Time,* print media, media, magazines, last week's *Time*
6. professionals, workers, medical professionals, Doc Wallace, doctors
7. engaging in physical activity, Pete Rose getting his record-breaking 4,192nd base hit, playing sports, batting, getting a base hit, playing baseball
8. animals, dogs, canines, black Labrador retrievers, purebreds, Labrador retrievers, Tom's lovable black Lab Otis

■ Choosing Between General and Specific Language

Good writers are able to mix general and specific language, depending on their purpose and their audience, two parts of the writing situation that you will remember from Chapter 1. Let's look to the sentences below and the discussions that follow.

> This week I had to spend about *$150* on *books,* so already I have only *$25* left of the money I saved before coming *here.*

If a college student living away from home wrote this sentence in a letter to her parents, the language would be fine. There are two very general words — *books* and *here* — but they need not be specific. The student's parents, as audience, will assume she means college textbooks, and she does not name the books because her purpose in writing the sentence is to show how she has had to spend most of the money she saved. If her purpose was to tell her parents that she is learning many new subjects, she might have named the books specifically to give her parents an idea of the variety of her studies. But since her purpose is to show she is going broke, the specific titles of the books are not important. Similarly, she can refer to her school generally as "here" because her parents already know where she is.

In contrast, notice how the writer refers to money in specific amounts. She tells her parents exactly how much she has spent and exactly how much she has left. If you guessed that in her next sentence she asked her parents for more money, you guessed right. And probably she got it. But would her parents have sent her more if she had written, "I spent a lot of money and don't have much left"? Perhaps they would have sent some, but since they would not know how much "a lot" is and what "much left" means, they might not have seen how badly their daughter needed money. Also, without the specific reference to textbooks, the parents would not know the student used the money for something important. By using specific details, this student makes sure her parents know that she has not wasted her money and needs and deserves more.

The following sentence comes from a student essay telling about a disappointing experience the student had on a blind date:

On Saturday night, July 19, 1989, I went on my first blind date.

While the mention of the date is very specific, do readers really need to know exactly when the date took place? Probably not, since the purpose of the essay is to entertain the audience with the story of the date.

Suppose we cut the specific reference to the day, leaving the sentence to read: "On Saturday night, I went on my first blind date." Now we have another problem — the sentence is too general. It sounds as if the date took place on the Saturday evening before the student wrote the essay. That cannot be true because the student wrote the essay during the third week of fall semester but went on the date the previous summer. Of the following groups of words, which would fit best at the start of this sentence?

1. One time
2. One Saturday night last summer
3. One night last summer
4. One night

Numbers 1 and 4 are too general. Though the essay will focus on dating, not time, the words *one time* and *one night* do not give the reader any idea of when the date took place or how old the student was at the time. Number 3 is good because it locates the date on a summer night, and we often associate summer nights with romance. Number 2 is even better. It does everything number 3 does but also adds a little to the focus on romance and dating because Saturday night is usually a time for going out on dates.

E X E R C I S E 2.2 In the following sentences, the italicized words are either too general or too specific. Cross each one out and replace it with a more fitting word. Following each sentence is a reference to the kind of writing in which the sentence occurs. When you make each change, ask yourself the purpose of the writing and the needs of its reader.

1. *OSWALD*
   A man shot President Kennedy in 1963. (an elementary school history book)
2. As you stir the spaghetti sauce, add *some spices*. *OREGANO* (a cookbook)
3. Congress passed a law that would lower funds for *elementary* *EDUCATIONAL INSTITUTIONS* *schools, middle schools, high schools, community colleges, and state universities*. (a newspaper article on lower funding for education)
4. When you arrive, report to the *big building* on *campus* for freshman orientation. (a letter to a freshman entering college)

■ Showing Versus Telling

Showing: Language shows when it uses detail to give a specific idea of something: On the campus quadrangle, the flower beds circling the flagpole contrast brightly with the green of the neatly trimmed lawn and the white of the concrete paths.

Telling: Writing tells when it gives only a general idea: The landscaping is pretty on the campus quadrangle.

Language can get too specific if it shows something readers already know or something they do not need to know. (Remember the student's reference to the exact day of his date?) If you read carefully and did the exercises, you also know that specific language shows more than general language. Although there are exceptions, most of the time when you write you should prefer specific language because it **shows** what you are writing about, while general language merely **tells**. Suppose the advertisement for the used car had read:

> 1976 Honda, engine runs good but steering wheel shakes and brakes are worn, body and interior in fair condition but body has a crumpled fender and severe rust and the interior has a torn driver's seat patched with tape. Speedometer shows 46,000 miles but has not worked for two years.

The seller of the car would never write such an ad because no one would come to see the car. He can't *show* the car in writing and expect anyone to come see it. It is not in his interest to be specific. But unless you are selling a junky old car, it is best to be specific in your writing because specific language shows that you have knowledge of a subject.

When you think of your need to show or tell, you are considering your audience. If you remember the discussion of audience in Chapter 1, you remember that you have to consider what the audience wants to know and what it needs to know, as well as what you the writer want to show the audience.

The following are paragraphs from two different drafts by the same student on the same subject. Both come from drafts of an essay about a blind date, and in each the writer describes an experience at a restaurant. Her purpose is not only to convey the experience of the date but also to put the audience in her place. Read the paragraphs and compare the use of language according to the writer's purpose.

Paragraph 1

I was really disappointed that my date took me to a fast food joint. I was all dressed up and thought we would go someplace good. The place was really crowded, so I felt even dumber in my fancy clothes. When we ate, he turned out to be a pig. He bought a lot of food and just stuffed himself. His table manners were gross too.

Paragraph 2

Since Nancy had told me that Greg was a little older and had a lot of class, I thought he would take me to a fancy place such as Richard's Townhouse or at least the Golden Steer. Needless to say I felt like a fool walking into Pizza Hut in my low-cut purple satin dress and high heels. Bratty little children with pizza sauce on their chins looked at me and giggled, while some young guys in their blue jeans and T-shirts stared and mumbled to one another. After we were seated and our food arrived, I liked Greg even less. He began devouring slices of pepperoni and mushroom pizza, in two gulps, and talked about weight lifting through the whole meal. I don't know what was worse, his bragging about how much he could bench press or the strands of cheese and chunks of pepperoni sticking between his teeth.

Both paragraphs talk about a bad experience for a young woman on a date. The first paragraph, however, *tells* about the experience, but the second *shows* it. Contrast the two paragraphs on the following points:

the restaurant
the way the writer was dressed
the people in the restaurant
the food
the conversation

The second paragraph brings the experience to life — it does not just tell that the young woman was disappointed; it shows the reasons for her disappointment. As readers, we can feel her problem because she puts us in her place by using specific language that shows rather than using general language that only tells.

E X E R C I S E   2.3   Read the following pairs of sentences and on a separate sheet of paper, write down which one you think is better and the reasons for your choice.

1. a. My parents did not understand my brother when he went New Wave.
   b. My parents threatened to send my brother to a psychiatrist when he dyed his hair blue, got a Mohawk haircut, and started listening to bands with names such as Dead Kennedys.
2. a. Ellen has to work all day as a paralegal, tidy up around the house, care for her child, attend law school at night, make sure her homework is done, and get enough sleep each night.
   b. Ellen is very busy and has many responsibilities.
3. a. Last week's party was fun.
   b. At the party Saturday night, about fifty people went through twenty pizzas and danced to live music until 3 A.M.
4. a. My parents always sent me to church but I never went.
   b. On Sunday mornings, I always went to the bowling alley to spend the dollar my parents gave me for the collection plate at church.
5. a. Good writing should be lively.
   b. Good writing uses specific details that show the reader your experience or opinions.

E X E R C I S E   2.4   Rewrite the following sentences so that they show rather than tell. In other words, make the language more specific.

1. My third grade teacher was always nice to me.
2. I get mad when it is noisy while I'm trying to study.
3. After my first day of work, I felt very tired.
4. Christmas is a time of togetherness in my family.
5. This year I hope my favorite team will have the best team in football.
6. Lunch was lousy today.
7. My books for this semester were expensive.
8. Jim was wearing a nice suit.
9. I had a delicious meal at a seafood restaurant.

E X E R C I S E   2.5   Rewrite one of the following paragraphs so that it contains more specific details, that is, so that it shows rather than tells. If you have trouble, go back to the ladder diagram that explains general and specific language. Also do not feel that you need to change every word.

1. Studying at home is not always easy. There is a lot of noise sometimes. I get distracted very easily because of the members of my family. Also I am more likely to take breaks when I study at home. I usually plan to get a lot of studying done but end up not doing much.

2. I am going to school so that I can improve my life. I want to get a good job in some growing field so that I will be able to afford a better life. Also I hope to learn many things that will make me handle problems better and get more enjoyment out of life. Educated people seem to enjoy life because they understand more and go more places.

■ Making Your Writing Specific

Sometimes you may have trouble thinking of a more specific word to replace a general word, especially if you do not know much about the topic you are writing about. If you do not follow professional basketball, for instance, you might have trouble making the following sentence more specific: "In the 1980s, the Los Angeles Lakers and the Boston Celtics were the best teams in basketball." Someone who followed basketball during the eighties might write: "During the 1980s, the Los Angeles Lakers and the Boston Celtics won more championships than any other team in basketball." This change improves the sentence somewhat because it specifies the teams' accomplishments.

This example shows that the writer's knowledge of a subject helps him or her to be specific. The more the writer knew about basketball, the more specific the sentence was. Writing well in your college classes often depends on knowing the material. Compare the following answers given on a history examination on the causes of the Revolutionary War. The question is "What was the Stamp Act and how did it help unify the colonies against Great Britain before the Revolutionary War?"

Answer 1

The Stamp Act was passed by the British Parliament in 1765. It required that the American colonists pay a tax ranging from a half penny to one pound on all public papers, including legal documents, advertisements, pamphlets, business papers, and so on. This law caused more trouble than earlier taxes because it taxed the businesses inside of the colonies, while earlier taxes had only added to the cost of goods imported from Britain. Since this tax affected powerful people such as businessmen, bankers, lawyers, and journalists, the protest against it was forceful. These men organized into "Sons of Liberty" organizations that tried to stop the British Admiralty Court from enforcing the act. Merchants organized boycotts against British products, colonial legislatures drew up resolutions against the tax, and great speakers such as Patrick Henry and Samuel Adams made public speeches to stir the public against it.

Representatives of nine colonies met in Massachusetts and sent a protest to Parliament, claiming that the law was illegal. Because they were not represented in Parliament, they demanded that taxes inside the colonies should only be passed by colonial legislatures. These protests, the boycott, and Benjamin Franklin's speech before Parliament convinced the British that the Stamp Act was doing more harm than good.

When the Stamp Act was then repealed, there were celebrations all over the colonies. The reaction to the Stamp Act is important because it showed the Americans, for the first time, that they could stand up to the British if they united together.

Answer 2

The Stamp Act was another tax that the colonists thought was unfair. A lot of important people from all over the colonies got together to protest it, and there were speeches made to stir everyone against it. The colonists saw this law as a violation of their rights that was illegal according to the British constitution. Then they boycotted British products until Parliament repealed the Stamp Act, and they all celebrated together.

After reading these two answers, you would not have any trouble figuring out which one got the better grade. Although the information in the second answer is correct, without the details the history teacher has no way of knowing if the student knows any more than he or she has written. In contrast, the first answer gives the date of the Stamp Act, tells exactly what it taxed, tells whom it affected most, names important people involved in the protest, shows why the colonists thought it was illegal, and then states why it was important in uniting the colonies against Britain.

How did the first student write such a good answer? Obviously this student knows the subject, but in studying for the exam and in preparing an answer he may have been helped by using some kind of invention strategy. As you read in Chapter One, invention strategies are methods which help you to examine a subject systematically. One strategy, as you may remember, is the journalist's "five W's plus H" method, with which you organize your thoughts before writing by asking, Who? What? When? Where? Why? How?

Since the student knew that the test would be on causes of the Revolution, he could have used the journalist's questions to study each cause. He could have applied them to the Stamp Act as follows. (Notice that he adds questions for each *W* so that he covers everything he needs to know.)

What happened? *What* was it? The Stamp Act, which taxed public documents such as wills and business papers. The tax ranged from a half penny to one pound. It was the first tax on something other than British imports. The colonies banded together in protest. There were boycotts of British goods and speeches against it. Also the "Sons of Liberty" groups were organized to prevent the tax from being enforced. When the tax was repealed, there were celebrations all over the colonies.

When did it happen? 1765

Who did it? British Parliament. *Who* had to pay it? Businessmen, lawyers, merchants, anyone who wrote public papers. Many of these people were rich and powerful. Patrick Henry, Samuel Adams, and Benjamin Franklin all made many of the protest speeches against the tax.

Why? Parliament passed the tax to make money from the colonies. The colonists protested because they felt that the tax was illegal since they had no representation in Parliament. They thought taxes on things inside the colonies should be passed only by colonial governments.

Where? The protests against the law happened all over the colonies. Nine colonies met in Massachusetts to send a protest to Parliament. Franklin spoke before Parliament in England.

How did the tax and the repeal affect the colonies? It made them even more angry at England, brought them closer together, and let them know that if united they could stand up to England.

This student may have had such a knowledge of the Stamp Act that using the five *W*s + *H* method would not have been necessary. But even if he did know the material that well, going through the journalist's questions would help him remember the specific details that make his answer so good. In contrast, the student who wrote the weak answer probably could have improved it a great deal if he had used the questions when studying.

On an exam or an essay written in class, you would not have time to write out all the journalist's questions before writing your answer, but you could use the questions to jog your memory and get your thoughts going. Or you might quickly use a brainstorming list or a clustering diagram.

For essays or paragraphs assigned to be written out of class, you can and should always take the time to use some kind of invention strategy to help get your thoughts flowing. The invention strategy will help you think of ideas and remember details. It will help you to be specific, to show rather than tell.

At the end of this chapter is a short essay describing Albert Einstein followed by a writing assignment that asks you to write a paragraph 150–200 words long on someone who is important to you. The following is a sample of how a student named Tracy worked through that topic, using one of the invention strategies to come up with specific details. Tracy chose the journalist's questions.

Who? My grandfather

What? I liked him almost more than I liked my parents.

Why? He took me places they wouldn't. He let me stay up late and
watch TV and eat junk snacks. He had a wood shop in his
basement and taught me to use power tools. He always thought of
the best presents to get me on holidays.

When? When I was a child, say from the time I was eight to the time I
was fifteen.

Where? In Edwardsville, Illinois, where we lived, a few miles across
the river from St. Louis, Missouri.

How? In his car.

Drawing on her notes, Tracy had enough to begin writing a paragraph:

When I was a child in Edwardsville, Illinois, from the time I was
eight until I was fifteen, I liked my grandfather almost more than
my parents. He would always take me places where they didn't
want to go. He let me stay up late watching TV and eating snacks.
I learned to use power tools in the wood shop in his basement,
and he always thought of the best gifts to buy me on holidays.

This paragraph covers the reasons why Tracy liked her grandfather.
It sticks to the topic and gives reasons for her liking him, but as a piece
of writing it is really rather weak because she never gets very specific.
While she has used the journalist's questions, she has not *limited* the
topic enough to be very specific. Where did her grandfather take her?
How late did he let her stay up? Did she get to watch TV programs she
could not watch at home? What snacks did he let her have? What power
tools did she learn to use and why was using them fun? What gifts did
she get on what holidays?

Tracy certainly had many reasons for liking her grandfather. Her
problem was that she had so many that she did not have room to develop
them specifically in the small space of only one paragraph. In fact, if she
treated each reason specifically, she could probably have written a whole
essay of five or six paragraphs. Alternatively, she could have written one
paragraph on *one* of the reasons. That's what she did. But first she used
the journalist's questions to develop each reason:

Who? Grandpa

What? When I was a child, I liked him almost more than my parents.

Why? He took me to St. Louis a lot.

Where? To Cardinal baseball games at Busch Stadium. To Six Flags
amusement park. Downtown St. Louis for shopping.

When? Ballgames about six times during the summer, usually on Friday
nights or Sundays. Six Flags in the summer, usually twice.
Christmas shopping downtown.

How? In his car, a big Oldsmobile, a 1965 or 1966.

Tracy again had plenty of details to write a specific paragraph, but now she had limited the topic to the places she went. Notice in her final paragraph that listing these details reminded her of even more.

When I was a child, I liked my grandpa almost more than I liked my parents because he would take me to St. Louis. During the summers, we went to Busch Stadium to the Cardinal baseball games. My parents never liked baseball and thought it was only for boys, but Grandpa taught me all the rules and told me all about the great players, like Lou Brock, my favorite. Grandpa also would buy me all the hot dogs and Cokes I wanted. For a special treat, once or twice a summer, he would take me to Six Flags amusement park, where we would ride the Screamin' Eagle, a wild roller coaster. In December, we would go Christmas shopping downtown. I always felt in the spirit as I watched all the people and went into the big department stores with decorations all over and the carols playing.

Tracy wrote a paragraph of approximately 150 words. She did not have to worry about having enough to write about because she had used an invention strategy to develop a limited topic. As a result of her efforts, she showed her readers the places her grandfather took her and thus convinced them of one of the reasons she liked him so much.

Why is this paragraph better than the first one she wrote? It is better because it shows her audience her experience with her grandfather. Readers can put themselves in her place and feel the special relationship she had. This paragraph brings her days with her grandfather to life. Readers do not have to ask where he took her or what was special about these places because she has communicated her experience. She has achieved her purpose in writing by meeting the needs of her audience.

When you write your paragraph for the assignment at the end of this chapter, use one of the invention strategies first to develop ideas. Then go over the paragraph, as Tracy did, and see if any of the sentences are general enough to develop specifically into another paragraph. The kind of specific writing that Tracy did is the kind of writing that will communicate your experience to others and win the praise of your instructor.

Essay for Reading

Albert Einstein
Banesh Hoffman

Banesh Hoffman was a student of Einstein's. He was also a mathematician and a teacher at Princeton University, the University of Rochester, and Queens College. In this essay, he discusses his first meeting with Einstein, perhaps the greatest scientist of all time and the man whose theory of relativity changed the way scientists think of time and space.

Vocabulary Cues

essence: the most important ingredient, the quality that gives someone or something its identity
instinctively: naturally, according to some quality one was born with
extraordinary: more than ordinary, uncommon
carte blanche: a blank check, permission for anything one wants
dismay: a feeling of trouble
inflection: a raising or lowering of tone of voice
characteristically: typically, displaying a quality or feature typical of a person or thing
endearing: likable, inspiring affection
vestiges: traces, last remaining signs

Questions to Guide Your Reading

1. What was Einstein's essence, according to Hoffman?
2. Why was the director of the institute surprised at the salary Einstein asked for?
3. How did Hoffman feel about Einstein before he met him? After he met him?
4. What did Einstein do that changed Hoffman's view?

He was one of the greatest scientists the world has ever known, yet if I had to convey the essence of Albert Einstein in a single word, I would choose *simplicity*. Perhaps an anecdote will help. Once caught in a downpour, he took off his hat, and held it under his coat. Asked why, he explained, with admirable logic, that the rain would damage the hat, but his hair would be none the worse for its wetting. This knack of going instinctively to the heart of a matter was a secret of his major scientific discoveries — this and his extraordinary feeling for beauty.

I first met Albert Einstein in 1935, at the famous Institute for Advanced Study in Princeton, N.J. He had been among the first to be invited to the Institute and was offered *carte blanche* as to salary. To the director's dismay, Einstein asked for an impossible sum: it was far too *small*. The director had to plead with him to accept a larger salary.

I was in awe of Einstein and hesitated before approaching him about some ideas I had been working on. When I finally knocked on his door, a gentle voice said, ''Come'' — with a rising inflection that made the single word both a welcome and a question. I entered his office and found him seated at a table, calculating and smoking his pipe. Dressed in ill-fitting clothes, his hair characteristically awry, he smiled a warm welcome. His utter naturalness at once set me at ease.

As I began to explain my ideas, he asked me to write the equations on the blackboard so he could see how they developed. Then came the staggering — and altogether endearing — request: ''Please go slowly. I do not understand things quickly.'' This from Einstein! He said it gently, and I laughed. From then on, all vestiges of fear were gone.

Questions for Study and Discussion

1. Hoffman's purpose in writing is to show that
   a. Einstein was the world's greatest scientist.
   b. Einstein was a great scientist but a simple and gentle man.
   c. Einstein didn't want a large salary.
2. Which of these points is not mentioned specifically in the essay?
   a. Einstein's theory of relativity changed scientific thought.
   b. The Institute for Advanced Study wanted to pay Einstein a large salary.
   c. Einstein best understood mathematics if the problems were explained slowly.
3. In the first paragraph Hoffman states that *simplicity* is the word that describes Einstein best. This word is general. What does Hoffman say in paragraph 1 to support his point specifically? How does the example show Einstein's simplicity?
4. Paragraph 2 is written in specific language. Express the main idea of the paragraph in one general statement. Is the main idea more specific or less specific than the idea that Einstein was a simple man? How does the main idea of the paragraph help show that Einstein was a simple man?
5. What is the main idea of paragraph 3? How does it help show Einstein's simplicity?
6. What is the main idea of paragraph 4? How does it help show Einstein's simplicity?
7. ''Albert Einstein'' is a short *essay,* a piece of writing with more than one *paragraph.* The whole essay has been condensed into the following paragraph. Read the paragraph and explain why it only *tells* about Einstein, in contrast to the essay, which *shows* his simplicity.

Einstein was a simple man. He did not ask for a large salary when he was hired by Princeton. He acted very naturally with people even when he was in his office. Even though Einstein was brilliant, he did not always understand things quickly. As a result, people who weren't as smart were not afraid he would think they were dumb.

Writing Assignment

Hoffman uses specific language in his essay to show that he liked Einstein because of his simplicity. Similarly, Tracy uses specific language in her paragraph on her grandfather to show that going places with him made her like him a great deal. Now it's your turn. Write a paragraph that *shows* one reason you like someone you knew in your past. The following sentence can serve as a pattern for stating your main idea:

_____ was my favorite person because (*one general reason*).

Even though the reason you fill in will be more general than the specific examples that support it, don't make the reason too general.

Not this: When I was playing football in high school, Coach Ott was my favorite person because he was a great guy.
This: When I was playing football in high school, Coach Ott was my favorite person because he taught me the value of discipline.

The problem with the first sentence is that it is so general that to develop the idea of greatness would take many examples. You would have to mention just about everything from Coach Ott's sense of humor to his knowledge to the generosity he showed in having the whole team over to his house for a spaghetti dinner.

To cover all the specifics that constitute greatness, you would have to write hundreds, maybe even thousands, of words. You don't have time (or the desire) to write so much. And even if you did have the time and desire, a paragraph is only a small piece of writing and doesn't have room for everything that made Coach Ott great.

If you did write about his greatness in a paragraph of normal size, you would have to be very general, and you would end up with the kind of paragraph that Tracy first wrote about her grandfather or the kind on Einstein in question 7. Neither of those showed readers much.

The second sentence on Coach Ott could work well for one paragraph full of specific details because all you have to cover is how Coach Ott taught discipline. You might have specific examples of the way in which his studies of game films long after practice influenced you to put extra time into your own work. You might show how he would bench even the star players in big games if they were late for practice or cut class.

You have to cover only the points about Coach Ott that taught discipline and then end the paragraph with a general statement about how learning to discipline yourself has increased your maturity. Because you limit the paragraph to discipline, you do not have to worry about the spaghetti dinners or anything else about Coach Ott.

Writing a limited paragraph requires that you really go over your memories to come up with specifics. The invention strategies can help. Use them. And then use them again, once you have the first draft of the paragraph written.

If you have trouble getting started, try some freewriting. Just put pen to paper and write anything that comes into your head about the subject (in this case the person). Once you have some thoughts written down, read over the paragraph and pick out one idea that is important to you and apply the invention strategies to that idea.

The trick is not to confuse the freewriting with the finished paragraph. The freewriting is just a warm-up, like the stretching exercises a ballerina does before dancing or a football player does before going into a game.

Now it's your turn. Remember to be specific. Show, don't tell. Good luck!

CHAPTER 3

Writing Essays

Essay: A short piece of writing in which the writer purposely presents ideas and information to influence an audience on a single topic.

The **essay** is one of the most common writing products of the college writer, in English classes and other subjects. This chapter defines the essay and emphasizes the process of writing an essay to enable you to produce the finished piece. Before discussing the process, we define the product. After all, to make a pizza you have to know what a pizza is.

■ What Is an Essay? The Product

You may already know what an essay is. You may have written the essay in the assignment at the end of Chapter 1; and you have read two essays in this book — Pamala Gasway's on writing and Banesh Hoffman's on Albert Einstein. You may have read essays in magazines or have written them in high school. If you are familiar with what an essay is, this section will review and clarify your ideas. If you do not have a definition of *essay* clearly in mind, this section will help you form one.

An essay is a short piece of writing in which the writer purposely presents ideas and information to influence an audience on a single topic. We can break down this definition into various elements that contribute to an essay.

Length

When we say that an essay is short, how short is short? An essay could be as short as 250 words. That's about one typed page or two to four handwritten pages, depending on the size of the handwriting. An essay also could run to thousands of words, say forty typed pages. Usually, the essays you write for college classes will run anywhere from one to twenty pages. Don't be alarmed about that twenty-pager. Usually such essays are assigned only in upper-level courses in your major. So by the time you have to write one, you will have plenty of experience as a college writer and also a solid knowledge of the subject area. In a beginning writing class, your essays will probably range from about 200 words to as long as 1000 (about four typed pages).

Essays Versus Paragraphs

Although an essay is usually thought of as a short piece of writing, it is longer than a paragraph. In fact, unless it is very short, an essay contains more than one paragraph. The next chapter discusses ways to improve the paragraphs in your essays. For now, it is enough to know that essays are divided into paragraphs to help the reader.

If you read newspapers or magazines, you are familiar with the ways paragraphs help you as a reader. They show you when the writer is moving to a new point, and they allow you to rest your eyes a bit as you read. To grasp this point, imagine if this book were written without any breaks for paragraphs. You would have to read line after line without a break for your eyes. You would probably get tired and quit reading. Unless your instructor assigns a short, one-paragraph essay like the one in the Chapter 2 assignment, be sure to divide your essay into paragraphs.

Essays and the Writer's Purpose

What do we mean when we say an essay "purposely" presents the writer's ideas? As we discussed in Chapter 1, a writer has a *purpose* for writing. The purpose can be as simple as wanting to inform the reader about how to change a flat tire or as complicated as wanting to change the audience's views on a political issue. Whatever the purpose, the essay presents the writer's ideas on some aspect of real experience. If an essay is well written, you should be able to tell what the writer's purpose is. For instance, in reading Gasway's essay on writing, you probably realized that she was trying to show other student writers how following a process makes writing easier. Similarly, in reading Hoffman's essay on Einstein, you probably saw, by Hoffman's choice of examples, that his purpose was to show his readers how a great genius was, in many ways, just like the rest of us.

Essays Versus Stories

Story: A newspaper story presents real events, but, unlike an essay, it does not present the writer's opinions and ideas. A fictional story does not present real events, though it presents the writer's ideas and opinions.

Sometimes beginning students will talk about the stories they are reading in their textbooks or about the stories they are writing as if those stories were essays. Such students are confused about what an essay is. An essay is not a **story**.

There are two basic types of writing that we refer to as stories — newspaper stories and fiction stories. A newspaper story deals with real events that a reporter writes about — a presidential trip or a natural disaster, for example. Newspaper stories present the events themselves, not the writer's ideas about the events. Thus, a newspaper story is not an essay. In a fictional story, the writer may make up all or some of the events. Fictional stories may present ideas, but they are not essays because the events, though possibly based on real life, are changed and shaped by the writer's imagination. You probably will read fictional stories in some of your college English classes. These stories can teach you a lot about life, and they can be fun to read, too. But when you talk about essays, use the word *essay*, not *story*, because there is a difference between the two. Knowing the difference will help you be a better reader and writer.

Other words are sometimes used to refer to an essay. When written in a writing course, an essay is sometimes called a theme or a composition or simply a paper. So if your teachers or classmates use these terms, know that they are talking about essays.

The Audience of an Essay

An essay, like most pieces of writing, is written for an audience. As discussed in Chapter 1, the audience will influence what goes into the essay. If you write an essay telling working parents how to choose a day care center, the financial status of the audience is important for you to consider. If the essay is written for low-income parents, you will offer information about free or low-cost centers provided by public and private agencies. If your audience is high-income parents, you probably will spend more time discussing expensive private centers. If your audience includes both high- and low-income parents, you need to include information on all types of centers. After you have had some practice reading essays, you will be able to tell whom the writer has in mind as an audience. If someone read your essay on day care centers and found that it covered only expensive centers, he or she could assume it was written for wealthy people. When an essay is well written, the reader can easily identify the audience for whom it is written.

The Essay Topic

Topic: A limited part of a subject area that can be fully developed in an essay. A topic is what an essay is about.

Subject: A general area that usually cannot be covered in a short piece of writing.

The definition of an essay says that an essay is written on a single **topic.** Simply defined, a topic is part of a larger **subject.** For example, causes of the American Revolution are one topic in the subject area of American history. Track and field is a topic in the larger subject area of sports. Pole vaulting is a topic within the larger subject area of track and field. Essays are a topic in the larger subject area of writing. A subject is general; a topic is more specific.

The topic of an essay focuses on one part of a larger subject. As a result, the topic often determines the length of an essay. The larger the topic, the longer the essay. When a topic is too large for the length of an essay, writers say the topic is too broad. When a topic is too broad, an essay usually ends up being too general to say very much. Recall Tracy writing about her grandfather in Chapter 2. Her first attempt tried to say everything she liked about him but ended up saying very little. When she limited herself to writing about her trips to St. Louis, she was able to be very specific. If you wrote the paragraph for the assignment at the end of Chapter 2, you have some experience in limiting your topic.

Suppose that you were assigned to write an essay of about 500–600 words with the purpose of describing your hometown to your classmates. If you tried to cover the whole town in 500–600 words, you would have to be very general. You might end up with 100 words on the types of housing, another hundred on recreational facilities, another hundred on businesses, and so on. Because the essay would be so general, your town would not sound any different from any other town of the same size. As a result, your audience would not be getting any information about towns the size of yours that they do not already know. Thus, they would gain little from reading the essay, and there would be little purpose in your writing it.

But let's say the assignment were narrowed down to require you to pick one thing about your hometown and to write an essay with the purpose of showing why this thing would make your hometown a good place to visit. Now, your hometown would be your subject, but the one thing you picked to write about would be your topic. For example, you might pick a local park. Because there is not as much to say about a park as there is about a whole town, you could probably write a specific essay in 500–600 words. With your specific details, this park would not sound like any other park, so you would have an easier time showing your audience why the park makes your town worth visiting.

The Essay Thesis

Thesis/thesis sentence: A thesis is the main point an essay makes about its topic. The thesis sentence states the main point. A thesis needs to be argumentative or demonstrable.

Simply defined, a **thesis** is the main idea of an essay. Many times this idea is stated in one sentence, called the **thesis sentence.** A thesis is not the same as a topic. A topic is the thing you are writing about; a thesis is the point you make about that topic. Deming Park in Terre Haute, Indiana, could be a topic. But to develop a thesis, a writer needs to ask, "What about Deming Park?" Here is one thesis sentence on Deming Park:

Deming Park is an ideal place for a family picnic.

Here are two more thesis sentences:

Deming Park provides a variety of facilities for anyone interested in sports.

Deming Park is the most popular park in Terre Haute.

Each of these thesis sentences says something about Deming Park, and each could be developed into an essay if the writer was familiar with the park. Finding a thesis is sometimes difficult for beginning writers. When beginners have a topic, they tend to want to write everything they know about it. When they do this, they end up with a paper that either has no point or has so many different points that the audience cannot tell what point the essay is trying to make.

As a written product, an essay should have a topic that can be covered within the length of the essay and a clear thesis that says something about the topic. To ensure that it has both, you must give careful consideration to both the topic and the thesis during the process of writing.

■ Writing an Essay: The Process

In this section, we will apply the writing process as discussed in Chapter 1 to the writing of essays.

Finding a Topic

College writing assignments can be different from one another. Sometimes a teacher may assign you a topic. For example, an economics teacher might assign an essay asking you to show whether stocks are a good or bad investment during times of inflation. When a teacher assigns such a specific topic, your job is easier because you do not have to start with a broad subject and then find a limited topic.

Sometimes, however, a teacher might give you a broad subject area to write about, and you have to limit the subject to a topic. Consider a class in world politics in which students spend about a third of the semester studying the United Nations. At the end of the unit, the instructor asks them to write a ten-page term paper on some aspect of the United Nations. Given all that they have learned about the United Nations, they cannot say much about the whole organization in ten pages. So from the subject area of the United Nations, one student came up with a topic on the influence of the Soviet Union in the UN, which he was able to cover in fairly specific detail in the ten pages.

In some cases, an instructor will just assign a paper on something covered in the course. In this case, you have to start with a very broad subject area — the whole course — limit that broad area to a smaller subject area that interests you, and then finally limit the smaller subject to a topic. One student was taking a course in black American history and was told to write a five-page essay on any aspect of the course. Beginning with the subject of black history, she limited herself to the life of W. E. B. DuBois, a black sociologist and writer. She realized, however, that since DuBois had done so much in his life, she could never cover his whole life in five pages. After thinking about the subject of DuBois's life, she finally limited her topic to how DuBois overcame extreme prejudice to become the first black person to earn a degree from Harvard University.

Learning how to limit a topic takes practice and experience. The more you write, though, the easier it becomes. The first thing to keep in mind is that a topic is usually much more specific than a subject area. However, you also have to be careful not to limit your topic so much that you do not have enough to say to produce an essay as long as you want. Working through the following exercise will begin to show you what writers have to consider in moving from subject to a limited topic.

E X E R C I S E   3.1   The following items could be subjects or topics. Following each is a specified number of typed pages. Identify each item as a subject or a topic, and then briefly explain why the item would or would not make a good topic for an essay of the length specified. Before doing the exercises, read the examples carefully.

Example 1   Choosing a tuxedo (15 pages). This is a topic, but it is probably too limited for a fifteen-page essay because even though there are different types of tuxedos for different occasions, the writer would run out of things to say unless he or she went into details that the reader would not need.

Example 2   The Apollo missions to the moon (4 pages). This is a subject because it is too broad for a four-page essay. There were many missions, and four pages would not allow the writer to be specific about any of them.

Example 3   Reasons for dropping a class (3 pages). This is a good topic for an essay of three pages. The writer could explain that students sometimes get bad advice, that teachers might make poor first impressions, and that the class might not be what a student expected. The writer could provide specific examples for each reason.

1. The music of the Beatles (4 pages)
2. How urban street gangs pressure youths to join (3–4 pages)
3. Abraham Lincoln (10 pages)
4. Deciding to go college (3–4 pages)
5. The fun of reading to children (3 pages)
6. Changing a flat tire (10 pages)
7. A music video (2 pages)
8. High school studies (3 pages)
9. The exterior appearance of the local courthouse (3–4 pages)
10. The nutritional value of a fast food burger (2 pages)

Using Invention Strategies to Find a Topic

The discussion of invention strategies in Chapter 1 went through the process of finding a topic, though the focus was on how to use the strategies rather than specifically on finding a topic. In the example throughout that section, we began with the broad subject area of smoking and eventually limited the subject to the topic of quitting smoking. Here you will see how the invention strategies can be used as a way to limit a subject area down to a topic that you can cover in an essay of 500–600 words.

Brainstorming   We start with the subject Deming Park and use the brainstorming strategy to limit it to one topic. The following is a brainstorming list on Deming Park:

Deming Park
sports

good place to go in nice weather
softball

duck pond	miniature train for kids
swimming pool	picnic facilities
tennis courts	clean and safe
well patrolled	course for Frisbee golf
children's playground	no drinking alcohol
basketball courts	nature trails
first aid station	lots of trees and wooded areas

Some of the items in the list are general, such as sports; some are more specific, such as the miniature train ride for children. If you sorted all of these items out and grouped related items together, you could probably write an essay describing the whole park. However, since you have only 500–600 words to work with, such an essay might still be too general. You might look over the list and discover that you are most interested in the facilities for families. Limiting your audience to families, you can then list the items that would appeal most to them:

good place to go in nice weather	duck pond
miniature train for kids	swimming pool
clean and safe	well patrolled
course for Frisbee golf	picnic facilities
children's playground	no drinking alcohol
first aid station	nature trails
lots of trees and wooded areas	

You could also have come up with this topic using any of the other invention strategies. Rather than work through each strategy completely, we present the first step in using each one.

Clustering   An example of clustering is shown at the top of the next page.

The Journalist's Questions

Who? All kinds of people, families, people wanting to play sports, picnickers, young couples, groups of teens

What? Go to Deming Park for fun

When? Spring, summer, whenever it is warm

Where? Deming Park, in picnic areas, around duck pond, on sports facilities (tennis and basketball courts, softball diamonds, swimming pool, Frisbee golf course)

Why? To have a good time, to picnic, to exercise

How? Safely, because of rules, park patrols, and first aid

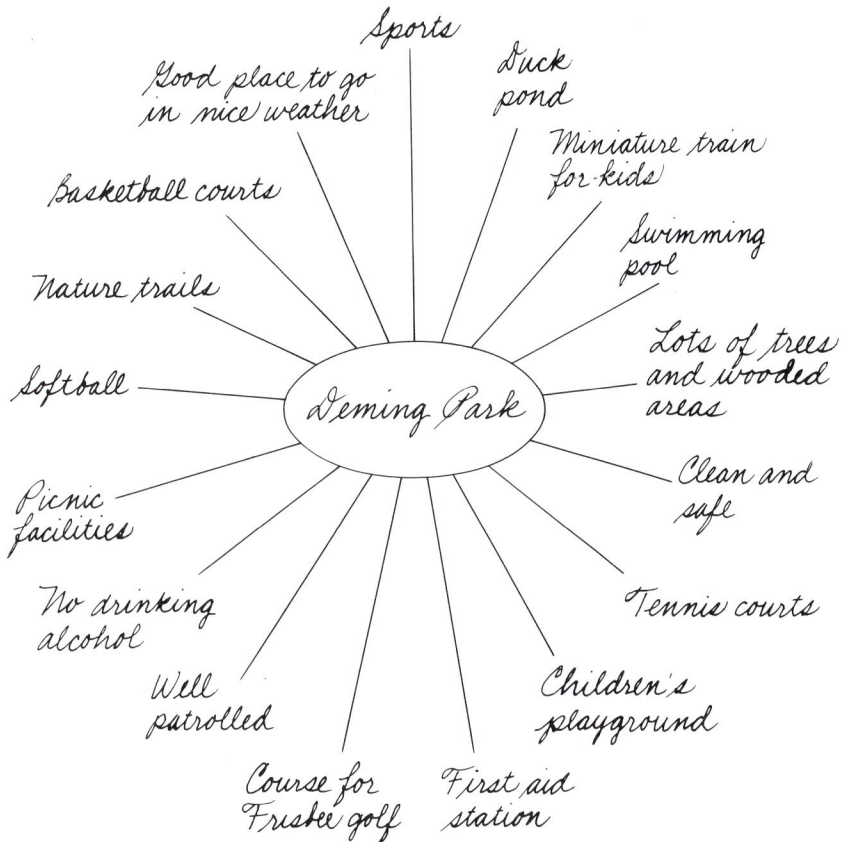

A clustering diagram with "Deming Park" in the center oval, connected to: Sports, Good place to go in nice weather, Basketball courts, Nature trails, Softball, Picnic facilities, No drinking alcohol, Well patrolled, Course for Frisbee golf, First aid station, Children's playground, Tennis courts, Clean and safe, Lots of trees and wooded areas, Swimming pool, Miniature train for kids, Duck pond.

Freewriting

Deming Park is one place that makes Terre Haute, Indiana, worth visiting. Especially in the summer. It's good for picnics. There's a lot to do there, play tennis, softball or basketball, or jog. Families go a lot. To have picnics. It's safe and clean because of the park patrol. There's the Frisbee golf course too, which kids seem to like. Also they are always feeding the ducks or riding on that train. I guess it's a good place for picnics, or playing sports.

Any of the invention strategies could help you explore the broad subject of Deming Park. But, of course, you would then have to limit yourself to one topic with the purpose of addressing a specific audience.

E X E R C I S E   3.2   Choose as a subject something you are good at — a sport, a hobby, a job, a leisure activity, a school subject. Don't overlook your skill in any area;

students have written this essay on everything from chemistry to shooting pool. Once you have made your choice, try each invention strategy to come up with a topic and notes limited enough to be covered in an essay of about 500 words.

Writing the Thesis Sentence

As discussed earlier, a thesis is the main idea of an essay, and a thesis sentence states that main idea. Once you have the topic, you need to say something about it in a complete sentence. As you write the thesis sentence, you need to make sure you do not slip back into referring to the subject instead of the topic. Suppose, for example, you wrote the following thesis:

People can have a lot of fun at Deming Park.

Although this sentence is true, it is too general and too broad. "People" could refer to anyone who enjoys the park, and "fun" is not specific enough to get across what you want to say about how families enjoy the park. Since you have limited your topic and audience to families, the thesis has to be specific enough to match the topic and address it to the audience.

Going back to your earlier examples of thesis sentences about the park, you might pick this one:

Deming Park is an ideal place for a family picnic.

This sentence does not sound bad, but as you look it over carefully and compare it with your final brainstorming list, you see that the list covers more than picnics. Although the paper will include picnics, it will also cover family recreation, amusements for children, and so on. Your problem is that in stating the thesis you have been too specific; you need to be more general. Perhaps you could change *picnic* to *activities*. This more general word seems a better choice, but as you look it over, it seems a bit too general because the word *activities* could cover anything pleasant that families do together. So you try *outings,* ending up with this thesis:

Deming Park is an ideal place for family outings.

With this thesis, you have hit the mark. Not only have you specified that you are writing about families, but with the word *outings* you are being general enough to cover everything from picnicking to swimming. Yet the word is specific enough to let the audience know what you mean.

The following summary of the qualities of a good thesis sentence can help you test any thesis sentence you come up with for an essay.

A Thesis Is Limited   A thesis is limited according to the topic and the length of the essay. For instance, a short essay of around 500 words needs a very limited thesis:

Too Broad	There are serious objections to grading systems in American colleges and universities.
Limited by Place	There are serious objections to the grading system at State College.
Limited by Number (One Problem)	Many students at State College value grades more than learning.
Limited by Time	In recent years, students at State College have begun to value grades more than learning.

EXERCISE 3.3   The following thesis sentences are too broad and need to be limited. Limit each one by place, time, or number.

1. Living in a small town causes less stress than living in a large city.
2. The space program needs to be more careful about safety.
3. City services need to be upgraded.
4. The University of Oklahoma has a history of great football teams.
5. Political conventions to nominate the president are dull and needless exercises.
6. Dogs make good pets because of their loyalty.
7. Wearing pierced earrings has become very popular.
8. American students know very little about geography.
9. Tuition costs are too high.
10. Subway trains can be an efficient means of transportation in large cities.

A Thesis Is Neither Too General Nor Too Specific   A thesis sentence should be general enough to cover all aspects of the topic, but specific enough to let the reader know exactly what point the writer wants to make. When a thesis sentence is too general, the reader does not quite know what the paper will say about the topic. When a thesis sentence is too specific, it usually contains details that should come later in the essay or that have nothing to do with the writer's purpose and should be cut altogether.

Too General	Many students are too concerned with grades.
Too Specific	Many students at State College just cram for tests and don't care what they learn. (Cramming would

probably be only one point used to support your thesis).

Just Right   Many students at State College value grades more than learning.

To make sure your thesis is not too general, try to avoid using vague words such as *interesting, bad, neat, unique, great,* and so on. Also, save your details for the body of the paper.

EXERCISE 3.4   Some of the following thesis sentences are too general, and some are too specific. Rewrite each one to make it more effective.

1. Pontiacs are good cars.
2. Seven of ten twelfth graders at Jefferson High School could not find Florida on a map of the United States.
3. My elementary school principal, Ms. Glass, who was very tall and always wore gray suits, could strike fear into the hearts of any kid from a kindergartener to an eighth grader.
4. In the 1980s, people tended to be selfish.
5. Comic books can be interesting.
6. The Honda Civic, because it costs little to maintain and gets thirty-five miles to a gallon in town, provides inexpensive transportation.
7. Cajun cooking is famous for such spicy dishes as jambalaya, red beans and rice, gumbo, blackened redfish, and seafood étouffée.
8. Cajun cooking tastes great.
9. Richard Hatcher, Tom Bradley, Andrew Young, Kenneth Gibson, and Harold Washington, black mayors of large cities, have shown that blacks can excel in high political office.
10. Blacks make good mayors of big cities.

A Thesis Is Argumentative or Demonstrable   A thesis should not be an obvious fact that your audience will accept without support. A thesis can be a controversial argument such as a claim that abortion is right or wrong, or it can be a sentence that just needs to be demonstrated for the reader to accept it.

Fact   New York has the largest population of any American city.

Thesis   A person must make at least $50,000 a year in New York to live a middle-class lifestyle.

Fact   My paper will explain the trade of carpentry.

Thesis   Carpentry is a well-paying and fulfilling occupation.

Fact	University *A* is larger than University *B*.
Thesis	Students can get just as good an education at University *B* as they can at University *A*.

E X E R C I S E   3.5   The following are some possible thesis sentences. Indicate which sentences are arguable or demonstrable theses and which are facts. For each sentence that's a fact, write a sentence that could be argued or demonstrated about the same topic.

1. I like bass fishing.
2. The Louvre in Paris contains more art than anyone can see in one day.
3. Disney World is in Orlando, Florida.
4. Tuition costs $7500 at Jefferson College this year.
5. Stripping and refinishing furniture is a time-consuming but worthwhile hobby.
6. The bald eagle is the symbol of the United States.
7. Designer jeans are a needless waste of money.
8. Cable television offers more programs than network television, but network shows are free.
9. The number of computer science majors today could lead to a poor job market in computers in the future.
10. My paper is about the Soviet Union having a larger area of land than the United States.

E X E R C I S E   3.6   Tell why each of the following sentences would or would not make a good thesis sentence for a paper of around 500 words.

1. *Raiders of the Lost Ark* was a very interesting movie.
2. Male-female relationships can be very complex.
3. Peer pressure is the major reason teens get into drugs.
4. Poor coaching contributed heavily to the poor record of the South Central basketball team last season.
5. This paper will discuss the space shuttle.
6. The proper grip is the key to an effective golf swing.
7. John F. Kennedy was the youngest president in U.S. history.
8. My paper is about getting a pilot's license.
9. Children should learn to swim at as early an age as possible.
10. Ice skating is fun.

E X E R C I S E   3.7   In Exercise 3.2, you formulated a topic for an essay about something you are good at. Now write two possible thesis sentences for your essay —

one bad one and one good one that you could use in writing the essay. Be ready to explain why the one is bad and the other is good.

Keeping Your Audience in Mind

In the process of planning your essay, as you use the invention strategies, form a topic, and write a thesis sentence, you need to remember your audience at all times. If you look back over previous discussions, you will notice that the audience is mentioned often. While you think of your audience throughout the process, you should also spend some time analyzing the audience directly.

Chapter 1 presented a series of questions for analyzing an audience. When you write essays, you should refer to those questions. The three major questions were the following:

1. Who is your audience?
2. What are your audience's attitudes toward your writing?
3. How is your audience going to use your writing?

If you apply these questions to the topic on Deming Park, they can help you to consider the topic more fully. Since the essay was assigned in a writing class, you can assume an audience of classmates. Which of those classmates is your essay directed toward? Those with families? Any who live close enough to the park to visit it for a family outing? What is their attitude toward the topic? Most would probably be neutral to receptive. In other words, you do not have to worry about hostility, but still you need to show the park well enough to convince the audience that it is worth visiting. How is the audience going to use this essay? One way might be to make a decision on whether to visit the park. Given this purpose, the audience would want to know where it is, if there are any costs for activities, if they need to reserve picnic areas in advance, if the park is safe, and so on.

You have now come up with some points that did not appear when you used the invention strategies — for instance, the possibility of costs and reservations. This does not mean you have to add additional sections to the essay. It does mean, however, you have to work the audience's concerns into the sections you already have. For instance, in discussing the picnic areas, you could tell the audience in a brief sentence how to reserve a picnic area — either by arriving early or making reservations if needed.

Do not lose sight of your audience as you write. Spending some time analyzing the audience will help you to keep it in mind, and you will write a better essay.

EXERCISE 3.8 Using the full set of audience analysis questions in Chapter 1, analyze the possible audience for your essay on something you do well.

Organizing Your Invention Notes

Once you have come up with a set of invention notes, formed a topic, written a thesis sentence, and analyzed your audience, you are ready to begin **organizing** your draft. At this point, you should return to your notes and think about the order in which you want to present the material and then group related information together. For instance, in looking over your brainstorming list for the family activities in Deming Park, you could organize the items in a list like this one:

Beauty of the Park
lots of trees and wooded areas
nature trails

Family Recreation
swimming pool
Frisbee golf course

Children's Amusements
feeding ducks in pond
riding the miniature train
playing on the playground

Picnic Facilities
picnic tables
shelters cover most tables
barbecue grills provided

Safe Family Environment
no alcohol allowed
well patrolled
first aid station

From this list you can begin to plan a rough draft. You have to decide in what order you want to put the groups of material. Also, you might find while you are drafting that you want to change the order.

E X E R C I S E   3.9   Organize the notes you have been making for your essay on something you do well.

Drafting the Essay

Keeping the Draft Organized   As you write the draft of the essay on Deming Park, you should stay aware of the way you are organizing it. The notes on the essay are put into groups. Each group forms a class of items that would appeal to a family wanting to enjoy an outing in a park. You should try to put each class into a separate paragraph or two so that the audience would not have to sort out all the reasons Deming Park is a good place for family outings. For instance, under the class called "Amusements for Children," you might be tempted to discuss the swimming pool because children enjoy it. But since adults also like the pool, it fits better under the class "Recreational Activities" because that class can include adults and teenagers as well as children.

You might find that one or two of the classes could be mixed. Suppose that as you discuss each family activity, you find that you are integrating details about the beauty of the park — the trees and grassy banks around the pond, the rustic logs of the picnic shelters, and so on. In other words, if you refer to the beauty in your discussion of family activities, you would not have to discuss it in a separate section of the essay. Similarly, the points about safety could be worked into each discussion of family activities — the lifeguards at the pool, the patrols in the picnic areas, the tameness of the ducks, and so on. These two items — beauty and safety — could be mixed in because neither of them is a family activity. But the other items would need to be kept in separate classes. A reader would be confused if you jumped from barbecue grills to the swimming pool to the train all in the same paragraph. Organizing the essay carefully is crucial.

Developing the Draft   *Developing* the draft means that you include enough information to meet the needs of your audience and to support the claim made in your thesis sentence. Your invention notes would give you a start, but you would have to develop each point in your notes more fully in your draft. You could not, for instance, simply say that Deming Park provides nice picnic shelters where a family can have a barbecue. You would have to be more specific and detailed if you expected the audience to accept your thesis. It would be necessary to tell how to reserve a shelter. It also would be wise to include some details to let the audience know that there are different sizes, ranging from small ones with only one table, which would be suitable for a small family, to very large ones with up to six tables, which would be suitable for a family reunion. You could then describe what the shelters look like and what kind of barbecue grills are provided.

Also you should try to bring details to life. For instance, it would be pretty dull if you wrote, "There's a pond where children can feed the ducks." Instead you might try, "In the southeast corner of the park, ducks populate a tree-lined pond, often waddling up the grassy banks, where children enjoy feeding them everything from bread to potato chips."

Including details in your draft is important. If you have your topic clearly in mind, you can draft from your invention notes. But if you think you might forget some of your details, you could use any of the invention strategies to develop one of your points further before you write or as you write. If you need details about feeding ducks, for instance, you could make another brainstorming list to come up with the details that are included in the sentence in the previous paragraph, or you could use a more ordered invention strategy, such as the journalist's questions:

Who? Children
What? Feed ducks
Where? On the banks of the pond in the southeast corner of the park
When? Anytime, doesn't matter
Why? For enjoyment
How? Giving the ducks bread, potato chips

You may think at this point that you have gone backward, that when you are supposed to be drafting you are back to invention. That's true.

Recall from Chapter 1 that the parts of the writing process often overlap. Even if you do not write notes for each point, as you did with the feeding of the ducks, it will help to have the invention strategies in mind as you draft each point.

EXERCISE 3.10 Take one of the points from your notes on your topic and jot down additional information and details that you would use to develop that point to meet the needs of your audience.

Revising

Once you have completed a draft, you need to revise it. The same considerations apply when you revise as when you draft: thesis, audience, organization, development. Chapter 5 covers revision in depth, but for now consider the following strategies.

Revising the Thesis   Sometimes when you complete a draft, you will find that your thesis no longer covers everything you have written. Suppose in writing the paper on family outings that you discovered that you spent most of your draft on the swimming pool at Deming Park. If you have enough information on just the pool, you could cut everything else and end up with a thesis that states that Deming Park pool provides a pleasant and safe place for families to swim. This would be a major change — in fact, a change of the whole topic. Sometimes such a change is necessary because no matter how much invention you do, at times you do not discover what really concerns you until you begin drafting. At other times, you might need to make only small adjustments in your thesis, but always reconsider the thesis after you have completed your draft.

Revising for Better Organization   If you organize your notes well, you should have a pretty good idea of the way the parts of your draft will fit together. However, when you complete your draft, you might find that paragraphs could be put in a different order, combined, or separated.

You saw how you might integrate the beauty and safety of Deming Park into the sections on family activities. In that sense, you would have been revising while drafting. But you might not have made the discovery until after the draft was complete. Similarly, suppose in ordering your notes that you had placed the section on picnic facilities last, thinking that since it was a major attraction of the park you would want the reader to remember it most. In reading the draft suppose you discovered that many of the other activities would be done in relation to picnicking — children feeding ducks as their parents prepare food, swimming or Frisbee golf after eating, and so on. As a result, you would want to discuss the picnicking first to set up the activities that follow.

Revising for Development   When you revise the way your essay is developed, you either add information and details or cut them according to your purpose. Your purpose in the park essay is to show the variety of family activities. Suppose on completing the draft you discover that in discussing the swimming pool you left out the fact that there is a water slide in the pool area. Certainly you would want to add such an attraction to your discussion of the pool. On the other hand, suppose in discussing the miniature train ride for children that most of your paragraph described in detail how authentic the engine looks and sounds. If this description is so long and detailed that the audience would forget the purpose of the essay, you would need to cut out some of the details about the train.

A student of mine once wrote an essay with a thesis stating that a trip to Florida with friends showed him he was not as mature as he thought. He had notes on points to support this thesis, such as how he did not have enough sense to take in the sun gradually and so was severely burned and how he mismanaged his money. Yet he spent the first three pages of the paper writing about how he and his friends prepared for the trip and made the drive. His details on these points were fine, but they had nothing to do with his thesis.

As a beginning writer, you may hate to cut anything because perhaps you fear that you cannot get enough written down to develop an essay. However, if you fully develop the points that support your thesis and meet your audience's needs, you will have no problem cutting unneeded material.

Revising for Your Audience   Any revising to improve your essay's thesis, organization, and development is done for the benefit of your audience. In addition, you may need to make other revisions to account for your audience's knowledge of your topic. For instance, you might include the location of Deming Park. You could probably get that into the beginning of your essay even before you state your thesis.

Many times in an essay on a topic with which you are familiar, you refer to things that you know about as if your audience knew about them too, but that's not always true. For example, in reading the brainstorming list about Deming Park, you may not have known what Frisbee golf is. Although many people play the game on courses around the country, Frisbee golf is not exactly the national pastime, and you could not assume that all your readers would be familiar with it. In revising the essay, you should add a brief description of the game if you have not included one while drafting.

Along with making sure the audience is aware of the meaning of your references, remember also to revise any language that does not fit the writing situation. Though written for a writing class, the Deming Park essay could be rather informal because it deals with informal activities. Thus, if in reading your draft you begin to find big words and long sentences, you could try to use more familiar words and shorter sentences to make the essay less formal.

Once you revise the draft, you would write a second draft and begin editing for errors and misspellings. Chapter 5, which focuses on revision, and Chapter 10, on editing, can give you more tips if you need them. Once you are satisfied, you would type or neatly write the final copy and proofread it once more before turning the essay over to your audience.

■ Essay Strategies

Essay strategies: Ways of thinking about and organizing the information in an essay.

Many **strategies** exist for organizing an essay. These strategies are often identified as patterns of organization in completed essays. You may have heard someone say an essay is an example of narration, process analysis, comparison-contrast, description, classification, or argument. Once an essay is written, we can identify its pattern of organization, and in doing so, as readers we can better understand the essay.

In writing essays, however, you need to think of these patterns as strategies that you can use in writing essays. You do not usually start out thinking that you are going to write a classification essay or a comparison-contrast essay. Rather, these patterns result from your thoughts about your topic. For example, if your essay on Deming Park contained a section on picnicking, a section on children's amusements, and another on recreation, the essay would be considered an example of classification because you would have broken down the large category of family activities into different classes of activities. In other words, the topic and the way you thought about it during the writing process would have resulted in a classification essay, a pattern you could identify in the finished product.

Narrating

Narrating: An essay strategy in which the writer presents information in chronological order.

Chronological: According to the order of time.

Even though an essay is not a story, when you are **narrating,** you are telling a story. A narrative essay is based on true events and also contains your feelings and opinions about those events. Therefore, a narration can be an essay. In narrating, you present the material in your essay in **chronological** order, that is, according to the order of time.

If you were to use narration to develop an essay on family activities at Deming Park, you could tell the story of one family's day at the park. You could use your own family or a typical family. You would ask what the family does first, second, third, and so on until you have covered all that the family does from the time it arrives until the time it leaves. For this narrative essay your notes from the brainstorming list might look like this:

arrives and chooses picnic area
unpacks food and sets up at table
while Dad starts fire, Mom and kids go to duck pond
family eats
whole family goes swimming

after swimming, family returns to picnic area and eats the last hot
    dogs and hamburgers
family begins to pack up to leave
horsing around child slams finger in cooler top and is taken to first
    aid station
family leaves

     As you draft this essay, you would follow your list, adding details; but the point is that you would follow the family hour by hour through the outing at the park. This essay would certainly be different from the version that classified family activities.

     Which essay would be better, the classification or narration? The strategy you choose for organizing your paper depends on your purpose. You determined that your purpose in this essay was to show one place that makes the town worth visiting. Part of that purpose is to show all the features of the park that would interest families. In classifying the features, you would be able to cover them all. In narrating, you would be limited to what the family did on one particular outing, and they might not have used all the facilities. For instance, the family in the preceding list did not use the Frisbee golf course or put the small children on the miniature train. Both of these features were covered when you grouped family activities into classes.

     This does not mean that classifying is always a better strategy for organization than narrating. Many topics lend themselves to narrating. For example, suppose a science professor asked you to write a report on an experiment you did. Your purpose would be to show how you did the experiment and what its results were. In this case, you could use narration to take your audience, the professor, through each step in the experiment.

E X E R C I S E 3.11 Take some part of your topic on something you are good at and try to make a brainstorming list in which you organize the whole essay or some part of it chronologically. As you make the list, consider whether narration would be an effective strategy in view of your purpose.

Analyzing a Process

Analyzing a process:
An essay strategy in which the writer shows how to do something, how something works, or how something is done.

Analyzing a process, like narration, uses chronological order. In analyzing a process, you organize your topic step by step. There are two types of process analysis. In one, commonly called the "how-to" essay, a writer tells a reader how to perform some task, such as changing a tire, making bread, tying a knot, swinging a golf club, and so on. In this type, you assume that your audience is going to perform the task you are writing about. In the second type, the writer shows how something is or was done. In this type, you assume that your audience is not going to perform the task but wants to know how something works.

The second type of process analysis could help you in certain college papers.

For instance, a business professor might ask you to write a paper showing how a company develops and sells a new product. In a political science course, you might be asked to show how laws are made in a certain country. In an electrical engineering course, you might have to write a paper showing the workings of something as simple as a flashlight or as complicated as a computer. In a biology course, you might be asked to show how a certain bacteria grows. Analyzing processes is a widely used method of writing because audiences are often interested in how something is done or how something works.

When you analyze a process, you have to consider these questions:

1. What is (or was) needed for the process to occur?
2. What are the steps in the process?
3. Are there smaller processes in the larger process?
4. In what order do the steps occur?
5. How does one step affect other steps?
6. What is the result of the process?

If you think back to Chapter 1, you should remember the discussion of the writing process. We can apply each of these questions both to our discussion of the writing process in Chapter 1 and to an essay analyzing how an automobile carburetor works.

What Is Needed?   For writing to occur a writing situation must exist in which the writer has a purpose, role, and audience. If you are writing about a carburetor, you would have to show what is mixed in it — air and vaporized gasoline — and the parts needed to do the mixing.

What Are the Steps?   By now you probably know quite well that the writing process consists of invention, drafting, revising, and editing. In the carburetor essay, you would trace the steps in which the parts work to create a mixture of air and vaporized gasoline that is then drawn into the cylinders of the engine.

Are There Smaller Processes in the Larger Process?   Certainly there are processes within the writing process. Each invention strategy, for instance, is itself a process with steps to be followed. The way gasoline enters a carburetor is also a process itself, which is a step in the larger process of mixing the vaporized gasoline and air.

In What Order Do the Steps Occur?   Although the steps in the writing process can overlap, we ordered them chronologically in Chapter 1 to show that invention usually comes first, drafting second, revision third, and editing last. In the carburetor, the air and gas have to enter before they can be mixed together.

How Does One Step Affect Other Steps? Good invention strategies can make drafting easier. Also, one step in the process can overlap with another. Writing about the carburetor, you would have to show how the steps of air and gas entering the carburetor must occur at the same time because it takes both to make the vapor that the engine burns.

What Is the Result of the Process? Even though the result is the last part of the process, in organizing an essay you put the result first. That way the audience does not have to guess what the process is leading up to. Did you ever see a recipe that does not tell you what you are making before giving directions on how to make it? In the essay on the carburetor, you would want the reader to know early that a carburetor is a device that produces a combustible vapor to be burned in the cylinders. Likewise, different kinds of writing are the results of the writing process.

E X E R C I S E   3.12 Consider the topic you came up with in Exercise 3.2, and think about it as a process. Jot down some notes that would help you analyze the topic as a process. For example, how does someone become good at the thing you are good at?

Analyzing Causes

Analyzing causes: An essay strategy in which the writer shows why something happened.

Analyzing causes is a very common strategy in writing. Because human beings are naturally curious, we like to know why things happen. If something bad happens, knowing the causes can perhaps help us to prevent it from happening again. If something good occurs, knowing the causes may help us make it happen again. Writing often analyzes causes. An editorial in a newspaper may analyze why the government set a certain policy. College writing also analyzes causes. Consider an essay on why the United States entered World War I or an essay on why an experiment produced certain results.

When you analyze causes, you start with the result of a chain of events. This result is called the *effect*. You then work backward, looking for the reasons — causes — for this effect. A brainstorming list can be helpful. Suppose you are analyzing why a college basketball team had a poor season. Your list might look like this:

star players graduated
poor coaching
tough schedule
newer players lacked teamwork on offense
weak defense
players fought among themselves
injuries

No matter what your topic, you would then have to analyze your causes and divide them into major causes and minor causes. Here is where your judgment comes in. While you might see poor coaching as a major cause of the team's performance, another writer might place less blame on the coach. You also need to explore how one cause might have led to others. Was the team's weak defense caused by the coach's inability to teach defense or by the players' lack of talent and determination?

In analyzing causes, you must always take care not to simplify your analysis. While you may see coaching as the major cause of the team's poor season, you would have to admit that other causes were beyond the coach's control — players graduating, injuries, and inexperience, for instance. Still, even admitting this, you might want to show that the coach was the major cause. You could organize your causes like this:

Minor Causes	*Major Causes*
star players graduated	poor coaching
tough schedule	no teamwork on offense
injuries	weak defense
	players fighting among themselves

In drafting the essay, you could cover the minor causes first. Next you could argue that even with these problems the team should not have had as bad a season as it did. You could then move to the major causes, and if you wanted to single out the coaching as *the* major cause, you could show how poor coaching led to the lack of teamwork, the poor defense, and the players fighting among themselves.

One way to grasp the way causes are analyzed is to remember that an essay that analyzes causes usually has a thesis that is argumentative. In contrast, an essay analyzing processes usually has a thesis that needs only to be demonstrated.

EXERCISE 3.13 Make a brainstorming list that shows the causes of your success in the area you chose in Exercise 3.2. Then divide the list into major and minor causes and put the items in the order that you would use if you were to write an essay analyzing causes.

Comparing and Contrasting

Comparing and contrasting: An essay strategy in which the writer shows the similarities and differences between two things.

Comparing and contrasting is a strategy you use all the time in your thinking. In comparing and contrasting things, you come to know them, and thus you can make judgments and form opinions about them. If you are buying a sweater, you might find two that you like and compare them at the same price while contrasting the color. You compare and contrast people, places, books, classes, TV shows — the list is endless.

Because comparing and contrasting is so basic to the way we think, it is also a very common type of writing, both in college and in the workplace. An executive writes a report comparing last year's sales figures with this year's; a student writes a research essay comparing the early years of U.S. involvement in Vietnam with the U.S. presence in Latin America.

Like all strategies for organization, comparing and contrasting is the result of the writer's purpose. You do not need to compare and contrast Deming Park with other parks because you want to show only its attractions. But suppose you are majoring in recreational studies and are asked to write a paper showing what makes a good park and what makes a bad park. Given this purpose, you could compare and contrast Deming Park with a less attractive park.

If you have a topic that requires you to compare and contrast, you can organize your draft in two different ways: successive coverage and alternating coverage.

Successive Coverage If one thing succeeds another, it follows another. In comparing and contrasting using successive coverage, you would make all your points about one thing and then all your points about another. Notes for an essay comparing and contrasting two parks — say, Deming Park and Fairbanks Park, also in Terre Haute — might look like this:

Deming Park	*Fairbanks Park*
sports facilities	sports facilities
family facilities	family facilities
natural beauty	natural beauty

As you draft this essay, you would first cover all the points about Deming Park before covering the same points in the same order about Fairbanks Park. Successive coverage works well when you do not have many points of comparison and contrast and when your essay will be relatively short.

If you have a lot of points to compare and contrast, successive coverage will not work well because the reader will have to remember everything about the first item in the essay while reading about the second much later. When you have many points, alternating coverage works better.

Alternating Coverage As the name implies, when you use alternating coverage, you alternate between the items you are comparing and contrasting. Rather than presenting all the information about one and then all about the other, you list the points of comparison and contrast and then alternately discuss each item that you are comparing. Your notes for an essay on the parks might look like this:

Sports Facilities
Deming Park
Fairbanks Park

Family Facilities
Deming Park
Fairbanks Park

Natural Beauty
Deming Park
Fairbanks Park

Using alternate coverage, you could discuss as many points as you wanted without worrying that the reader has forgotten what you said about one of the items being compared and contrasted. Thus, you could use alternating coverage for longer essays that compare and contrast.

EXERCISE 3.14 Choose one of the following pairs and make two sets of notes, one using successive coverage, the other using alternating coverage.

1. Two children
2. Two athletes
3. Two different ways of performing the same task
4. Two cars
5. Two courses or teachers
6. Two styles of dress
7. Two breakfast cereals

EXERCISE 3.15 Use comparison and contrast to explore the topic you have been working with in previous exercises. For instance, compare and contrast the basic and advanced knowledge in this area. Or compare and contrast the area you chose with another. When you have your notes, ask yourself if comparison and contrast would be a good way to get across what you want to say about your topic.

Classifying

Classifying: An essay strategy in which the writer divides the information into classes.

As you worked through the essay on family outings in Deming Park, you got some experience in **classifying.** The final divisions in the planning of that essay, as you remember, classified the types of activities that would interest families. As the name suggests, in classifying, you divide items into classes or groups. To set up a system of classification, you need at least three groups. The items in each group should share some quality that places them in that group, but they do not have to be exactly the same. For instance, if you have a dresser with socks in one drawer, underwear in another, and sweaters in another, you have a classification system. But within one class, say the sock drawer, the items can have differences.

Human beings classify constantly. Like comparing and contrasting, classifying is a way of thinking. It is a way of putting things in order and of seeing differences between one group and others.

Because people often think in terms of classification, they often write the same way. In classifying, the writer usually wants the reader to see the differences between classes for some purpose. In the essay on Deming Park, by classifying the types of family activities, you could show a variety that could appeal to different families.

Classifying occurs primarily in two ways: by built-in qualities and by imposed qualities. When you classify by built-in qualities, the differences in the groups are already there. For instance, if you group teachers according to the courses they teach, you would use the built-in classes of math teachers, English teachers, history teachers, science teachers, and so on. But if you group teachers as good teachers, average teachers, and poor teachers, you would be imposing the qualities on each class. In other words, your judgments would form the classes.

Sometimes an essay can use both systems. If you classify automobiles according to the country where they are produced, you might come up with the following classes: American cars, Japanese cars, German cars, Italian cars, and British cars. Then once you have these classes, you can divide each class by imposing qualities on the cars in it. For each class, your divisions might then look like this: American cars you like, American cars you consider average, American cars you do not like.

You might end up with classes within a class. That can happen, too. Suppose you had a drawer full of sweaters. They form one class of your clothes. Then suppose you put heavy sweaters on the left side of the drawer, medium-weight sweaters in the middle, and lightweight sweaters on the left. You would be classifying items that are part of the larger class, sweaters.

EXERCISE 3.16 Pick one of the following items and, using built-in qualities, classify it into at least three groups. Then using imposed qualities, divide each group into at least three more classes.

1. breakfast cereals
2. television programs
3. restaurants
4. books
5. printed T-shirts
6. soft drinks

EXERCISE 3.17 Use classification to explore your topic on something you are good at. For instance, classify the people in your area into beginners, intermediates, and experts; or classify the tasks in your area according to levels of difficulty.

Defining

Defining: An essay strategy in which the writer shows the audience what something is by placing it in a class and then showing how it differs from other members of that class.

Sometimes the purpose of an essay is to provide the audience with a definition. When AIDS first burst into the forefront of the news several years ago, many news magazine articles appeared that defined the disease. However, it is more common for **defining** to be used as part of an essay. Analyzing a process, you might have to define a term so the audience can follow your analysis. If you are analyzing how a carburetor works for an audience unfamiliar with auto mechanics, you would have to define the parts of the carburetor or your analysis would mean little to the audience.

In defining, your first step is to place a thing in its class. For example, wool is a natural fiber. Your second step is to show how the thing differs from other members of that class: wool is a natural fiber that comes from sheep. You can also add the function of the thing: wool is a natural fiber that comes from sheep and is often used for making clothing and blankets. You can also define by comparison: wool is a natural fiber about the same weight as alpaca. Or by contrast: wool is a natural fiber that is heavier than cotton.

As you can see, the strategies overlap. Your purpose was to define wool, and in defining it you compared and contrasted it with other fibers. Definitions can be as short as one sentence, as in the previous paragraph, or they can be extended, as in the following paragraph.

Frisbee golf is a game played on a grassy course similar to a golf course. But instead of using golf clubs to hit a ball into a hole, players throw a Frisbee with the object of landing it in a chain net mounted on a pole about four feet high. The distance to the net on a Frisbee course is anywhere from 25 to 100 yards, in contrast to the 100-to-500-yard distances between the tees and holes on a regular golf course. Frisbee golfers begin each "hole" with a long toss, attempting to get as close to the net as possible. Depending on where the first toss lands, players then make one or more short tosses until they land the Frisbee in the net. Scoring is the same as in golf; the player with the lowest number of tosses wins.

The primary purpose of this paragraph is to define. The paragraph starts by placing Frisbee golf in the class of game and then compares and contrasts it with regular golf. The definition also includes some analysis of the way the game is played.

In college, you may sometimes be asked to write fully developed definitions. The essay question on the Stamp Act in Chapter 2 is one such instance. But rarely would you write a whole essay that is only definition; if you did, you would need the other strategies for organization. While the other strategies enable you to define, remember that short definitions may be necessary when you write essays using the other strategies.

E X E R C I S E   3.18   Pick three of the following items and write a short definition, one or two sentences, that places the item in a class and shows how it differs from other members of the class.

1. spatula
2. antifreeze/coolant
3. any one of the strategies for organization
4. stick match
5. wristwatch

E X E R C I S E   3.19   Choose some term used in the area for your topic and define it according to class, difference, and function.

Mixing Strategies

If you read an essay, you can often identify the organizing strategy that the writer has used. At times, however, you can see more than one strategy. In analyzing causes, a writer might compare and contrast one cause with another. Or an essay using any of the strategies might stop to define something for the reader. Sometimes, though, one strategy will clearly dominate the essay, and you will be able to identify the essay by the strategy it uses. Thus, people sometimes speak of a classification essay or a definition essay or a process analysis.

In contrast, many essays will use two or more strategies within the same essay. This does not mean that the essay lacks organization but that the subject requires the writer to think about it and present it in many ways. Examine the following two paragraphs on home computers.

> The two most popular types of personal computers are those using floppy diskettes and those with hard diskettes. The floppy diskettes, as the name implies, are flat, flexible $5\frac{1}{4}$ " squares with a hole in the center. They look something like a 45 rpm record in its jacket, though the jacket of the floppy diskette is soft plastic that cannot be removed. The smaller, hard diskettes are $3\frac{1}{2}$ " squares, feel like hard plastic, and are covered with a smooth substance that looks like stretched tin foil.
>
> Computers using floppy diskettes have become very popular, but the computer industry is promoting the smaller hard diskettes. When Apple introduced the revolutionary Macintosh computer, it used the hard diskettes. Following the Macintosh, IBM introduced hard diskette systems, and industry analysts predicted that the

floppy diskette would soon be obsolete. These predictions seemed true when nearly all the new laptop computers came out with the hard diskettes. However, since so many people already own machines that use the floppy diskettes, they remain widely used today.

In the first paragraph, the writer is comparing and contrasting the two types of diskettes by how they look and feel. In the second paragraph the writer shifts to narration to show how the hard diskette was introduced to replace the floppy. The purpose of the whole essay might be to compare and contrast the two diskettes; in the third paragraph, the essay might shift back to comparing and contrasting the two on the basis of how much data they hold, or it could include a process analysis on how each one works. The writer's purpose may require many strategies to complete the overall strategy of comparing and contrasting.

It is important to remember that the strategies are ways of thinking. During invention, the writer of the two paragraphs probably thought about what each diskette looked like, how each was introduced, the advantages and disadvantages of each, and so on. This range of thinking led to the mixed organization.

Though we can identify the strategies as organizational patterns in the writing, if you think of the strategies only in this way, they become products. To use the strategies as you write, you must focus on them as thinking processes and remember that the topic and your purpose determine what strategy you use. Sometimes you need not even be aware that you are using a strategy. If you direct a stranger how to get somewhere in your hometown, you do not stop and say to yourself, "My topic is getting to point *B,* so I will analyze the process of traveling from point *A* to point *B.*" Rather, your mind automatically thinks in terms of process because of your purpose and your audience's need.

Sometimes your topic and purpose in writing are not so clear-cut. During invention and drafting, you may discover that your purpose requires you to approach the topic using one or more of the strategies; or during revision, if you find that your draft reflects a certain strategy, you can apply it more carefully.

E X E R C I S E   3.20   Pick one of the topics in Exercise 3.16 and think about how various strategies could be used in writing about it.

■ Writing Timed Essays

The essays we have discussed so far allow you a tremendous luxury — time. Writers often have time. If an executive has to write a report each month, he or she has thirty days between reports. When a student writes a term paper, the assignment is usually announced weeks or months before it is due. Even a short essay written overnight allows you a few hours to draw on the process. Yet many writing situations do not offer writers the luxury of time: a reporter must meet a deadline, a police officer must file a report on a crime, a businessperson must write a memo to address an immediate problem. Usually such people do this kind of writing so often that they have internalized the writing process for such situations. That is, they have had so much practice that they go through the process almost unconsciously. In college you are faced with basically two situations in which you must write against the clock: in-class essays and examination questions. Though you may not do your best writing in these situations, you can learn some tips that will help you through them.

In-Class Essays

In-class essays are often assigned in English classes so that you gain experience in writing against the clock. Sometimes the topic is assigned a few days before the writing, and you might be allowed to bring in a page of notes. When this is the case, the essay is not too difficult. You can take the topic home, work through your invention strategies, write a thesis sentence, and plan a pattern of organization. Even in this situation, you have to draft the essay in fifty minutes or an hour, and more than likely the draft will have to stand as the final copy (even though you may be given the opportunity to revise it at some other time). Though you can't do much, if any, revision in such a short time, it is wise to try to plan the essay so that you have at least five, preferably ten, minutes to read over and edit your paper before turning it in. You probably won't catch all your errors, but you may fix a few that could distract a reader.

Impromptu essay: An essay written in one class period without the writer knowing the topic beforehand.

A more difficult type of in-class writing is the **impromptu essay.** The word *impromptu* comes from the French, meaning "at hand." In English, it means "not rehearsed" or "spontaneous." In a writing class, it means that the instructor gives you a topic, or a choice of topics, and asks you to write an essay in class. Impromptu essays are difficult because they do not allow much time for the writing process, but you can use parts of the process to guide you.

Invention and Impromptu Essays   In an impromptu situation, the writing topic itself can sometimes suggest a thesis and a strategy for organization. Here are two impromptu topics assigned by one instructor near the end of a first-semester writing course:

1. Define a problem on campus and explain what could be done to solve it.
2. What has been your best course (excluding this one) and why?

If you look carefully at these topics, you will notice that the second one is a question but the first one tells you to do something. This difference is important. The first assignment just about gives you a strategy for organizing the essay. You are to start by defining a problem and end by explaining how to solve the problem. For each of these parts of the paper, you could quickly make a short brainstorming list. Then once you had the list, you could write a thesis sentence and begin writing by following your brainstorming list.

The second topic, because it is phrased as a question, could lead you immediately to a thesis if you answered both parts of the question. Here are two possible thesis sentences. Notice how the first part of each answers the "what" of the question while the second part answers the "why."

> Introduction to Chemistry was my best course last semester because Professor Dailey's unconventional teaching style made a difficult course fun.

> My best class last semester was Afro-American Studies because I discovered how I take equality for granted when there is still much prejudice and racism.

Once they have a thesis sentence, the students writing these essays could then come up with a brainstorming list, see what strategy for organization the list suggests, and begin drafting.

How long should you spend on invention for an impromptu essay? For an hour-long class, no more than ten minutes. Because you have so little time it is probably best to use brainstorming lists because they are faster than other invention strategies. Of course, you don't have time to make multiple lists. Rather, make just one and then number the points according to the order in which you will present them. Impromptu essays do not allow you much time for invention, but the few minutes you spend on it are worthwhile. If you just start writing as soon as you've read the topic, there is no telling where you might end up. Remember, most readers would rather read something short but organized than something long but rambling.

Drafting an Impromptu Essay   When you draft an impromptu essay, you have to move quickly, but you can't just rush through as if you were freewriting. Keep checking your invention list, and try to stick to it unless you come up with strong additional points as you are writing. However, try not to get too far off track because, unlike a draft written out of class, an impromptu essay does not allow time for moving paragraphs around or reshaping your organizational strategy. That's why invention is so important in an impromptu assignment. As you draft, you should probably stop after each paragraph and reread it quickly. Doing so can help you remember where you want the next paragraph to go. However, do not stop and mull over individual sentences unless you are really stuck. Unless you catch an obvious error, save editing for last.

Revising an Impromptu Essay   Impromptu essays do not allow time for revision, unless perhaps you are given a couple of hours to write. In most cases, your first draft is the only draft. However, you can do some revising of the brainstorming list, perhaps changing the order of a paragraph or two. Or perhaps when rereading a paragraph you might quickly combine a few sentences if needed. Otherwise, impromptu essays do not leave you time for major revision.

Editing an Impromptu Essay   If you leave yourself five or ten minutes to edit an impromptu essay, you will probably catch and correct some errors. But which ones? It is best to know what you are looking for. For example, if you know you have trouble with pronoun usage, concentrate on finding errors in such usage. Also keep an eye out for major sentence errors such as fragments, comma splices, and run-on sentences because these can be the most distracting to your reader. You won't catch every misused comma or misspelling, but if you concentrate on errors that usually give you trouble and on major sentence errors, you can clean up your essay quite a bit in five or ten minutes.

■■■■■■■■■■■■■

E X E R C I S E   3.21   Pick one of the following impromptu topics and prepare a brainstorming list and thesis for it in less than ten minutes. Time yourself.

1. It is sometimes said that during the first semester of college, a student matures more than he or she has through four years of high school. Do you agree or disagree with this statement?
2. Older students who return to college often work harder and earn better grades than traditional freshmen even though they often have responsibilities such as jobs and families. Why do you think this statement is generally true?
3. Compare and contrast two actors, actresses, teachers, parents, or athletes.
4. Define a problem in your town or neighborhood and explain what should be done to solve it.
5. Students learn about many processes in their classes: how a certain war started, how a company becomes a corporation, how a certain muscle functions, how a product is marketed. Pick a process you learned about in another class and analyze it.
6. Classify the students in your classes in terms of *one* of the following features: academic ability, clothing, body type, social background.
7. What is the most important problem facing America today and why?
8. Who is the most overrated athlete in a certain sport and why?
9. Who is the most underrated athlete in a certain sport and why?

Essay Questions   Although you will find all kinds of questions on your college examinations — true-false, multiple choice, one-word answer, matching

— essay questions are one way college instructors test their students' knowledge. Essay questions may range from requiring a short paragraph of five or six lines to a two- or three-page essay, depending how much time is allotted for the exam. In a one-hour class period, you might be expected to write one or two essays along with some short answers. In a final exam period, which can run two hours, you might have to write two or three longer essays. Though the idea of writing for an examination is scary, essay questions are not as difficult as impromptu essays.

When you write an impromptu essay you must come up with ideas about the topic quickly. When you write in response to an essay question, if you have kept up with the course and have studied sufficiently, you already have much information at hand when you begin the exam. Of course, you won't know the questions beforehand, but there is a lot you can do to answer them well.

Preparing for Essay Questions   First, when you study, use the invention strategies to review the material. Go over your class notes and textbooks and pick out the points you believe are important. Think back to the points the professor has stressed in class. Then using pen and paper, go through some invention strategies on these points. In the answer to the question on the Stamp Act in Chapter 2, the use of the journalist's questions helped the student review and organize the material. Be sure to use pen and paper because when you write things down, you review them more carefully and remember them more easily when the exam comes. Just rereading your text and notes and thinking about them won't help nearly as much as using pen and paper.

Second, list significant points and begin to think about them using the strategies for organization. This will help you see relationships between points and enable you to anticipate questions. For instance, are there issues or people the instructor might ask you to compare and contrast? Are there points that can be classified? What items might the instructor ask you to define? Have you covered anything that could be analyzed as a process? This type of thinking and listing is extremely important because the strategies reflect the way people think — the professor as well as you — and thus they can reflect the kinds of questions you will be asked.

Third, write some sample questions. In an introductory psychology course, you would have studied many different theories of psychology. Write a question asking that students classify the theories. Write another question asking that students compare and contrast two major theories. Write another question asking students to define one theory. Write one asking students to analyze the process of one of the famous experiments you studied. In writing these questions, you may get lucky and write one that will show up on the test, but that's not the point. Rather, by writing questions, you think about the important relationships in a given subject. Finally, if you have time, you can practice writing sample answers to the questions you have written.

Writing the Exam Essay   When you receive your exam, read all the questions first, noting how many points each is worth (that information is often listed) and which questions you know the most about. Figure out roughly how much time you can spend on each question. This is important. Some students will foolishly spend the time to write two or three pages on a short essay question worth only ten points and then have time to write only a page on a question worth thirty. Finally, begin answering the question you know most about, numbering it so that the professor knows which question you have started with (rarely do professors care about the order in which you answer the questions). Writing about the question you know most about has two purposes: it will give you confidence and it may jog your memory on points that apply to questions you do not know as much about.

When you begin to answer the question, just as when writing an impromptu essay, you should examine the question to see if it suggests a thesis or an organizational strategy. The following questions come from various subjects, and the way each is worded could help you organize an answer.

Explain how a fuel injection system works. (Automotive technology)

Compare and contrast the design of the 1920s flapper skirt with the miniskirts of the 1960s. (Fashion design)

What is an ''arbitrage house,'' and how does it make profits on the stock market? (Economics)

What was the ''back to basics'' movement of the 1970s and how is it similar to and different from the ''cultural literacy'' movement of the late 1980s? (Education)

Why did President Truman relieve General MacArthur of his command during the Korean War? (History)

If you know what to look for, these questions tell you how to organize them. The first question obviously wants you to analyze a process: how something works. The second clearly requires a comparison-contrast. The third and fourth, however, are a little trickier since each has two parts, but you can assume in each that you will begin with a definition before writing the process analysis of how an arbitrage house profits from the stock market or the comparison-contrast of the back to basics and cultural literacy movements. The fifth question allows you to start immediately with a thesis, which you could then develop with specific causes.

Unfortunately, not all essay questions will immediately suggest a pattern of organization. Compare these questions with the preceding ones on the same subject:

Discuss the design of the 1920s flapper skirt and the design of the 1960s miniskirt.

Discuss "arbitrage houses."

Examine the "cultural literacy" movement of the 1980s in light of the "back to basics" movement of the 1970s.

In these questions, the words giving you directions — "discuss" and "examine" — are not as specific as those in the first set of questions. Does "discuss" mean that you are to compare and contrast the skirt designs? Does it mean you are to define and analyze how arbitrage houses work? Does "examine" mean that you are to compare and contrast the two educational movements? Show how one caused the other? When you get a question worded as generally as these, don't just begin writing all you know on the subject. Take a minute to think about how you could organize what you have to say. Though general questions do not clearly say so, they are probably looking for specific and well-organized answers.

Some Additional Tips Sometimes problems will arise when you are taking an essay exam. One major problem is running out of time even when you have tried to plan your time. If you run out of time and still have more to say, add a sentence telling what additional points you would have covered given the time. Suppose in comparing the flapper skirt and miniskirt, you had covered the length of hemlines, the types of waistbands, the fit of each, and so on, but you still had much to say about the kinds of fabrics each were made of. Instead of not mentioning fabric at all, you would be wise to add a sentence saying something like this: "I was getting ready to compare the fabric types for the skirt when time ran out." Such a sentence will not get you full credit, but it lets the professor know that you knew more about the question than you were able to write in the time allotted. Who knows? You may earn an extra point or two.

Another common problem can occur when you have finished an answer and realize you have left out something in the middle of the essay. If you have time, you can write the paragraph at the end of the essay and then draw an arrow and write a note showing where it goes. While this is not great form, it allows you to show what you could have done if you were not writing against the clock.

Finally, the worst problem of all can arise. Suppose you read a question and feel as if you can't answer it at all. Rather than skip it, you should start writing something about any part of the question you know anything about. Suppose you cannot remember any of the reasons that Truman fired MacArthur but you do remember MacArthur's success as commander earlier in the war. While you would not be answering the question by writing on his success, in doing so you might begin to remember more about him and that information might help you remember the events that led to his being fired. In this sense, you would be "writing your way into the question," for as you know, when writing you often jog your memory, recall information, and come up with ideas. And even if you do not end up answering the question, you would at least show that you know something about MacArthur.

Anxiety and Timed Writing

Writing can cause anxiety even when you have as much time as you need. When writing against the clock, you may feel even more anxious, especially when you know that an essay question will affect your grade or that an impromptu essay will be graded by your writing instructor. There are some consolations, though. Most writing teachers do not expect your best work on impromptu essays, and as experienced writers themselves, they will read (and grade) your paper knowing the difficulties you faced. As for essay exams, the better an answer is written, the higher grade it will usually receive. At the same time, most graders of essay exams do not expect an essay written in twenty or thirty minutes to be a masterpiece. If your essay answers the question, is fairly well organized, and includes specific details, you will probably do well. Though timed essays do not allow you the luxury of using all you know about the writing process, what you do know about it can help.

E X E R C I S E 3.22 Read a chapter from one of your textbooks and write three essay questions that you think you would be asked if you were being tested on the chapter.

E X E R C I S E 3.23 Most writing courses do not give essay exams on the textbook and class discussions; instead, you are graded on the essays you write for class. However, for practice, try to answer these essay questions on what you are learning about writing. Time yourself according to the suggested number of minutes specified for each question.

1. Analyze the writing process. (30 minutes)
2. Compare and contrast brainstorming and freewriting as invention strategies. (15 minutes)
3. Explain the difference between general and specific writing, providing examples of how each works in an essay. (25 minutes)
4. What are the journalist's questions, and what are the advantages and disadvantages of them as an invention strategy? (20 minutes)

Essay for Reading

How Children Form Mathematical Concepts
Jean Piaget

Jean Piaget was born in 1896 and died in 1980. He was a Swiss educator particularly interested in how the mind develops as a person grows, and he wrote a great deal on this subject. His theories of learning are highly respected and remain important to today's students of psychology and educational development.

Vocabulary Cues

impose: force something on someone or something
prematurely: before someone or something is ready; too early
essential: basic
simultaneously: at the same time
receptacle: a container, such as a glass, empty can, or box
conserved: saved, remaining the same, not changing

Questions to Guide Your Reading

1. When do children truly begin to understand mathematical concepts?
2. What does Piaget mean by "conserved" and "conservation"?
3. What is the "concept of number"?
4. What experiments does Piaget describe to show how children learn the concept of number?

It is a great mistake to suppose that a child acquires the notion of number and other mathematical concepts just from teaching. On the contrary, to a remarkable degree he develops them himself, independently and spontaneously. When adults try to impose mathematical concepts on a child prematurely, his learning is merely verbal; true understanding of them comes only with his mental growth.

This can be shown easily by a simple experiment. A child of five or six may readily be taught by his parents to name the numbers from 1 to 10. If ten stones are laid in a row, he can count them correctly. But if the stones are rearranged in a more complex pattern or piled up, he no longer can count them with consistent accuracy. Although the child knows the names of the numbers, he has not yet grasped the essential idea of number: namely, that the number of objects in a group remains the same, is "conserved," no matter how they are shuffled or arranged.

On the other hand, a child of six and a half or seven often shows that he has spontaneously formed the concept of number even though he may not yet have been taught to count. Given eight red chips and eight blue chips, he will discover by one-to-one matching that the number of red is the same as the number of blue, and he will realize that the two groups remain equal in number regardless of the shape they take.

The experiment with one-to-one correspondence is very useful for investigating children's development of the number concept. Let us lay down a row of eight red chips, equally spaced about an inch apart, and ask our small subjects to take from a box of blue chips as many chips as there are on the table. Their reactions will depend on age, and we can distinguish three stages of development. A child of five or younger, on the average, will lay out blue chips to make a row exactly as long as the red row, but he will put the blue chips close together instead of spacing them. He believes the number is the same if the length of the row is the same. At the age of six, on the average, children arrive at the second stage; these children will lay a blue chip opposite each red chip and obtain the correct number. But they have not necessarily acquired the concept of number itself. If we spread the red chips, spacing out the row more loosely, the six-year-olds will think that the longer row now has more chips, though we have not changed the number. At the age of six and a half to seven, on the average, children achieve the third stage; they know that, though we close up or space out one row of chips, the number is still the same as in the other.

In a similar experiment a child is given two receptacles of identical shape and size and is asked to put beads, one at a time, into both receptacles with both hands simultaneously — a blue bead into one box with his right hand and a red bead into the other with his left hand. When he has more or less filled the two receptacles, he is asked how they compare. He is sure that both have the same number of beads. Then he is requested to pour the blue beads into a receptacle of different size and shape. Here again we see differences in understanding according to age. The smallest children think that the number of beads has changed; if, for instance, the beads fill the new receptacle to a higher level, they think that there are more beads in it than in the original one; if to a lower level, they think there are fewer. But children near the age of seven know that the transfer has not changed the number of beads.

In short, children must grasp the principle of conservation of quantity before they can develop the concept of number.

Questions for Study and Discussion

1. Now that you have read the essay, answer the Questions to Guide Your Reading.
2. What is the one sentence in the essay that you think best expresses Piaget's thesis?
3. Piaget says that when a child of five or six counts from 1 to 10, he does not readily understand the concept of number. Why not?

4. Into how many age groups does Piaget divide children in the experiment with the red and blue chips? How does each age group react in the experiment?
5. How many age groups does he use in the experiment with the beads? Why is it that the younger children think there are more or fewer beads when they pour the beads into a different receptacle?
6. The first example about the chips seems to make Piaget's point. Why then do you think he uses the second example on the beads?
7. What is the lesson parents and teachers can learn from this essay?
8. How can you tell that this essay was written for the general public rather than for other scientists?
9. What organizational strategy seems to be working in this essay? Are there any other strategies used too?

Writing Assignment

Throughout this chapter the exercises asked you to work with a topic on something you are good at. Use the invention notes that you made for one exercise to write a rough draft. Then revise your draft using the strategies discussed in the chapter. Plan to write a final paper of about 500 words.

CHAPTER 4

Writing Paragraphs

J ust as you probably had some idea of what an essay is before you read
about essays in Chapter 3, you probably have some idea of what paragraphs are. The discussion in this chapter will expand and clarify your
definition, show you how paragraphs work, and provide strategies for
writing them.

■ What Is a Paragraph?

Paragraph: A relatively
short piece of writing that
can stand alone but
usually is part of an essay.

We start with a short definition to focus the discussion: A **paragraph** is
a short piece of writing on a very limited topic. Although some paragraphs can stand alone, most are part of a larger piece of writing such as
an essay.

Length

The length of a paragraph varies according to a writer's purpose. You
will notice that newspaper reporters often use one- or two-sentence paragraphs. These short paragraphs do not strain the eyes of readers. Because
newspapers have long, narrow columns of small print, writers have to
indent often. Otherwise, the reader would have difficulty separating line
from line.

But in essays, college essays included, the length of the paragraph
depends on its purpose as part of the essay. Usually, writers use a paragraph to develop a point in an argument, to signal a shift in time in a
narrative, to cover one step in a process, and so on. If you were writing
an essay on the causes of the American Revolution, you might have a
section on the unjust laws that angered the colonists. In this section, you
would explain each law and its effect. You would probably use one para-

graph for each law. Thus, the indentations for paragraphs in your essay would not be governed by the reader's eyes but by your purpose. In reading an essay, your audience expects a shift in the topic when a new paragraph begins.

Once in a while, an essay writer will use one- or two-sentence paragraphs to emphasize an idea or to make a transition from one section of the essay to the next, but most often paragraphs in essays continue until the point or step is fully developed or explained.

Because the writer's purpose governs the length of paragraphs in essays, a paragraph can run anywhere from 50 to 200 words. These numbers are rough estimates, and it would be foolish to count words in paragraphs to see if they fit the definition. But to develop a point in detail, a writer usually needs at least 50 words. And unless a paragraph is very well written, many readers will have difficulty following a paragraph beyond the 200-word length. Again, you need not count words. Just think that a paragraph usually should not run longer than three-quarters of a typed page or one full handwritten page.

If you are covering a point in a paragraph in your essay and you find that the paragraph is getting rather long, see if you can divide it in two at some logical place. If you were writing about the tea tax as a cause of the American Revolution, you would define the law and then analyze its effect, probably ending with the Boston Tea Party, telling how some colonists disguised themselves as Indians, sneaked onto some British tea ships docked in Boston Harbor, and threw the tea in the harbor to protest the law. In writing your paragraph on the tea tax, you might find that you spent about 175–200 words just defining the tax and another hundred to talk about the Boston Tea Party. In this case, it would be wise to start a new paragraph for your discussion of the tea party. Even with this break, each paragraph would still have a single topic — one on what the tea tax was and another on the protest.

E X E R C I S E   4.1   The following paragraph is about suntanning. It runs a bit long. Read the paragraph carefully, and then mark the spot where you think it could logically be divided into two paragraphs.

Many people today will do anything to look attractive, and one thing they often do is to get a suntan. Seeing the bronzed models in the ads for suntan lotions, these people think that having a tan makes them look healthier and sexier, and many will spend their summer hours tanning on the beach, in parks, or in their own backyards. In the winter or on cloudy days, they go to tanning salons to use the tanning beds. These tan fanatics also spend a lot of money on creams and lotions that promise a faster or deeper tan. There are many risks in tanning. When a person is lying in the sun, the rays are actually killing off skin cells. Some doctors say that too much tanning can cause skin cancer. Even if tanning does not result in skin cancer, it can cause the skin to be freckled, to turn yellow, to have dry rough spots, and to wrinkle prematurely. For example, I once worked with a woman who always had a tan. I thought she had a naturally dark complexion, and I also considered her very attractive for a woman of forty. Another co-worker told me that the woman was actually thirty and that she got her "natural" complexion at a local tanning parlor.

Just as paragraphs can be too long, they can be too short. Examine the following paragraphs.

People who cannot help being exposed to harmful sunlight need to take precautions. For example, farmers, sailors, and construction workers often work long hours out in the sun.

Because their uncovered arms, necks, and faces are constantly exposed to the sun, their skin becomes coarse and leathery. These workers need to use creams that block the sun, and they should apply lotions to exposed areas after working.

In reading through these two paragraphs, you can identify their topic in the first sentence: that outdoor workers need to take precautions against prolonged exposure to sunlight. The second paragraph contains the same topic still being developed in the effects of sunlight on the skin and in the remedies mentioned in the last sentence. Because both paragraphs discuss the same topic, they should be combined. By combining them, you would not have to worry about creating a paragraph too long for readers to follow. If you left the paragraphs separated, you would end up with a choppy effect, but worse, you would confuse readers because when they see a new paragraph, they expect some change in the topic.

As you draft and revise your essays, you need to consider the length of your paragraphs. Sometimes you won't have any trouble if you have spent a lot of time on invention. At other times you will need to consider whether paragraphs need to be separated or put together as you read over your completed draft.

Paragraphs Versus Essays

Occasionally you may be given a writing assignment that asks you to write only one paragraph, such as a short question on a test or an answer to a question on reading assigned for homework. Most writing assignments in college require essays. You already have some idea of the differences between the two, and perhaps you have recognized some similarities as well. Knowing the differences and similarities can help you write both essays and paragraphs.

How Are Essays and Paragraphs Different?   A paragraph is usually part of an essay. For instance, in Chapter 3, the essay on Deming Park was to show how its various facilities make it a good place for family outings. In fulfilling this purpose, you would have to cover various family activities in the park. Each paragraph then would cover an activity or facility. Together, all the paragraphs would add up to support your thesis about Deming Park.

As a part of an essay, naturally the paragraph is shorter than an essay. Thus, a paragraph will have a more limited topic than an essay will. Recall Tracy writing about her grandfather in Chapter 2. Her first attempt at a paragraph tried to cover everything about him, and as a result it was too general to tell readers much. Moreover, her second attempt was much more detailed and developed because she limited the topic of the paragraph to the trips she and her grandfather took to St. Louis.

Topic sentence: A sentence that states the main idea of a paragraph.

How Are Essays and Paragraphs Similar?   First, a paragraph, like an essay, covers one topic, even though that topic is more limited than an essay topic. Just as an essay must develop its topic according to the writer's purpose and the readers' needs, each paragraph in the essay must also work to fulfill the writer's purpose and readers' needs. Second, just as an essay often states its main idea in one sentence called a thesis sentence, a paragraph often states its main idea in one sentence called the **topic sentence.**

Be careful here. The word *topic* is used to refer to what the essay is about, and it also is used to refer to the main sentence of a paragraph. The following discussion of topic sentences will help you clear up any confusion.

■ Topic Sentences

A topic sentence is a sentence that states the main idea of a paragraph within an essay. The topic sentence is also a subpoint of the point made in the thesis. For instance, if you start with the thesis stating that Deming Park is an ideal place for family outings, one of your paragraphs might have a topic sentence saying that the park offers clean and convenient picnic facilities. This would be one specific point used to develop the thesis. Remember that a topic sentence is more specific than a thesis sentence. On Hayakawa's ladder diagram on general and specific language (Chapter 2), think of the topic sentence as a rung or two below the more general thesis sentence.

Although a topic sentence is more specific than a thesis sentence, it is more general than the rest of the information in the paragraph. For example, after stating the topic sentence on the clean and convenient picnic areas in Deming Park, you would need specific examples to support your claim.

E X E R C I S E 4.2 The following groups of sentences could form paragraphs if the sentences were arranged in the right order. Read each group and underline the sentence that would be the topic sentence if you arranged the sentences in order to form a paragraph. Remember that the topic sentence should be the most general sentence in the paragraph.

1. Gas burns more cleanly than oil.
   Natural gas is the best way to heat a home.
   Gas is less expensive than electric heat.
   The air does not dry out from gas heat as much as it does from oil heat.
2. Computers can help people improve their writing.
   Writers can revise as they go along, and then they can check a printed draft before making more revisions.
   With a computer, a writer does not have to worry as much about making mistakes because it is easy to correct them.
   Computers also allow writers to move sentences and paragraphs to parts of the essay where they would fit more effectively.
   Unlike staring at a blank page, working on a computer can be fun, and when people like to write, they will improve.
3. Because the roads are so slick, drivers can easily lose control of the car.
   Also, icy roads produce a glare that lessens the driver's ability to see.
   Icy roads pose certain dangers for even skilled drivers.
   Drivers must press the gas pedal lightly, or the car might go into a spin.
   Although radial tires can improve traction, they cannot always prevent skidding and spinning.

E X E R C I S E 4.3 The underlined topic sentence in each of the following paragraphs is so general that it is vague. Rewrite the topic sentence to make it more specific and thus more closely related to the information in the paragraph.

One time in high school, I was really embarrassed. We had a math teacher, Mr. Toro, who could not see well. When he took the attendance, he squinted, hunched toward the class, frowned so that he looked like a prune, and then called our names in a squeaky voice. One day, I had heard he was absent for the first period class, so I figured we would have a substitute. When I got to class, there was no teacher there, so I sat at Toro's desk and began imitating him. I was hunched over so far that my nose was almost on the desk, I had my face screwed up so that my eyes were slits, and I was calling out everyone's name in Toro's squeaky voice. Everyone was cracking up until who should walk in but Toro himself! He had been to the dentist first period and returned to finish the day.

The Pontiac GTO was a neat car in the 1960s. It had a 389-cubic-inch engine and could be ordered with either a large four-barrel carburetor or three two-barrels. With either setup, the engine rumbled at even cruising speeds. Most GTOs also had four on the floor with Hurst power shift linkage, enabling a hot driver to get rubber in every gear. The styling was as impressive as the car's power, with sleek lines, a low-slung chassis, and an air scoop in the middle of the hood.

Old movie stars were great. Who can forget Humphrey Bogart's performances as the suave Rick Blaine in *Casablanca* or as the tough but vulnerable Sam Spade, private eye? Gary Cooper brought a quiet strength and unquestionable morality to his characters in such films as *The Lou Gehrig Story* and *High Noon*. And then there was Clark Gable, who makes today's leading men look like pretty boy wimps. Yet for all his ruggedness, Gable played perhaps the most romantic character in film history — Rhett Butler in *Gone With the Wind*.

Placement of Topic Sentences

Topic sentences can be placed almost anywhere in a paragraph: first, second, or third, or even last. Sometimes writers split them, revealing part of the main idea in the first sentence before completing the idea in the last sentence of the paragraph. Chapter 6 gives numerous examples of the different places where a topic sentence may appear. That chapter emphasizes how to find main ideas as you read, but after completing this section you might want to look ahead at the variety of examples. For now, we will look at some basic ways to place a topic sentence.

Topic Sentence First   Beginning writers often like to place the topic sentence first in a paragraph. Experienced writers use this method too. One advantage of placing the topic sentence first is that the reader will know what is coming. Look over these two paragraphs.

Working in a metal-plating factory was dangerous. When metals are plated, they are dipped in vats of different chemicals which give off terrible odors. At times I could hardly breathe, and I worried about my lungs. Also some of the chemicals were hot, and if they splashed on somebody they could cause serious burns. Even worse were the acids which could burn the skin.

Weeds put up a good fight against people. Pull up a dandelion and miss the taproot and you get another dandelion. Often, in our struggle against ragweed, we end up actually aiding the ragweed. Spraying herbicide on a clump of ragweed is to do nothing more than recreate the disturbance that permitted the ragweed to grow in the first place. A healthy new crop of ragweed will replace the old crop.

John Kricher, "In Praise of Weeds"

In each paragraph, the writer begins with a general point in the topic sentence and then follows with specific examples for support. Such paragraphs are fairly easy to write and read. You can't go wrong when you place the topic sentence first.

Topic Sentence Second or Third   Sometimes a writer will use a sentence or two to lead up to the topic sentence. Usually the initial sentence or two refers to the discussion of the previous paragraph in the essay. It provides a sort of bridge. The paragraph on the dangers of the metal-plating factory was followed by this paragraph:

> Because of the dangerous chemicals, the workers had to be very careful, and sometimes people got burned. Wearing the proper clothing was the best protection against injury. Even in hot weather, we wore heavy jeans and long-sleeved flannel shirts, which gave us some protection against the less powerful acids. To protect our hands, we used rubber or canvas work gloves, and as for shoes, we usually wore heavy boots.

You can see that the first sentence cannot be the topic sentence because it talks about people being careful and getting injured while the rest of the paragraph describes the workers' protective clothing. The first sentence, though, leads up to the topic sentence, placed second, on protective clothing.

Topic Sentence Last   Sometimes a writer can use arguments, examples, or specific details to lead up to the topic sentence. This method can be effective because the topic sentence works as a "clincher" to emphasize the point of the paragraph. Consider this paragraph:

> My psych teacher assigned three chapters this week and promised a test on Friday. My English teacher hit us with another essay assignment. My golf teacher told us we have to play one round this week and have our scorecard signed by the clubhouse attendant. I have to interview people in three different professions this week for my career counseling class. It seems most college professors think their class is the center of a student's life.

There would be nothing wrong with putting the topic sentence first in this paragraph, but it is probably more effective coming last because after the series of examples, the sentence on professors packs more punch than it would if it came first.

E X E R C I S E 4.4   Underline the topic sentence in each of the following paragraphs.

1. The keyboard of the word processor has extra keys to perform word processing functions, but most keys are arranged the same way as on a typewriter. On most word processors the "touch" of the keys is a little lighter, but not that much different than the touch of the keys on an electric typewriter. Thus, if you already know how to type, learning to work on the word processor can be fairly easy.

2. Grant and Lee had, to begin with, the great virtue of utter tenacity. Grant fought his way down the Mississippi in spite of acute personal discouragement and profound military handicaps. Lee hung on in the trenches at Petersburg after hope itself had died. In each man there was an indomitable quality, the born fighter's refusal to give up as long as he can still remain on his feet and lift his two fists.

Bruce Catton, "Grant and Lee: A Study in Contrasts"

3. After the handgun, the criminal's next weapon of choice is the knife, but it is such a far second that guns used in crime outnumber knives used in crime by at least three to one. The handgun, especially one with a relatively short barrel, is the preferred weapon of crime because it is both so lethal and so easily concealed. Stuck inside the belt, only the grip of the handle is visible, and a jacket or suitcoat or sweater can easily cover that small bulge. Also, the handgun slips easily into a coat, jacket pocket or purse. The inside of an automobile offers any number of handy hiding spots.

Pete Shields, "Why Do People Own Handguns?"

4. Cats are loose in their morals, but not consciously so. Man, in his descent from the cat, has brought the cat's looseness with him but has left the unconsciousness behind — the saving grace which excuses the cat. The cat is innocent, man is not.

Mark Twain, "The Lowest Animal"

Implied topic sentence:
A topic sentence that is not stated in a paragraph. All the information in the paragraph points to one idea that is not stated.

Implied Topic Sentences   Sometimes a paragraph will not state a topic sentence. This does not mean that the paragraph does not have a topic but that for some reason the writer has not felt the need to include it in the paragraph. When this is the case, we say the topic sentence is **implied.** Consider the following paragraph.

The decor at Florio's includes plush carpet of a deep maroon, candlelit tables, and elegantly framed paintings adorning the walls. Waiters clad in white jackets and black bow ties take your order from a menu which boasts such entrees as beef Wellington, broasted pheasant, and lobster thermidor among others. Prices begin at $25.00 per entree, and the wine list offers vintages costing as much as $200.00 a bottle.

In reading this paragraph, you probably noticed that each sentence contains specific details — the color of the carpet, the dress of the waiters, the samples of the entrees, and the cost of food and wine. Yet there is no one sentence that tells the point of the paragraph. Nevertheless, we can see the point: Florio's is a very fancy restaurant.

Implied topic sentences can save the writer from stating an obvious point, but if you choose to leave your topic sentence implied, make sure that the information in the paragraph clearly points to one idea that readers can see without confusion.

EXERCISE 4.5 In each of the following paragraphs, the topic sentence is implied. For each, write a sentence that expresses the implied topic sentence.

1. The hot cheese bubbles as it mixes with the bright red sauce and clumps of tomato, all surrounded by a rising rim of golden crust. The sausage and pepperoni dot the surface glistening with a hint of oil, while slices of peppers and onions crisscross through the cheese. All the ingredients contribute to the unmistakable aroma that tickles the nostrils and tantalizes the taste buds.

2. There was, for example, the turn-of-the-century trainman who replaced a faulty coupling with a pair of jeans, the Wyoming man who used his jeans as a towrope to haul his car out of a ditch, the Californian who found several pairs in an abandoned mine, wore them, and discovered they were sixty-three years old and still as good as new. . . . And then there is the particularly terrifying story of the careless construction worker who dangled fifty-two stories above the street until rescued, his sole support the Levi's belt loop through which his rope was hooked.

Carin Quinn, "The Jeaning of America — and the World"

3. To install a new air filter, first open the hood of the car and look on the top of the engine for a large circular part that resembles a covered pan. This is the air filter housing. On top of the housing in the center there will be a wing nut. Loosen it with a pair of pliers and remove it with your hand. Once you have the wing nut removed, using both hands lift off the cover of the housing. Inside you will see the old air filter. It is circular and looks like the new one you have purchased. Remove the old filter by merely picking it up with your hands. Set the new air filter in the same position as the old one was. Put the cover of the housing back in place, and secure it with the wing nut. Close the hood.

**Topic Sentences
and the
Writing Process**

As you plan, draft, and revise the paragraphs in your essays, pay close attention to your topic sentences. Consideration of your topic sentences can occur at any point in the writing process. Some writers, for instance, plan possible topic sentences once they have a thesis and a set of invention notes. Other writers begin with the notes and do not worry about topic sentences until they are drafting.

Whatever you do, always reconsider and evaluate your topic sentences during revision. This set of questions can help:

1. Does the topic sentence express the main idea of the paragraph clearly?
2. Is there anything in the paragraph that does not fit the point of the topic sentence?
3. Is the topic sentence more specific than the thesis sentence of the essay?
4. Is the topic sentence more general than the other sentences in the paragraph?

Also during revision, check the placement of your topic sentences. For example, adding a lead-in sentence before the topic sentence can create a needed connection between a paragraph and the one before it. Maybe a topic sentence can be moved to the end to emphasize your point. Sometimes you might want to place the topic sentence first to make sure the reader knows where the paragraph is going. At other times, you may find you can cut a topic sentence and leave the point implied, or you might want to add a topic sentence when the implied point is not quite clear.

■ Three Qualities of a Good Paragraph

As you draft and revise paragraphs in your essays, you will need to consider three qualities that make a paragraph effective: *development, unity,* and *cohesion.*

Development

Development: The process of providing enough information — examples and details — in a paragraph to enable the readers to see the main idea.

From our previous discussions, you already have some sense of paragraph **development.** A paragraph shows adequate development when it fully covers a limited topic to meet the writer's purpose and the readers' needs. In this sense, development has to do with specific details and examples, which we discussed in Chapter 3. Recall the student's paragraph on the blind date, Tracy's paragraph on going to St. Louis with her grandfather, and the essay answer on the Stamp Act. All were developed in enough detail to serve each writer's purpose and meet each audience's needs.

Exercise 4.5 contained a paragraph instructing readers how to install a new air filter in an automobile. Suppose the paragraph had been written like this:

Take the cover off the air filter housing first. Then take the old air filter out and put the new one in. Close the hood and you are done.

Only a person who knew a lot about cars could follow these directions because the paragraph lacks development. Such a person would not need directions to begin with. In contrast, the directions in the paragraph in Exercise 4.5, because they are fully developed, could instruct someone who knew nothing about cars.

E X E R C I S E   4.6
The following paragraphs lack development. Choose one and revise it for an audience that knows very little about the topic it covers.

1. Nowadays, little boys, as well as girls, play with dolls. But these dolls are called action figures. There are many kinds of action figures, and few people would think the boys are sissies for playing with them.

2. Keeping a house clean is easier if everyone in the family helps out. While the mother does some of the cleaning, the father should help too. Even the children can help.

3. TV game shows are entertaining. The hosts and hostesses usually act silly, and the contestants get really excited when they win. Some of the questions are interesting, and it's fun to try to answer them before the contestants.

Unity

Unity: The characteristic of a paragraph that sticks to its main idea.

When a paragraph has **unity**, it has one topic and does not shift from that topic, even though the examples may differ. For instance, the following paragraph talks of three different baseball players, yet the topic focuses on one main idea that applies to all three players:

Great home run hitters often strike out a lot. Babe Ruth, for example, led the American League in strikeouts as often as he led it in home runs. Mickey Mantle did the same, and Reggie Jackson, one of the most consistent home run hitters of the 1970s and early 1980s, holds the major league record for strikeouts in a career. Not all home run hitters strike out as often as these three did, but usually a player who hits thirty to forty home runs in a season will strike out over 100 times.

When a paragraph has unity, it sticks to the topic it develops without getting off track. This means that all the development works to support the topic sentence. In the preceding paragraph, you can see that from the first sentence to the last it focuses on the idea that home run hitters strike out a lot.

When you are drafting an essay, keeping a paragraph unified can be difficult because one example or idea can lead to another that does not fit the topic of the paragraph. For instance, in writing the preceding sample paragraph, when the writer reached the example on Reggie Jackson, he might have been tempted to add that in addition to striking out a lot, Jackson usually did not have a high batting average. That's true, but since the topic of the paragraph focuses on home run hitting and striking out, the point about batting average does not belong.

As you revise your draft, consider the unity of each paragraph. If you have examples that do not fit your topic, remove those examples to unify the paragraph. Consider the possibility of using the examples elsewhere in the essay. Although the point on batting average does not fit the preceding sample paragraph, the writer could write another paragraph on the relationship between home run hitting and hitting for average, if that topic had some connection to the thesis of the whole essay.

E X E R C I S E   4.7   In each of the following paragraphs, indicate any sentences that break up the unity of the paragraph.

1. If tourists are unfamiliar with a large city, they can easily find their way around by following a map. City maps show all streets by name or number. Bold lines trace the routes of major highways, and arrowheads usually mark the exits. If tourists have not driven in a large city before, they should be very careful and wear seat belts because often there is a lot of traffic, especially during rush hour. City maps also show the location of points of interest, such as parks, zoos, sports arenas, and museums. Some maps even list libraries, churches, and universities. With a map, tourists can quickly find the locations of various attractions and the easiest ways to get to them.

2. Bicycling is terrific exercise. When you ride a bike, you exercise all of the leg muscles and most of the muscles of the upper body. In addition, bicycling exercises the lungs and the heart. Thus, bicycling is both a muscular and aerobic exercise. The best bicycles are ten-speeds.

3. William Blake was not only a famous poet but a great painter. Blake often paints religious themes, using bright colors and bold forms which result in paintings that are as stunning as they are beautiful. "The Tyger" is probably Blake's most widely known poem. Many of Blake's paintings hang in the British Museum in London. Blake was a religious mystic, who at times thought he saw angels in trees.

Cohesion

Cohesion refers to the way parts work together to form a whole. Often the word is used in its adjective form, *cohesive.* In a cohesive family unit, family members work together to keep the family whole. If a sportscaster speaks of a cohesive team, he or she means that players work well together as a group.

Paragraphs need cohesion. Cohesion occurs in a paragraph when one sentence follows logically and clearly from the one before it, while leading to the sentence following it. As a result, all the sentences work together. For a paragraph to be cohesive, first it must have unity. The sentences you omitted in the previous exercise did not follow from the sentence before or lead to the sentence after.

In addition, paragraphs achieve cohesion through transitions. Simply defined, transitions are words that signal the connections between paragraphs in an essay and among sentences in a paragraph. You should be aware of two types of transitions: (1) *the repetition and variation of key words* and (2) *transitional words and phrases.*

Repetition and Variation of Key Words When you write a paragraph, if you stick to the topic you will often repeat the key words in your idea without thinking about doing so. Sometimes you will vary the key words, however. You might substitute "riding a bike" for "bicycling." Look at the paragraph on bicycling in Exercise 4.7. The topic sentence focused on bicycling as exercise, so *bicycling* and *exercise* are the key words. As you reread the paragraph, note the connections between key words that are in bold type and italics.

> **Bicycling** is terrific *exercise.* When you **ride a bike,** you *exercise* all of the leg muscles and most of the muscles of the upper body. In addition, **bicycling** *exercises* the lungs and the heart. Thus, **bicycling** is both a muscular and aerobic *exercise.*

From these connections, you can see how the repetition throughout the paragraph holds together the two parts of the idea in the topic sentence — bicycling and exercise. This is also an example of variation in the second sentence when *bicycling* is changed to *ride a bike.*

Seeing the connections in the bicycling paragraph should have been easy because the idea was fairly simple. The following is a more difficult paragraph. Read the topic sentence first, and note the key words: references to home run hitters are in bold type; references to the big swing are italicized; and references to strikeouts are circled. Examine the way these words are repeated and varied.

> **Home run hitters** need a *big, powerful swing,* but such a *swing* reduces the chances of making contact with the ball and thus leads to more (strikeouts) **Babe Ruth** had a compact *swing,* but **he** *swung* very hard with a *quick, snappy stroke* of the bat

that either knocked the ball into the stands or (missed it completely.)
Like **Ruth, Mickey Mantle** took a *powerful cut* at the ball, but **he** also *swung* with a much longer arc, bringing the bat back farther, stretching his arms farther from his body, and ending with a long follow-through. Anyone who ever saw **Reggie Jackson** bat knows how hard he *swung*. **He** seemingly began his *swing* from somewhere back behind the catcher and often ended it with *a wild sweep*. *This swing* either launched the ball into the upper deck or left **Jackson** on one knee as the umpire called (strike three.)

This paragraph is fairly long, yet because of the repetition and variation of the key words, readers are able to follow it. It contains more variation than the previous example. For instance, *big, powerful swing* is varied a number of times, but the variations still convey that part of the idea. Likewise, *strikeout* appears as *missed it completely* and *strike three*.

EXERCISE 4.8 Read each of the following paragraphs carefully and then circle the key words in the topic sentence. Finally, indicate connections between those words and the repetitions and variations in the rest of the paragraph.

1. At one point along an open highway, I came to a crossroads with a traffic light. I was alone on the road by now, but as I approached the light, it turned red, and I braked to a halt. I looked left, right, and behind me. Nothing. Not a car, no suggestion of headlights, but there I sat, waiting for the light to change, the only human being for at least a mile.

Andy Rooney, "In and of Ourselves We Trust"

2. The third class of objects — those that don't work — is the most curious of all. These include such objects as barometers, car clocks, cigarette lighters, flashlights, and toy train locomotives. It is inaccurate, of course, to say they never work. They work once, usually for the first few hours after being brought home, and then quit. Thereafter, they never work again.

Russell Baker, "The Plot Against People"

3. Even though each broken marriage is unique, we can still find the common perils, the common causes for marital despair. Each marriage has crisis points and each marriage tests endurance, the capacity for both intimacy and change. Outside pressures such

as job loss, illness, infertility, trouble with a child, care of aging parents, and all the other plagues of life hit marriage the way hurricanes blast our shores. Some marriages survive these storms and others don't.

Ann Roiphe, ''Why Marriages Fail''

4. How does one determine whether a law is just or unjust? A just law is a man-made code that squares with the moral law or the law of God. An unjust law is a code that is out of harmony with the moral law. To put it in terms of St. Thomas Aquinas: An unjust law is a human law that is not rooted in eternal law. Any law that uplifts human personality is just. Any law that degrades human personality is unjust. All segregation statutes are unjust because segregation distorts the soul and damages the personality.

Martin Luther King, ''Letter from Birmingham Jail''

Transitional Words and Phrases

Transitional words and phrases: Words and phrases that show connections between sentences. Examples: however, consequently, indeed, in fact, as a result, in addition.

Transitional words and phrases are any words or phrases that purposely show connections between sentences. They work like highway signs, signaling to readers that here is a place to turn or that the discussion will continue this way. You have probably used these words often in conversation and writing, probably without thinking about them. Sometimes they emerge naturally as you think and write. At other times you might have to add them while revising to tighten the connection between one sentence and another. Study the following list and examples of transitional expressions.

In addition, also, moreover, furthermore, and, indeed, in fact. This group signals that you are adding another point or example.

My sister maintained an A average in high school. *In fact,* she had the highest average in her graduating class. *Furthermore,* her combined SAT scores totaled 1300.

Thus, therefore, consequently, as a result. These words signal an effect that comes from a cause in the previous sentence.

As a result, my parents were always praising my sister and comparing her achievements to my lack of interest in school.
My parents, *consequently,* were always praising my sister and comparing her achievements to my lack of interest in school.

Of course, no doubt, certainly, doubtless, granted. These words concede a point or recognize a point just off your main point.

Of course, she deserved the praise because she had worked hard in school all her life.
She *certainly* deserved the praise because she had worked hard in school all her life.

Still, nevertheless, notwithstanding. These return to stress a point you are making after you have left it.

Still, it got on my nerves when my parents compared her to me.
Her achievements *notwithstanding,* it got on my nerves when my
parents compared her to me.

Yet, however, but, on the other hand, on the contrary, in contrast.
These words signal a contrast.

In contrast, my sister herself never made me feel bad because I
did poorly in school.
But I could not help resenting her success sometimes.

Consider how some of these sentences can be put together to form
a paragraph:

My sister maintained an A average in high school. *In fact,* she
had the highest average in her graduating class. *Furthermore,* her
combined SAT scores totaled 1300. My parents, *consequently,*
were always praising my sister and comparing her achievements to
my lack of interest in school. She *certainly* deserved the praise
because she had worked hard in school all her life. *Still,* it got on
my nerves when my parents compared her to me. My sister,
however, never made me feel bad because I did poorly. *On the
contrary,* she always encouraged me and tried to help. *Yet* I could
not help resenting her success sometimes.

This paragraph conveys the writer's conflicting feelings about her
sister. On the one hand, she seems proud of her sister; on the other hand,
she resents her success. Because of this conflict, the writer's ideas shift
back and forth between pride and resentment. The transitions help make
those shifts flow smoothly. Read the paragraph without the transitions
and notice how choppy and unconnected many of the ideas seem.

My sister maintained an A average in high school. She had the
highest average in her graduating class. Her combined SAT scores
totaled 1300. My parents were always praising my sister and
comparing her achievements to my lack of interest in school. She
deserved the praise because she had worked hard in school all her
life. It got on my nerves when my parents compared her to me.
My sister never made me feel bad because I did poorly. She always
encouraged me and tried to help. I could not help resenting her
success sometimes.

Though the same ideas are still in the paragraph, readers must sort
them out and piece together the conflict. There are no signposts to tell
readers which way the writer's thought is going.

Although transitions are important, every sentence you write need
not contain transitional words and phrases. In fact, sometimes too many
can confuse the reader, just as too many road signs in one place can
confuse a driver. Often, the repetition and variation of key words will

make your paragraph cohesive. Still, it is helpful to become aware of transitional words and phrases and the ways they add cohesion.

When you are drafting a paper, some transitional words and phrases will appear naturally in your writing because your thought patterns often add and shift information. When you are revising a paper, you might find that adding a transitional word or phrase can tighten the relationship between sentences and make your point clear.

E X E R C I S E 4.9 Add a transitional word or phrase to the second sentence of each of the following pairs to tighten its connection to the first sentence.

1. Writing can be difficult. It can cause anxiety.
2. Students know the writing will be graded. They fear their reader as a judge. They should imagine their reader as a person who wants to be informed and entertained.
3. The teacher has to evaluate the paper. If students forget about evaluation and concentrate on writing, good grades will follow.

E X E R C I S E 4.10 Write a short paragraph using the sentences from exercise 4.9.

■ Paragraph Checklist

We have said so much about paragraphs that you cannot possibly remember it all as you revise your paragraphs. The following list of questions can help you recall the general considerations that you need to be aware of as you revise.

1. Does the paragraph have a purpose? In other words, what is the one point it is trying to make? How is that point connected to the thesis of the whole essay?
2. Does the paragraph have a single identifiable topic? In other words, is there one main idea that it is trying to get across?
3. Is the main idea expressed clearly in a topic sentence? If the main idea is implied, will it be evident to the reader?
4. Is the topic of the paragraph limited enough to be covered specifically?
5. Is the topic fully developed, given your purpose and the readers' needs?
6. Does the paragraph have unity? Is there any information that could confuse readers because it does not belong in the paragraph?
7. Is the paragraph cohesive, with key words repeated and varied and transitional words and phrases used when needed?

8. Should the paragraph be divided into two or more paragraphs?
9. Should the paragraph be combined with another paragraph?

■ Special Kinds of Paragraphs

Body paragraph: Any paragraph that follows the introduction and leads to the conclusion of an essay. Each body paragraph helps develop and support the thesis of the whole essay.

The paragraphs we have discussed so far are often called **body paragraphs.** That is, they are paragraphs that make up the body of an essay once the topic has been introduced and the thesis has been stated. They also lead up to a final paragraph or two that concludes the essay. In a relatively short essay, a paragraph called an *introductory paragraph,* or simply an *introduction,* comes before the body paragraphs. Another paragraph, called the *conclusion,* follows the body paragraphs and closes the essay. In longer essays, introductions and conclusions may be two, three, or more paragraphs long. For now, though, you can think of an introduction and a conclusion as one paragraph each. Introductions and conclusions have different purposes than body paragraphs but work together with them to create the overall structure of the essay.

Introductions

Introduction: A paragraph that gets the reader's attention, limits the topic of the essay, and states the essay's thesis.

How do I prepare the introduction? Many writers have asked themselves this question. And many beginning writers are often so stumped by the question that we will start by discussing how *not* to begin. The weakest introductions discuss the writer's difficulty with the topic or talk directly to the instructor:

> When you assigned us to write about a community problem, I really had trouble because the small town where I live is really nice and we don't have many problems. But then I came up with this idea for the thesis that our town needs a law so that people don't let their dogs run loose.

The problem with this introduction is that it disregards the audience. In fact, for the writer, the instructor is the only audience. Though the instructor may be your reader, you should write as if you are writing to the whole class. Also, the audience is not really interested in the trouble the writer had with the topic. Rather, the audience wants to know about the town and the problem — the topic of the essay.

Another problem occurs in introductions when writers start too far from the topic:

> Since there was medicine, doctors have always tried to help people. Hippocrates in ancient Greece wrote an oath which doctors still take, and in it they swear to help others. Back in the eighteenth and nineteenth centuries, many doctors worked with little or no pay to find cures for diseases. But today's doctors seem to care more about their fees than about their patients.

This writer is on the right track in that she defines her topic in the introductory paragraph, but she needs to begin closer to the issue of her thesis — doctors' attitudes today. Going back to the beginning of medicine does not get her or her readers to the thesis very quickly, and by covering so many years — actually centuries — she ends up with a vague and general opener.

Introductions are not easy to write, but because they provide readers with a first impression of your essay, they are certainly important and you should take much care in writing them. It is often best to write them last. That way, you know what the body of your paper says and you can make sure that your introduction leads into it effectively. If you do write the introduction first, it is wise to revise it carefully after you have written the body.

But whether you write the introduction before or after the body of the paper, your readers will expect one. You do not just plunge into a hot bath; you get in gradually. Readers like to get into an essay the same way. That's why a paragraph to introduce your topic and set up your thesis will add to the effectiveness of your essay.

Introductions serve four purposes:

1. To get readers' attention.
2. To move readers into your essay while showing what you are writing about before you state the thesis, which is the essay's main idea, or topic.
3. To limit your essay by moving from a general discussion of the topic to the specific thesis that your essay will illustrate.
4. To state your thesis before moving to the body paragraphs that illustrate it.

The following paragraph is a possible introduction for the essay on Deming Park, discussed in earlier chapters. To show you how one type of introduction works, each sentence is numbered and an explanation of its purpose follows.

(1) People who know Terre Haute would not consider the city a vacation spot, or even a place to visit. (2) These people, however, do not realize that the city offers an excellent park system. (3) Perhaps the most attractive park in the system is Deming Park, on the city's east side. (4) During the warm months, people of all types and ages enjoy the park's many facilities. (5) The park is particularly popular with families because *it is an ideal place for family outings.*

1. The first sentence raises the subject area of Terre Haute and the question of the city as a place to visit. Recall that the assignment asked for an essay showing why a particular town would be a good place to visit.
2. This sentence limits the subject to parks in Terre Haute.

3. The third sentence introduces the topic of Deming Park.

4. Here the topic is limited further to people who use the park.

5. The first part of this sentence limits the topic even further, and the second part, which is italicized, is the thesis — what the paper will say about the topic.

This type of introduction is sometimes called a "funnel" because it begins with a wide subject area and gradually narrows down to the limited topic. It starts very general and becomes more specific with each sentence until it finally reaches the specific thesis.

The funnel is a common and effective way to begin an essay, but there are many strategies for writing an introduction. In fact, the number of strategies is limited only by the writer's imagination. Clever writers are always coming up with new ways to begin. Here are a few strategies that students have used effectively. The thesis is italicized in each to show you how the introduction leads to it. In your own essays, do not underline the thesis unless your instructor asks you to do so.

Selecting This strategy begins with a straightforward statement about the subject area. It gives brief but specific examples within the subject area, and the final example becomes the thesis of the paper.

> In the 1980s, the National Football League had many top-notch coaches. Anyone who ever saw a Dallas Cowboys game heard the announcers praising Tom Landry and saw Landry calmly send in the players that led his team to numerous victories. Mike Ditka of the Chicago Bears rebuilt one of the league's worst teams into a Super Bowl champion. Bill Walsh of the San Francisco 49ers, though not as well known as Landry and Ditka, revolutionized the passing game with his multiple-receiver offense. However, *year in and year out, the best coach of the eighties was Don Shula of the Miami Dolphins.*

The opening sentence introduces the subject of the essay as NFL coaches in the eighties and limits it to top-notch coaches. The writer then gives three brief examples of top coaches before introducing his thesis on Don Shula. Note the transitional word *however*. It is used to contrast the thesis and the introductory examples; that is, it *selects* Shula from a group of coaches and limits the essay to him.

Narrating Another way to introduce your thesis is to tell a brief story — to narrate — about you or people you know. In the following introduction, the student uses his experiences on a summer job to set up a thesis about surviving his first semester of college.

> Last summer while working construction, I met a lot of guys who were going to college. They knew I would be attending Louisiana State in the fall, so they would always try to impress me by telling me how hard college was. They spoke of really tough

tests, hours and hours of homework, and mean professors who cared nothing for their students. I must admit that they had me scared, but now that I have been at Louisiana State for a semester I know that *freshmen can do well if they attend class regularly, don't overdo the social life, take good notes in class, and develop a regular schedule for study.*

Although the student's summer construction job had little to do with his success in college, he used the story of his experience to lead up to the thesis.

Describing   Simply describing a person, place, or thing can effectively introduce your thesis.

Person

He was a fairly large man, who always appeared in dark suits that made his cocoa brown skin seem even darker. He had a kind face with a high forehead and sensitive eyes. While he looked like a man with a great capacity for love and understanding, he also projected an image of strength with his sturdy body and determined walk. His voice could be soft and soothing, or it could be powerful enough to rouse thousands of people to action. This man was Martin Luther King, *an American hero whose birthday should be commemorated as a national holiday.*

Place

The room was about twenty by forty feet, with a floor of scuffed linoleum and bare walls of a light indefinite color, which may have been green or blue, or even a sick beige. Leading to the counter at the far end were lines of people, some complaining to each other, others just waiting for the lines to move. This was my first time at the unemployment office. Three months later, I was a regular. *Living without a job means living without self-respect.*

Thing

Loops of steel hurtle fifteen stories in the air like the tentacles of some technological monster. Long spines of track zigzag from one loop to the next. It's the "Vortex," King's Island's largest roller coaster, and *riding it is one of life's most exciting two minutes.*

In each introduction, the writer has used specific details to bring the topic to life and set up the thesis. A descriptive introduction can work with more serious topics, such as those in the first two examples, or with an informal topic such as a narrative on riding a roller coaster. Whatever the topic, you need vivid details to get the readers' attention.

Asking Questions   You can usually begin an essay by raising a question or a series of questions. Because a question appeals to the natural curiosity of people, it can be a handy way of getting your readers' attention and introducing the topic.

Single Question

If I were to give you an exam from a class you took last year and made good grades in, do you think you could pass it? Many students probably couldn't. These students remember information just long enough to pass a test, but after the test forget most of what they've studied. We are going to college to learn, but I think too many of us just memorize and forget. Everyone wants good grades, but *too many students place grades above learning.*

Series of Questions

Do you want to live in the country? Do you want to wake up in the morning to the fresh air and sound of birds? Sound great? Do you want to drink well water that tastes like the pipes which carry it into your home? Do you want to drive five to ten miles to the nearest store for a bag of potato chips? Do you want to haul your weekly garbage another ten miles to the nearest dump? If you still want to live in the country, then you will have to find out for yourself that *country living is not as pleasant as most people think.*

Beginning with questions is fairly easy, but don't overuse the strategy. There's nothing wrong with it, but students sometimes fall back on it too often and thus do not get practice with the other strategies. As you develop as a writer, you should learn to use all the strategies and even come up with some new ones of your own.

Shocking or Surprising Readers   This strategy attempts to get readers' attention quickly with the opening statement. The statement can range from something mildly surprising to something downright shocking. When most people hear something surprising or shocking, they immediately want to hear more.

Surprising Statement

Only a little over half of entering college freshmen ever earn a degree. It is not that freshmen are unintelligent. Young students living away from home may simply get homesick, students who are parents may want more time for their families, and other students may leave for economic reasons. Yet a large number of students do leave for academic reasons. *More of these students would succeed if they took advantage of the help offered by professors and tutorial programs.*

Shocking Statement

Hitler was a hero. Maybe not to people today, but in the 1930s, for many Germans he was the man who was leading Germany back to prosperity and greatness. Of course, these Germans later found out their leader was a monster. We always hear how societies need heroes, but *when taken too far, hero worship destroys both hero and followers.*

In both examples, the first sentence opens the readers' eyes (and ears). In the first, an essay written for freshmen, most readers will want to read on to find out how to avoid becoming one of the many who do not earn a degree. The second introduction comes from a term paper written for a psychology professor. The rest of the paper analyzed how the dynamics of hero worship can be destructive. There was nothing startling about the analysis itself, but you can bet that after the opening sentence, the student had the professor's attention.

Quoting   If you are familiar with a quotation from a famous person or even a well-known celebrity, quoting that person can help move readers into your essay. Readers will quickly identify with widely known quotes, such as John F. Kennedy's "'Ask not what your country can do for you'' or Martin Luther King's "I have a dream." If the quotation is not widely known, it will still add authority to your introduction.

The American philosopher John Dewey once said that the job of the educational system in a democracy is "to teach students how to think, not what to think." Dewey's point, however, is not always upheld in our schools as *teachers sometimes impose their own political and even religious beliefs on unsuspecting students.*

When you use a quotation, be sure that it fits your thesis. In the preceding introduction, the quotation is used as a contrast. Sometimes your thesis might agree with the quotation. If you are arguing that some class does teach students how to think, you could use the quotation from Dewey to lead up to the thesis in praise of the class.

Referring to Something You've Read   As a college student, you have been doing a lot of reading. Often your reading can help you begin an essay of your own. In the following paragraph, the writer uses Banesh Hoffman's point about Einstein to set up his own thesis:

In Banesh Hoffman's essay "Albert Einstein," Hoffman tells how, as a student, he was intimidated by Einstein and afraid to approach him. When Hoffman finally did call on Einstein in his office, he found a kind and simple man who was glad to help him. While all teachers are not as kind as Einstein, *students should not be afraid of calling on teachers during office hours because the students can benefit greatly from individual conferences.*

Referring to something you've read can be an effective introductory strategy. By comparing your thesis to someone else's, you can see your own ideas more clearly. Also, your readers will begin with the impression that you have some authority on the topic because you have read about it. Your reading will support your personal experience.

EXERCISE 4.11 The following are some possible thesis sentences. If a thesis sentence has a blank, rewrite the sentence filling in the blank with words of your choosing. Then pick one thesis and write two different introductions for it using two strategies discussed in this section. For example, you could write one with a famous quotation and another with the funnel method. Choose any two types of introductions you want, but make sure you choose only one thesis.

1. _____ is the toughest course for entering freshman at

   _____.

2. It is necessary that every educated person have experience and skill in writing.

3. _____ is the best athlete in _____.

4. Some television preachers pervert Christian principles.

5. Many young people today have more concern for others than most people think.

6. Too many young people today seem to care only about themselves.

EXERCISE 4.12 Write a new introduction for one of the essays you have previously written for this class.

Conclusions

Conclusion: A paragraph that stresses the importance of the thesis, gives the essay a sense of completeness, and leaves a final impression on readers.

Just as an essay should begin with an introductory paragraph, it should end with a concluding paragraph, a **conclusion**. And just as introductions can be weak, so can conclusions. As with introductions, avoid discussing your troubles in concluding.

> I have said all I know about why MTV is not harmful to children. I can't think of anything else, but I think my examples prove my point, and I think you should agree.

Like the introduction that gave the writer problems, this conclusion shares the writer's troubles with readers. If the examples did prove the writer's point, they should stand on their own and he should not be telling his readers to agree.

Another type of weak conclusion lacks development and states the obvious:

Everyone should get a lot of exercise. Exercise is fun and it makes people live longer, so everyone who is able should have a good program of exercise.

This writer has the right idea in restating her thesis, but the sentences lack punch. They are obviously true, but without development the conclusion is flat and will not leave much of an impression on an audience. Remember that a conclusion is the last thing the audience reads; thus it should leave a lasting impression.

Purposes of Conclusions   Concluding paragraphs have several main purposes:

1. They enable you to stress the importance of the point made by your essay. Often they repeat your thesis, but in different words to emphasize it once more.
2. Conclusions give your essay a sense of completeness so that readers do not feel that you have dropped the topic abruptly before developing it fully.
3. Conclusions give you one final chance to leave a lasting impression on your readers.

Qualities of Conclusions   The most effective conclusions share several characteristics:

1. Often they restate the thesis in different words or imply the thesis.
2. In most cases, they are more general than the body paragraphs.
3. Like introductions, conclusions for short essays (500–700 words) should be fairly short, no more than 100–150 words.

Like the strategies for beginning an essay, the strategies for ending one are limited only by the writer's imagination. Writers are always coming up with new ways to write conclusions. The following are a few strategies that some students have used effectively.

Solving a Problem   If your essay has discussed a problem, one easy way to conclude it is to present a way to solve the problem. Sometimes, even if you are not discussing a problem, you can show how your topic is nevertheless a solution to one.

Without the presidential debates, the voter sees the candidates only in paid political advertisements, which are usually biased, or in brief news footage accompanied by the newscaster's comments. Neither of these allows the voter to hear the candidates addressing issues for any longer than a minute or so. The debates, in contrast, enable the voter to see the candidates, head to head, discussing the important issues. In the debates, the candidates cannot evade questions or sidestep issues without looking foolish. Thus, the debates provide the voter with two hours of unbiased information about the candidates.

The body of this essay argued that debates during presidential elections are necessary to help voters make an informed choice. In most of the essay, he discussed how debates clarify the candidates' positions on issues, reveal their personalities, and show their ability to think quickly and speak well. In other words, he did not discuss the debates as a problem. Still, in showing how the debates provide a more accurate view of the candidates than news reports and commercials do, he implies that without the debates voters would have a harder time making an informed choice — and that is his thesis.

Challenging Your Readers   Another effective way to conclude is with a challenge, asking your readers to take action or to change the way they think. In the following conclusion, also from an essay on presidential debates, this writer challenged readers to watch the debates.

> Instead of complaining that the debates cut into *Dynasty* or some other favorite program, we should watch them. We are free to vote for any candidate we please, but if we are responsible citizens, we will make sure that our decision is based on knowledge of the candidates and their ideas. The presidential debates can provide that knowledge, and as conscientious citizens, we owe it to ourselves and our free society to make sure we vote wisely.

Echoing Your Introduction   Sometimes you can conclude a paper by recalling your introduction for your readers. Your conclusion, then, becomes a sort of echo. This strategy works because along with reminding the reader of your thesis, it gives the essay a kind of wholeness. The writer who introduced his thesis by narrating a story about his construction job concluded his essay this way:

> Next summer I hope to return to my construction job, and if I do, chances are that I will be working with high school graduates preparing for college, as I was last summer. Although I am tempted to scare them just like the guys scared me, I will probably be more honest with them. I will tell them that college is difficult but that students can do well if they work hard and take their courses seriously.

The writer retells the story as it may happen in the future, but this time he is the experienced college student. Note also how the concluding narration leads to a restatement of the thesis in different words.

Looking to the Future   Most of the time an essay will cover a topic from the past or in the present. To conclude the essay, you can look ahead to the future, predicting possible outcomes from your topic. The preceding example predicts the writer's future behavior as it echoes his introduction. While echoing the introduction is a nice way to conclude, you do not have to do it in order to look to the future. The following conclusion, for example, came from a research essay discussing the problem of drinking on college campuses.

> As they mature, college students will learn to drink in moderation. If they learn fast enough, they will manage to stay in college while also developing self-confidence in social matters. Others, however, will continue to believe their popularity is equal to the amount of alcohol they consume. Out of these students the most intelligent will make it through college, but they probably won't do as well as they would if they drank less. The less intelligent will eventually flunk out, and they won't leave with a degree. All they will have are memories of the night they won a chugging contest and had to be carried home.

This writer wrote a powerful conclusion. It works well because much of the discussion in the body of her paper supports the predictions she makes. That is crucial. If you use this strategy, make sure that your predictions are within reason. Don't exaggerate, but at the same time don't be afraid to predict possible outcomes of your topic.

Posing Questions   Just as you can start an essay with a question or series of questions, you can also conclude an essay this way. (However, if you use questions in your introduction, it is not wise to use the same strategy in your conclusion.) The following examples show variations within this strategy: one uses questions at the beginning of the concluding paragraph, and one uses them at the end.

Questions First

> Why do so many college students drink? Why do they drink so much? Psychologists might say that drinking enables them to overcome their social problems, providing a false sense of confidence. Sociologists might say that students are like the rest of American society, where per capita alcohol consumption is among the highest in the world. The students themselves might say that they are just trying to find a release from academic pressures. Whatever the reasons, drinking on college campuses has reached epidemic proportions.

Question Last

> The debates help us to pick the best candidate. We see the candidates under pressure, hear them state their positions on the various issues, and get an idea of their personal leadership

qualities. The debates provide so much information that they challenge us to be informed voters. Are we up to that challenge?

Both writers use questions effectively. In each conclusion, the questions enable the writer to emphasize the main point of the essay.

E X E R C I S E   4.13   Write two different conclusions for a paper that you have already written for this class, using two different strategies discussed in this section.

Essay for Reading

Black and Well-to-Do

Andrea Lee

Andrea Lee grew up in an upper-middle-class neighborhood, which she discusses in this essay. She has written a book, *Russian Journal,* and she now writes for the *New Yorker* magazine. This essay first appeared in the *New York Times.*

Vocabulary Cues

bourgeoisie: middle to upper middle class

Martha's Vineyard: an island off the coast of Massachusetts, whose year-round and summer populations are largely upper middle class

enclaves: communities separated from the rest of society

speculators: investors and developers

pastoral: pleasantly calm and free of trouble

Dick and Jane readers: elementary school readers of the 1950s that presented life as carefree and pleasant

extraordinarily: out of the ordinary

discounted: not counted or considered

avidly: with great interest and intensity

Birmingham, Selma, Greensboro: southern cities where civil rights protests took place in the 1960s

radicalized: made politically radical

dashikis: loose, colorful shirts commonly worn in Africa

alienated: made to feel like a stranger

vied: competed

complacency: a feeling of well-being and satisfaction with no desire for change

repository: a storehouse

Questions to Guide Your Reading

1. How did Lee view her neighborhood as a child?
2. What did she begin to sense as she got older?
3. How did Lee and her friends change after college?
4. How does Lee finally think of her neighborhood?

I grew up in the kind of town few people believe exists: a black upper-middle-class suburb full of colonial-style houses and Volkswagen Rabbits. Yes, Virginia, there is a black bourgeoisie, it has existed for years, and it summers on Martha's Vineyard.

The Philadelphia suburb of Yeadon, my home through childhood and adolescence, is one of many black enclaves that someday will make a very interesting study for a sociologist.

After World War II, housing speculators found it profitable to scare off white residents and sell whole streets of Yeadon to black professionals who were as eager as anyone else at that time to pursue the romantic suburban dream of fieldstone patios and eye-level ovens. In the 1950s, half the black doctors and lawyers in Philadelphia crowded into this rather small town, which was one of the few integrated suburbs, and we Yeadon kids grew up with tree houses and two-car garages and fathers who commuted into the city.

Our parents had a vision of pastoral normalcy for their children that was little different from the white ideal laid out in the Dick and Jane readers. Their attempts to provide this and to protect us from the slightest contact with race prejudice left us extraordinarily, perhaps unhealthily, sheltered: we were sent to Quaker schools and camps where race and class were discounted with eager innocence. When the Yeadon Civic Association (my father was president) discovered that a local swimming club was discriminating against blacks, the parents in my neighborhood simply built another club, which they christened "The Nile Swim Club." When we asked about the name, my father explained gravely: "This is a club only for Egyptians."

Childhood in Yeadon was a suburban idyll of shady streets and bicycles and ice cream from a drugstore called Doc's. This was the early 1960s, and as my friends and I grew older, we became dimly aware that the rest of the world was not necessarily Yeadon. Most of our parents were active in the civil rights movement, and at gatherings we listened avidly to their campaign references: Birmingham, Selma, Greensboro.

Occasionally, we kids would travel into the city and stare in horrified fascination at slums. When my generation of Yeadon preppies was graduated from high school in the late 1960s and early 1970s, however, we quickly realized that our vague concern was not enough, and many of us became radicalized. (Most of us were attending Ivy League colleges, and this increased our sense of guilt.)

During college holidays, Yeadon's driveways were colorful with dashikis and other, more complicated African garments, and a great deal of talk went on about the brothers and sisters of the urban community. Yeadon parents were edgy and alienated from their children at this time, and a common conversation between mothers began: "Yes, she used to look so *sweet,* and now she's gone and gotten one of those . . . Afros."

In the 1970s our guilt evaporated, and Yeadon became a place where parents vied with one another to produce tidbits about surgeon daughters and M.B.A. sons. Now early in the 1980s, I find that in some circles, Yeadon is a synonym for conservatism and complacency, a place famed as being the hunting ground of the AAP (Afro-American Prince or Princess), but I don't care.

Yeadon was a great town to grow up in, was as solid a repository of American virtues and American flaws as any other close-knit suburban community; moreover, it had, and still has, its own peculiar flavor — a lively mixture of materialism, idealism, and ironic humor that prevents the minds of its children from stagnating. I feel a surge of well-being when I return there in the summer to hear the symphony of lawn mowers to find that the Nile Swim Club remains ''for Egyptians only.''

Questions for Study and Discussion
1. Answer the Questions to Guide Your Reading.
2. How are the people of Yeadon similar to suburban whites? How are they different?
3. What is the thesis of this essay?
4. What type of introductory strategy does Lee use?
5. Which of the body paragraphs state topic sentences? Which imply a topic sentence?
6. Point to two examples of how Lee uses specific details to support and develop a point in a paragraph.
7. Are there any paragraphs that you think could be developed further? In other words, is there any point that you, as audience, feel you need to know more about?
8. Point out uses of the repetition and variation of key words that add cohesion in Lee's third paragraph. Do the same in her fourth paragraph.
9. Give at least three examples of the use of transitional words and phrases.
10. Compare and contrast the strategy in Lee's concluding paragraph with any of the strategies covered in this chapter.

Writing Assignment
In writing about her neighborhood, Lee illustrates the thesis that a black middle class existed at a time when most people, especially whites, did not think one did. She sees her neighborhood in the early and mid-1960s as being a typical American middle-class neighborhood, except that most of the residents were black. Think about the place where you grew up. How is it typical? different? What thesis does it illustrate?

Write a short essay (500 words) showing how your neighborhood illustrates, or does not illustrate, something about the way Americans live. Be specific in developing your paragraphs so that your neighborhood does not sound like any similar place. Give much attention to your introduction and conclusion as well as to the body paragraphs.

CHAPTER 5

Revision

B y now you have a general idea of what revision is about. In Chapter 1, you learned that revision is part of the writing process — the part when you re-see your writing and make changes according to your purpose and your audience's needs. And in other chapters, you saw how revision can make writing more specific or be used to improve an essay or paragraph. Before proceeding into a detailed discussion of revision, let's review what you know already.

First, you know that revision is not the same as editing. When you edit, you check your writing for misspelled words, grammar errors, punctuation errors, and so on. When you revise, you change larger matters having to do with the content, organization, and style. Second, you know that revision is the part of the writing process that usually comes after drafting, but you also know that because the parts of the process sometimes overlap, some revision can take place as you are writing your draft. Third, you know that you need to wait a while between writing your draft and revising it — at least a few hours, if not overnight. This period of waiting will enable you to re-see the draft so that you can make the necessary changes. Finally, during revision it is important to receive feedback from others — friends, relatives, classmates, your instructor — by having them read and respond to your essay.

Along with knowing something about revision, you have seen examples of revised writing. Recall Tracy's paragraph about her grandfather in Chapter 2. She revised to focus her topic on the one activity she enjoyed most with him — going to St. Louis. She expanded that point from a first draft that contained many general ideas about her grandfather but very little focus and few specific details. In revising — re-seeing — her first paragraph, Tracy realized that to make her audience understand how she felt about her grandfather, she would have to develop each general idea she wrote in her first paragraph. Thus, her revisions consisted of separating the general ideas and developing each one with additional details in a paragraph of its own. In short, she made changes — separating ideas and adding details to fulfill her purpose and to meet her audience's needs.

With the writing you have done in this or other courses or on your own, you have probably gained some experience in revising. If you think about that experience, you know that in revising you consider many different aspects of your writing — from as large a matter as reorganizing the paper to as small a matter as rewriting part of a sentence. Good revision, in other words, requires many different considerations. And though part of the larger writing process, revision is a process itself — a process within a process.

■ Revision as Process

Revision leads to changes, and change implies a process. You have probably heard the expression "in the process of change," or you may have heard someone say something "changed in the process." These expressions can apply to almost anything — the changes in someone's outlook during the education process, the changes in the design of a house during the building process. Such changes are the result of re-seeing — the student seeing his or her ideas about democracy differently as the result of a political science course, the architect seeing his or her ideas about a house differently once the house has begun to take shape.

Writers make those kinds of changes also. A former writing teacher of mine once said, "For a good writer, a piece of writing is never finished; it's just abandoned." He meant that good writers are always re-seeing what they have written and looking for ways to say it better. But finally, because of a deadline, the writer must "abandon" the writing and let it stand as it is. Of course, if the writer has allowed time to revise and done necessary revisions, the writing will probably be a successful product. The point is that experienced writers are always looking at — re-seeing — possibilities for making their writing even better. They see their writing as always in the process of change until a deadline prevents them from changing it anymore.

While most experienced writers revise a great deal, beginning writers usually do not revise much. As discussed in Chapter 1, beginners tend to think that experienced writers just sit down, write something, and are finished. The beginning writers then try to write this way themselves because they do not realize how much experienced writers revise, either while drafting or after completing a draft. I sometimes tease beginning writers by telling them that their final paper is just their rough draft copied over neatly. Usually this joke makes them realize that they need to make changes in the rough draft before thinking about a final copy.

Revision, as experienced writers know, is hard work. Most beginning writers avoid revision not because they are lazy but because they do not know how to revise or what to revise. In revising a first, second, or even third draft, it is necessary to reconsider and make necessary changes in the content, organization, and style of the essay. And all of these changes must be done according to the requirements of the writing situation — your purpose, role, and audience. It seems as if there are many things to consider in the revision process, and there are, but if you look at them one at a time, you will gain a better understanding of how and why you revise.

■ Revision and the Writing Situation

Any change you make on an essay relates directly to one or more of the elements of the writing situation: purpose, role, and audience. If you add more details to strengthen a point, you are assuming that your audience needs those details and will not get the point without them. If you cut a sentence, you are assuming that the audience does not need the sentence to make sense of what you are saying. Suppose you start with a thesis that points out a problem, but then in revising you change the thesis to one that calls for a solution to a problem. As a result, your purpose in writing changes. If in revising a term paper, you substitute a neutral or formal word for a slang word, you are making the substitution to conform to your role as college student: you know that students do not use slang in term papers. Nor does your audience, the professor, expect slang. Thus the substitution is the result of both your role and your audience.

Revising for Your Audience

As you can see in the preceding examples, it is difficult to separate your purpose and role from your concerns about audience. But when you revise, it is wise to reconsider your initial thoughts about your audience. The audience analysis questions from Chapter 1 can help during revision:

1. Who is your audience?
   a. What do members of your audience know about the topic?
   b. What references can you assume they will know?
   c. What references must you explain?
2. What are your audience's attitudes toward what you are writing?
   a. Are members of the audience most likely to agree?
   b. Are they most likely to disagree?
   c. Are they neutral?
3. How is your audience going to use your writing?
   a. To inform themselves?
   b. To entertain themselves?
   c. To make a decision?

d. To examine or solve a problem?

e. To change their behavior?

If you review these questions *after* you complete your draft, you can often see the places in your writing that need revision. I once wrote a letter to a company from which I purchased a stereo that developed a problem. My letter described the problem in reasonably good detail. I closed the first draft of the letter by telling the reader — the company official — that I hoped he or she would help me. But how? I never said. Did I want a new stereo? Did I want my money refunded? Did I want the name of a local service center that could fix the stereo? I had taken the stereo to the local service center twice, and neither time was it repaired properly, so I wanted the reader to authorize either a replacement of the stereo or a refund. When I revised the letter I made this clear, but if I had not, the company probably would have told me to go to the same service center I had gone to in the first place.

In my first draft, I was not aware of what I wanted the reader to do. If the reader saw the first draft, he or she would have assumed that the stereo needed to be fixed and would have *solved the problem* by sending me to the service center. However, I wanted the reader not only to solve the problem but to do so by *making a decision* about a refund or a replacement. In this case, keeping in mind *how the reader was to use the writing* (question 3 on audience analysis) was extremely important.

E X E R C I S E   5.1   Assume that you are writing a letter asking a company to replace a faulty stereo. Your audience is a consumer affairs representative for a national chain of electronics stores. The stores sell various brands and products ranging from telephone answering machines to wide-screen televisions, and your audience must deal with complaints about all of them. Examine the items below. Indicate which you think should be included in the letter and which should not. Explain your answers.

1. The exact date of purchase
2. The brand and model number
3. The color of the stereo
4. The name and address of the store where the stereo was purchased
5. Reference to other items that you have purchased at that store
6. The specific problem with the stereo
7. The number of times and dates repairs were made
8. What songs were playing when the stereo malfunctioned
9. The name and address of the service center
10. Your taste in music

The following is a draft of a letter written in response to Exercise 5.1. It is badly in need of revision. Revise the letter using what you have learned from the previous discussion and exercise.

August 17, 1989

Ms. Mary Tune
Consumer Affairs
Electroland Stores
Oxnard, California 93030

Dear Ms. Tune:

Last month, I bought a stereo at my local Electroland Store. I was really happy to buy it because I am into rhythm and blues music, and I knew to get the best sounds from my large collection of R&B albums, I needed a good stereo.

At first, the stereo played real well, and I particularly enjoyed the bass sounds, but then the turntable started slowing down, distorting the music. Of course, I was bummed out, so I took the stereo back to Electroland. They sent me to another place to get it fixed. I was told the problem was just a loose belt and that it would be fixed in a couple of days. It was fixed, and the stereo worked well for a week or two, but then the turntable started slowing down again. I then had the turntable fixed again, but in a few days it was slowing down again. So I went back to the Electroland store where I bought the stereo, but they told me they couldn't do anything and that I had to write to you. That's how I got your address.

I hope you will help me out. I'm tired of all this hassling around, and I just want to be able to listen to my favorite records.

Examine a paper written for this or any class. Find parts in the paper that need to be revised to meet the needs of your audience more effectively. Using the audience analysis questions, revise the paper as needed.

Revising to Clarify Your Role and Purpose

As you revise a paper to meet the needs of your audience, you will also be reconsidering your role and purpose. In the writing situation in Exercise 5.2, the writer left out some information the reader needed while including other information that the reader did not need. You should be able to identify the writer's role as dissatisfied consumer, but in the unneeded information you can also see that the writer has mixed in another role: rhythm and blues fan. Though the writer may love this type of music, the reader, who reads dozens of letters a day, probably does not care what kind of music the writer likes. The reader, as a consumer affairs representative, is concerned with the writer as consumer and should not be asked to spend time seeing the writer in another role. Also, since the writer's purpose is to have the stereo replaced, the love of rhythm and blues is not part of the purpose of the letter.

As you read through the following paragraph, see if you can identify the writer's role and purpose. Then look for information that does not fit either one.

Driving a tractor-trailer is not an easy job. First of all, the driver must be able to shift a transmission which can have anywhere from ten to twenty-four different gears. Each shift must be double-clutched, meaning the driver must push down the clutch, move the gearshift to neutral before releasing the clutch, and then push down the clutch again before shifting to the next gear. All this must be done in a split second so that the truck does not stall. Peterbuilt, the best brand of truck, also has the easiest transmission to shift because the gears are very smooth and the clutch has a hydraulic release. Also, truck drivers must be skillful at using their brakes. Unlike a car's brakes, truck brakes are controlled by air, and thus they are very powerful and can throw the truck into a skid if a driver applies them too quickly. Yet a truck without air brakes would be a menace to highway safety. Along with knowing how to apply the brakes, a truck driver must learn how to steer properly, using a very large steering wheel to keep the semi in its lane and to guide it safely around corners.

You probably did not have much trouble seeing that the writer's role is that of someone knowledgeable about truck driving and that the purpose of the paragraph is to inform a less knowledgeable audience about the difficulties of driving a tractor-trailer. Perhaps the writer wants the reader to respect truck drivers more. But what is the writer's role and purpose in the sentence about Peterbuilt trucks? Is the writer now persuading or informing? Does the sentence stick to the paragraph's purpose? Also, how does the statement about trucks without air brakes fit the writer's role and purpose? As this paragraph shows, when you revise your writing, just as in the invention stage, you must keep your role and purpose clearly in mind.

EXERCISE 5.4 The following paragraph was written to explain why insurance companies set particular rates for automobile insurance for different groups of drivers. The writer's role is that of student. His purpose is to show the professor that he knows why rates are highest for single males from age eighteen to twenty-five. Revise the paragraph to fit this role and purpose. What information does not belong? What wording needs to be changed?

> Insurance rates for single males from eighteen to twenty-five are the highest of any group of drivers, and there are many reasons. These dudes have the most accidents, and they are most often arrested for driving and drinking. No one should drive drunk, and anyone who does should be put in jail. Drivers at this age also rank among the highest in number of speeding tickets, and a large proportion of these males are gear heads who like to drag race with high-performance cars. Single males between eighteen and twenty-five buy the largest percentage of high-performance cars. A lot of them should not even be allowed on the road.

EXERCISE 5.5 Choose any topic you like and write a paragraph of about a hundred words. Make sure your role and purpose are clear, but then add a sentence or two that does not fit either the role or the purpose. When you are finished, trade paragraphs with a classmate and identify the information that does not fit the writer's role and purpose. Be prepared to explain why.

EXERCISE 5.6 Examine a paper written for this or any class that you feel would be improved with more revision. Find information that does not fit your role and purpose in writing the paper. Revise any parts of the paper where this problem occurs.

■ Revising for Better Content

When you revise your writing to meet the needs of your audience more effectively or to clarify your role and purpose, you are often tinkering with the *content* of the paper so that it meets the needs of the writing situation. However, sometimes you may have your role, purpose, and audience clearly in mind, but still the content of your paper does not do the job of communicating what you want to say. The content of the paper has more to do with *what* the writer says and less with *how* he or she says it. (How something is written is important too, and it is discussed later in this chapter.)

Adding and Expanding Information and Ideas

Adding and expanding:
In revision, putting in missing information, examples, and ideas or elaborating on material already in the essay.

Sometimes the problem with a piece of writing is that it does not say enough to meet the audience's needs. In that case, **adding** or **expanding** information becomes necessary. The following paragraph is from the first draft of an essay on popular music in the 1960s.

> A lot of sixties music had a protest message. Bob Dylan's songs dealt with racism and war, such as "The Ballad of Emmett Till" and "Masters of War." Richie Havens was another protest singer. The Beatles had some protest songs too, such as "Bungalow Bill."

This paragraph was written by a student in his early thirties and directed to an audience of classmates in their late teens and early twenties who knew little about sixties music. The writer's purpose was to educate the audience to see the value of the music, so his role was that of an authority on the subject. The role, purpose, and audience seem clear, and the paragraph has a clear topic sentence backed by some examples. But most of the students in the audience had questions. How were the Dylan songs about war and racism? Who was Richie Havens? Were there other protest singers? And even though the writer's audience was familiar with the Beatles, most of the young students had never heard "Bungalow Bill." In short, if the writer was to fulfill his purpose in educating the audience and his role as authority, he would have to consider what additional information his audience would need. His revised paragraph looked like this:

> A lot of sixties music had a protest message. Bob Dylan wrote songs against racism and war. For instance, "The Ballad of Emmett Till" told the story of the awful lynching of a young black man in Mississippi. Also, "Masters of War" condemned people who made money from wars. Richie Havens was another protest singer. He was black and his most famous song, "Freedom," was often sung at civil rights demonstrations. Joan Baez had a hit with "I Shall Be Released," a song written by Dylan about the unjust imprisonment of protesters. Even the Beatles wrote and sang protest songs. "Bungalow Bill" made fun of General William Westmoreland, who was the commander of American troops in Vietnam.

In this revised version of the paragraph, the writer added another example, on Joan Baez, and expanded and explained the previous examples. His audience now knows what the Dylan songs were about, who Richie Havens was and why he was important at the time, and what "Bungalow Bill" was about. Although the writer still gives only a sample of protest songs in the sixties, this sample provides enough information to enable his audience to see his point.

Using Invention Strategies to Add and Expand

In the discussion of the writing process in Chapter 1, invention strategies were placed first because when faced with a writing assignment the first thing you have to do is to come up with — invent — ideas and information about your topic. You can also use the invention strategies to help you add and explain information during revision.

In revising the paragraph on protest in sixties music, the student could have used brainstorming, clustering, or even the journalist's questions to come up with the information that he added to the paragraph. For example, in the draft he mentioned that Richie Havens was another protest singer, a statement that did not tell his readers much. By brainstorming or clustering about Havens, he might have come up with the following list and cluster diagram.

Brainstorming List: Richie Havens
Strong voice
Not a lot of hit songs
Well known mostly in the late sixties
Black man
Often wore African dashikis
Best song "Freedom"
"Freedom" often sung at civil rights protests

Cluster: Richie Havens

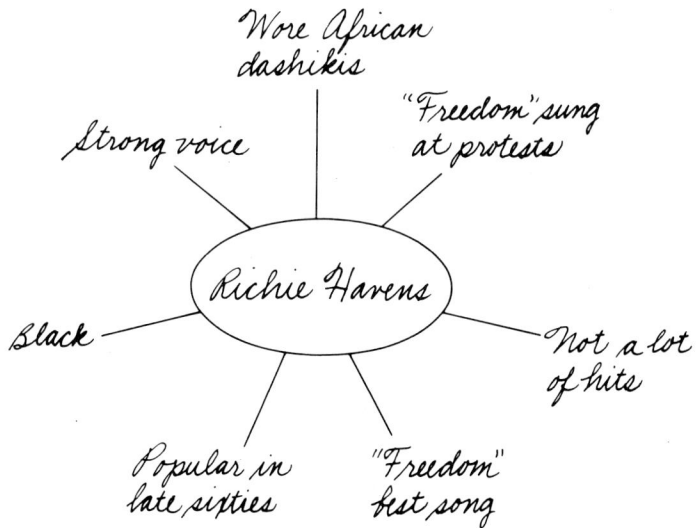

Journalist's Questions: Richie Havens
Who: Richie Havens
What: Sang protest songs, particularly the song "Freedom"
When: Late sixties
Why: To protest problems of civil rights; he was black

Where: In concerts and at civil rights protests
How: With a real strong voice, wearing African dashiki

Any of the invention strategies would have given the student the details he needed. From these he would have picked the details that best supported his topic sentence stating that much of the music of the sixties carried a protest message. He could then have jotted these details in the appropriate places in his draft and included them in the revised version of the paragraph. Of course, revision does not always require that you go back to the invention strategies, but when you see a need for more information, or readers ask for it, the strategies can help you discover it.

E X E R C I S E   5.7   The following three paragraphs need information added or expanded. For each paragraph, make a list of questions that could help the writer revise. Do this exercise on your own or with two or three other students.

1. Trains are not a very good way to travel long distances. They take too long to get from one place to another. If you have to sleep overnight on the train, you probably won't be very comfortable. You see nice scenery, but after a long time, even the scenery gets boring.

2. My son's paper route helped him make money, but it was an inconvenience for me. I always had to make sure he was up on time to deliver the papers before he went to school. People would call our home bothering me when he forgot to leave their paper. Sometimes when he could not deliver the papers, I delivered them for him, and he had a big route with many customers. It wasn't worth the money he made.

3. Going to college part time has its difficulties. You have to work either during the day or at night when you are not in school. Also you do not have much time for your family if you have one, or for a social life if you are single.

E X E R C I S E   5.8   Choose one of the paragraphs in Exercise 5.7 and revise it by adding information that would make it more informative. Use the invention strategies if you have trouble coming up with information. Once you have the paragraph rewritten, ask a classmate to point out how the information you have added improves the paragraph and what information is needed to improve it even more.

E X E R C I S E   5.9   Revise a paragraph from an essay you have written for this or another class, adding and expanding information where needed.

Cutting Unnecessary Information

Cutting: Taking out information, examples, or ideas that stray from the purpose and thesis of an essay or that are not needed for the audience's understanding.

Some of the revisions you made in earlier exercises required you to cut material, such as the letter writer's references to rhythm and blues. Beginning writers, and many experienced writers too, often find that **cutting** is the most painful part of revision. After all, whether beginners or experts, writers put a lot of work into writing. Many times, however, cutting information can improve a piece of writing significantly. Among the many reasons to cut information, two stand out:

1. you have more details or examples than the reader needs to get the point, or
2. you have unnecessarily repeated an idea.

Cutting Unnecessary Details   In Chapter 3, you learned about the need to be specific in your writing. Specific writing requires that you use enough examples to enable the reader to see your point. When you think that your readers will disagree with you, you probably need more examples to convince them to accept or at least consider your point. When readers will agree or be neutral, fewer examples will probably suffice. When do you have enough examples and details? When do you have too many? It takes practice and experience to know exactly. A good rule of thumb is that it is better to have too much information than too little, but if you consider the needs of your audience carefully, usually you know when you have too much. Consider the following paragraph.

In the past few years McDonald's has tried to improve the decor of its restaurants to make them seem like fancy restaurants. Recently I was in a McDonald's in northern Indiana which was decorated to look like the dining room of an old riverboat. It had many mirrors edged in an imitation gold leaf, brass bells and replicas of gas lanterns on the walls, and scalloped moldings and railings. There were about a dozen of the mirrors, and the bells and lanterns were over each booth. Another McDonald's I visited, this one in Ohio, had a modern decor. The walls were done in pink and mauve, there were numerous plants, and modern paintings hung above each booth. These paintings were not Picasso copies or anything that radical. Instead, they abstractly portrayed mountains or beaches, done suggestively in bold lines and broad patches of color rather than in the realistic detail of landscapes. Another McDonald's was decorated to suggest an old railroad station. . . .

This writer obviously has an eye for detail, but as you read through this paragraph, you may have begun to forget the writer's main point —

that McDonald's is upgrading the decor of its restaurants. Even if you didn't lose sight of this point, do you really need the estimate of the number of mirrors or the location of the lanterns and bells in the restaurant decorated like a riverboat? Doesn't just knowing they were there enable you to get the point? Similarly, do you need a detailed description of the paintings to see that the second restaurant had a modern decor? Don't forget, as you learned in Chapter 2, show rather than tell, but remember that showing doesn't mean losing your point — and the reader — in a forest of details.

E X E R C I S E 5.10 Revise the following paragraph, cutting unnecessary details.

As kids, we shuddered when we walked past old Mr. Speers's house, for we were sure it was haunted. In front of the house there was a fence with sharp pointed spikes on top of it. It was about five feet high. A path of broken stones crossed a yard full of dead weeds and leafless thorny bushes. The porch sagged across the front of the house, and there were spaces where spindles were missing from the broken railings. The rickety steps led to a carved oak door with a heavy brass knocker. I never looked, but I was sure the carvings on the door were pictures of fiends and devils. The dusty velvet curtains in the windows looked like they belonged in an old funeral parlor. But it was hard to see the curtains because of the thick cobwebs in the windows themselves. The roof of the house was high and peaked with turrets on each side. These turrets were pointed at the top. Under the eaves of the roof, blackbirds nested and screamed like tormented souls. These birds would swoop down as if they wanted to attack us. All the gutters around the roof were rusty. The house had once been painted a pale gray, but the paint was faded and chipped. In some spots, the bare weathered wood showed through the paint.

Cutting Unnecessary Repetition of Ideas Sometimes in a piece of writing you may repeat yourself to make sure the reader gets the point. At other times, you may repeat yourself too much. Readers lose patience when they are told something more times than they need to know it. Consider the following paragraph, for example.

The design of baseball mitts has changed tremendously since the game was first played, making fielding much easier. The first mitts, used in the latter part of the nineteenth century, were little more than a leather glove, like those worn today in cold weather. Without padding or webbing, they offered little protection and thus hindered a player's ability to field sharply hit balls. Because the old mitts were just five-fingered gloves made of leather, they were effective only in catching slow ground balls or pop flies, so players could not field as well. Today's mitts are much larger, sometimes measuring as much as eighteen inches from the heavily padded heel to the top of the wide basketlike webbing that bridges the forefinger and thumb. They still have five fingers, but the fingers are as much as eight inches long, stiffly padded, connected to each other by a rawhide stitch, and hinged at the palm to allow the player to smother the wickedest grounder or the sharpest line drive. The large size and heavy padding of modern gloves enables players to be better fielders. Today's baseball gloves are far superior to the first gloves and make fielding easier.

The purpose and point of this paragraph are clear: the writer is comparing the original baseball mitts to today's to show how the changes in the design make fielding easier. We get this idea in the topic sentence, but then it reappears three times in the last two sentences of the paragraph. Also, in the middle of the paragraph, the writer says the old gloves were like the leather gloves people wear in winter. He then repeats himself by saying they were just five-fingered leather gloves. Part of this writer's problem is that he is afraid to let his specific details show his general ideas; thus he unnecessarily repeats them.

E X E R C I S E   5.11 The following paragraph repeats its general idea more than it should. Revise it to eliminate repetition.

Nursing is not the glamorous job that the media sometimes shows it to be. In movies and television shows, female nurses are usually pretty women with cheery smiles and great dispositions. They flirt with doctors and usually end up marrying or having a romance with one. Sometimes, they are shown making life and death decisions about a patient when the doctors are not around. This is a very glamorous picture, but it doesn't happen that way. A nurse's job is not very glamorous. In reality, because the nurse may often work long hours, or even double shifts, she won't care whether she looks pretty or not, so she is not very glamorous. These hours, along with the never-ending demands of the patients, can wipe the smile off the face of even the most cheerful nurse. As for romances with doctors, the nurse's life is not this glamorous. The truly professional nurse is not on the job to flirt with doctors. And instead of making life and death decisions, the average nurse spends most of her time emptying bedpans, administering medication, filling out charts, and moving heavy patients so the bed linen can be changed, which is not glamorous either. So a nurse's job is tough, not glamorous like on TV or in the movies.

Rearranging Information

Sometimes a paragraph or essay may have all the information it needs, but the information may not be presented in the best possible order. It needs **rearranging**. You might be using a narrating strategy and might place some material out of chronological order, or you might be persuading but not have your points arranged to create the most impact. Compare the first draft and revised versions of the following paragraph.

First Draft

When I returned from Christmas break, a water pipe had burst, and my dorm room was a mess. There was a big puddle of dirty water in the middle, and the tiles were all coming up. The bottom mattress had stains on it, and there was a rusty spring hanging down from the soaked bunk above. Then I looked up and saw all these wet stains on the ceiling. The dresser had mold all over it, and there were some soggy old magazines in front of it. They smelled from all the dampness from the water.

Revised Version

When I returned from Christmas break, a water pipe had burst and my dorm room was a mess. The floor tiles were coming loose in a big puddle of dirty water. This puddle started in the middle of the floor and ran into a pile of soggy magazines in front of the dresser. As for the dresser, there was slimy gray mold all over it. When I turned around, I saw the bunks. The mattress on the top one was soaked, and it had a rusty spring hanging from it. Even the bottom one had water stains. The whole room had a sickening moldy smell. Then I looked up and saw a stain that covered almost the whole ceiling and cracks that the water had dripped through from the pipes.

These paragraphs may not seem very different to you. You probably notice a few added details, such as the words "slimy gray" describing the mold or the expansion of the example about the ceiling. However, if you look more closely, the examples have been rearranged quite a bit to improve the organization. Notice that in the second sentence of the revision the writer reverses the order of the loose tiles and the puddle. Readers now see the tiles *in* the puddle, and mentioning the puddle second allows the writer to lead into the third sentence, which is also about the puddle. That sentence then gives readers an idea of the size of puddle but also leads over to the magazines and the dresser, which is described in the fourth sentence. The writer then includes the details on the bed and the ceiling. Overall, the revision moves across the floor to one side of the room where the dresser is, back to the other side where the bed is, and finally up to the ceiling to the cause of the problem, the broken pipe, first mentioned in the topic sentence. In other words, readers see the room as the student did. Because the rough draft presents the details randomly, it is more difficult to follow.

In Chapter 4, you learned that coherence in a paragraph is achieved when one sentence follows logically from the one before it. The revised paragraph of the preceding pair works better because it has coherence. You also learned in Chapter 4 that transitions — both transitional words and repetition of key words — add to coherence. When you rearrange information in a paragraph or a whole essay, it is important that you check your transitions. Sometimes the rearrangement requires that new transitions be added.

In the preceding revision, notice the transitional phrases added at the beginnings of sentences four, five, and seven: *As for the dresser, When I turned around, Even.* The first two help locate readers as the writer's eyes move about the room, and the last emphasizes the extent of the damage. So while the rearranged examples improve the paragraph, the transitions help readers to see the rearrangement.

E X E R C I S E 5.12 The following are some questions that can help you judge whether sentences in a paragraph need to be rearranged. Apply these questions to each of the sentences in a paragraph you have written. Jot down notes about the purpose and place of each sentence in the paragraph. Then revise the paragraph for the best possible arrangement.

1. Is the sentence the topic sentence? If so, is the topic of the paragraph clear and limited? Is the sentence smoothly written?
3. Is the sentence an example? If so, is the example concrete and specific?
4. Is the sentence one part of a longer example? If so, is it linked clearly to the other parts?
5. Does the sentence follow clearly from the sentence before it? If not, why not? Should a transition be added or should the sentence be moved?
6. Does the sentence lead to the sentence following it? If not, why not? Should a transition be added or should the sentence be moved?

All the examples so far have discussed content in paragraphs, assuming that the paragraphs were parts of a larger essay. Whether you are adding, cutting, or rearranging content, the same principles that apply to individual paragraphs apply to the whole essay. One student, for example, wrote a term paper for an Afro-American studies course. The purpose of her paper was to show how Tuskegee Institute, the first black college in America, started out as a vocational school and gradually developed into a full-fledged university. She had received the paper back with a poor grade, but the professor was allowing her to revise and resubmit it. When she went over the paper with her writing instructor, she was able to see that she had done a good job showing Tuskegee's original vocational curriculum and its broad curriculum of the last few decades. However, she had skimmed over the 1930s, a decade when the school increasingly added liberal arts courses. In her revised version of the paper she added more than two pages of discussion on this important period in the school's development.

While this student added much material to her essay, some students cut whole paragraphs, and even pages, when the information is not relevant to the purpose of the paper and the needs of the audience. If rearranging information makes a better paper, there is nothing wrong with moving a paragraph or more from the end of the paper to the beginning, from the beginning to the end, from the middle to the end, and so on. You should strive to put your paragraphs in the best possible order.

At the end of this chapter is a case study of one student's revisions. As you read through it comparing her drafts, notice that she applies the same principles of revision to the whole of the essay as she applies to its individual parts.

■ Sentence Combining

When you are satisfied with the larger matters of your paper, you should begin to look at individual sentences. Revising sentences can clarify your point. For beginners, revision often requires **sentence combining.**

Combining Short Sentences for a More Mature Style

The first books you read as a child contained very short sentences:

> See Dick run. See Jane run. See Spot. See Spot run. Dick and Jane run with Spot.

Sentence combining: A technique in which short sentences can be joined into one sentence, usually in various ways. Longer sentences also can be combined to show contrasting, coordinate, or cause-and-effect relationships.

Written for first graders, these sentences fit the audience, but to an adult they seem ridiculous. As a beginning writer in college, you would never write such sentences. Because you are older, you naturally have developed a more sophisticated control of sentences. In fact, in speaking, you probably use much more complex sentence structure than you realize. For instance, if you had to express the action of the short sentences above, you would probably say something like, "Dick and Jane are running after their dog, Spot."

In writing, however, beginners sometimes need to combine sentences so that their written style is as mature as the way they speak. Consider the following examples.

> My first grade teacher made me want to become a teacher. Her name was Mrs. Green. I was in her class at Honey Creek Elementary School.

I am majoring in broadcasting. It is a growing field. I hope some day to be a TV newswoman.

In each set, the sentences are too short, creating a choppy effect that would be annoying to most adult readers. The sentences could easily be combined:

Mrs. Green, my first grade teacher at Honey Creek Elementary School, made me want to become a teacher.

I am majoring in broadcasting, a growing field, and I hope to become a TV newswoman.

In both examples, three sentences were combined to make one. Learning how to combine sentences can improve your style and make your writing more mature.

EXERCISE 5.13 Combine each group of sentences into one sentence. Feel free to change the order of the information. Just concentrate on writing the best sentence you can from the short sentences.

Example

Clark Kent wore glasses.
The glasses were thick.
The glasses were black-framed.
He appeared meek.
He appeared mild.

Combined: Clark Kent, who wore thick, black-framed glasses, appeared meek and mild.

1. Superman was born on Krypton.
   Krypton is a planet.
   Krypton is imaginary.
2. Superman comics have been popular.
   This popularity has gone on for many years.
3. Jimmy Olsen appears in Superman comics.
   He is a reporter.
   He is young.
   Jimmy works for the *Daily Planet*.
   It is the newspaper of Metropolis.
4. Perry White is an editor.
   He is the chief editor.
   He works for the *Daily Planet*.
   He yells at Jimmy Olsen.

He yells at Clark Kent.

He yells at them often.

5. Some people like Batman.

   They like him more than they like Superman.

6. Batman has a sidekick.

   His name is Robin.

   Robin helps him fight.

   They fight against crime.

7. Superman fights villains.

   Batman fights villains.

   The villains are strange.

   The villains are powerful.

8. There are many superheroes today.

   Batman has been around longer than them.

   Superman has been around longer than them.

9. The Incredible Hulk looks like a monster.

   He has huge muscles.

   He has green skin.

   He has bulging eyes.

10. The Hulk has strength.

    His strength is great.

    He uses his strength to fight.

    He fights criminals.

    The criminals are diabolical.

In working on Exercise 5.13, you may have thought that you do not write such short sentences. You are right: Because you are an adult, your sentences are never so short. Combining such sentences, however, can help you realize how longer sentences are made from several short ones. Also, you may have realized that each group of short sentences could be combined in more than one way. To revise a sentence, you have to realize that you can say the same thing in different ways. Compare the different ways the example sentences in Exercise 5.13 can be combined:

Clark Kent, who wore thick, black-framed glasses, appeared meek and mild.

Clark Kent, who appeared meek and mild, wore thick, black-framed glasses.

Appearing meek and mild, Clark Kent wore thick, black-framed glasses.

Wearing thick, black-framed glasses, Clark Kent appeared meek and mild.

Clark Kent, wearing thick, black-framed glasses, appeared meek and mild.

Clark Kent, appearing meek and mild, wore thick, black-framed glasses.

Meek and mild appearing Clark Kent wore thick, black-framed glasses.

As you can see, there are many ways to write this sentence, and you might be able to think of even more. The more possible versions of a sentence you can see, the easier it is to revise.

E X E R C I S E 5.14 Rewrite three sentences from Exercise 5.13 in as many ways as you can. Some sentences will allow for more versions than others, so there is no correct number of revisions.

Combining Longer Sentences to Show Relationships

Combining short sentences can help you to see how sentences work and to avoid a childish style. Often, though, you have longer sentences that can be combined to make your meaning easier to understand. Examine the following pairs of sentences.

Tuition at two-year colleges seems to get higher each year. Two-year colleges still charge less than most four-year schools.

I learned to use a word processor last year. Writing became much easier.

The pairs in each set of sentences are related. In the first set, the second sentence contrasts with the first, but because the sentences are separate, readers must draw the contrast themselves. In the second set, there is a time relationship, but again readers must figure out the connection. Compare the following combined versions to the original pairs.

Tuition at two-year colleges seems to get higher each year, but two-year colleges still charge less than most four-year schools.

When I learned to use a word processor last year, writing became much easier.

The combined versions do not add new information, but, when combined, the sentences show the connections between the first piece of information and the second. In the first set, the transitional word *but* lets the reader know that the second part of the sentence contrasts with the first part. In the second set, adding *when* to the first part makes the time relationship clear. Combining longer sentences makes connections for readers. In addition, the combined versions eliminate the choppy and seemingly immature style of the first sets.

The transitional words that are used to draw relationships between sentences in paragraphs can also work as sentence connectors. The following transitional words are especially useful as sentence connectors.

Connectors Used with a Comma	*Connectors Used with a Semicolon*
, but	; also
, and	; accordingly
, for	; consequently
, nor	; furthermore
, or	; moreover
, so	; nevertheless
, yet	; then
	; thus
	; therefore
	; still

Whether you choose a connector that takes a comma or a semicolon depends on the writing situation. The connectors used with semicolons tend to be more formal, so if the writing situation is formal, use one of them. In less formal situations, prefer connectors that can be used with the comma.

Combining to Show Contrast The following combining words — *contrast* — show a difference between — information in one sentence and a sentence that follows: *yet, but, however, nevertheless, still.*

Jim loves to sleep late in the morning, *yet* he rises at six each day to go to work.

The first part of the sentence shows something Jim does not like to do, while the second part shows that he does it every day. Thus, the sentence expresses a contrast between Jim's desire (wanting to sleep late) and his behavior (getting up early for work). Many of the connectors in the preceding list could show this contrast:

Jim loves to sleep late in the morning, *but* he rises at six each day to go to work.

Jim loves to sleep late in the morning; *however,* he rises at six each day to go to work.

Jim loves to sleep late in the morning; *nevertheless,* he rises at six each day to go to work.

Jim loves to sleep late in the morning; *still,* he rises at six each day to go to work.

Remember that sentences combined with *however, nevertheless,* and *still* are punctuated with a semicolon.

Sometimes one connector may work better than another. You could write, for example:

The children wanted to go on a picnic, but it was raining.

The same sentences connected with *nevertheless* would not sound quite right:

The children wanted to go on a picnic; nevertheless, it was raining.

When you use connectors to show contrast, make sure the contrast is clear.

E X E R C I S E   5.15   The following pairs of contradictory sentences are taken from students' writing. Combine each pair of sentences twice to show contrast, using a different connector each time. Compare the sentences. Are some connectors better than others in certain sentences?

Example   People usually think of dogs as smart animals. Many other animals are smarter than dogs.

People usually think of dogs as smart animals, but many other animals are smarter than dogs.

People usually think of dogs as smart animals; still, many other animals are smarter than dogs.

1. In high school I thought I would become a pro football player for sure. After playing college ball, I learned that very few players have the talent to make the pros.
2. My sociology teacher was so boring that he put me to sleep and made me hate the subject. I read the textbook for the class and found that sociology is fascinating.
3. *Doonesbury* is a popular comic strip. You have to be up on politics to get all the jokes.
4. I don't think I'll ever like writing. I like writing in this journal because I can say what's on my mind.
5. Mr. Mengelt kept the students in line sometimes. Usually they were so wild he was afraid to try.
6. My parents were not rich. They always bought me nice clothes if the other kids had them.
7. I didn't expect it to rain. On my way back from my first class I got caught in a downpour.

8. I think the essay explained a thesis sentence. I had trouble reading it, so I don't understand.

■■■■■■■■■■■■■■■
E X E R C I S E   5.16 Using the sentences in Exercise 5.15, connect the sentences by placing one of the following words at the beginning of the first sentence: *although, even though, granted that*. Then join the second sentence to the first with a comma.

Example People usually think of dogs as smart animals. Many other animals are smarter.

Although people usually think of dogs as smart animals, many other animals are smarter.

In Exercise 5.16, by adding *although, even though,* or *granted that* to the first sentence, you turned it into a dependent clause. A *dependent clause* has a subject and verb, but it depends on another piece of information to complete its meaning. (See Chapter 10 for more discussion of dependent clauses.) For instance, if you simply wrote *Although people usually think of dogs as smart animals,* a reader would ask, "So what?" When you add the word *although* to the first part of the sentence, it now needs the second part to form a complete idea: that people do not realize that many animals are smarter than dogs. Thus, the first part of the sentence, one clause, depends on the second part, another clause, to complete the contrast.

■■■■■■■■■■■■■■■
E X E R C I S E   5.17 Revise the following paragraph by combining sentences to show contrast where needed. Try to use both methods discussed in the text.

Secretaries receive much lower pay than their bosses. Often they know more about their office than the boss does. The boss may be responsible for decision making. The secretary must know the day-to-day routines and procedures of the business. Secretaries deserve more recognition and higher wages.

■■■■■■■■■■■■■■■
E X E R C I S E   5.18 Revise a paragraph or section of a paper you have written for this or any other course by combining sentences to show contrast where needed.

Combining to Show Causes and Effects   Just as combining sentences can show contrast between sentences, it can help you show a *cause-and-effect relationship* between sentences. In the following pair of sentences, what happens in the first sentence *causes* the effect expressed in the second:

> I had on sneakers, cutoffs, and a Bud Light T-shirt. I was embarrassed when everyone else came to the barbecue in fancy sportswear.

Most readers can guess that the clothing described in the first sentence causes the embarrassment expressed in the second sentence, yet readers have to make the guess, have to do the work that the writer should have done. Thus, the writer should combine the sentences to show the cause-and-effect relationship that they imply. One way to combine them is by using the following punctuation and connecting words

, so
; consequently
; therefore
; thus

> I had on sneakers, cutoffs, and a Bud Light T-shirt, *so* I was embarrassed when everyone else came to the barbecue in fancy sportswear.

> I had on sneakers, cutoffs, and a Bud Light T-shirt; *consequently,* I was embarrassed when everyone else came to the barbecue in fancy sportswear.

> I had on sneakers, cutoffs, and a Bud Light T-shirt; *therefore,* I was embarrassed when everyone else came to the barbecue in fancy sportswear.

> I had on sneakers, cutoffs, and a Bud Light T-shirt; *thus,* I was embarrassed when everyone else came to the barbecue in fancy sportswear.

No matter which connector you choose to combine the sentences, the combination draws a cause-and-effect relationship. However, the best choice here is *so* preceded by a comma because it is less formal and fits the informal subject.

E X E R C I S E   5.19   In each of the following pairs of sentences, the first states a cause and the second states an effect. Combine each pair to show a cause-and-effect relationship.

1. Before I came to the university, I had never seen people from other countries. I thought the foreign students here were strange at first.
2. Nuclear waste remains toxic for thousands of years. Scientists must find a way to dispose of it safely.
3. The recruiters said that my education, not basketball, was most important. My mother thought they cared about me.
4. A lot of people think teenagers from the ghetto just want to fight and steal. These people won't give ghetto kids a job.
5. There is a shortage of nurses throughout the nation. Hospitals are raising nurses' salaries.
6. Financial aid benefits were reduced during the Reagan administration. Students are finding it more difficult to secure funds to pay for their education.
7. During the late sixties and early seventies, there was much publicity about the consequences of overpopulation. People began planning smaller families.
8. In the late nineteenth century, workers earned low wages and had no rights or benefits. Labor unions were formed to combat injustices in the workplace.

You can also show cause-and-effect relationships by adding *because* or *since* to the beginning of the first sentence and then replacing the period between the sentences with a comma:

> *Because* I had on sneakers, cutoffs, and a Bud Light T-shirt, I was embarrassed when everyone else came to the barbecue in fancy sportswear.

In this revision, the first clause now becomes dependent on the second; that is, the second clause describes the effect of the cause expressed in the first clause. Thus, both parts of the sentence are tightly linked, enabling readers to see the cause-and-effect relationship.

E X E R C I S E   5.20   Rewrite the sentences in Exercise 5.19, this time adding *because* to the first clause and changing the period between the sentences to a comma.

Combining to Coordinate Information   When you combine sentences that contain related information, you are *coordinating,* putting together similar pieces of information. Each of the following sentences states a piece of information about ways to pay for a college education:

Many state and private scholarships are available.

The government offers low-interest loans for students who do not qualify for scholarships.

These are not bad sentences by themselves, but they are closely related. Thus, they could be joined to stress the relationship between them. There are two ways to link them:

1. join them with a comma and *and,*
2. join them with a semicolon and either *furthermore, moreover,* or *in addition.*

Coordinating related sentences can help you to connect ideas so that your readers can see the relationship between them. Also, coordination helps avoid a choppy style and adds sentence variety to your writing.

EXERCISE 5.21 Combine the following sentences to coordinate related information.

1. Wrigley Field is one of the oldest stadiums in baseball. Just as stadiums were in old times, it is located in a residential neighborhood.
2. The Camaro has a powerful engine. It looks very sporty with its long and low design.
3. My sister got high grades in high school. She was also in the National Honor Society.
4. Some students played radios in class. Other students would start dancing before the teacher took the radio away.
5. Tuition costs a lot. The books, dorm, and living expenses add even more to the cost of college.
6. You have to get up early on a farm. You have to be willing to work hard for long hours.
7. Learning a trade such as plumbing does not take as long as earning a four-year degree. Plumbers make as much money as — or even more than — many college graduates.
8. The sky was black. The rain was coming down in sheets.
9. The cost of homes is rising rapidly. Interest rates are going up too.
10. The home we are planning to buy needs a new furnace. The roof will have to be replaced in a few years.

■ Revising Unclear Sentences

Sometimes sentences do not need to be combined but do need to be rewritten because they do not make your point clearly or they simply sound awkward. The following sentences were taken from a paper that a student wrote for a class in educational counseling. The student was assigned to discuss some aspect of peer pressure that high school counselors need to know about. The main idea of his paper is that peer pressure can cause teenagers to have sex before they want to and are ready for it. The following three sentences are different versions of the beginning of a paragraph on how peer pressure occurs in the locker room:

> There are many specific areas where peer pressure to have sex are noticed, the locker room being one of these.

> In the locker room, guys always pressure each other to have sex.

> In the locker room, young men always pressure each other to talk about their sexual experiences with their girlfriends.

In looking over the first sentence, the student decided that it had many problems. Earlier in the paper he had said that the peer pressure occurs in many areas, so he did not need to say that again. He also discovered that he had no people in the sentence and that the locker room, the place being discussed, was tacked on to the end of the sentence. He made some improvements in writing his second sentence; he identified the locker room and the people in it at the beginning of the sentence. But the student saw that this sentence also needed revision, first because it sounded as if the young men were trying to have sex with each other, and second because the writer found the word *guys* rather casual for his audience. The third sentence solves both problems. It is clear and appropriate to the writer's purpose and audience.

As you draft a paper, sometimes you can catch a problem sentence and revise it before you go on, but after writing the paper you should read all your sentences aloud. Are there any that could be smoother? clearer? Can you change the order of any parts of any sentences? cut words? You need to ask these questions when you find a sentence that does not sound quite right.

EXERCISE 5.22 Read over the papers you have written for this class. Find three to five sentences that sound unclear or awkward and revise them.

■ A Student Revising

On the following pages are samples of one student's work in revising a paper. Elaine Pies wrote "From Full Time Mom to Re-Entry Woman" when she was a thirty-eight-year-old sophomore at Indiana State University. Her purpose was to show other married women how she and her family adapted to the changes that her return to school brought about in their lives. The complete essay appears first, followed by sections from different drafts. Read the essay first and then examine the sections from the drafts and the explanations that follow.

From Full Time Mom to Re-Entry Woman
Elaine Pies

According to Jeanne Fisher-Thompson and Julie A. Kuhn in an essay on the status of women in higher education, the reentry woman is defined as "any woman who has interrupted her education after high school or during college for at least a few years, and is now re-entering or seeking to re-enter a college or university for the purpose of completing a degree." After more than twenty years of marriage and seventeen years of childrearing, I am assuming this identity, namely, "reentry woman." As a full-time student at Indiana State University, I find this role to be both challenging and satisfying. In addition, I have discovered that the reentry students are the focus of much research, and researchers have found that campus support groups are needed to meet the financial, emotional, and educational needs of women with families. Without the necessary reassurance that such groups offer, many women drop out of college. But I have found on my own that another support group may be even more important: the family itself. So I feel fortunate to have a very effective support system in my own home. Not only is my husband in favor of my enrollment at ISU, but our four sons share much enthusiasm for my commitment to earning a college degree even though my enrollment makes our home life hectic, to say the least.

My first experience of entering postsecondary education began when I enrolled in the women's external degree program at Saint Mary-of-the-Woods College. There was much flexibility in this program due to the off-campus, self-directed study which allowed me to remain in my home. But though I could remain home, taking courses required my family and me to make many adjustments. The time I generally set aside for reading an extra story or watching another television program with the boys was spent in a cloistered area (if such a place can be found in a busy household). My daily chores, which my family had once taken for granted, now seemed important as the heaps of laundry accumulated in the basement while an assignment in Introduction to Philosophy couldn't wait. Consequently, the entire family developed an understanding of domestic chores and also began to realize that Mom was very serious about her new career. They soon learned that study time was sacred and knew I tolerated few interruptions. However, when seven-year-old Zachary brought me a cup of tea while I was muddling my way through my psychology textbook, I couldn't refuse his act of love and took advantage of that intrusion to share a treasured moment with an inquisitive child.

Since I have been reading articles about reentry women, I noticed that child care is cited as a common problem. The year I was taking courses through St. Mary's external degree program, I was also providing day care for three children besides my own. Three of my four were in school most of the day, but with the three I was taking care of, plus my youngest, I still had at least four children around the house all day. But I needed the day care money to pay for my courses, so I had to do the best I could. Each day as I cleared away the remnants of lunch and mopped up rivulets of milk that ran down chair legs, I looked forward to the children's nap time. These peaceful interludes in my hectic days provided times to read assignments or work on papers that always seemed to be due immediately. I was amazed at the amounts of work that I could accomplish before my school-age boys burst through the front door in a flurry of papers and backpacks, signaling the end of naps and study time. What a transition! Within five minutes I went from Cardinal Ratzinger's theological concepts to little boys' hugs and *Cartoon Carnival.*

When my youngest son, Daniel, entered grade school, I decided to give up the day care service and enroll at Indiana State University part time, and by the next semester full-time enrollment seemed appropriate. Again, this change in my status brought many changes for me and my family. Meeting class schedules, preparing assignments daily, and interacting with the younger students were only a few of the adjustments that I had to make. (My family had a different list, of course.)

What a sense of relief I experienced as I learned that most of my professors understood many of the complications that an older student encounters. Just beginning a new semester, a project, or preparing for exams seemed to be enough to stimulate a series of family illnesses or other crises. The possibilities and probabilities of confusion were often overwhelming, but fortunately most of my professors understood when Daniel's virus or Zachary's flu caused me to miss class or to ask for permission to complete an assignment late.

Prior to becoming a student at Indiana State, I had not considered the possibility of individual attention and consideration from the professors. Now I am experiencing the benefit of instruction and guidance from men and women who will help me to realize my potential. The professors at Indiana State have been, and continue to be, constant sources of motivation and affirmation. Perhaps being a nontraditional student heightens my eagerness to take advantage of the open communications with my professors. How reassuring it is for me to know that I can schedule a conference without difficulty, or that I might drop in during office hours with my questions and problems. Without such contact from the faculty, my education would not be nearly as pleasant.

Now that I have been on campus for three semesters, I also feel accepted by the younger students. Being labeled a "curve buster" and harassed by a few students in a psychology class is the only unpleasant response that I have encountered. This incident occurred on the first day of my first semester on campus. I was the last person to enter the classroom due to a trek across the unfamiliar campus. As I came into the room one of the young men turned, looked at me, and feigned a headache. "Oh no, a curve buster. There goes our chances of a low curve in here!" he groaned. I didn't understand why he found me threatening. Later, a friend informed me that the younger students know that most older students take their courses very seriously, so this young man assumed I would earn top grades, thus raising the grading scale. As the semester progressed, I began to make friends in this class — even with the young man who didn't want me to be a part of it — and by the end of the term, I was asked to join the study session that was planned before finals.

Although attending college full time can be fulfilling, there are also various discontinuities and role conflicts that reentry women must understand and resolve whenever possible. For example, sometimes I feel guilty and question my ability to fulfill both roles, mother and student. "Am I neglecting my home and my family?" Or "Will I ever be able to prepare for an exam the way that I want to?" Finding time for a seemingly insignificant task, such as pegging Clint's Levi's or mending my husband's blue jacket, often seems impossible. However, the little projects seem to be the ones that frequently mean the most to my crew. Obviously, when seventeen-year-old Greg wants a high school term paper typed and needs it the next day, I don't experience guilt for refusing his request. But when he is involved in a school activity, the role of mother dominates the role of student. Besides, the mom in me enjoys seeing the ninth-grade play that Clint directed or discussing Zach's book report more than the student in me enjoys exploring Merton's "modes of adaptation" for Sociology 200. Still, there are times when I'm with the kids that I feel I should be studying and times when I'm studying that I feel guilty for not being with the kids.

Planning and organization are surely important to maintaining a moderate sense of order in the family, and remaining flexible is the only way that I have learned to cope with the stress that is inevitable. Regardless of the course load that I take, Zachary must be taken to the orthodontist or Daniel to his trumpet lessons. Or I have to attend Greg's track meets (I wouldn't miss such an exhilarating experience!) or take the snake (the one Daniel has in a big glass jar) to school for show and tell. The list is endless. With so much "running" to be done, contrary to the attitudes of some parents, I am thrilled that my teenage son, Greg, can drive! Now that leaves us to shuffle the family vehicles.

This can present as much stress as Greg's driving alleviates. For example, one day Greg took his father to work and then took the truck to meet his own work schedule, while I drove the car to the college library. So Mark, my husband, was left without a way home from work. Greg and I each thought the other one was to pick Dad up. Consequently, as I drove home the figure that I thought I recognized walking down the road was indeed familiar! Mark had walked most of the four miles home. Why hadn't he "phoned home" and left a message? Between Clint, Zachary, and Daniel talking to their friends, our phone was easily tied up for some time, even with calls supposedly limited to ten minutes each. How fortunate for Mark (and the boys) that the weather was warm and pleasant for his evening stroll.

Such scheduling mishaps seem comical in retrospect, just as unused symphony tickets and declined dinner invitations continue to be a necessity if I am to achieve the quality of education that I desire. Without a doubt, many students in similar situations wonder, "How will we accomplish everything?" When I feel this way, I just think that if parenthood did not help me to learn how to defer gratification, pursuing a college education certainly has.

Despite the upheavals my education sometimes causes, my going to college has also benefited my sons. As Greg, Clint, Zachary, and Daniel watch my efforts and see my determination to earn a college degree, I believe they will be affected in the best possible ways. Certainly they are responsible for more of the mundane household chores than when I was at home all of the time, and the older boys are becoming very good cooks. All of the boys' work around the house will provide them with practical skills that they will use as adults. Furthermore, they are helping me toward my goal, learning to be responsible for themselves, and continuing to realize the importance of setting goals and getting an education.

For several years before I began my college education in Saint Mary-of-the-Woods College off-campus program and then at Indiana State University, I wondered if attending college was possible for a full-time mother and a woman in her thirties. Definitely! Even on those days when I don't get all of the assignments handed in, or when spaghetti is on the menu for the third time in one week, my education is worth the effort. The reentry experience provides a sense of accomplishment and creative involvement in my own life that is exceptionally satisfying. Being a college student over thirty is a fantastic part of my life, whether I am referred to as nontraditional student, reentry woman, or my favorite label — MOM.

Revisions of Paragraphs

On the following pages, you can compare Pies's revisions of paragraphs from one draft to another. Following each revision are explanations of the changes based on conversations I had with her. As you read and compare the paragraphs, see if you agree with her strategies.

Introduction: Draft 2

According to Jeanne Fisher-Thompson and Julie A. Kuhn in a paper on the status and education of women, the re-entry woman is defined as "any woman who has interrupted her education after high school or during college for at least a few years, and is now re-entering or seeking to re-enter a college or university for the purpose of completing a degree." After more than twenty years of marriage and seventeen years of childrearing, I am assuming this identity, namely, "re-entry woman." As a full-time, nontraditional student at Indiana State University, I find this role to be both challenging and satisfying. In addition, I have discovered that the reentry students are the focus of much research. *and researchers* ~~Our various~~ *have found that campus support groups are needed to* ~~needs— financial, emotional, and educational —are studied in~~ *meet the financial, emotional, and educational* ~~depth. From this information one significant fact appears~~ *needs of women with families.* ~~repeatedly. The need for support groups exists, whether~~ ~~ad~~vocating revised financial aid or promoting curriculum ~~changes~~ that are more compatible ~~with the routines~~ of women with ~~families~~ and jobs. Without the necessary reassurance ~~that such~~ *But I have found that another support group may be* ~~groups offer, many women drop out of college,~~ So I feel ~~that my~~ *even* *fortunate that* *more* ~~good fortune is apparent.~~ I have a very effective support system in *important the* my own home. Not only is my spouse in favor of my enrollment *family* at ISU, but our four sons (10 to 17 years old) share much *itself.* enthusiasm for my commitment to earning a college degree, *even* *though my enrollment makes our home* *life hectic, to say the least.*

Introduction: Draft 3

According to Jeanne Fisher-Thompson and Julie A. Kuhn in a paper on the status of women in higher education, the re-entry woman is defined as "any woman who has interrupted her education after high school or during college for at least a few years, and is now re-entering or seeking to re-enter a college or university for the purpose of completing a degree." After more than twenty years of marriage and seventeen years of childrearing, I am assuming this identity, namely, "re-entry woman." As a full-time student at Indiana State University, I find this role to be both challenging and satisfying. In addition, I have discovered that the re-entry students are the focus of much research, and researchers have found that campus support groups are needed to meet the financial, emotional, and educational needs of women with families. Without the necessary reassurance that such groups offer, many women drop out of college. But I have found that another support group may be even more important: the family itself. So I feel fortunate that I have a very effective support system in my own home. Not only is my husband in favor of my enrollment at ISU, but our four sons (ten to seventeen years old) share much enthusiasm for my commitment to earning a college degree even though my enrollment makes our home life hectic at times, to say the least.

Elaine does not make major changes from the second to the third (and final) draft of her introduction, but the changes are important. In the first sentence, she merely changes a few words to make the sentence read more smoothly, but in the middle of the paragraph she combines a lot of information on support groups into one sentence. However, the two most important changes come at the end of the introduction. First, she adds the sentence stating that she has discovered that the family may be the most important support group. Second, by adding to her thesis the point about how hectic school has made her family's life, she expands the thesis to cover much of what the paper is about.

Third Paragraph: Draft 1

As I continued to read articles about the re-entry woman, I noticed that child care was cited as the most common concern among this group. Being enrolled in an external degree program alleviated that worry for me. Moreover, I could continue as caregiver for other children. That service provided an income which paid much of my tuition. Each day as I cleared away the remnants of lunch and mopped up rivulets of milk that ran down chair legs, I looked forward to the children's nap time. These peaceful interludes in my hectic days provided times to read assignments or work on papers that always seemed to be due

Make clear how many kids I took care of and how many were home at once.

immediately. I was amazed at the amounts of work that I could accomplish before the older children burst through the front door in a flurry of papers and backpacks, signaling the end of naps and study time. What a transition! Within five minutes I went from Cardinal Ratzinger's theological concepts to little boys' hugs and *Cartoon Carnival.*

Third Paragraph: Draft 2

The year I was taking courses through St. Mary's external degree program, I was also providing day care for three children besides my own. Three of my four were in school most of the day, but with the three I was taking care of, plus my youngest, I still had at least four children around the house all day. But I needed the day care money to pay for my courses, so I had to do the best I could. Each day as I cleared away the remnants of lunch and mopped up rivulets of milk that ran down chair legs, I looked forward to the children's nap time. These peaceful interludes in my hectic days provided times to read assignments or work on papers that always seemed to be due immediately. I was amazed at the amounts of work that I could accomplish before my school-age boys burst through the front door in a flurry of papers and backpacks, signaling the end of naps and study time. What a transition! Within five minutes I went from Cardinal Ratzinger's theological concepts to little boys' hugs and *Cartoon Carnival.*

Comparing these two paragraphs, you can see that Pies makes notes to herself to revise the paragraph so that it is clear how she was earning money providing day care and how many children she still had at home. In the first draft, the term "caregiver" is confusing, and readers can't tell how many of her own children Pies is taking care of. She knows how many, but she also knows her audience needs to know.

She cuts her first sentence completely. Why? At the time the paragraph refers to, she had not yet begun to read articles about re-entry women. She also feels that at this point her paper is focused primarily on her experience. But she puts the sentence back in the final draft. There, however, she revises it to make clear that she only recently began reading the articles. In addition, though the paragraph still focuses on her experience, the first sentence indicates that other reentry women are concerned about child care, too. Thus, putting the sentence back in enables Pies to more effectively follow her purpose: to show re-entry women that others share their problems. In short, the first sentence helps to show that Pies's experience is typical.

Fourth Paragraph: Draft 1 (cut from following drafts)

The new role that I found so stimulating also required me to carefully consider the projects that I volunteered for or the sewing jobs that I accepted. As an "at-home-mom," I was frequently asked to mend costumes, cushions, or curtains for one or another of the teachers at the school that my sons attended. I suppose "yes" had become a conditioned response. Thus, when Mrs. Nation (the principal) asked me if I would mend an article for the children, I said, "Certainly." The article was delivered in a bag; however, it was not the usual brown bag from our neighborhood grocery but an ominously large black trash bag! The object of my stitchery was a parachute — a massive, survival orange parachute that the children used for playground activities! It took more than an hour to locate all of the tears in the fabric. Just the thought of the precious nap times that the mending would consume impressed the importance of investigating a request more thoroughly before committing myself to volunteer my time now that I was taking courses.

Though this paragraph is very specific and tells an interesting story relating to Pies's thesis, it is cut out of the final draft because the example is not typical enough and Pies has already made the point on balancing home life and off-campus courses. She also needs to get on to the discussion of enrolling in Indiana State because on-campus study would be more typical of the experience of other reentry women. So in cutting the paragraph, Pies again kept her purpose and audience in mind.

Revising the Organization of the Whole Essay

The order of the paragraphs in the final copy of Pies's essay represents a major reordering of the sections of earlier drafts. Pies's first draft was handwritten in different sections, and after revising numerous sentences in it, she then arrived at the order on the left in the following list. Compare it with the final order on the right and read the discussion that follows.

Draft 2	Final Draft
Introduction	Introduction
Paragraph 2: initial family adjustments to off-campus courses	Paragraph 2: initial family adjustments to off-campus courses
Paragraph 3: day care, nap and study time	Paragraph 3: day care, nap and study time
Paragraph 4: parachute mending	Paragraph 4: enrolling in ISU part time and then full-time
Paragraph 5: enrolling in ISU part time and then full-time	
Paragraph 6: role conflicts and guilt	Paragraph 5: support of faculty at ISU

The organization of the second draft is not bad. Once Pies begins discussing her entry into ISU, she presents all the difficulties in paragraphs 6, 7, and 8. Then paragraph 9, because it shows the difficulties as comic, allows her to make a transition to the benefits of enrollment. While this order works, the organization of her final draft is even better because after paragraph 4 on enrolling in ISU, she discusses the benefits of on-campus enrollment, moves to the difficulties, but then returns to the positive side to show how her enrollment has also benefited her sons. Thus her readers move back and forth between the difficulties and benefits, just as Pies does in her own experience.

Pies is a mature student, and by the time she wrote this essay she was a fairly experienced writer. But as her revisions show, experienced writers, whether students or professionals, revise and revise and revise.

Essay for Reading

The Maker's Eye: Revising Your Own Manuscripts
Donald Murray

Donald Murray has written numerous magazine essays, poems, and novels. As an editorial writer for the *Boston Globe,* he won the Pulitzer Prize, and he has been a contributing editor for *Time.* In addition to working as a writer, Murray teaches writing at the University of New Hampshire.

Vocabulary Cues

typographical: having to do with typed writing
prolific: producing a great deal
progression: a series of things, one following from another
implications: points or ideas implied or suggested but not stated directly
detachment: absence of bias or emotional involvement
euphoric: elated, having a feeling of well-being
excise: cut, take out, delete
spontaneity: the quality of doing something on impulse, without planning, all of a sudden
tentative: experimental, uncertain, likely to be changed
nuance: slight degree of difference

Questions to Guide Your Reading

1. How do professional writers think of drafts?
2. What seven things does Murray say to look for in revising?
3. What is "the maker's eye"?

When the beginning writer completes his first draft, he usually reads it through to correct typographical errors and considers the job of writing done. When the professional writer completes his first draft, he usually feels he is at the start of the writing process. Now that he has a draft he can begin writing.

The difference in attitude is the difference between amateur and professional, inexperience and experience, journeyman and craftsman. Peter F. Drucker, the prolific business writer, for example, calls his first draft "the zero draft" — after that he can start counting. Most productive writers share the feeling that the first draft — and most of those which follow — is an opportunity to discover what they have to say and how they can best say it.

To produce a progression of drafts, each of which says more and says it better, the writer has to develop a special reading skill. In school we are taught to read what is on the page. We try to comprehend what the author has said, what he meant, and what are the implications of his words.

The writer of such drafts must be his own best enemy. He must accept the criticism of others and be even more suspicious of it. He cannot depend on others. He must detach himself from his own page so that he can apply both his caring and his craft to his own work.

Detachment is not easy. Science fiction writer Ray Bradbury supposedly puts each manuscript away for a year and then rereads it as a stranger. Not many writers can afford the time to do this. We must read when our judgment may be at its worst, when we are close to the euphoric moment of creation. The writer "should be critical of everything that seems to him most delightful in his style," advises novelist Nancy Hale. "He should excise what he most admires, because he wouldn't thus admire it if he weren't . . . in a sense protecting it from criticism."

The writer must learn to protect himself from his own ego, when it takes the form of uncritical pride or uncritical self-destruction. As poet John Ciardi points out, ". . . the last act of the writing must be to become one's own reader. It is, I suppose, a schizophrenic process, to begin passionately and to end critically, to begin hot and to end cold; and more important, to be passion-hot and critic-cold at the same time."

Just as dangerous as the protective writer is the despairing one, who thinks everything he does is terrible, dreadful, awful. If he is to publish, he must save what is effective on his page while he cuts away what doesn't work. The writer must hear and respect his own voice.

Remember how each craftsman you have seen — the carpenter eyeing the level of a shelf, the mechanic listening to the motor — takes the instinctive step back. This is what the writer has to do when he reads his own work. "The writer must survey his work critically, coolly, as though he were a stranger to it," says children's book writer Eleanor Estes. "He must be willing to prune, expertly and hard-heartedly. At the end of each revision, a manuscript may look like a battered old hive, worked over, torn apart, pinned together, added to, deleted from, words changed and words changed back. Yet the book must maintain its original freshness and spontaneity."

It is far easier for most beginning writers to understand the need for rereading and rewriting than it is to understand how to go about it. The publishing writer doesn't necessarily break down the various stages of rewriting and editing, he just goes ahead and does it. One of our most prolific fiction writers, Anthony Burgess, says, "I might revise a page twenty times." Short story and children's writer Roald Dahl states, "By the time I'm nearing the end of a story, the first part will have been reread and altered and corrected at least 150 times. . . . Good writing is essentially rewriting. I am positive of this."

There is nothing virtuous in the rewriting process. It is simply an essential condition of life for most writers. There are writers who do very little rewriting, mostly because they have the capacity and experience to create and review a large number of invisible drafts in their minds before they get to the page. And many writers perform all of the tasks of revision simultaneously, page by page, rather than draft by draft. But it is still possible to break down the process of rereading one's own work into the sequence most published writers follow and which the beginning writer should follow as he studies his own page.

Many writers at first just scan their manuscript, reading as quickly as possible for problems of subject and form. In this way, they stand back from the more technical details of language so they can spot any weaknesses in content or in organization. When the writer reads his manuscript, he is usually looking for seven elements.

The first is *subject*. Do you have anything to say? If you are lucky, you will find that indeed you do have something to say, perhaps a little more than you expected. If the subject is not clear, or if it is not yet limited or defined enough for you to handle, don't go on. What you have to say is always more important than how you say it.

The next point to check is *audience*. It is true that you should write primarily for yourself, in the sense that you should be true to yourself. But the aim of writing is communication, not just self-expression. You should, in reading your piece, ask yourself if there is an audience for what you have written, if anyone will need or enjoy what you have to say.

Form should then be considered after audience. Form, or genre, is the vehicle which will carry what you have to say to your audience, and it should grow out of your subject. If you have a character, your subject may grow into a short story, a magazine profile, a novel, a biography, or a play. It depends on what you have to say and to whom you wish to say it. When you reread your own manuscript, you must ask yourself if the form is suitable, if it works, and if it will carry your meaning to your reader.

Once you have the appropriate form, look at the *structure,* the order of what you have to say. Every good piece of writing is built on a solid framework of logic or argument or narrative or motivation; it is a line which runs through the entire piece of writing and holds it together. If you read your own manuscript and cannot spot this essential thread, stop writing until you have found something to hold your writing together.

The manuscript which has order must also have *development*. Each part of it must be built in a way that will prepare the reader for the next part. Description, documentation, action, dialogue, metaphor — these and many other devices flesh out the skeleton so that the reader will be able to understand what is written. How much development? That's like asking how much lipstick or how much garlic. It depends on the girl or on the casserole. This is the question that the writer will be answering as he reads his piece of writing through from beginning to end, and answering it will lead him to the sixth element.

The writer must be sure of his *dimensions*. This means that there should be something more than structure and development, that there should be a pleasing proportion between all of the parts. You cannot decide on a dimension without seeing all of the parts of writing together. You have to examine each section of the writing in its relationship to all of the other sections.

Finally, the writer has to listen for *tone*. Any piece of writing is held together by that invisible force, the writer's voice. Tone is his style, tone is all that is on the page and off the page, tone is grace, wit, anger — the spirit which drives a piece of writing forward. Look back to those manuscripts you most admire, and you will discover that there is a coherent tone, an authoritative voice holding the whole thing together.

When the writer feels that he has a draft which has subject, audience, form, structure, development, dimension, and tone, then he is ready to begin the careful process of line-by-line editing. Each line, each word has to be right. As Paul Gallico has said, ". . . every successful writer is primarily a good editor."

Now the writer reads his own copy with infinite care. He often reads aloud, calling on his ear's experience with language. Does this sound right — or this? He reads and listens and revises, back and forth from eye to page to ear to page. I find I must do this careful editing at short runs, fifteen or twenty minutes, or I become too kind with myself.

Slowly the writer moves from word to word, looking through the word to see the subject. Good writing is, in a sense, invisible. It should enable the reader to see the subject, not the writer. Every word should be true to what the writer has to say. And each word must be precise in its relation to the words which have gone before and the words which will follow.

This sounds tedious, but it isn't. Making something right is immensely satisfying, and the writer who once was lost in a swamp of potentialities now has the chance to work with the most technical skills of language. And even in the process of the most careful editing, there is the joy of language. Words have double meanings, even triple and quadruple meanings. Each word has its own tone, its opportunity for connotation and denotation and nuance. And when you connect words, there is always the chance of the sudden insight, the unexpected clarification.

The maker's eye moves back and forth from word to phrase to sentence to paragraph to sentence to phrase to word. He looks at his sentences for variety and balance in form and structure, and at the interior of the paragraph for coherence, unity and emphasis. He plays with figurative language, decides to repeat or not, to create a parallelism for emphasis. He works over his copy until he achieves a manuscript which appears effortless to the reader.

I learned something about this process when I first wore bifocals. I thought that when I was editing I was working line by line. But I discovered that I had to order reading (or, in my case, editing) glasses, even though the bottom sections of my bifocals have a greater expanse of glass than ordinary glasses. While I am editing, my eyes are unconsciously flicking back and forth across the whole page, or back to another page, or forward to another page. The limited bifocal view through the lower half of my glasses is not enough. Each line must be seen in its relationship to every other line.

When does this process end? Most writers agree with the great Russian novelist Tolstoy, who said, "I scarcely ever reread my published writings, but if by chance I come across a page, it always strikes me: all this must be rewritten; this is how I should have written it."

The maker's eye is never satisfied, for he knows that each word in his copy is tentative. Writing, to the writer, is alive, something that is full of potential and alternative, something which can grow beyond its own dream. The writer reads to discover what he has said—and then to say it better.

A piece of writing is never finished. It is delivered to a deadline, torn out of the typewriter on demand, sent off with a sense of frustration and incompleteness. Just as the writer knows he must stop avoiding writing and write, he also knows he must send his copy off to be published, although it is not quite right yet — if only he had another couple of days, just another run at it, perhaps. . . .

Questions for Study and Discussion

1. What, according to Murray, is the difference between beginning writers and professional writers?
2. What is the purpose of the first draft for professional writers?
3. How are writers similar to other craftsmen such as carpenters and mechanics?
4. Briefly summarize Murray's definitions of subject, audience, form, structure, development, dimensions, and tone?
5. How do Murray's definitions relate to what you have learned about purpose, role, and audience?
6. How does Murray say writers must read their drafts?
7. What did Murray say he first learned from wearing bifocals?
8. What does Murray mean when he says, "A piece of writing is never finished"?
9. Compare Murray's ideas on revision with Elaine Pies's revisions of her essay on balancing college and home life. Did Pies seem to follow strategies Murray recommends?

Writing Assignments

1. Changing your audience, revise an essay written for this or another class.
2. Write a letter to a friend about something related to college — grades, studying, social life, and so on. Then revise the letter so that it would be appropriate to send to your parents.
3. Write an essay advising beginning freshman writers on what they need to know about revision. Consider the purpose, need, and strategies for revision.

CHAPTER 6

Reading for Writing

Just as writing is a process of making meaning out of experience, reading is also a process of making meaning. Reading can help you to become a good college writer. In fact, some people have become good writers just by reading. Over a period of time, people who read a lot become familiar with the ways different kinds of writing look, sound, and fit together. They absorb this information about writing almost without knowing it. Learning to write well this way takes years, and as a college freshman you don't have years to learn. Still, as you improve your reading skills, your writing skills will improve too, not only in this course but in all your college courses.

Studies have shown that students with strong reading skills usually are better writers than students who have trouble reading. Some freshman students claim that they rarely read at all, that they won't read something if it is more than a couple of pages, or that they have never read a book from cover to cover. These students admit that they have never liked to read. Usually, these students also have trouble writing.

If you have trouble writing, perhaps you may have trouble reading too. Maybe you, like the students just mentioned, never liked to read. Yet if you think about reading, you probably will realize that you have read more than you think. In addition to reading for school, do you ever read the newspaper? Do you read sections of the newspaper such as news, features, fashion, sports? Did you read the school newspaper when you were in high school? Do you read your college newspaper? Do you read magazines about fashion, music, world affairs, or any other subject? Do you ever read the articles in *TV Guide?* You may not feel that you are a good reader, but if you answered yes to any of these questions, you have a desire and need to read. You probably also have more skill at reading than you think.

College and most jobs after college require that you develop good reading skills. Even in the short time you have been at college, you probably have had a lot of reading assigned for homework. Perhaps you sometimes think too much reading is assigned, but reading is an important part of learning. Although your professor's lectures and classroom discussions can teach you a great deal, the reading you do in your textbooks will give you the background knowledge you need to understand what goes on in the classroom.

On the job after college, people read all the time. Businesspeople read every day — letters, memos, company reports, articles in magazines and newspapers about business trends. Doctors read studies of new ways to treat patients. Laywers read law briefs. Engineers read research reports. Actors read scripts. And many of these people, having learned to read well, pick up a book and read for pleasure in the evenings or on weekends. As you can see, reading is a part of life for the college graduate as well as the college student.

If you are not a good reader, do not get discouraged by the fact that success in college and life depends a great deal on reading. If you have the desire to learn to read better, you can learn to read well. This chapter will help you. If you are a good reader already, the chapter will provide some hints to improve your reading.

■ Active Reading

Active reading: The process of concentrating while reading, asking questions, separating main ideas from details and examples, paying close attention to context, and making judgments.

People rarely think of reading as an activity. Reading is not, of course, a physical activity like jogging, swimming, cleaning the house, cutting the grass, or even taking a walk. But reading *is* an activity — that is, **active reading** is an *active* process in which the reader must do much of the work.

Students often do not see reading as active. You might think that in reading you sit back passively and just receive the author's meaning as you read. In some ways, this is how you watch television. You don't need to think much because the picture is there before you, and you can hear the words of the actors. You might, for instance, wonder what will happen next in a situation comedy, but you do not have to wonder what a character sounds like or what a room looks like because it is there before your eyes and ears.

Making Meaning

Reading, unlike watching TV, takes concentration and thought. Even though the words are there on the page, you have to put them together to make sense of what the author means. If you are not familiar with the subject or the words the author is using, you ask yourself questions as you read, and you try to predict what the author means. In other words, you fill in with your own experience to try to make sense of the information. In this way, you make meaning. Therefore, as a reader, you are active. Sometimes the meaning you make might differ from what the author wanted to say. When readers sense that they do not understand, weak readers give up while strong readers read the material again.

Read the following paragraph and then answer the questions. As you read, try to notice how each sentence helps or confuses you as you try to make sense of the information.

> On my return, I had learned that Professor Agassiz had been at the Museum, but had gone, and would not return for several hours. My fellow-students were too busy to be disturbed by continued conversation. Slowly I drew forth that hideous fish, and with a feeling of desperation again looked at it. I might not use a magnifying-glass; instruments of all kinds were interdicted. My two hands, my two eyes, and the fish seemed a most limited field. I pushed my finger down its throat to feel how sharp the teeth were. I began to count the scales in the different rows until I was convinced that that was nonsense. At last a happy thought struck me — I would draw the fish, and now with surprise I began to discover new features in the creature. Just then the professor returned.
>
> Samuel H. Scudder

1. Given the people mentioned — a professor and students — where does the action take place? What details tell you so?
2. Is Scudder using the word *Museum* differently from the way it is used today?
3. At what point in the paragraph did you know where the action was taking place? What was the first clue that told you?
4. What is Scudder's assignment?
5. At what point in the paragraph did you know Scudder's assignment? List the clues that helped you figure it out?
6. What clues tell you that Scudder was first having trouble with the assignment? What clue tells you he began to do better?
7. If you could read the next paragraph of the essay, what do you think the professor's response would be?

If you read the passage carefully and answered the questions, you probably figured out that Scudder was a college student in a laboratory who was assigned to learn about a fish. At first he was not doing well, but he began to do better when he decided to draw the fish.

The exercise may have seemed easy to you, or it may have seemed puzzling at times, but you can probably see that you had to make much of the meaning to answer the questions. For example, you probably were able to tell that Scudder was in some kind of laboratory or classroom because he mentioned a professor and students. But to answer the question about the word *Museum,* you had to take all the clues — references to the students, the professor, and the assignment — and use them to set aside your own idea of a museum. In figuring out that Scudder was a student, you were able to draw on your experience of being a student. But to figure out that for Scudder, using the word *Museum* was a way to refer to a kind of laboratory, you had to use the clues from the paragraph, rather than your experience, because you probably don't think of a school building as a museum. The point is that you helped make the meaning of the paragraph as you read. You were *active.*

Responding to Meaning

As you read, the process of making meaning includes your **reading responses,** your feelings about what you understand the author to be saying. You agree with some things you read, you disagree with others, you are confused by others, you confirm and question your beliefs with others. As you read through the paragraph by Scudder, many thoughts may have crossed your mind. You may have thought the assignment was silly. Why is Scudder just looking at the fish? Why can't he use a magnifying glass? Why is the professor not around to help his students? Any questions you ask or opinions you form make up your response. Together with the ideas on the page, your responses contribute to the total meaning of the writing.

Reading responses: Opinions readers form about what reading material says and the ideas that they develop as a result of reading.

Of course, for your responses to be taken seriously, you must understand what you read. Some years ago on the comedy program *Saturday Night Live,* a character named Emily Latella gave opinionated responses to things she read in the newspaper. She never understood what she read, so her responses were very funny. One night she started her response asking, "Why is everyone against *violins* on television?" She went on and on about how she liked violin music and about how it should be allowed on television. When she was finished, she was told that people were against *violence* on television, not *violins.* She then said, "Never mind." Week after week, Emily ended her act with "Never mind" because after giving her opinion she found that she had not understood what she had read. So while responses are extremely important, they must be based on a clear understanding.

■ Comprehension

Comprehension: The ability to understand reading material.

Being an active reader helps reading **comprehension.** Simply defined, *comprehension* means "understanding." If you comprehend something, you understand it. That applies to comprehension in reading as well. If your reading comprehension is good, you can make sense of what you read.

Your comprehension differs according to what you are reading. If you are interested in the stock market and know a good deal about it, your comprehension will be high if you are reading the *Wall Street Jour-*

nal. If you know little or nothing about sociology, your comprehension will probably be low the first time you read a sociology textbook.

Comprehension is affected by a number of things. Three of the most important are (1) your frame of reference and context, (2) your ability to pick out main ideas, and (3) your ability to understand individual words.

Frame of Reference and Context

Context: The relationship between the parts of the reading material and the knowledge of the reader as they form the total meaning. Readers understand writing in the context of their knowledge, or they build context as they read.

Some readings are more difficult than others. When you know a lot about a subject, you refer what you read to the knowledge you already have on the subject; in short, you fit what you read into the frame of reference that you already have. When you have little knowledge of a subject, the context you build while reading becomes your frame of reference.

A **context** is the way things fit together and are related to one another within a subject area. If you can recognize context, you have a frame of reference that enables you to make sense of things. For instance, if you have knowledge of how to do laundry, you know what a rinse cycle is. If a friend said that the rinse cycle was broken on his washing machine, you would refer to your knowledge of doing laundry and know that if your friend tried to use the broken machine, his clothes would come out full of soap. In college, you are learning about many new subjects that you are not familiar with. When material is unfamiliar, you have to try to build a context as you read.

As you read, you build a context by paying careful attention to the meaning that each sentence adds. For instance, reading Scudder's paragraph on the fish, you were able to figure out that Scudder was a college student, even though college in his time was much different from what it is today. As a result, if you were to read the next paragraph of Scudder's essay, the professor's compliments on Scudder's work would make sense because you would refer them back to the previous paragraph in which you built the context that Scudder was in a college laboratory completing an assignment for his professor.

Context is very important to comprehension because a sentence, paragraph, or paragraphs may have a different meaning if read out of context. Politicians often complain that reporters take their remarks out of context. A senator may be quoted as saying, "I want to cut funding for schools." Standing alone, this quotation makes her seem to be against providing money for education, but notice how the meaning of her statement changes in the context of a paragraph:

> I want to cut funding for schools when I see money being wasted on extracurricular frills and trendy new programs that quickly go out of date. But when I see money being spent to reward talented teachers who can make students want to learn or money being spent to provide students with a pleasant learning environment, then I am committed to educational funding.

As you can see, the senator's statement about wanting to cut funding for schools changes completely when it appears in the context of all her remarks.

As a reader, you build context as you read. In reading the first sentence of the senator's statement, for example, you begin to see that the paragraph will be about funding for schools, and at first you may also think that the senator is against school funding. But by the time you reach the end of the paragraph, you have recognized a larger context that shows that she is not against all school funding, just funds for extracurricular activities and trendy programs.

An easy way to understand context is to think what would happen if you opened a book on an unfamiliar subject and tried to understand one of the paragraphs. Without the context of what comes before and after the paragraph, you would have a hard time making sense of what the paragraph means. In the paragraph on Scudder and the fish, for example, you might have been confused at first about what was going on. Why are there students in a museum? Why does Scudder seem nervous and frustrated at first? Who is the professor? By reading the paragraph, you were able to build a context for the action. But if you had read the beginning of the essay — read the paragraph in context — you would have had a much easier time because the beginning of the essay says that Scudder was a student at Harvard University studying under Louis Agassiz, a famous professor, who gave Scudder a fish and without any other directions told him to look at it. In other words, the context of the whole essay would have given you the knowledge to fully understand the parts of the essay.

When you write, you must also build a context for your reader. Scudder began his essay with a description of how he enrolled at Harvard, entered Agassiz's laboratory, and was assigned to look at a fish. As a result, when readers see him struggling nervously through the assignment, they know why he is doing it. When at the end of the essay Scudder says that he learned to observe and concentrate from studying the fish, the assignment that at first seemed foolish is shown to be valuable, and Agassiz is shown to be a good teacher. But readers can recognize these points only after reading the whole essay and building its overall context.

As you write, you always need to make sure that you are providing context for your points. Otherwise, you will leave your reader guessing. As you know, the writing process contains overlapping parts. Some of the overlapping involves reading. To make sure that your writing is supplying the context that your reader needs, you must read and reread your work as you are writing. You can then see if what you have written in one sentence or paragraph makes sense within the context of what you have written before it. Also by rereading as you write, you can begin to predict what you need to write next. In this way writing itself becomes a means of discovering ideas.

E X E R C I S E   6.2   The following sentences do not make much sense out of context. Provide a context — a sentence or two — so that the statements make sense.

In other words, add a sentence or two so that the first sentence makes sense.

1. The cheerleader cried.
2. The man took off his jacket quickly.
3. Not thinking of anything, the driver sped through the busy intersection.
4. Family room, three bedrooms, two-car garage.

Picking Out Main Ideas

You probably have seen your classmates at times underlining or high-lighting sentences in their textbooks. If these students are skilled readers, they were probably marking the main ideas — the thesis and topic sentences. As you know, writers support and develop a main idea with examples. While the examples are needed to help the reader understand the main idea, if the reader cannot tell what the main idea is, then the examples will not make sense. Without the main idea readers also do not have a chance to respond to the writer.

Your practice in writing paragraphs with topic sentences should tell you that you can place the main idea at different points in different paragraphs. It would be impossible to list all the ways in which paragraphs, essays, or textbook chapters state main ideas, but the following are a few common ways. If you have covered the chapter on paragraphs, some of these methods will be familiar.

Main Idea First   Stating the main idea first and then following it with specific examples for support is a common pattern of communication. This pattern is often used in speech. For instance, a young woman might say she is glad she has chosen to go to college and then follow this statement with examples of the career opportunities her education will offer. A sportscaster might say that a certain player is the best in the league and then follow with statistics to support his claim. You use the pattern every day. If you are working and attending college, you might state that it is difficult to do both and then give your listener specific examples of how the hours you spend at work prevent you from studying or how studying late after work makes it difficult to stay alert in an early morning class. More than likely, you have also used this pattern in developing paragraphs in your essays. Professional writers also often begin with a main idea and follow with examples for support. As a reader, you need to be alert to this pattern because if you miss the main idea, the examples that follow may not make much sense. Examine the following paragraph.

Consider the many hats we expect the President to wear, rapidly switching them like some quick change artist. The President simultaneously is the chief administrator of the entire federal government, the chief diplomat and foreign policy spokesman, the Commander-in-Chief of the Armed Forces, the head of his political party, the key legislative leader, and the shaper of public opinion.

Paul A. Dawson, American Government

If you read this paragraph quickly, you will notice all the references to the different roles of the president. However, not one of these examples, by itself, is the main point of the paragraph. It would not be wise to say, for instance, that the main point is that the president is the nation's "key legislative leader." He is, but that role is just one he plays in the context of this paragraph. That one role, however, added to all the other roles, gives us the main idea — that the president plays many different roles — "wears many hats," for the public. Each of the individual roles is one example of this main idea.

As you read your college textbooks, try always to separate main ideas from examples or details because to respond to the reading you need to respond to its main ideas. You know how making your ideas clear helps your reader understand your writing. As a reader, locating the writer's main ideas will make the information clearer to you. When you recognize a main idea beginning a paragraph, you can then respond by judging the examples to see if they convince you to accept the main idea, although the main idea does not always come first.

Main Idea Delayed   In the paragraph on presidential roles, the main idea came first. Chapter 4 presented examples of paragraphs in which one sentence or even two or three sentences were used as a lead-in to set up the main idea in a topic sentence. In reading, you need to be very careful to separate any lead-in sentences from the topic sentence. Read the following paragraph and try to identify the main idea.

Air conditioning began to spread in industries as a production aid during World War II. Yet only a generation ago a chilled sanctuary during summer's stewing heat was a happy frill that ordinary people sampled only in movie houses. Today most Americans tend to take air conditioning for granted in homes, offices, factories, stores, theaters, shops, studios, schools, hotels, and restaurants. They travel in chilled buses, trains, planes, and private cars. Sporting events once associated with open sky and fresh air are increasingly boxed in and air cooled. Skiing takes place outdoors, but such attractions as tennis, rodeos, football, and, alas, even baseball are now often staged in synthetic climates like those of Houston's Astrodome and New Orleans' Superdome.

Frank Trippett, "The Great American Cooling Machine"

Most of the examples in this paragraph support one claim: "Today most Americans take air conditioning for granted." Notice that two sentences come before this statement. Both give readers an idea of how limited air conditioning was in the past. These sentences can't be the main idea of the paragraph, however, because most of the examples talk about how people use air conditioning *today*. Yet the sentences lead to the topic sentence by providing a contrast to the past.

Main Idea Last When the main idea is stated in a topic sentence at the end of the paragraph, all the examples lead up to it. If you begin reading a paragraph and find specific examples, stay alert for the idea at the end, as in the following paragraph.

> The television set casts its magic spell, freezing speech and action, turning the living into silent statues so long as the enchantment lasts. The primary danger of the television screen lies not so much in the behavior it produces — although there is danger there — as in the behavior it prevents: the talks, the games, the family festivities and arguments through which much of the child's learning takes place and through which much of his character is formed. Turning on the television set can turn off the process that turns children into people.
>
> Urie Bronfenbrenner, "Who Cares for America's Children?"

This paragraph begins with examples of the effect of television and discusses the ways in which TV can cast a spell on people and stop them from talking or acting. The paragraph then continues with more examples of what watching TV prevents — family games, talks, arguments — and then introduces the idea that all the examples are what children need to learn to grow up and develop character. Finally, the main idea is stated: that TV can prevent children from participating in the growth process that makes them people.

Unlike the paragraph on presidential roles, this paragraph gradually builds up to its main idea. If you moved the last sentence to the beginning of the paragraph, you would have a paragraph similar to the one on presidential roles. But this writer chose to lead up to the main idea.

When you read this type of paragraph, you need to be careful because sometimes the examples will lead you to accept an idea you do not totally agree with. For example, Bronfenbrenner makes a strong claim against television. Though it may have some effects on children, does it prevent them from becoming people? Is there anything on TV that may help them become people? Raising such questions helps you to evaluate claims that are made as the result of a series of examples.

Main Idea Implied In the preceding sample paragraphs, the main idea was stated. Sometimes, however, a paragraph may consist of only a group of examples, details, or facts. Together, these imply a main idea without ever stating it in a topic sentence. When an idea is *implied*, it is suggested but never stated directly.

If you have been writing such paragraphs yourself, you are probably familiar with the concept of implication. If not, you still may not be familiar with the words *implied* or *implication*. However, you are familiar with the practice of implying ideas or stating them by implication. On the news you may hear a reporter give several examples of a politician breaking campaign promises. Though the reporter never says so, the examples *imply* that the politician was not honest with the people. Common everyday occurrences often imply ideas. A neat room, a clean car, good grades in school, a regular routine of exercise, and an active social life imply that the person who has these is organized and disciplined. The details and examples of the person's life enable you to make a judgment about him or her. This judgment is an idea implied by examples about the person.

As you saw in Chapter 4, to imply a main idea a writer often needs several examples. You can't imply something strongly with one example. By itself, having a clean car does not imply that a person is disciplined or organized in general. He or she just may be a car lover and be sloppy about everything else. But if you add the single example to many others that suggest organization, you imply a general pattern of behavior — a main idea.

Writers often let examples imply the idea. In doing so, they show respect for the intelligence of their audience by not stating a point that is obviously implied. To imply an idea successfully, the writer must have a good knowledge of the audience. If the audience cannot get the main idea from the examples, and the writer does not state the main idea, then communication will fail. However, if the examples do imply the idea effectively, the writer is saved from stating the obvious. Examine the following paragraph.

> Areas that traditionally fall into the province of economists include inflation, taxes, unemployment, international trade, and economic growth and development. More recently, economic analysis has been applied to other areas ranging from marriage and the family to explanations for criminal behavior and war, from aspects of our political and legal systems to questions about environmental quality, discrimination, and professional athletes' salaries.
>
> Ralph T. Byrns and Gerald W. Stone, *Economics*

If you read through this paragraph counting the examples of areas studied by economists, you would find well over a dozen. What does this imply? Well, one implication is the idea that economics is a wide and varied field. Another implication is that because economics deals with many areas, it is a difficult field to define. The writer never states either idea, but the examples imply both.

Main Idea Split   Although this method was not covered in the chapter on paragraphs, a writer often splits the main idea, giving the first half of it in the first sentence and the second half near the end of the paragraph. In a way, this method cuts the topic sentence in half, combining the strategies of main idea first and main idea last. Consider the following paragraph.

Life is filled with low-level frustrations. Your pencil breaks during an exam, you get stuck in traffic, or you forget to set your alarm clock for an important appointment. To what extent do these minor irritations pile up to become stressors that play havoc with your health? The answer is: to a bigger extent than we imagine.

Philip G. Zimbardo, *Psychology and Life*

The last two sentences of the paragraph complete an idea started in the first sentence. If you were to state the main idea in one sentence, you would take part of the first sentence and parts of the last two. You might discover a sentence like this: Low-level frustrations can cause stress that harms our health more than we imagine. In the paragraph this idea is split by the examples in between.

This type of paragraph is common because it allows a writer to develop an idea gradually, working in examples before the idea is complete. It is particularly common in textbooks because an idea can be related in parts rather than all at once. Also, completing the idea at the end of a paragraph enables the writer to move smoothly into other points. For instance, the preceding sample paragraph, from a psychology textbook, was followed by a discussion of experiments to support the idea developed in the paragraph. Readers need to follow how such an idea develops, to see what the paragraph says as a whole. Therefore, readers must pay attention when new information expands on a point already stated.

Picking out main ideas takes practice, but the more you read, the easier you will be able to find main ideas. Remember that a main idea is just that: an idea. Therefore, it must be stated as a complete sentence, just as when you write you state your thesis and topic sentences in complete sentences. In one of the previous examples, the topic or subject of the paragraph was economics. But you could not say that the main idea of that paragraph was economics because economics is not an idea; it is a field of study. To have an idea you must *say something about something else.*

Also, you as a reader cannot respond to just a topic. If someone simply says to you, "Economics," you will probably think he or she is crazy. What about it? But if the person tells you to major in economics because you will make a good salary after graduation, you could respond in a number of ways. The paragraph on economics contains two implied ideas: (1) economics is a wide and varied field, and (2) it is difficult to define economics because it covers many areas.

Once you see the main idea, you can respond. In this case, you might think that because economics covers so many areas, it might be a good field to enter because it offers much to choose from and many job possibilities. Or you might conclude that the writer's definition is not very good because it does not pin down a common point that draws all these areas together under economics.

E X E R C I S E   6.3   Read each of the following paragraphs. Then write what you think is the main idea of each paragraph. If the idea is stated in the paragraph, just copy it down. If the idea is implied or split, write a sentence of your own that expresses the idea. Make sure each answer is a complete sentence. Once you have the main idea, write a short response to it.

1. Life in the urban slums destroys families. In the south central section of Los Angeles called Watts, where 14 percent of the citizens resided in 1964, over half the children under eighteen years of age lived in broken homes — with only one parent or with neither. One-quarter of all families received public assistance. The divorce rate was one and a half times that for Los Angeles as a whole, difficult as it is for the poor to finance a divorce. The number of households headed by a female was far higher than elsewhere in the city. Other areas in other cities were worse off.

Ramsey Clark, *Crime in America*

2. Unlike the white high school, Lafayette County Training School distinguished itself by having neither lawn, nor hedges, nor tennis court, nor climbing ivy. Its two main buildings (main classrooms, the grade school and home economics) were set on a dirt hill with no fence to limit either its boundaries or those of bordering farms. There was a large expanse to the left of the school which was used alternately as a baseball diamond or basketball court. Rusty hoops on swaying poles represented the permanent recreation equipment, although bats and balls could be borrowed from the P.E. teacher if the borrower was qualified and if the diamond wasn't occupied.

Maya Angelou, "Graduation"

3. The dying of a field mouse, at the jaws of an amiable household cat, is a spectacle I have beheld many times. It used to make me wince. Early in life I gave up throwing sticks at the cat to make him drop the mouse, because the dropped mouse regularly went ahead and died anyway, but I always shouted unaffections at the cat to let him know the sort of animal he had become. Nature, I thought, was an abomination.

Lewis Thomas, *The Medusa and the Snail*

4. Female infants speak sooner, have larger vocabularies and rarely demonstrate speech defects. (Stuttering, for instance, occurs almost exclusively in boys.) Girls exceed boys in language abilities, and this early linguistic bias often prevails throughout life. Girls read sooner, learn foreign languages more easily, and are more likely to enter occupations involving language mastery.

Richard Restak, "The Other Difference Between Boys and Girls"

5. In the United States, there is some disagreement (to say the least) over the risks and benefits of nuclear power. There can be

no question that with our electrical power needs increasing rapidly, we cannot rely indefinitely on the earth's remaining fossil fuel supply. The question is, can we safely shift our reliance to nuclear fission power plants — considering the present state of our technology. The American public has, in the past few years, developed a rather strong consensus regarding this question. Nuclear power has fallen into disfavor.

Robert A. Wallace, Biology: The World of Life

Handling Words You Do Not Know

While vocabulary building is important to your development both as a reader and as a student, many students often worry too much about coming upon words they don't know. Sometimes a teacher will tell students to read with the dictionary by their sides so that when they come to a word they don't know, they can stop to look up its meaning. This can be helpful for an experienced reader who rarely sees an unknown word and who has a good reading speed. But for someone who reads slowly or often sees unknown words, stopping to look up every word can slow the reader down so much that he or she loses the general meaning of the sentence or paragraph.

The two best ways for a slow reader to deal with unknown words are to try to guess the meaning of the word from the context or to circle the word *after* finishing the sentence or paragraph and look up the circled words in the dictionary after reading the whole essay or chapter.

Guessing from Context Millions of people have learned countless new words without ever having looked them up in the dictionary. Small children learn new words almost every day, and they learn them from hearing the words spoken in context. This is not meant to discourage you from using your dictionary — it is a valuable tool — but to stress the power of context. Think of all the words you learned throughout your life by hearing them spoken in context. You can learn more words if you pay close attention to context as you read.

Suppose you were from a non–English speaking country and you were just learning English. Suppose you read the following sentence:

IBM executives were disappointed with decreasing sales this year.

Now assume you know every word in the sentence except *decreasing*. Could you figure out its meaning? Certainly. You would know that more sales would not disappoint company executives, so you could guess that *decreasing* means "becoming fewer or less." Now read the same sentence with one word changed, and notice how the context gives you clues to what may be an unfamiliar word:

IBM executives were disappointed by diminishing sales this year.

Just as the context of a sentence can give you the meaning of a word, so can the context of a paragraph. In fact, sometimes you can't guess the meaning of a word from just the context of a sentence. Try guessing the meaning of *purloined* in this sentence from a student essay:

> Just then a clerk grabbed my arm and snatched the *purloined* cap from my head.

If you do not know the meaning of the word, the sentence does not provide much help. But try again, this time using the context of a paragraph:

> When I was nine I learned a lesson I will never forget. All the guys on my block were getting Cubs caps. I had a baseball cap that my mom had brought home for me. It had a silly Little Leaguer sign on it. I hated to wear it around the guys, but my mom thought it was fine and told me I would have to save my own money if I wanted another cap. I didn't have any money, but I had a plan. I went down to the mall on Saturday afternoon and entered a busy sporting goods store. Trying not to be noticed, I surreptitiously made my way to the back of the store near the caps, and when the nearest salesman was showing some woman some jogging shoes, I put a Cubs hat on my head. I tried to look calm as I walked out the door. I thought I was home free. Just then a clerk grabbed my arm and snatched the purloined cap from my head.

With the sentence in the context of a paragraph, you now can make a pretty good guess about the meaning of *purloined*. What do you know about the cap? (1) It is a Cubs hat. (2) It is new. (3) It is stolen. Since it is unlikely that *purloined* means "Cubs," it has to mean either "new" or "stolen." Either could be the answer, but given that the paragraph begins a story of learning a lesson and proceeds to describe a scene of shoplifting, the word in question probably means "stolen." In fact, it does.

Another word in the paragraph can be guessed from context. The student says he "surreptitiously" went to the back of the store. Although this word is probably too formal for the paragraph, you should try to find out what the writer means. What else do you know about what he was doing in the store? He was planning to shoplift, and he says he was "trying not to be noticed." Given this information, what do you think "surreptitiously" means? In a sneaky way? Quietly? Secretly? If you guessed that the word combines all three meanings, you are catching on.

▪▪▪▪▪▪▪▪▪▪▪▪▪

E X E R C I S E 6.4 Using the context of the sentence, try to guess the definition of each italicized word. Write out your definitions, and when you are finished check the word against the meaning in your dictionary.

1. Three days after the storm, the flood waters finally *abated*.
2. When the suspect was stopped for speeding, his *vociferous* protests to the officer only got him into more trouble.
3. Everyone thought Shirley was brilliant, for she made the dean's list with a *modicum* of effort each semester.
4. Because of their *divergent* positions and *irascible* personalities, the debate between Congressman Lodge and her opponent, Ed Wentz, resulted in a mud-slinging match *injurious* to the image of politicians everywhere.
5. Reading a 500-page book in a week can be a *formidable* task if one is not used to reading.
6. In settling the lawsuit out of court, the lawyers tried to work out an agreement that would be *amenable* to both parties.
7. When the reporter misquoted the mayor in the morning edition, she was severely *rebuked* by her editor.

EXERCISE 6.5 The following paragraph contains some italicized words. Read through it once, guessing the meanings of the words. Then write down the definitions you guessed, and compare your definitions with those in the dictionary.

Often terms that have been *discarded* from the soul people's vocabulary for one reason or another are reaccepted years later, but usually with completely different meaning. In the Thirties and Forties, "stuff" was used to mean vagina. In the middle Fifties, it was *revived* and used to refer to heroin. Why certain expressions are thus *reactivated* is practically an *indeterminable* question. But it is not difficult to see why certain terms are dropped from the soul language. Whenever a certain term becomes popular with whites it is common practice for the soul folks to *relinquish* it. The reasoning is that "if white people can use it, it isn't hip enough for me."

Claude Brown, "The Language of Soul"

As you worked through Exercises 6.4 and 6.5, you probably found that some of your guesses weren't quite right. You may have come close to the meanings at times; at other times you may have guessed wrong altogether. But you probably guessed many of the meanings correctly or at least came close enough to get the sense of the sentence.

Guessing from context is helpful, but you can't rely on it totally. A student once wrote a paper on teenage drinking habits. He had read some magazine articles about research studies on teen drinking and used information from them in his paper. But in writing about one of the studies, he said that researchers had found that when the drinking age is twenty-one rather than eighteen there are fewer accidents from drunk driving. However, the study had actually said that the research study *refuted* the idea that a higher drinking age reduces alcohol-related accidents. In error, he had guessed that *refuted* means "proved" when actually it means "showed that an argument is *false*." You can imagine the problem the wrong guess caused in the student's paper. Once you have finished reading, it is wise to use the dictionary to make sure that your guesses are right.

Using a Dictionary   If you do not already own a good dictionary, you should buy one to use throughout college and beyond. Avoid small pocket-sized dictionaries. They usually do not contain all the information a good dictionary should. Though you need a good dictionary, you need not spend a fortune to get one. If you can afford a large hardbound dictionary, buy one, but you can also get a good paperback dictionary at a reasonable price. Your instructor may require a particular dictionary for the class. If not, here are a few of the many to choose from. Each is available in paperback.

The American Heritage Dictionary of the English Language
Merriam Webster's Collegiate Dictionary
The Random House Dictionary of the English Language
Webster's New World Dictionary

Although most people use the dictionary to find the meaning or spelling of a word, dictionary definitions can tell you much more. The following is a definition from *The American Heritage Dictionary of the English Language.* All the parts are labeled.

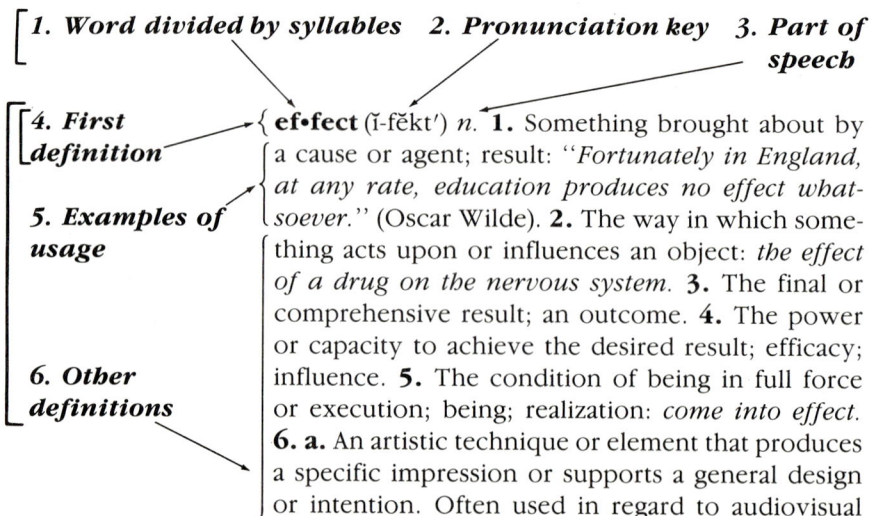

1. Word divided by syllables   *2. Pronunciation key*   *3. Part of speech*

4. First definition

5. Examples of usage

6. Other definitions

ef•fect (ĭ-fĕkt′) *n.* **1.** Something brought about by a cause or agent; result: *"Fortunately in England, at any rate, education produces no effect whatsoever."* (Oscar Wilde). **2.** The way in which something acts upon or influences an object: *the effect of a drug on the nervous system.* **3.** The final or comprehensive result; an outcome. **4.** The power or capacity to achieve the desired result; efficacy; influence. **5.** The condition of being in full force or execution; being; realization: *come into effect.* **6. a.** An artistic technique or element that produces a specific impression or supports a general design or intention. Often used in regard to audiovisual

7. Idiomatic usage and definitions ⟶ techniques: *The effectiveness of the animated cartoon depends on special effects.* **b.** The impression produced by an artifice or manner of presentation. **7.** The basic meaning or tendency of something said or written; purport: *He said something to that effect.* —**in effect. 1.** In fact; actually. **2.** In essence; virtually. **3.** In active force; in operation.— **take effect.** To become operative; gain active

8. Second part of speech and definitions ⟶ force. —*tr. v.* **1. effected, -fecting, -fects. 1.** To produce as a result; cause to occur; bring about: *"If he is taught to fear and tremble, enough has been effected."* (De Quincey). **2.** To execute; to make: *"important change of ancient custom can only be*

9. Cross-references ⟶ *effected by act of Parliament"* (Winston Churchill). — See Synonyms at **perform.** — See usage note at **affect.** [Middle English, from Old

10. Etymology ⟶ French, from Latin *effectus,* past participle of *efficere,* to accomplish, perform, work out; *ex-,* out

11. Other forms and suffixes ⟶ + *facere,* to do (see dhe-¹ in Appendix*)]—**ef fect' er** *n.* —**ef fect' i ble** *adj.*

12. Synonyms and explanations of different meanings ⟶ **Synonyms:** *effect, consequence, result,* and *outcome, upshot, sequel, consummation.* These nouns denote occurrences, situations, or conditions that are traceable to something antecedent. An *effect* is that which is produced by the action of an agent or cause and follows it in time immediately or shortly. A *consequence* also follows the action of an agent and is traceable to it, but the relationship between them is less sharply definable and less immediate than that between a cause and its effect. A *result* is. . . .

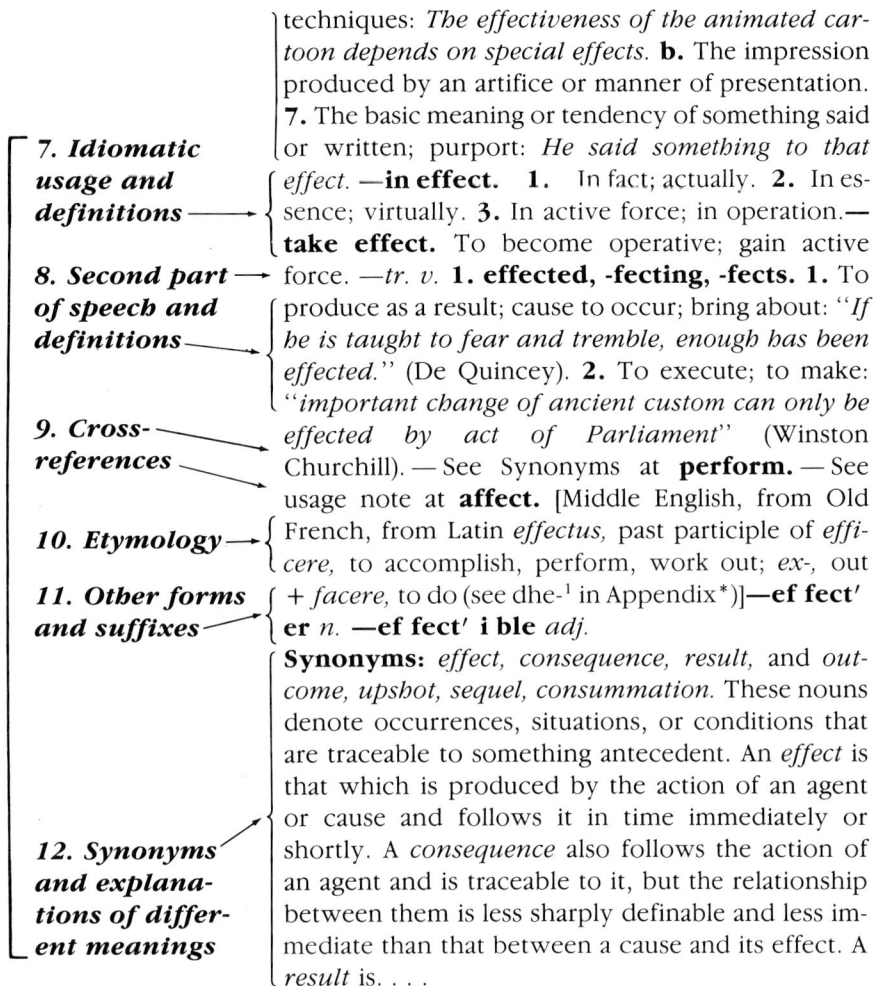

As you can see, dictionary definitions can tell you a lot. And they can seem complicated! However, all the parts of a definition and the way parts are presented are explained in the introduction at the front of the dictionary. The explanation of the parts of this definition will help you get an idea of how dictionaries work.

1. Word divided by syllables: The entry for each word in a dictionary breaks the word into parts (syllables) according to the way the word is pronounced. Syllables are separated by dots. Paying attention to the syllables can help you spell the word.
2. Pronunciation key: The dictionary gives, in parentheses, the phonetic spelling of the word. That is, the word is spelled and marked according to the way it is pronounced. Some of the symbols may seem confusing. To find out how to pronounce them, you can check the chart in the front of the dictionary or

look at the bottom of the page. Beginning on the bottom of the left-hand page and running across the bottom of the right is a list that uses common words to give examples of the sounds (sometimes the list is just on the bottom of one page). For instance, "âr/c**ar**e" means the *ar* in a word is pronounced like the *ar* in *care*, rather than like the *ar* in *bar* or *carry*.

3. Part of speech: In the example, *n.* is for noun because *effect* is defined first as a noun. Other abbreviations are *v.* for verb, *adv.* for adverb, *adj.* for adjective, and so on. A complete list of abbreviations is in the front of the dictionary.

4. First definition: The front of the dictionary tells what the order of definitions means. It is important to know because some dictionaries list the definitions beginning with the one most widely used and then moving to the one used least. Other dictionaries arrange the definitions historically, beginning with the way the word was first used and then moving to the more modern uses. In this arrangement, definitions in use today would come last, and the first few definitions might not be in use anymore.

5. Examples of usage: Sometimes, but not always, the definition shows how the word is used in a phrase or sentence. Sometimes the sentence in the example comes from a famous writer, whose name then appears in parentheses.

6. Other definitions: Often a word has more than one definition. Good dictionaries list most or all meanings. Poor dictionaries might only give a few, and you may not find the meaning you need.

7. Idiomatic usage and definitions: An idiom is an expression peculiar to a particular language. A word used idiomatically is used in combination with another word or other words. For instance, the phrase *come over* in "come over for dinner" is an idiom because those words are used together in that way only in the English language. Most languages have idioms of their own. A few common ones in English are *take up, carry on, turn off, sleep in, stay up, wait out.* A good dictionary defines words in idiomatic usage.

8. Second part of speech and definitions: Often a word is used as more than one part of speech. The dictionary usually gives definitions first for the part of speech in which the word is most often used. The definition of *effect* first gives definitions of the word as a noun because the word is used most frequently as a noun. Then *effect* is defined as a transitive verb (*tr. v.*). Notice that the definitions start again at number 1 when the word is defined as a different part of speech.

9. Cross-references: Cross-references usually begin with the word *see* and direct you to another part of the dictionary for more information. In the definition of *effect,* one cross-reference tells you to "See usage note at **affect.**" People often confuse the words *effect* and *affect,* so the usage note that appears with the

definition of *affect* contains information to help readers avoid that error. Another cross-reference tells you to see the Appendix, a section at the back of the dictionary that tells more about the words.

10. Etymology: The etymology of a word is its history, from its first use to its most recent. The etymology tells you what languages the word came from before it became part of English. Unless you become a language historian, you might not find etymology very useful, but it can be fascinating at times to know where words come from. For instance, the word *sandwich* comes from the Fourth Earl of Sandwich, the eighteenth-century Englishman who invented that particular way of eating food so that he would not have to leave the gambling table to eat his meals.

11. Other forms and suffixes: Suffixes are parts added to the ends of words to change their form or meaning. For example, the *-er* added to the word *farm* to make *farmer* is a suffix. Often dictionary definitions contain suffixes.

12. Synonyms and explanations of different meanings: Words that have similar definitions are called *synonyms*. Some definitions in the dictionary include lists of synonyms, as in the case of *effect*. The synonyms are usually defined and small differences in meaning explained.

13. Labels: The sample definition of *effect* has no labels, but labels are worth knowing about. There are two types of labels. The first type notes specialized uses of a word, that is, the way it is used in a certain field or activity. For example, under the word *down,* one definition reads, "*Football.* Any of a series of four plays during which a team must advance at least ten yards to retain possession of the ball." This type of label often refers to areas of study from architecture to zoology and tells how people in a given field use the word. It can be helpful because often textbooks use words in specialized ways. The second type of label tells if a meaning is nonstandard, slang, informal, vulgar, poetic (used only in poems), regional (used only in a certain region), obsolete, and so on.

As you can see from the discussion of the *American Heritage* definition of *effect,* a dictionary can give a lot of information about a word. You probably will use the dictionary most to find out the meanings of words, but to find meanings it helps to be at least familiar with the parts of dictionary definitions.

E X E R C I S E   6.6   Use your dictionary to answer the following questions. If you have trouble, refer to the introduction at the front of your dictionary for help.

1. How is the word *ramification* divided into syllables?
2. What languages are listed under the etymology of *oil* in your dictionary?

3. List and translate all the abbreviations for the parts of speech under your dictionary's definition of *down*.
4. What symbols represent the two *a*'s in paramount?
5. Write a word that has an *a* sound like the second *a* in paramount and circle the letter that represents the sound.
6. What is the label for the definition of *ain't?*
7. List the suffix forms given in the definition of *convulse*.
8. What field does the word *phlebotomy* come from, and what part of speech is it?
9. Find a word in your dictionary that lists synonyms. Choose one of the synonyms and explain how it is different from the word you have chosen.
10. Does your dictionary list definitions historically from the first usage to the latest, or does it list them according to how frequently they are used?

Because a word may have different meanings, you need to be careful when using the dictionary. When you look up a word, you need to find the meaning that fits the context in which the word is used. I remember as a young boy reading a Western story and being puzzled when the book said that some outlaws were trying to rob a stagecoach full of *bullion*. I did not know what *bullion* meant, and when I asked my mother, she told me it was a kind of soup. She was thinking of *bouillon,* which is a broth or clear soup. I became even more confused. Why and how would a stagecoach carry soup? Why would anyone want to steal soup? Finally I looked in the dictionary and found that the word *bullion* refers to gold or silver bars. With the proper definition, things made sense. Just as context alone cannot always give you the meaning of a word, neither can the dictionary. The dictionary gives you meanings. You need to match the proper meaning to the context.

E X E R C I S E   6.7   Look up the meaning of the word italicized in each sentence and write the definition that fits best given the context.

1. The Harmony Hill Commune was one of the last *bastions* of the hippie lifestyle.
2. Professor Lavent was *ignorant* of his students' abilities.
3. When the savings bonds *mature,* Linda will have plenty of money to pay for her education.
4. Three *matrons* were injured in the riot at the state penitentiary for women.
5. Philip could not believe John was so *base* a man until John tried to *fleece* him of his savings.

The dictionary also provides correct spellings of words. Had I spelled out the word *bullion* for my mother, she probably would not have told me it meant "soup." Some students wonder about teachers' instructions to use a dictionary to check the spelling of a word. How, they ask, can they find the word in the dictionary if they don't know how to spell it. That's a good question.

Usually when you misspell a word, you are off only by one or two letters, and rarely, almost never, do you miss the first letter. So you do have a place to start in the dictionary. Suppose you write *discribe*, and your instructor marks the word wrong. Begin in the dictionary under *d,* but do not, of course, look at all the words. Start with words beginning *di,* and then if you do not find the word there (you won't), ask yourself what other letter might follow the *d.* Use vowels — *a, e, i, o, u* — first. If you try *a,* you will probably recognize quickly that it does not fit, especially if you are a native speaker, because *da* does not produce the sound "disk" like the sound in *discribe.* So try *e,* which seems plausible. When you look under *de* in the dictionary, you will find *describe,* properly spelled. Like everything else, using the dictionary to find correct spellings takes practice.

E X E R C I S E   6.8   Using your dictionary, find the correct spelling for each of the following misspelled words.

1. manacal	7. benifit
2. latle	8. atitude
3. calander	9. impatients
4. develope	10. attendence
5. prefered	11. mistery
5. critisize	12. fullfil

Annotating Your Texts

Annotating: Making marks or notes in a book to record comprehension or responses. Annotating includes underlining, bracketing, and making marginal notes.

Annotating your texts means writing in them. The word *annotating* has the word *note* in it. When you annotate, one thing you do is make notes in the margins of your books. You may find it strange to be encouraged to write in your books. In high school, you were probably told never to write in a book. Those books were not yours; they belonged to the school and would have to be used again the next year by another student. Similarly, you should never write in a book borrowed from a library. But since you buy your college textbooks, they are yours, and you can make notes in them as you read.

Even though students own their books, many still do not want to write or make markings in them. Some of these students may be afraid that the college bookstore will not buy the books back at the end of the semester or will give them less for the books if they are not "clean." The cost of a textbook seems like a small sum compared with the hundreds of dollars it costs to take a course. Annotating textbooks helps students learn and understand much more than they normally would. If they are to get the most out of courses that are costing hundreds of dollars, they really should learn to write in their books. As an active reader, you read to understand and make meaning out of what you read.

Annotation can help you (1) understand what you are reading and (2) record your responses to what you read.

Different readers have different methods of annotation. Some use felt-tip highlighters; others use pens or pencils. Readers also may use different kinds of markings and comments. As you become experienced as an active reader, you may develop your own system of annotation. The following is one system to get you started.

Underlining   If the main idea is stated in a paragraph, whether it is in the beginning, middle, or end, draw a line under it. If the main idea is stated a second time in the paragraph or stated again in the essay, underline it again. However, avoid too much underlining. When you underline or highlight whole paragraphs, nothing stands out; everything seems important. If a whole paragraph seems important to the essay or chapter you are reading, then draw a line along one side of it. That way the paragraph will stand out in the whole piece of writing, but you still will be able to underline its main point.

Bracketing   Often key words or phrases are repeated in a chapter or essay. For instance, the phrase *active reading* was used very often early in this chapter and has been repeated throughout the chapter. The first time key words are mentioned in this book they are printed in bold type to help you remember them. Sometimes textbooks use bold type and sometimes they don't; other kinds of books rarely do. Without the bold type to help, you need to pick out key words and phrases and make them stand out. One way to do this is by drawing brackets around them. Brackets looks like this: [active reading]. To find key words and phrases, look for words that are repeated. You need not use brackets every time, but once you figure out that something is a key word or phrase, bracket it a couple of times so that you will remember it when you see it again.

Making Marginal Notes   While you are underlining and bracketing, you should also be making notes in the margins. If you want to make long notes as you read, you will need separate sheets of paper. But the small white spaces of the margins of a book can give you a place to write notes to help you understand and respond to your reading.

One type of *marginal note* is called a *summary note*. This note simply sums up the main idea in a paragraph or section. A summary note for the paragraph that defined economics as a varied field might read simply, "Econ. a varied field." Or stressing how the variety makes economics difficult to define, you might write, "Econ. hard to define." Your summary notes need not be complete sentences, but they should briefly get across the idea you find in the reading.

Another type of marginal note is simply a *question mark*. If you do not understand what an idea means or why a certain example is used, put a question mark next to the sentence. The paragraph by Samuel Scudder in which he looks at the fish raises some questions when read out of the context of the whole essay. You might have placed a question mark next to the sentence where Scudder says he is in a museum or the sentence where he says he was not allowed to use a magnifying glass.

Question marks can be helpful in two ways. First, sometimes as you read further, your questions will be answered. Then when you look back over what you read, you can often connect your question to an answer. Second, if you have marked a textbook chapter with questions, you can look for answers to those questions in your professor's lecture. If the lecture does not provide the answers, you are ready with specific questions when the professor asks if anyone has questions. If he or she does not ask, you can raise the questions on your own. Do not be afraid to ask. A question will not make you look stupid, as students often think. On the contrary, a question based on the reading will show your professor that you have read the material carefully and are thinking about it.

Another type of marginal note is the simple *yes/no note*. If you agree with an idea, write "yes" in the margin; if you do not agree, write "no." You can also expand on these notes briefly. In reading Ramsey Clark's paragraph on how urban slum life destroys families, someone who comes from a strong but poor family background in the urban slums might write, "No, not true at all." Another person whose family was torn apart by urban poverty might write, "Yes, like my family." Of course, not everything you read will cause you to write a yes/no comment, but this type of note is a good way to respond to what you are reading.

A fourth type of note is the *cross-reference*. If you are reading something and the same or a similar idea was also stated earlier in the reading, you can write *cf.* (which stands for *confer,* meaning "compare" in Latin) or *cp.* (which stands for *compare*). After the abbreviation, you can write the page number where the similar or related idea also appears. In addition to the page number, you can add a brief note. For instance, Ramsey Clark's paragraph on broken families in the urban slums is part of a larger discussion of how slum life and poverty cause crime. If you read a paragraph in which Clark talks about juvenile crime in the slums, you might write next to it: "cf. p. 10, point on poor family life." You would thus make a connection between broken homes and juvenile crime, and you would be beginning to see Clark's overall point on poverty as a cause of crime.

Cross-references are perhaps the most difficult type of notes to make because they require you to think back to other points you read and not just deal with the ideas right in front of you. You should try making cross-reference notes because they will help you grasp the main ideas of whole essays or chapters. When you make cross-references, you are a very active reader because you are pulling ideas together to get to larger ideas.

In annotating what you read, you won't use every method in every paragraph, but try to annotate your reading as much as you can. You will develop better comprehension and be better able to come up with responses. Annotation is work, but it pays off.

■■■■■■■■■■■■■■■
E X E R C I S E   6.9 The following paragraph has been annotated, although it does not use every kind of annotation. Each annotation is numbered. Study this paragraph and then identify each type of annotation and briefly write down why you think the reader made the annotation.

(1) aggression
belligerent
behavior
(2) cause is
competition

(5) yes, like groups
of people who
fight among
themselves.

First, we should note that <u>aggression is belligerent behaviour</u> *(3)* that normally arises as a <u>result of competition.</u> An animal shows aggression mainly toward other individuals that tend to utilize the same resources. Thus, it is likely to be aggressive toward those*)? (4)* most like itself. Those most like itself are, of course, of the same species and sex. And most aggressive interactions occur within species, between members of the same sex.

Robert A. Wallace, *Biology: The World of Life*

■■■■■■■■■■■■■■■
E X E R C I S E   6.10 The following paragraph is from a psychology textbook. It discusses memory. Annotate it.

The order in which you receive information affects your retention of it. You tend to remember the information you first receive — a tendency called the primacy effect — and material that you last receive before recall — a tendency called the recency effect. You typically forget the material in the middle. The first items in a list of to-be-remembered words get your attention; the last ones are still in short term memory when you attempt to recall them. The words in the middle of the list enjoy neither advantage, and so you are more likely to forget them.

Sandra Scarr and John Vander Zanden, *Understanding Psychology*

■ Reading Speed

The speed of your reading can also affect your ability to make meaning from and comprehend the words on the page. Students who have difficulty understanding what they read usually are reading too slowly. They read word by word. Studies have shown that when reading speed falls below 180 words per minute, comprehension is much lower than at higher rates. In an essay at the end of this chapter, Bill Cosby provides three techniques for improving your reading speed. Here you will find more detailed explanations of two of these techniques — skimming and clustering — and some exercises to help you practice them. The third technique — previewing — is covered fully in Cosby's essay.

Remember that your goal in increasing reading speed is to increase comprehension, not just to read faster. Remember also that reading speed and comprehension will differ according to your familiarity with the material and the level of difficulty of what you read. Skimming and clustering, the two techniques described here, if used properly, can improve speed and comprehension.

Skimming

Skimming: The process of moving the eyes quickly across a page to pick up key words. It is used to read short, easy material and to get a general idea of context before carefully reading difficult material.

Bill Cosby shows you how you can use **skimming** to quickly read something short and simple. College textbooks are not short and simple, as you know. But skimming can help you with college reading if you use it right. That means skimming *before* you read something *carefully*. If you skim material before you actually read it carefully, you pick up some general terms and ideas that can help you improve your speed and comprehension when you do read carefully.

How do you skim? You move your eyes quickly through a line, trying to pick out the key words, the words that give you a sense of what the passage is about. You ignore short words such as *the, a, an, of,* and so on and words that connect sentences such as *but, when, because,* and the like. Examine the following passage. The key words are underlined.

> In the <u>forties</u>, <u>black</u> <u>writers</u> began to <u>document</u> the <u>effects</u> of the <u>Depression</u> on the people of <u>Harlem</u>. The <u>neighborhood</u> was <u>never</u> to <u>recover</u> from its heavy toll or <u>regain</u> the <u>innocence</u> <u>and</u> <u>optimism</u> of the twenties. By the <u>fifties</u>, however, two towering literary figures, <u>Ralph Ellison</u> and <u>James Baldwin</u>, were to <u>come to</u> <u>grips</u> with <u>Harlem</u>, transmuting it in <u>their</u> <u>writing</u>. <u>Today</u>, again in a period of <u>heightened</u> <u>consciousness</u>, <u>black</u> <u>writers</u> are <u>rediscovering</u> their <u>literary</u> <u>past</u> and attempting to <u>build</u> <u>cultural</u> <u>institutions</u> in <u>Harlem</u> that <u>will</u> <u>survive</u> where those of the <u>twenties</u> <u>did</u> <u>not.</u>
>
> Susan Edmiston and Linda D. Cirino, *Literary New York*

In the following list of the underlined words from the preceding paragraph, you can see how they can give you a general idea of what the paragraph is about.

forties black writers document effects Depression Harlem. neighborhood never to recover regain innocence and optimism twenties. fifties Ralph Ellison and James Baldwin come to grips Harlem their writing. Today period of heightened consciousness black writers rediscovering literary past build cultural institutions in Harlem will survive twenties did not.

E X E R C I S E   6.11   The following are some words skimmed from a paragraph. Read them and see if you can answer the questions that follow.

> Today better coverage national and international events. television companies added more trained men improved equipment. Full crews reported Vietnam. reporters middle of battles brought horror of war into homes. reporters wounded.

1. List two ways television news has improved coverage of national and international news.
2. How did news coverage change in the Vietnam War?
3. Give an advantage of this change.
4. Give a disadvantage.

You probably were able to answer the questions in the exercise without too much trouble. But remember that skimming is not a substitute for reading. It can help you only to get the general idea of a chapter or an essay, so that before you read it completely you have some understanding of the context. Compare the following complete paragraph with the words skimmed from it in the exercise:

> Today, better coverage of national and international events has been achieved by television news staffs. The broadcasting companies have added more trained men and have constantly improved their picture transmission equipment. Full crews reported the Vietnam War as the United States sent officers and troops to aid the South Vietnamese. The telecasters, both news reporters and camera men, stood in the middle of the battles in jungles, in rice paddies and in the streets of Saigon, the gunfire bursting all around them. They brought the horror of war right into the homes of millions of American viewers. A number of television and newspaper reporters and photographers were wounded while on their jobs.
>
> Sidney Kobre, *Development of American Journalism*

Even though the skimmed words allowed you to get a general idea about changes in reporting during the Vietnam War, the whole paragraph brings those general ideas to life. The paragraph gives you the details of changes in reporting, the daring and bravery of reporters, the pictures of the war brought into American homes, and the price many reporters paid for their work. These kind of details help you remember the general ideas that you would need to know for a test if you were taking a course in the history of journalism.

EXERCISE   6.12   Skim the following sentences. Then list the words that you picked out as important.

1. After years of low profits, Wall Street investors gladly welcomed the rising profits of the bull market of the mid-1980s.
2. Willie Mays began his career disastrously, going without a hit in his first twelve at bats, but his first hit was a home run against the Boston Braves, and it was a preview of the many more homers he would hit.
3. The cerebrum is the part of the brain located just above the forehead; it is responsible for controlling learning, thinking, and memory.
4. At large colleges, campuses usually have a large grassy area called a quad, which is surrounded by buildings but which also provides a collegiate playground of sorts where students meet with friends, toss Frisbies, or sun themselves in the warm months.

EXERCISE   6.13   Now that you have skimmed some sentences, try skimming the following paragraphs. Then write down the series of words you picked out while skimming.

People who are myopic (nearsighted) cannot focus distant objects properly, while those who are hyper-metropic (farsighted) cannot focus nearby objects well. As people get older, the lens gradually loses its elasticity, so that it cannot become thick enough for close vision. After about age 45, the blur point — the closest point at which you can focus clearly — gets progressively farther away. When this happens, people who never needed glasses before begin to need them for reading and other "close work," whereas people who already wear glasses may need to switch to bifocals (glasses that have a near focus in the lower part and a far one in the upper part).

Philip G. Zimbardo, *Psychology and Life*

Companies such as Whirlpool and American Motors have made warranties and consumer satisfaction a major part of their product strategies. Whirlpool and many other companies have "800" toll-free telephone numbers that consumers can use to make complaints, ask questions, or find out the location of the nearest service center. Although these after-the-sale programs are costly, they can contribute additional sales and profits, because consumers value the companies' products more highly because of these services.

Thomas C. Kinnear and Kenneth L. Bernhardt, *Principles of Marketing*

Clustering

As you learned in Chapter 1, one type of clustering is an invention strategy involving diagrams. Another type of **clustering** is a technique for reading. In skimming you move quickly through a passage picking out key words. In clustering, you read all the words, but you group related words together as you read. This method helps you to keep your rate of speed high enough for comprehension. Good readers tend to read words in groups rather than word by word. When people read word by word, they often have trouble understanding because they do not see the sentence as a whole unit of meaning made up of sections. By the time they get to the end of the sentence, they have forgotten what they read at the beginning. You may be used to reading word by word, and you may think that reading a few words at a time will be more difficult. Actually, reading more than one word at a time, after a little practice, makes reading easier. Notice how the groups of words go together in the following sentence: [Our family] [has a picnic] [on my grandfather's farm] [every Fourth of July.] Now read the following paragraph, grouping words set off in brackets.

[Years ago,] [college women] [were sometimes said] [to be studying] [for a MRS. degree,] [meaning they were] [in college] [just to find] [a husband.] [To say] [such a thing] [today] [would not] [only be sexist] [but also inaccurate.] [Young women] [today] [are seriously studying] [for degrees] [in a wide variety] [of majors] [from aviation] [to zoology.]

Reading a paragraph with the words bracketed off in clusters may seem hard at first. After all, in real reading there are no brackets around the words to get in your way. But by reading this way, perhaps you found that clustering makes you train your eyes to see the words in groups. With practice, you will find that clustering helps you read faster as well as understand what you read more easily.

E X E R C I S E   6.14   Read each of the following sentences and try to cluster the words as you read. After you read a sentence, go back and draw brackets around the words you clustered.

1. Napoleon's army was defeated by the British at the Battle of Waterloo.
2. The Duke of Wellington commanded the British forces at Waterloo.
3. As a result, the Duke of Wellington went down in British history as a national hero.
4. Today in London there is a separate museum honoring the Duke of Wellington and his victory over Napoleon.

5. We can understand the importance of the victory if we remember that before Waterloo, Napoleon had conquered nearly all of Europe.
6. If Napoleon had beaten the British at Waterloo, the course of European history would have been changed.

Now try a paragraph:

Women had fewer children in the 1970s than in earlier decades. The birthrate, which had peaked at over 3.5 births for every woman of childbearing age in the late 1950s, dropped to less than 2 by the mid-1970s. This trend toward smaller families was related to the great increase in working wives, an increase that was intensified by the economic pressure caused by inflation in the 1970s. Many women who pursued careers put off childbearing, waiting until they had established themselves professionally, while others simply decided to forgo children entirely. The drop in the birthrate also reflected the later age of marriage in the seventies, as well as the ever larger number of single women.

Robert A. Divine et al., *America, Past and Present*

Previewing: A technique of reading the first two paragraphs, any headings, the first sentence of every paragraph, and the last two paragraphs of a long piece of writing.

As Cosby tells you in the following essay, clustering takes practice. At first you should try it on easy reading material, but if you practice enough and master the technique, it can help you with all but the most difficult reading. Also, he discusses **previewing**.

Essays for Reading

How to Read Faster
Bill Cosby

> You probably know Bill Cosby as a comedian and star of the popular *Cosby Show*. But along with his many talents as an entertainer, Cosby holds a doctorate in education from Temple University in Philadelphia. Cosby's tips provide a humorous but useful review of some of the techniques presented in this chapter.

Questions to Guide Your Reading

1. How much did Cosby read as a child?
2. How have his reading habits changed as an adult?
3. How do you preview and what is the purpose of previewing?
4. For what type of reading does Cosby recommend skimming?

When I was a kid in Philadelphia, I must have read every comic book ever published. (There were fewer of them then than there are now.)

I zipped through all of them in a couple of days, then reread the good ones until the next issues arrived.

Yes indeed, when I was a kid, the reading game was a snap.

But as I got older, my eyeballs must have slowed down or something! I mean comic books started to pile up faster than my brother Russell and I could read them!

It wasn't until much later, when I was getting my doctorate, I realized it wasn't my eyeballs that were to blame. Thank goodness. They're still moving as well as ever.

The problem is, there's too much to read these days, and too little time to read every word of it.

Now, mind you, I still read comic books. In addition to contracts, novels, and newspapers. Screenplays, tax returns, and correspondence. Even textbooks about how people read. And which techniques help people read more in less time.

I'll let you in on a little secret. There are hundreds of techniques that you could learn to help you read faster. But I know of three that are especially good.

And if I can learn them, so can you — and you can put them to use *immediately*.

They are commonsense, practical ways to get the meaning from printed words quickly and efficiently. So you'll have the time to enjoy your comic books, have a good laugh with Mark Twain or a good cry with *War and Peace*. Ready?

Okay. The first two ways can help you get through tons of reading material — fast — without reading every word. And let you cut out an awful lot of unnecessary reading.

1. Preview — If It's Long and Hard

Previewing is especially useful for getting a general idea of heavy reading like long magazine articles, business reports, and nonfiction books.

It can give you as much as half the comprehension in as little as one tenth the time. For example, you should be able to preview eight or ten 100-page reports in an hour. After previewing, you'll be able to decide which reports (or which *parts* of which reports) are worth a closer look.

Here's how to preview: Read the entire first two paragraphs of whatever you've chosen. Next read only the *first sentence* of each successive paragraph. Then read the entire last two paragraphs.

Previewing doesn't give you all the details. But it does keep you from spending time on things you don't really want — or need — to read.

Notice that previewing gives you a quick, overall view of *long, unfamiliar* material. For short, light reading, there's a better technique.

2. Skim — If It's Short and Simple

Skimming is a good way to get a general idea of light reading — like popular magazines or the sports and entertainment sections of the paper.

You should be able to skim a weekly popular magazine or the second section of your daily paper in less than *half* the time it takes you to read it now.

Skimming is also a great way to review material you've read before.

Here's how to skim: Think of your eyes as magnets. Force them to move fast. Sweep them across each and every line of type. Pick up *only a few key words in each line.*

Everybody skims differently.

You and I may not pick up exactly the same words when we skim the same piece, but we'll both get a pretty similar idea of what it's all about.

To show you how it works, I circled the words I picked out when I skimmed the following story. Try it. It shouldn't take you more than 10 seconds.

My brother Russell thinks monsters live in our bedroom closet at night. But I told him he is crazy.

"Go and check then," he said.

I didn't want to. Russell said I was chicken.

"Am not," I said.

"Are so," he said.

So I told him the monsters were going to eat him at midnight. He started to cry. My Dad came in and told the monsters to beat it. Then he told us to go to sleep.

"If I hear any more about monsters," he said, "I'll spank you."

We went to sleep fast. And you know something? They never did come back.

Skimming can give you a very good *idea* of this story in about half the words — and in *less* than half the time it'd take to read every word.

So far, you've seen that previewing and skimming can give you a *general idea* about content — fast. But neither technique can promise more than 50 percent comprehension, because you aren't reading all the words. (Nobody gets something for nothing in the reading game.)

To *read faster and understand most* — if not all — of what you read, you need to know a third technique.

3. Cluster — To Increase Speed and Comprehension

Most of us learned to read by looking at each word in a sentence — *one at a time.*

Like this:

My — brother — Russell — thinks — monsters . . .

You probably still read this way sometimes, especially when the words are difficult. Or when the words have an extra special meaning — as in a poem, a Shakespearean play, or a contract. And that's O.K.

But word by word reading is a rotten way to read faster. It actually *cuts down* on your speed.

Clustering trains you to look at *groups* of words instead of one at a time — to increase your speed enormously. For most of us, clustering is a *totally different way of seeing what we read.*

Here's how to cluster: Train your eyes to see *all* the words in clusters of up to 3 or 4 words at a glance.

Here's how I'd cluster the story we just skimmed:

My brother Russell thinks monsters live in our bedroom closet at night. But I told him he is crazy.

"Go and check then," he said.

I didn't want to. Russell said I was chicken.

"Am not," I said.

"Are so," he said.

So I told him the monsters were going to eat him at midnight. He started to cry. My Dad came in and told the monsters to beat it. Then he told us to go to sleep. "If I hear any more about monsters," he said, "I'll spank you."

We went to sleep fast. And you know something? They never did come back.

Learning to read clusters is not something your eyes do naturally. It takes constant practice.

Here's how to go about it: Pick something light to read. Read it as fast as you can. Concentrate on seeing 3 to 4 words at once rather than one word at a time. Then reread the piece at your normal speed to see what you missed the first time.

Try a second piece. First cluster, then reread to see what you missed in this one.

When you can read in clusters without missing much the first time, your speed has increased. Practice 15 minutes every day and you might pick up the technique in a week or so. (But don't be disappointed if it takes longer. Clustering *everything* takes time and practice.)

So now you have 3 ways to help you read faster. *Preview* to cut down on unnecessary heavy reading. *Skim* to get a quick, general idea of light reading. And *cluster* to increase speed *and* comprehension.

With enough practice, you'll be able to handle *more* reading at school or work — and at home — *in less time.* You should even have enough time for your favorite comic books — *and War and Peace.*

Questions for Study and Discussion
1. What kinds of material does previewing help you to read?
2. Can you think of times when it could help you in college?
3. How would you preview a textbook chapter?
4. What kinds of materials does skimming help you read? Can you think of times when it could help you in college? How is Cosby's use of skimming different from the use discussed in this chapter?
5. In what cases would skimming not be helpful for college reading?
6. How does clustering change the way you usually read?
7. How does Cosby recommend you practice clustering?
8. How can you tell if clustering is improving your speed?

Writing Assignments
1. As Cosby recommends, practice clustering for fifteen minutes a day for one week. After each reading, make notes on progress you feel you are making and on any difficulties you are having with the technique. At the end of the week, use your notes to write an essay that recommends, or does not recommend, clustering to other college freshmen.

2. Read a chapter in a textbook *without* previewing or skimming it first. Then read a chapter in the same textbook, this time previewing and skimming before you read. Write an essay that recommends, or does not recommend, these techniques to other college freshmen.

From *Hunger of Memory*

Richard Rodriguez

Richard Rodriguez was born in 1944 and grew up in San Francisco. His Mexican-American parents spoke Spanish at home. In his autobiography, *Hunger of Memory,* he tells how his fascination with English led him to conventional success as a Ph.D. and teacher at the University of California. At the same time, he tells how his success was painful in separating him from his ethnic background.

Vocabulary Cues

assurance: lacking doubt, feeling sure, certain
breadth: wide or great extent, large scope
disheartened: discouraged
earnestness: sincerity, serious determination
embarked: started out
epigram: a short statement of a single piece of wisdom
essence: the most important ingredient, the crucial element
grandiose: great but foolish intent
irony: use of words to mean the opposite of their usual meaning; sarcasm

Questions to Guide Your Reading

1. What does Rodriguez first feel is the purpose of reading?
2. Why does he read a lot?
3. Does he enjoy reading?
4. How does he judge books?
5. Does Rodriguez's attitude about reading change at the end of the essay?

In our house each school year would begin with my mother's careful instruction: "Don't write in your books so we can sell them at the end of the year." The remark was echoed in public by my teachers, but only in part: "Boys and girls, don't write in your books. You must learn to treat them with great care and respect."

OPEN THE DOORS OF YOUR MIND WITH BOOKS, read the red and white poster over the nun's desk in early September. It soon was apparent to me that reading was the classroom's central activity. Each course had its own book. And the information gathered from a book was unquestioned. READ TO LEARN, the sign on the wall advised in December. I privately wondered: What was the connection between reading and learning? Did one learn something only by reading it? Was an idea only an idea if it could be written down? In June, CONSIDER BOOKS YOUR BEST FRIENDS. Friends? Reading was, at best, only a chore. I needed to look up whole paragraphs of words in a dictionary. Lines of type were dizzying, the eye having to move slowly across the page, then down and across. . . . The sentences of the first books I read were coolly impersonal. Toned hard. What most bothered me, however, was the isolation reading required. To console myself for the loneliness I'd feel when I read, I tried reading in a very soft voice. Until: "Who is doing all this talking to his neighbor?" Shortly after, remedial reading classes were arranged for me with a very old nun.

At the end of each school day, for nearly six months, I would meet with her in the tiny room that served as the school's library but was actually only a storeroom for used textbooks and a vast collection of *National Geographics*. Everything about our sessions pleased me: the edge of the long hallway outside the door; the green of the sun, lighting the wall; and the old woman's face blurred white with a beard. Most of the time we took turns. I began with my elementary texts. Sentences of astonishing simplicity seemed to be lifeless and drab: "The boys ran from the rain. . . . She wanted to sing. . . . The kite rose in the blue." Then the old nun would read from her favorite books, usually biographies of early American presidents. Playfully she ran through complex sentences, calling the words alive with her voice, making it seem that the author was somehow speaking directly to me. I smiled just to listen to her. I sat there and sensed for the very first time some possibility of fellowship between a reader and a writer, a communication, never *intimate* like that I heard spoken words at home convey, but one nonetheless personal.

One day the nun concluded a session by asking me why I was so reluctant to read by myself. I tried to explain; said something about the way written words made me feel alone — almost, I wanted to add but didn't, as when I spoke to myself in a room just emptied of furniture. She studied my face as I spoke; she seemed to be watching more than listening. In an uneventful voice she replied that I had nothing to fear. Didn't I realize that reading would open up whole new worlds? A book could open doors for me. It could introduce me to people and show me places I never imagined existed. She gestured toward the bookshelves. (Bare-breasted African women danced, and the shiny hubcaps of automobiles on the back covers of the *Geographic* gleamed in my mind.) I listened with respect. But her words were not very influential. I was thinking then of another consequence of literacy, one I was too shy to admit but nonetheless trusted. Books were going to make me "educated." *That* confidence enabled me, several months later, to overcome my fear of silence.

In the fourth grade, I embarked upon a grandiose reading program. "Give me the names of important books," I would say to startled teachers. They soon found out that I had in mind "adult books." I ignored their suggestion of anything I suspected was written for children. (Not until I was in college, as a result, did I read *Huckleberry Finn* or *Alice's Adventures in Wonderland*.) Instead, I read *The Scarlet Letter* and Franklin's *Autobiography*. And whatever I read I read for extra credit. Each time I finished a book, I reported the achievement to a teacher and basked in the praise my effort earned. Despite my best efforts, however, there seemed to be more and more books I needed to read. At the library I would literally tremble as I came upon whole shelves of books I hadn't read. So I read and I read and I read: *Great Expectations;* all the short stories of Kipling; *The Babe Ruth*

Story; the entire first volume of the *Encyclopaedia Britannica* (A–Anstey); the *Iliad; Moby Dick; Gone With the Wind; The Good Earth; Ramona; Forever Amber; The Lives of the Saints; Crime and Punishment; The Pearl.* . . . Librarians who initially frowned when I checked out the maximum ten books at a time started saving books they thought I might like. Teachers would say to the rest of the class, ''I only wish the rest of you took reading as seriously as Richard obviously does.''

But at home I would hear my mother wondering, ''What do you see in your books?'' (Was reading a hobby like her knitting? Was so much reading even healthy for a boy? Was it a sign of ''brains''? Or was it just a convenient excuse for not helping around the house on Saturday mornings?) Always, ''What do you see . . . ?''

What did I see in my books? I had the idea that they were crucial for my academic success, though I couldn't have said exactly how or why. In the sixth grade I simply concluded that what gave a book its value was some major idea or theme it contained. If that core essence could be mined and memorized, I would become learned like my teachers. I decided to record in a notebook the themes of the books I had read. After reading *Robinson Crusoe,* I wrote that its theme was ''the value of learning to live by oneself.'' When I completed *Wuthering Heights,* I noted the danger of ''letting emotions get out of control.'' Rereading these brief moralistic appraisals usually left me disheartened. I couldn't believe they were really the source of reading's values. But for many more years, they constituted the only means I had of describing to myself the educational value of books.

In spite of my earnestness, I found reading to be a pleasurable activity. I came to enjoy the lonely good company of books. Early on weekday mornings, I'd read in my bed. I'd feel mysterious comfort then, reading in the quiet dawn — the blue-gray silence interrupted by the occasional churning of the refrigerator motor a few rooms away or the more distant sounds of the city bus beginning to make its run. On the weekends, I'd go to the public library to read, surrounded by old men and women. Or, if the weather was fine, I would take my books to the park and read in the shade of a tree. A warm summer evening was my favorite reading time. Neighbors would leave for vacation and I would water their lawns. I would sit through the twilight on the front porches or in the backyards, reading to the cool, whirling sounds of the sprinklers.

I also had favorite writers. But often the writers I enjoyed most I was least able to value. When I read William Saroyan's *The Human Comedy,* I was immediately pleased by the narrator's warmth and the charm of his story. But as quickly I became suspicious. A book so enjoyable to read couldn't be very ''important.'' Another summer I determined to read the novels of Dickens. Reading his fat novels, I loved the feeling I got — after the first hundred pages — of being at home in a fictional world where I knew the names of the characters and cared about what was going to happen to them. And it bothered me that I was forced away at the conclusion, when the fiction closed tight, like a fortune teller's fist — the futures of all the major characters neatly resolved. I never knew how to take such feelings seriously, however. Nor did I suspect that these experiences could be part of the novel's meaning. Still, there were pleasures to sustain me after I'd finish my books. Carrying a volume back to the library, I would be pleased by its weight. I'd run my fingers along the edge of the pages and marvel at the breadth of my achievement. Around my room growing stacks of paperback books reinforced my assurance.

I entered high school having read hundreds of books. My habit of reading made me a confident speaker and writer of English. Reading also enabled me to sense something of the shape, the major concerns, of Western thought. (I was able to say something about Dante and Descartes and Engels and James Baldwin in my high school term papers.) In these various ways, books brought me academic success as I hoped that they would. But I was not a good reader. Merely bookish, I lacked a point of view when I read. I vacuumed books for epigrams, scraps of information, ideas, themes — anything to fill the hollow within me and make me feel educated.

Questions for Study and Discussion
1. Early in the essay Rodriguez does not like to read. Why not?
2. What in the way the old nun reads makes Rodriguez begin to like reading?
3. What does the old nun tell him reading can do for him? How does he interpret what she says?
4. As a youngster, how does Rodriguez choose books? As a man, he implies there was something wrong with the way he chose books. What was wrong?
5. Along with some "education," what else did Rodriguez get out of books? Why was he dissatisfied?
6. How did Rodriguez judge the value of a book? What do you think of his method of judgment?
7. What advantages did all of Rodriguez's reading give him in high school?
8. Why at the end of the essay does Rodriguez say, "I was not a good reader"? What in Rodriguez's approach to reading would make him say this?

Writing Assignments
1. Write an essay that discusses your own experiences with reading in your childhood and teen years. As Rodriguez does, consider both negative and positive experiences.
2. Write an essay that discusses the kinds of reading you do outside of school. Tell why you read the things you do and what you get out of them.

CHAPTER 7

Writing from Sources: The Mechanics

Source: Material that provides information for a college paper: most commonly, a textbook, a piece of literature, a newspaper article, a magazine article, or an interview.

So far in this course, you have been writing essays based on personal experience or observation. Even though you often read a professional author's essay first to get some ideas on how to write your own essay, your purpose in writing was to tell of your feelings and ideas about things you have *experienced* and *observed*.

Knowing how to write essays based on personal experience and observation can be helpful in college, but many of your writing assignments, especially in other courses, will ask you to write about something you have read. The material you have read is called the **source**.

■ Types of Sources

You can use many kinds of sources in your writing, ranging from newspaper articles to books. Before you write in response to sources, you should have some idea of the kinds of information that different sources provide.

Books

Books are obviously one type of source. But there are many different types of books, depending on their audience. Most of the books in the bookstores at the local mall are written for a general audience, as are many books in the library. Some books are written for experts and scholars and are more difficult to read but provide very specific information. You will find this type of source more useful as you gain knowledge in your major. Textbooks usually provide basic information on a particular subject and can be used as a source. Also knowing what is in a textbook can help you understand more difficult sources.

Newspapers

Newspapers contain four types of sources: news articles, features, editorials, and columns. News articles report some event that either took place or will take place. They cover news events, such as crime and world affairs. Features provide information on trends, food, people, and so on, rather than reporting a single event. Articles and features do not contain the writer's opinions; they just report the facts to provide readers with information.

In contrast, editorials and columns provide the writer's opinion on something. Editorials appear on the same page each day, aptly called the editorial page, and are usually written by one of the newspaper's editors. Columns are written by people called — what else? — columnists. A column by a particular writer may appear every day or on certain days of the week, and a column may appear in many different newspapers. Columns, like editorials, include the writer's opinion and are actually short essays. You may have heard of or read some of the better-known columnists, such as Mike Royko, Andy Rooney, George Will, and Ellen Goodman. Any of these sources from newspapers can be helpful if they cover the topic you are writing about.

Magazines

There are, of course, many kinds of magazines. Some, such as *Time* and *Newsweek,* report news events. Others include mostly features and are aimed at an audience with a special interest: *Sports Illustrated* for sports fans, *Parents* for parents, *Gentleman's Quarterly* for fashion-conscious men, and so on. Magazine articles can be helpful because they are usually well developed and specific. Because they are written for a general audience, they are not difficult to understand.

Scholarly Journals

Scholarly journals are similar to magazines in that they are published periodically and are paperbound. However, the essays in them are usually written by experts for a very specialized audience. Also, journals are not available at newsstands, as general-interest magazines are; rather, they are purchased by subscription or found in libraries. When you begin to gain a specialist's knowledge in your major, scholarly journals will be useful sources, but for someone with just a basic knowledge of a subject, they can be difficult to understand. Of course, that's how you will learn — by tackling what is difficult to understand — so you should not rule out journals completely. Yet if you find you have difficulty understanding them, don't feel bad; they are written for experts.

Interviews

Unlike the other sources, interviews usually are not printed. But if you are looking for information on a topic, why not ask an expert? Journalists do this all the time, but an interview can also be a good source for a college paper. Suppose that for an economics class you are asked to write a paper on the problems of small businesses. It would be useful and informative to interview some of the owners of small businesses in your town. When you conduct an interview, it is helpful to use a tape recorder if possible because you can't always write down everything a person says, and you won't remember it all. The recording allows you to go back and pick out the most important information.

In writing about sources, you will be writing about the ideas and opinions of others. But this does not mean that you will merely copy their ideas and present them. A good essay based on sources also will contain your opinions and ideas in response to the ideas and opinions in the sources. Sometimes you might agree with the writer of a source; at other times you might disagree.

Suppose you are taking a class in political science, and you read an essay arguing that American presidents should be able to serve more than two terms. If you disagree with the author, your essay will have to present the ideas given in the essay *and* the reasons that you disagree. If you agree that presidents should be allowed to serve more than two terms, you will have to give *your* reasons along with the author's. Either way, whether you agree or disagree with the source, you need to integrate your own ideas with those in the source. Source writing, in other words, requires that you respond to the ideas you read. But even though a source essay requires your response, your ideas mixed in with those of another writer, first you need to learn how to present the other author's ideas in your essay.

Avoiding Plagiarism

Plagiarism: Use of someone else's ideas or words as if they were your own.

Plagiarism can be defined as use of the words or thoughts of another person as if they were your own. In the public sector, plagiarism can result in lawsuits. You may be familiar with a few cases in the music industry a few years back. In one, a songwriter won a lawsuit against former Beatle George Harrison when the court ruled that Harrison used the music from the song "He's So Fine" in his song "My Sweet Lord." Plagiarism cases also involve words. During the primary elections for the 1988 presidential nominations, Democratic candidate Senator Joseph Biden had to drop out of the race when news media revealed that he had taken phrases and sentences from a speech by a British politician and used them in a speech of his own. These cases show that plagiarism is a serious matter.

Inexperienced writers sometimes think they can copy information from a source into their own essays word for word. That won't work. The words and information belong to the author, and to just copy them and hand them in as if you wrote them is plagiarism. In college, as in the public sector, plagiarism has serious consequences. At the very least, a student who plagiarizes in a paper will receive a failing grade on the assignment or be failed for the course; in some cases, students have been expelled from school for plagiarism.

You *can* use the words and ideas of a source if you do so in the right way. Also, and even more important, when you learn how to present the ideas of a source properly, you learn a lot about those ideas — much more than you would learn from merely copying them. These are the ways to present an author's ideas: *paraphrasing, summarizing, quoting,* and *documenting.*

■ Paraphrasing

Paraphrasing: Putting the ideas and points of a source in one's own words by (1) changing the sentence structure, (2) writing the paraphrase without looking at the source, (3) avoiding the use of more than three consecutive words of the source, (4) using synonyms for words in the source, (5) using common but key words from the source, (6) avoiding striking or catchy language from the source (unless you put quotation marks around it).

TV makes looks important
Losers looked bad on TV

Kennedy & Carter looked good: young

Eisenhower + Johnson looked fatherly

Paraphrasing means expressing someone else's ideas in your own words. It is a necessary skill when you write in response to a source you have read. In paraphrasing, you need to mention the author's name so that the reader knows you are discussing someone else's ideas, not your own.

To paraphrase properly, it is very important to read carefully and to make sure you understand what you read. You will then present the author's ideas accurately and clearly. One way to build your paraphrasing skills is through *annotation*. As you learned in Chapter 6, annotation means marking parts of a paragraph by underlining key words and sentences and by making notes in the margin.

To refresh your memory, read the following paragraphs and notice the annotations.

What effects does television have on the candidates themselves? It dictates priorities that are different from those of an earlier day. The physical appearance of the candidate is increasingly important. Does he or she look fit, well-rested, secure? Losing candidates like Adlai Stevenson, Hubert Humphrey, and Richard Nixon all seemed to look "bad" on TV. Nixon overcame this problem in 1972 with ads that featured longer shots of him being "presidential" — flying off to China. Close-ups were avoided.

Both John Kennedy and Jimmy Carter seemed more at home with the medium, perhaps because both were youthful, informal, physically active outdoor types. Dwight Eisenhower and Lyndon Johnson seemed to have a paternal, fatherly image on the small screen.

E. J. Whetmore, *The Selling of the President*

The notes in the margin condense and restate the sentences that are underlined. The first underlined sentence is the answer to the question Whetmore raises. That is the topic sentence and the main idea of the paragraphs. The underlining and the marginal notes about Whetmore's examples are useful because when the writer paraphrases — puts the paragraphs in his or her own words — he or she will need to show how Whetmore proves his point. The writer can then use the annotations as the basis for a paraphrase of Whetmore's paragraphs. Consider the following paraphrase:

> According to E. J. Whetmore, a presidential candidate's looks are becoming more and more important because of television. On television, voters can see if a candidate is healthy and if he seems secure. Whetmore says that unsuccessful candidates such as Stevenson, Humphrey, and Nixon did not look good on television. When Nixon won in 1972, he avoided close-ups on TV. Whetmore also shows that winning candidates did look good. Kennedy and Carter were young-looking, friendly, and athletic, while Eisenhower and Johnson looked fatherly on TV.

Notice that the paraphrase presents both Whetmore's main idea about the importance of a candidate's appearance on television and the examples Whetmore uses to support his point.

How to Paraphrase

To write a good paraphrase, you need to follow three steps.

Read Carefully Make sure you understand the material you are reading. Separate main ideas from examples, and try to figure out the relationship between them. Annotation can help; use the methods presented in Chapter 6.

Tag: A reference to the name of the author of a source used in a paraphrase or a quotation. Omitting a tag can result in plagiarism.

Use a Tag A **tag** is a reference to the name of the author who wrote the source. You use a tag so that readers know you are presenting someone else's ideas. In the previous example, Whetmore's name is mentioned: "According to E. J. Whetmore . . . , Whetmore says . . . , Whetmore also shows."

Using a tag is not difficult. You can write "According to _____" or "As _____ says." You can also use the author's name and a verb to lead in to your sentence: "_____ says. . . ." Here is a list of handy verbs that can be used easily with the tag:

argues	illustrates
asserts	offers
believes	says
claims	shows
contends	states
demonstrates	

Although using tags may be new to you, you have been using them all your life in everyday conversations. If as a child you said to a friend, "My mom said I can't come out to play," you used a tag. In your conversations with friends now, you use a tag every time you tell one friend something that another friend said. For example, "Pam claimed that she did not know she was supposed to meet me last night." Just for practice, listen to yourself and your friends speak today and try to notice the many times tags are used.

Put the Ideas in Your Own Words   While all of these steps are important, this one is probably the most difficult, but the following section gives you steps and exercises to help you learn how to put a source's ideas in your words.

Strategies for Using Your Own Words

Often you use your words to retell something that someone else has said. Suppose a friend named Mike tells you about a trip he has taken. Later that day you see another friend who also knows Mike. When you tell the second friend that you talked to Mike earlier, she asks if he said anything about his vacation. You then retell what Mike told you. However, in the retelling, the words you choose and the structure of your sentences will not be the same as Mike's.

A paraphrase is similar, but because the author's words and sentences are there on the page to keep reminding you exactly what the author is saying, putting the information into your own words can be difficult. The following strategies can help.

Change the Sentence Structure   Try not to use the same type and order of clauses and phrases that are used in the source you are paraphrasing.

E X E R C I S E   7.1   Rewrite the following sentences by reversing the order of the sentence structure. Don't worry now about writing a successful paraphrase; just concentrate on changing the sentence structure.

1. Like Napoleon before him, Hitler blundered when he ordered an invasion of Russia in the winter.
2. Because of the severity of the Russian winter, Napoleon's troops became sick and demoralized.
3. Hitler should have learned from the lesson of history.
4. Also the Russian invasion meant the Germans were fighting on two fronts; thus the German army was not at full strength on either front.
5. Historians generally believe that the Russian invasion marked the downfall of the German war machine.

Paraphrase "Blindly"   This means to read the whole paragraph (or paragraphs), make notes, and then write a paraphrase without looking back at the material. Paraphrasing blindly will help you to change the sentence structure because you often won't remember the structure of the author's sentences.

EXERCISE 7.2 Using the sentences in Exercise 7.1, read the first one carefully, cover it with a sheet of paper, and rewrite the sentence. Repeat the process for each sentence. Then compare these sentences to the first set you wrote. This set of sentences should contain more of your own words.

Do Not Use More Than Three or Four Consecutive Words of the Source Even when you try to change the sentence structure and use your own words, you will often find that your paraphrase still contains three- or four-word phrases that belong to the author. Unless these are very common phrases — for example, "in the morning" — you should rewrite the words or even the whole sentence.

EXERCISE 7.3 Compare the sentences you wrote in Exercise 7.2 with the original sentences. Underline any phrases in which you used more than three or four consecutive words from the original. Rewrite those sentences in which you did.

Use Synonyms A synonym is a word that means approximately the same thing as another word. In the following sentence the words *appeared* and *looked* are synonyms:

> Yesterday morning the patient appeared better, but by evening he looked ill again.

Students who lack experience in paraphrasing often think they can merely replace a few words in a source with synonyms and have a good paraphrase. Synonyms are helpful and should be used, but they are only one step in paraphrasing. Make sure that you follow the other rules for paraphrasing too.

EXERCISE 7.4 Read over the set of sentences you wrote in Exercise 7.3 and see if you can use synonyms for any of the words in your sentences.

Use Key Words from the Source While you need to paraphrase in your words, you cannot and need not substitute a different word for every word in the original. The paraphrase of Whetmore earlier in this chapter used the words *television* and *presidents*. Because these are common words in the English language and do not belong exclusively to

Whetmore, another writer can use them in a paraphrase. To substitute the slang word *tube* for television would be needless and silly. To substitute *chief executives of America* would also be needless and would sound unnatural. Whetmore is writing about television and presidents. Those are his key words, and the paraphrase must use them if it is to present the source clearly.

E X E R C I S E 7.5 In the following passage, underline the words that you think would be absolutely necessary to keep in a paraphrase.

> The scholars of the intellectual effects of television routinely insist that no more than an "association" can be verified between poor performance in school and hours of TV viewing. There's no scientific proof of cause and effect, they report. Some even scoff at the thought it might exist, pointing out that in the pre-TV era, those hours that kids now spend before the TV were devoted to radio listening and comic books.
>
> Daniel Greenberg, "Electronic Gizmos Make Us Stupid"

Striking or catchy language: Clever phrases that show the writer's imagination and originality. In writing about a source, writers must paraphrase or quote striking or catchy language.

Do Not Use Striking or Catchy Language In referring to **striking or catchy language,** we mean that some writers use clever phrases that most people would not think of. For instance, if ten students wrote a paragraph on Michael Jordan, the Chicago Bulls' basketball player, and one student described Jordan as "a whirling dervish in gym shorts," that student would be using striking or catchy language and you could not use those words in a paraphrase.

Striking or catchy language is a group of words that is original and imaginative. Think about your everyday conversations. Just joking around, you often hear people use striking or catchy phrases. Often you repeat them in your own conversation. That's okay because conversation is not published writing. But remember that when you paraphrase, you should not use another author's striking or catchy phrases. If you want to use them, you will need to put quotation marks around them (explained in later sections in this chapter).

Parenthetical Citation

Parenthetical citation: The page number of a source in parentheses following a paraphrase, summary, or quotation.

When you paraphrase a source, you need to tell your readers the page from which you have taken the information. **Parenthetical citation** means that you put the page number in parentheses following the material:

> Gideon E. Nelson says that there are two basic reasons why Americans have become strongly diet conscious: health and vanity (52).

Note the page number in parentheses following the last word in the sentence but coming before the period. You should also use parenthetical citation when you are summarizing or quoting sources, two methods covered later in this chapter.

EXERCISE 7.6 Rewrite the following sentences to eliminate the striking or catchy language.

1. Love thy neighbor as thyself.
2. Neither a borrower nor a lender be.
3. Jim awoke to a frog-drowning rain.
4. When want is mistaken for need, we fall the victim of greed.
5. I am having a Big Mac attack.

EXERCISE 7.7 The following passage is from an essay on the astronomy of the Mayans, a tribe of Indians living in Mexico from approximately A.D. 400 until the 1500s, when they were conquered by Spanish explorers. Following the paragraph are three student paraphrases. Read the original source and then the student paraphrases. One of the student passages is a good paraphrase. Mark it correct. The other two violate some of the rules of paraphrasing. If the paraphrase is not satisfactory, identify the rules that are violated by specific phrases.

Original Source

We know that Mayan astronomers of Mexico and Guatemala recorded and predicted eclipses long before European contact. One of three priceless Mayan manuscripts left after the Spanish conquest is a record of observed and predicted solar eclipses as well as other astronomical information, such as the motions of Venus. Tragically, because the Spaniards burned 27 other Mayan manuscripts in 1562, we may never know the extent of Mayan knowledge.

William K. Hartmann, *Astronomy: The Cosmic Journey,* p. 25

Student Paraphrase 1

We know that Mayan astronomers, who lived in Mexico and Guatemala, recorded and predicted eclipses before Europeans came to explore South America. One of three Mayan manuscripts left after the Spanish conquest of the Mayans shows that they predicted and observed solar eclipses as well as other astronomical knowledge. Unfortunately, because the Spanish destroyed 27 other Mayan manuscripts, we may never know the knowledge of these early astronomers (25).

Student Paraphrase 2

Hartmann explains that before the European exploration of South America, Mayan astronomers living in Mexico and Guatemala kept records of eclipses and even predicted them. This information comes from a Mayan manuscript that tells not only about eclipses but about other aspects of Mayan astronomy such as the movements of Venus. The Mayans may have known a lot more about astronomy, but we cannot tell because in 1562 the Spanish, who conquered the Mayans, burned 27 other manuscripts that might have told us more about Mayan knowledge (25).

Student Paraphrase 3

According to Hartmann, the Mayan astronomers of Mexico and Guatemala could record and predict eclipses before Europeans discovered the New World. A priceless manuscript that the Mayans left after the Spaniards conquered them tells of observing solar eclipses as well as other astronomical data. Unfortunately, the Spaniards burned 27 other Mayan manuscripts, so we will never know the extent or the depth of Mayan knowledge (25).

EXERCISE 7.8 The following is another student paraphrase of Hartmann's source on Mayan astronomy. It uses tags and is in the student's own words, but there is a major problem. Identify and explain why this is not a good paraphrase.

Hartmann shows that the Mayans, who lived in Mexico and Guatemala, were pretty good astronomers even before the Europeans came to the New World. An old manuscript from the time after the Mayans were conquered by the Spanish shows that the Mayans kept records of eclipses and were able to predict them. But we can't know how much the Mayans knew because of the Spanish. Hartmann says that the Spanish were too dumb to know that the Mayans were geniuses, so they burned the rest of the Mayan manuscripts because they could not understand them (25).

EXERCISE 7.9 Paraphrase each of the following sources. Follow these steps: (1) Read and annotate the source. (2) Jot down notes from your annotations. (3) Cover the source with a sheet of paper; write the paraphrase from the notes you jotted down. (4) Use a page number in parentheses to refer to the location of the information.

1. Despite the technological sophistication and excellence evident in today's stereo records, many aspects of records have

remained constant since 1894. Their color, for instance. The earliest discs were made of hard rubber, which was naturally black. Modern vinyl, naturally colorless, is dyed black, because people have always expected records to be black.

Dr. Demento, "Record Innovations over the Years Recalled," p. 6

2. The weight lifter, or those who emphasize isometrics or calisthenics, represent muscular fitness. These types who have the right motives but wrong approach are stuck with the myth that muscular fitness means physical fitness. This is one of the great misconceptions in the field of exercise. The muscles that show — the skeletal muscles — are just one system in the body and by no means most important. If your exercise program is directed only at the skeletal muscles, you'll never achieve real fitness.

Kenneth Cooper, *Aerobics,* p. 2

■ Summarizing

When you write a paraphrase, you present everything the author says in his or her sentence or paragraph. Paraphrasing can come in handy when all the specific examples are important to the main idea of the source or when you want to show how the author is using the specific examples. But when you write your own essay in response to a source, you cannot paraphrase the whole source. Imagine trying to paraphrase a whole textbook, or even one chapter! Your essay would be as long as the source, you would not have room for your own ideas, and your reader could just as easily read the original source rather than your paper.

Summary: A concise version of a source containing only its main ideas, not its examples.

Unlike a paraphrase, a **summary** is a short version of the source, presenting only the author's main idea. Because a summary is short, it is also general. As a short version of the source, the summary does *not* present all the specific examples as a paraphrase does. Again, you use summaries all the time in everyday conversations. Suppose you have taken a major examination. After class, you meet a friend and she asks about the exam. Because you don't have time to stop and tell her all about it, you say, "It was tough, but I think I did okay." Your answer is a summary. It gives your friend only a general idea of the exam. Compare this short summary answer to the longer, detailed answer you would give if you were having lunch with a friend who asked to hear all about your exam. Then you would probably tell how long the exam was, what the questions were like, how many questions there were, how long it took you to complete them, and so on. A summary leaves out these specific details. It tells rather than shows.

The section in Chapter 2 on specific writing told you to show rather than tell. In a summary, you do just the opposite. This does not mean that summaries are poor writing. Their purpose is to present the general idea or ideas of a source so that you can respond in your own writing.

Basically, when you summarize a paragraph, you pick out the main idea and, using your own words, state it in one or two sentences. When you summarize a whole essay, you begin by stating its thesis and then you state the main ideas from sections or paragraphs that support and develop the thesis, all in your own words.

Summary Length

Summaries are always much shorter than the original version. However, summaries can be different lengths. For example, you could summarize Banesh Hoffman's essay about Albert Einstein (Chapter 2) in one sentence or one paragraph:

One Sentence

Banesh Hoffman says that although Einstein was brilliant, he was a simple man who could make people feel at ease around him.

One Paragraph

According to Banesh Hoffman, Albert Einstein was a simple man. He did not ask for a large salary when he was hired by Princeton. He acted very casually with people even when he was in his office. Even though Einstein was brilliant, he did not always grasp mathematical problems quickly. Because he acted like an average person, people less intelligent than Einstein were comfortable when talking to him.

Summaries and Your Purpose

The length of a summary is related to your purpose. You can use any of the following strategies to write a summary.

1. Write a one-paragraph or a one-page summary of something you have read for a class, such as a textbook chapter. This kind of summary serves two purposes. First, by summarizing the material, you understand the main points of the source. Second, the summary can help you study when the time comes to be examined on the source.
2. Use a one-paragraph summary in a paper on a source. Your introduction to the paper might summarize the source before you move into a more detailed discussion of the source's points. In a longer paper on more than one source, you might use a one-paragraph summary in the body of your paper to set up a comparison of one source with another.
3. Write a one-sentence summary to show briefly the point of a source before you move to your own points. Such a one-sentence summary is too brief to use for study notes, but it can be very handy when you are writing papers on sources.

Whether you are using a one-paragraph or one-sentence summary, remember to cite it with the page number in parentheses.

EXERCISE 7.10 Write a one-sentence summary of each of the paragraphs in Exercise 7.9

EXERCISE 7.11 Pick one of the essays in this book and summarize it first in one paragraph of no more than 100 words and then in a sentence of 20–25 words.

EXERCISE 7.12 In a paragraph of 50–100 words, summarize one of the essays that you have written for this class. Then summarize your essay in a sentence of no more than 20 words.

■ Using Quotations from Sources

In paraphrasing and summarizing, you put the words of a source into your own words. Paraphrasing and summarizing are handy and necessary skills because you learn a great deal by being able to understand a source well enough to put it in your words. Also, when you write papers in college and on the job, you cannot copy a source word for word.

Sometimes, however, you might want to use the original words from a source for one of these reasons:

1. The language is so striking or catchy that you would like to have it preserved in your paper. It would be foolish, for instance, to paraphrase John F. Kennedy's famous statement "Ask not what your country can do for you, ask what you can do for your country." By quoting Kennedy word for word, you allow his language to have the same impact on your reader that it first had on you.
2. The language is too complex to paraphrase. In such a case, you might feel that if you were to paraphrase, you would change the meaning of the source. This problem comes up sometimes when you are working with highly technical material or with a subject that is difficult for you.
3. You want to give the reader a general idea of the language of the source. If you were writing about literature — a poem or a short story — using quotations would give your reader some idea of the style of the writer.

Quotation: Exact words from a source, indicated by quotation marks.

When you quote, you need to remember that the **quotation** must contain the *exact* words of the source. Whatever your reason for quoting a source, you set off the quotation with *quotation marks*. The quotation marks tell your readers that the words between the marks belong to the source.

When quoting, you also need to use tags. You can place a tag before the quote, as in paraphrasing: John F. Kennedy said, "Ask not what your country can do for you, ask what you can do for your country." Or you can place the tag in parentheses after the quotation at the end of your sentence: "Ask not what your country can do for you, ask what you can do for your country" (John F. Kennedy). Also remember to cite the page number in parentheses when you quote, just as you did when paraphrasing and summarizing.

<table>
</table>

Strategies for Quoting	You can use many strategies for quoting a source in your writing. The following discussions, examples, and exercises will help you learn to use the different strategies. As you study each strategy, remember that you must use the author's exact words; you must tag the quotation with the author's name, either in the wording of the sentence or in parentheses at the end of the sentence; and you must give the page number, in parentheses, where the quotation comes from in the source.

Quote a Small Piece of the Source in Your Sentence   This strategy allows you to include short phrases or sentences that use striking or catchy language or language that it would be too difficult to paraphrase.

> Many people get cheated on repairs, and one "gold mine for crooked repairmen" is air-conditioner repair (Purdy, 9).

> Holidays aren't what they used to be, yet greeting card companies, as Betty Rollin says, have come up with "an infinite variety of occasions about which to fashion a 50-cent card" (1).

> The average person pays his check after eating, but "it would be remarkably easy to wander away from a meal without paying" (Greene, 29).

When you quote a brief part of the source, make sure that it fits into your sentence correctly. Sometimes the use of a quotation can lead to an error in grammar if you are not careful. What is the error in the following sentence?

> The average person pays his check after eating "it would be remarkably easy to wander away from a meal without paying" (Greene, 29).

If you could not recognize the error right away, consider that the student's words make up one complete sentence: *The average person pays his check after eating.* And the quotation of author Bob Greene makes up another complete sentence: *"It would be remarkably easy to wander away from a meal without paying."* But the two sentences are run together without punctuation and a connecting word. Thus, the student has written a run-on sentence (see Chapter 10). If you compare the run-on sentence to the correct example preceding it, you will see that the comma and connecting word *but* allow the two sentences to be joined correctly.

Introduce a Quoted Sentence with a Colon   Using a colon is one way to avoid a run-on sentence when you are joining your sentence to a sentence from a source. Aside from helping you avoid an error, the colon is a useful strategy for quoting a source. Study the following examples:

> The punishment a man absorbs in a boxing ring is not always evident while the fight is taking place: "A prizefighter may be able to survive even repeated brain concussions, but the damage to his brain may be permanent" (Smith, 11).

> Jane E. Brody argues that marijuana has various effects on the brain: "a marijuana high impairs memory, learning, speech, reading comprehension, arithmetic problem-solving and the ability to think" (16).

The colon allows you to state a point and then support it with a quotation. When you use a colon, you must have a complete sentence before it.

Introduce a Quotation with the Word *That*   One of the easiest ways to quote a complete sentence from a source is to use a dependent clause beginning with *that*. As in the following examples, you begin with a tag and a verb and then connect the quoted sentence with *that*.

> Desmond Morris shows that "we evolved as tribal animals, living in comparatively small groups, probably of less than a hundred and we existed like that for millions of years" (66).

> Michel Foucault points out that "for a long time, one of the characteristic privileges of sovereign power was the right to decide life and death" (135).

You can also add information to the beginning of a sentence before you introduce the quotation with *that,* as in this example:

> In discussing public speaking, George Plimpton notes that "once the mood of an audience is set, it is difficult to change it, which is why introductions are important" (2).

Here the phrase before Plimpton's name provides a context for the quotation that follows. The quotation itself does not refer to public speaking and could in fact refer to writing, but the writer's opening phrase clarifies Plimpton's topic.

Block quotations: Long quotations (more than fifty or one hundred words) indented ten spaces from the left margin and presented without quotation marks.

Use Block Quotations   Sometimes you might want to quote more than a sentence or two. You use a **block quotation** for such long quotations. How long is long? Some style manuals say fifty words. Others recommend one hundred. Use fifty as a general rule unless your instructor specifies otherwise.

When you introduce a block quotation in a finished paper, drop down one extra space (a total of three spaces in a double-spaced paper). Then indent the quotation ten spaces from the left margin if you are typing and roughly one inch if you are writing by hand. If the quotation is the beginning of a paragraph, indent the first line three more spaces to show the paragraph. Do not use quotation marks around the quotation. The block form tells the reader that the information is quoted. The following is an example of a long quotation in a student paper. Notice how the student leads up to the quotation with her own sentence and then follows the quotation with a discussion of her point. Notice also that the quotation is *not* in quotation marks.

> Ken Purdy shows that dishonest repairmen will prey on women very often:
>
> > An Ellenville, N.Y., woman, Mrs. Marian Talken, had trouble with her clothes dryer. The repairman told her it needed a new drive-shaft and bearings. The bill was $72 and when the original trouble recurred, he wouldn't come back. Another repairman charged $13 to take the dryer apart and show Mrs. Talken that the same old drive-shaft was still in business at the same old spot (14).
>
> Mrs. Talken's experience is unfortunate and is one of many examples of women being victimized by repairmen. But this is happening less because women today are becoming wiser about cars and appliances as their interests broaden with their independence.

Block quotations enable you to include a fairly long piece of the source. You can often use them to support your thesis. Or, as this student did, you can use them to set up a point of disagreement. When you use a block quotation, make sure that you follow with some discussion of your own. Don't just put the quotation in and leave the reader to figure out why it is there. Also, use block quotations sparingly. A paper with many of them will look as if you are merely stringing together information from sources without using your own ideas.

Ellipsis points: Three spaced periods used in the middle of a quotation to show that some words have been omitted from the source's sentence.

Use Ellipsis Points in Quotations   Suppose you want to quote only part of a sentence. If you cut something from the beginning of the sentence, you simply work the quotation into your sentence without losing the meaning of the source. If you cut something in the middle or at the end of a quotation because you don't need the whole quotation, then you use **ellipsis points.** Ellipsis points are spaced periods that tell readers that something has been left out of the quotation. The following example shows how ellipsis points work in practice.

Source

      At a newly established taste and smell clinic at the University of Connecticut at Farmington, researchers are finding that the overwhelming majority of patients complaining of a loss of taste really have something wrong with their ability to smell. The clinic is one of two "chemosensory" research and treatment centers (the other is at the University of Pennsylvania) recently established under grants from the National Institute of Neurological and Communicative Disorders and Stroke, in part to help the more than two million American adults who cannot smell and taste normally.

Jane E. Brody, "What the Nose Knows," p. 1

Quotation in a Student Paper

      According to Jane E. Brody, at the University of Connecticut there is a taste and smell clinic which "is one of two 'chemosensory' research and treatment centers (the other is at the University of Pennsylvania) recently established . . . in part to help the more than two million American adults who cannot smell and taste normally" (1).

Notice that the ellipsis points in the middle of the sentence were used in place of the information about the clinics' grants. The student chose to cut this information because her purpose in the paragraph was to show how people with taste and smell disorders are being helped. She really did not need to say how the clinics were funded.

     Suppose the student's purpose had been to emphasize how medical clinics are funded. Then she might have quoted the information about the grants but cut the information about the people. Compare the following example with the one preceding.

Quotation in a Student Paper

      Recently, funding has been provided to clinics which study rare medical problems. According to Jane E. Brody, the University of Connecticut at Farmington has set up a clinic to study problems with taste and smell. This clinic "is one of two 'chemosensory' research and treatment centers (the other is at the University of Pennsylvania) recently established under grants from the National Institute of Neurological and Communicative Disorders and Stroke . . ." (1).

In this example the writer emphasizes funding, not the benefits of the clinic for people. The purpose of her paper was to show how funding supports medical clinics.

Use Square Brackets in Quotations   Sometimes a quotation will not make sense in your sentence unless you change a word to fit the context of your paper or the grammar of the sentence. Suppose you write:

> Ken Purdy says that "now it seems to me that it hasn't been done at all" (10).

Square brackets: Placed around a word or words that the writer has added to a quotation.

Seems to *you* or to Purdy? What hasn't been done? The pronoun *it* has no noun to refer to. Notice how the words in **square brackets** clear up these questions:

> Ken Purdy says that "now it seems to [him] that [repair work] hasn't been done at all" (10).

Although brackets can be handy in integrating quotations, avoid using them too much. Instead try to choose quotations that can be worked in without brackets or paraphrase the source. Reserve brackets for important quotations that won't fit any other way.

E X E R C I S E   7.13   Use the following passage to illustrate the six strategies for using quotations. Writing your own sentences, devise ideas that you want the quotations to support. Before writing your sentences, underline key points and annotate the paragraph.

> It is hard for us today to realize how very widely communities were separated from one another when they depended for transportation wholly on the railroad and the horse and wagon — and when telephones were scarce, and radios nonexistent. A town which was not situated on a railroad was really remote. A farmer who lived five miles outside the county seat made something of an event of hitching up and taking the family to town for a Saturday afternoon's shopping. (His grandchildren make the run in a casual ten minutes, and think nothing of it.) A trip to see friends ten miles away was likely to be an all-day expedition, for the horses had to be given a chance to rest and be fed.
>
> Frederick Lewis Allen, *The Big Change: America Transforms Itself, 1900–1950*, p. 96

■ Documenting Your Sources

If you paraphrase, summarize, and quote your sources correctly, you are on your way to writing a successful source essay and avoiding plagiarism. But to complete the job, you need to document your sources. This means to give credit to the writers whose ideas and words you have integrated into your essay.

When you use a source's ideas or words in your essay, you need to show the reader who and where they come from. If you include a tag, the reader will know whose ideas they are. You also need to use parenthetical citation, that is, to give the page number of the source where those ideas are found.

■ Preparing a List of Works Cited

List of works cited: This is a list of the sources that have been cited in a source essay. Each item on the list is called an entry and it must be written according to the form used for the kind of source it describes.

When you write in response to one or more sources, you usually include a list of the sources at the end of the paper with all the information about each source: author, title, date and place of publication, publisher, and so on. If readers want to read more of a source, they can find it and look up the pages cited in parentheses in your paper.

This list of sources is called a **list of works cited.** You begin it on a new page of your paper, and at the top of it you write ''Works Cited.'' For short papers in college, you may not be required to include this list if your instructor is familiar with the source or sources, as in the case of a paper written in response to a textbook chapter or some newspaper articles. For longer essays and term papers, you almost always need to include a list of works cited.

Each type of source has a particular form that you must use when putting it on the list. The following examples conform to the style of the Modern Language Association, an organization of English teachers. This style is widely used in many fields, but as you advance in your major, you should find out if your field has its own style. For most college writing this style is acceptable.

Entry: A listing of a source in a list of works cited.

Once a source is on the list in the proper form, it is called an **entry.** As you take more advanced writing courses, you will learn about the proper style for citing many different kinds of sources. This section presents a few of the more common ones.

A Book with One Author

A book with one author is the simplest of entries, and the same style is used no matter what kind of book you are entering, as long as it has only one author.

Gray, Michael. *Song and Dance Man: The Art of Bob Dylan.* New York: Dutton, 1974.

1. The author's name is written last name first followed by a comma, first name, and a period.
2. Second is the title of the book followed by a period. Titles of books are printed in italics, but when you type or handwrite them, underline them.

3. Third is the city where the book was published followed by a colon. (You do not need to add the state for books published in the United States.)
4. Next is the name of the publisher, in shortened form.
5. Last is the date the book was published.

The information about the city, the publisher, and the date is printed on the title page or copyright page of most books.

Notice that the first line of the entry is placed against the margin. Any line after the first is indented five spaces.

A Book with More Than One Author

When a book has two authors, use this form for your entry:

Kinnear, Thomas C., and Kenneth L. Bernhardt. *Principles of Marketing.* Glenview: Scott, 1986.

1. The first author's name is written with last name first, a comma, and first name, just as in an entry for a book with one author. The first author's name is the one that appears first on the title page of the book. (The names are not necessarily in alphabetical order.)
2. Write "and," the name of the second author in regular order, first name is first, last name last. Then put a period.
3. The rest of the information follows the same form used for a book with one author. Notice that *Scott* is the shortened form for the publisher Scott, Foresman.

For a book with more than two authors, use this form:

Divine, Robert A., et al. *America: Past and Present.* Glenview: Scott, 1986.

1. The first author's name is in the same form as in the other entries for books, but it is followed by a comma, the words "et al.," and a period. (*Et al.* means "and others" in Latin.)
2. The remaining information is in the same order as the information for books with one or two authors.

An Essay in a Book

Sometimes essays appear in books by other authors or in collections of essays put together by an editor. When you use such a source, write its entry this way:

Curtin, Sharon. "Aging in the Land of the Young." *Patterns of Exposition 8.* Ed. Randall E. Decker. Boston: Little, 1982. 255–58.

1. The name of the author of the essay follows the same pattern as in other entries: last name, comma, first name, period.
2. Next comes the title of the essay, followed by a period and placed in quotation marks.

3. After the underlined title of the book and a period comes "Ed.," the abbreviation for "editor," and then the editor's name, in regular order.
4. The city, publisher, and year of publication follow, and then the page numbers on which the essay appears followed by a period.

Sources in Magazines

Often you may use an article, essay, or column from a magazine. Entries for sources from magazines have different styles depending on whether the magazine is published each week or each month. For a source in a weekly magazine, use this form:

Zucker, Seymour. "The Good News Behind the Upturn in Interest Rates." *Business Week* 12 Mar. 1984: 83.

1. The author's name is written with last name first, a comma, first name, and a period.
2. The title of the article is followed by a period and is placed in quotation marks.
3. Next is the title of the magazine. Underline it, but do not put a period after it.
4. Next is the day of the month the magazine was published, followed by the month and year and a colon. There are no commas or periods between title, day, month, and year. All the months *except* May, June, and July are abbreviated to three or four letters.
5. Last is the page number on which the source appeared.

For a monthly magazine, use this form:

Crenshaw, Ben. "Make More Short Putts." *Golf* Sept. 1982: 58–61.

This is the same form as for a weekly magazine, except that the day of the month is not given.

Sources in Newspapers

Whether you are citing an editorial, an article, a feature, or a column, use the following form for a source from a newspaper:

O'Brien, Dennis. "It's Simply Classical Economics." *USA Today* 3 March 1987: sec. A: 4.

1. All the information up to the abbreviation "sec." (which stands for "section") is in the same form as in an entry for a source in a weekly magazine.
2. Following the abbreviation, the "A" indicates that O'Brien's column appeared in section A of the paper, and the colon separates the section letter from the page number. Some papers use letters for sections, others use numbers, and some do not mark

sections at all. If sections are not marked, just put the page number after the colon following the date.

Interviews

Sometimes interviews are printed in magazines, and sometimes you might interview someone yourself and then use the information in your paper, either paraphrased or quoted. In your paper, you do not use parenthetical references to an interview you conducted verbally, although you do use a tag and you place the interview in the list of works cited. There are two kinds of interview entries: one for a personal interview and another for a telephone interview.

Volkers, Judy. Personal interview. 21 June 1987.
Brackney, James, Police Commissioner. Telephone interview. 14 March 1988.

1. The name of the person comes first with last name first, a comma, and a period.
2. If the person's title is important, put that next followed by a period before indicating the type of interview.
3. Next indicate the type of interview.
4. Last is the date in this order: day, month, and year without commas between them and with a period at the end.

These are sample entries for common sources. There are, however, different forms for other kinds of sources, such as scholarly journals, books in volumes, government reports, and so on. If you use a source and you do not know how to make an entry for it, you can find the proper style in *MLA Handbook for Writers of Research Papers,* 3rd ed. (New York: MLA, 1988), or you can look in a grammar book or ask your instructor.

Essay for Reading

Symbols of Mankind
Don Lago

In this essay, Don Lago discusses the development of symbols for communication, from early pictures to modern writing. He also shows how humans will have to use pictures to communicate if we discover other civilizations in space.

Vocabulary Cues

binary: having two parts

embodied: represented in bodily form; in this essay, represented in readable form

ideograms: characters or symbols, such as Chinese writing symbols, that represent an idea or a thing without words

interstellar: between stars; in this essay, related to communication in space

massive: very large, huge

pictograph: a picture that represents a word or idea

profound: far-reaching, important, having depth and seriousness

syllabic: having to do with syllables, the distinct parts of words sounded in speech

Questions to Guide Your Reading

1. How did people first start to represent thoughts through symbols? Were these symbols letters or pictures?
2. In representing thoughts in symbols, what did early humans discover?
3. What happened when people developed letters and an alphabet?
4. How are humans now attempting to communicate with beings in outer space?

Many thousands of years ago, a man quietly resting on a log reached down and picked up a stick and with it began scratching upon the sand at his feet. He moved the stick slowly back and forth and up and down, carefully guiding it through curves and straight lines. He gazed upon what he had made, and a gentle satisfaction lighted on his face.

Other people noticed this man drawing on the sand. They gazed upon the figures he had made, and though they at once recognized the shapes of familiar things such as fish or birds or humans, they took a bit longer to realize what the man had meant to say by arranging these familiar shapes in this particular way. Understanding what he had done, they nodded and smiled in recognition.

This small band of humans didn't realize what they were beginning. The images these people left in the sand would soon be swept away by the wind, but their new idea would slowly grow until it had remade the human species. These people had discovered writing.

Writing, early people would learn, could contain much more information than human memory could and contain it more accurately. It could carry thoughts much farther than mere sounds could — farther in distance and in time. Profound thoughts born in a single mind could spread and endure.

The first written messages were simply pictures relating familiar objects in some meaningful way — pictographs. Yet there were no images for much that was important in human life. What, for instance, was the image for sorrow or bravery? So from pictographs humans developed ideograms to represent more abstract ideas. An eye flowing with tears could represent sorrow, and a man with the head of a lion might be bravery.

The next leap occurred when the figures became independent of things or ideas and came to stand for spoken sounds. Written figures were free to lose all resemblance to actual objects. Some societies developed syllabic systems of writing in which several hundred signs corresponded to several hundred spoken sounds. Others discovered the much simpler alphabetic system, in which a handful of signs represented the basic sounds the human voice can make.

At first, ideas flowed only slightly faster when written than they had through speech. But as technologies evolved, humans embodied their thoughts in new ways; through the printing press, in Morse code, in electromagnetic waves bouncing through the atmosphere and in the binary language of computers.

Today, when the Earth is covered with a swarming interchange of ideas, we are even trying to send out thoughts beyond our planet to other minds in the Universe. Our first efforts at sending our thoughts beyond Earth have taken a very ancient form: pictographs. The first message, on plaques aboard Pioneer spacecraft launched in 1972 and 1973, featured a simple line drawing of two humans, one male and one female, the male holding up his hand in greeting. Behind them was an outline of the Pioneer spacecraft, from which the size of the humans could be judged. The plaque also included the "address" of the two human figures: a picture of the solar system, with a spacecraft emerging from the third planet. Most scientists believe that when other civilizations attempt to communicate with us they too will use pictures.

All the accomplishments since humans first scribbled in the sand have led us back to where we began. Written language only works when two individuals know what the symbols mean. We can only return to the simplest form of symbol available and work from there. In interstellar communication, we are at the same stage our ancestors were when they used sticks to trace a few simple images in the sand.

We still hold their sticks in our hands and draw pictures with them. But the stick is no longer made of wood; over the ages that piece of wood has been transformed into a massive radio telescope. And we no longer write on sand; now we write our thoughts onto the emptiness of space itself.

Questions for Study and Discussion
1. The main focus of the essay is on
    a. communicating through pictures;
    b. different means of communication in the development of humans;
    c. communicating with beings from outer space.
2. List the most important steps in the development of writing.
3. How are we similar to our early ancestors? How are we different?
4. Why did the Pioneer spacecraft carry a pictograph rather than a written message?
5. Cite three instances of striking or catchy language that you would have to eliminate or quote if you were paraphrasing this essay.
6. Cite five key words that you would have to use if you were paraphrasing this essay.

Writing Assignments
1. Choose two of the paragraphs in Lago's essay and paraphrase them. Make sure you include all the examples as well as the main idea.
2. Rewrite your paraphrases from number 1, this time working in quotations. Do not quote too much, but try to choose the language that you quote carefully.
3. Write an essay that demonstrates why writing is or is not important in your chosen field. Try to use a few of Lago's ideas in your essay. Paraphrase or quote them and do not forget to use tags.

CHAPTER 8

Writing the Single-Source Essay

As you begin to write essays in response to sources, the methods you learned in Chapter 7 — paraphrasing, summarizing, using quotations — will help you convey the ideas in the source. However, after beginning writers have learned to paraphrase and summarize, they sometimes think that a source essay should merely retell what the source says, without including what they themselves want to say on the topic. Just the opposite is true. Along with what the source says, your opinions, observations, questions, and ideas will make up the content of your essay. If readers just wanted to know what a source says, they could simply read it instead of your essay. What you have to say is the most important part of your essay.

This chapter concentrates on writing in response to one source. This type of writing is common in daily communication as well as in college assignments. A plant manager might be asked to write in response to a government inspection that found unsafe conditions in the plant. A sales manager might write an explanation responding to a report showing decreasing sales in his or her department. An accountant might write a report responding to the Internal Revenue Service's review of a client's tax return. A doctor might write an essay supporting or refuting the published findings of another doctor's research.

In college, the single-source essay is equally common. An elementary education major might be asked to give her opinion of some educator's theory of teaching. An engineering major might write an essay arguing against a professional essay that says that plastic pipe works better than copper for certain types of plumbing. Or any student might be asked to write an essay giving an opinion of an idea stated in a textbook. You may already have had to write such an essay for one of your classes.

The process you learned for writing essays from personal experience and observation also works when you are writing in response to a source. You will use invention strategies to discover ideas about the source. You will have to read and reread your draft as you write. And you will revise and edit the essay before it is finished. Because you are integrating the ideas from the source with your own ideas, the content of the essay will differ from the content of a personal essay, and, therefore, the product will be different. The process, however, is very similar, except that the reading of the source will become part of the process. To write about a source you must know what it says and for what purpose the writer has written.

■ Finding the Purpose of the Source

Chapter 6 discussed various strategies for reading. As you read a source you are going to respond to in an essay, you will need to put these strategies to work: annotating, finding main ideas, building a context, and so on. Also, you will need to apply some of what you know about writing. For example, you know that writers have a purpose in mind as they write. As you read, look for the writer's purpose because knowing it will help you find your own purpose when you respond to the source.

The purpose for writing can vary. A writer may merely want to inform his or her audience by presenting information without opinions. Or the writer may want to persuade the audience or argue a point, giving his or her opinions about the information. Compare the following paragraphs.

> Drowning is the second leading cause of accidental death for people between the ages of 4 and 44, according to the American National Red Cross. Twenty-eight percent of those drowned are children under 15 years old. Seven out of ten of them are boys.
>
> Carla Stephens, "Drownproofing"

> For 30 years now, this nation has been on a relentless expensive high-technology binge, forging for itself the machines and systems that are supposed to underpin — and to presage — our 21st-century lives. The only trouble is that all this high technology not only doesn't seem to be solving our problems, it actually looks to be compounding them.
>
> Kirkpatrick Sale, "The 'Miracle' of Technofix"

Both paragraphs come from the beginnings of essays, and you can already guess the purpose of each essay. Stephens's statistics on drowning inform her audience of the danger it poses. In her essay she goes on to present methods for teaching children how to avoid dangerous situations when swimming. While she certainly wants the audience to realize the importance of teaching children water safety, she achieves her purpose by informing with facts. Sale, in contrast, begins with an attack on technology. His claim that it causes more problems than it solves is obviously an opinion because many people believe the opposite. Following this opinion, he presents a series of examples to try to persuade the reader to accept his argument against technology. As the essay continues, Sale argues that solutions to the world's problems must come from people, not technology.

If you are writing an essay arguing that some form of technology is more trouble than it is worth, you might be able to draw on Sale's essay for support. Suppose your essay argues that the possible dangers of nuclear power plants outweigh the value of the energy they produce. Though Sale covers technology in general, you might be able to use some of his opinions because your essay would have a similar purpose — to persuade people to question a form of technology. In contrast, if you are writing in favor of some form of technology — say, the use of computers in schools — you could show how Sale overlooks some of the benefits technology provides. But whatever your topic, recognizing Sale's purpose would help you come up with your own.

E X E R C I S E   8.1   Identify the writer's purpose in each of the following paragraphs.

A new car simply presents a new set of troubles, which may be more disturbing than the beloved, familiar old troubles the old car presented. With your old car, strange troubles do not take you by surprise, but a new car's troubles are invariably terrifying for being strange and unexpected.

Russell Baker, "Auto Suggestion"

A 1972 survey of the amount of mathematics taken by incoming freshmen at Berkeley revealed that while 57 percent of boys has taken four years of high school math, only 8 percent of girls had the same amount of preparation. Without four years of high school math, students at Berkeley, and other colleges and universities, are ineligible for the calculus sequence, unlikely to attempt chemistry or physics, and inadequately prepared for statistics and economics.

Sheila Tobias, "Who's Afraid of Math, and Why?"

Australia has many strange beasts, one of the oddest of which is the koala. Perfectly adapted to one specific tree, the eucalyptus, this living teddy bear does not need anything else, not even a drink! The moisture in the leaves is just right for the koala, making it the only land animal that doesn't need water to supplement its food.

Jean George, "That Astounding Creator, Nature"

One difference between football and war, though, is that there is little or no protest against football. Perhaps the most extraordinary thing about the game is that the systematic infliction of injuries excites in people, not concern, as would be the case if they were sustained at say a rock festival, but a collective rejoicing and euphoria. Players and fans alike revel in the spectacle of a combatant felled into semiconsciousness, "blindsided," "clotheslined" or "decapitated."

John McMurtry, "Kill 'Em! Crush 'Em! Eat 'Em Raw"

■ Invention and the Single-Source Essay

As you are discovering the purpose of a source, whether it is a magazine article or a textbook chapter, ideas come to your mind. If you are reading an article in *Time* magazine about a new trade agreement between the United States and Japan, you might wonder how the agreement will affect automobile prices. You also might question whether the agreement will create or eliminate jobs. In short, you will be thinking and trying to make your own sense of the article, for as you saw in Chapter 6, reading is an active process. Though you would not annotate an article you read just for information or pleasure, if you are reading something to write about it, annotation will help you to discover ideas. As a result, your annotations will be part of the invention stage as they become items on a brainstorming list, spokes on a cluster diagram, ideas for freewriting, or answers to the journalist's questions. In other words, annotation is the beginning of invention when you write in response to a source.

Read the following short essay, noting the student annotations and the brainstorming list that follows.

FROM *The Great Chain of Life*
Joseph Wood Krutch

Joseph Wood Krutch was born in 1893 and died in 1970. Throughout his life, he thought and wrote on a wide range of topics, from literature to politics to ecology. He worked as a newspaper columnist, professor, and naturalist. This essay is a small part of *The Great Chain of Life,* one of the many books Krutch wrote.

It wouldn't be quite true to say that "some of my best friends are hunters." Still, I do number among my respected acquaintances some who not only kill for the sake of killing but count it among their keenest pleasures. And I can think of no better illustration of the fact that men may be separated at some point by a fathomless abyss yet share elsewhere much common ground. To me, it is inconceivable that anyone can think an animal more interesting dead than alive. I can also easily prove, to my own satisfaction, that killing "for sport" is the perfect type of pure evil for which metaphysicians have sometimes sought.

Most wicked deeds are done because the doer proposes some good for himself. The liar lies to gain some end; the swindler and the thief want things which, if honestly got, might be good in themselves. Even the murderer is usually removing some impediment to normal desires. Though all of these are selfish or unscrupulous, their deeds are not gratuitously evil. But the killer for sport seems to have no such excusable motive. He seems to prefer death to life, darkness to light. He seems to get nothing other than the satisfaction of saying: "Something which wanted to live is dead. Because I can bring terror and agony, I assure myself that I have power. Because of me there is that much less vitality, consciousness and perhaps joy in the universe. I am the spirit that denies." When a man wantonly destroys one of the works of man, we call him "Vandal." When he wantonly destroys one of the works of God, we call him "Sportsman."

The hunter-for-food may be as wicked and as misguided as vegetarians say, but he does not kill for the sake of killing. The ranchers and farmers who exterminate all living things not immediately profitable to them may be working against their own best interests; but whether they are or not, they hope to achieve some supposed good by the exterminations. If to do evil, not in the hope of gain but for evil's sake, involves the deepest guilt by which man can be stained, then killing for killing's sake is a terrifying phenomenon and as strong a proof as we could have of that "reality of evil" with which present-day theologians are concerned.

killing for sport = "pure evil"

sport killer has no reason

power trip

No.

sport killing shows "Reality of evil"

Brainstorming List   When you make a brainstorming list from your own reading, start with your annotations but also include other points that come to mind. The annotations should be part of the list, but they should generate additional points and ideas. The following is a brainstorming list you might have written in response to Krutch's essay.

Sport hunting true evil to Krutch.
No reason to kill for sport.
What about hunting for food?
Food hunters have reason but still might be wicked.
Killing for sport shows ''reality of evil.''
Killing for food not as bad.
I agree killing for sport is a kind of power trip.
Sometimes hunting helps animals, like necessary thinning of deer
      herds so the herd won't starve.
What about hunting for profit?
Much depends on whether animals are endangered species.
Almost instinct to hunt.
Kids kill bugs and small animals before they learn better.

Like any brainstorming list, this one needs to be sorted out. One way to begin sorting it is to make two lists: one of the points you might agree with and another of points you might disagree with and points the source overlooks.

Possible Agreement	*Possible Opposition*
No reason to kill for sport.	What about hunting for food?
Sport hunting true evil to Krutch.	Food hunters have reason but still might be wrong.
Killing for sport shows ''reality of evil.''	Killing for food not as bad.
Killing for sport is a kind of power trip.	Sometimes hunting helps animals, like necessary thinning of deer herds so the herd won't starve.
	What about hunting for money? Much depends on whether animals are endangered species.
	Almost instinct to hunt.
	Kids kill bugs and small animals before they learn better.

A glance at the lists shows that you have more points in opposition to Krutch than in agreement with him. You agree that killing animals for pure sport is wrong. However, the second list raises questions about additional points such as hunting for profit, hunting as a necessary thinning of herds, hunting endangered species, and hunting as possibly an instinct. In comparing these lists, you can begin to discover a purpose: to show that Krutch is partly right about hunting but that in overlooking some aspects of it, he has not seen the reasons for hunting for food. From this purpose, you can then formulate a thesis: Hunting purely for sport is wrong, but in most cases there is nothing wrong with hunting for food and profit.

■ Finding a Purpose and Thesis in Responding to a Source

If you have written even a simple book report in elementary or high school, you have some sense of how the writer's purpose controls what he or she says about the source. In a book report, often your purpose was merely to show your teacher that you read and understood the book. You included a summary of the book's plot or main points, a brief explanation of what they meant, and an evaluation of whether the book was worth reading. The last part of the purpose also generated a thesis on the value of the book.

Likewise, in the examples mentioned at the beginning of this chapter, each writer has a purpose. The plant manager must explain why government inspectors found unsafe conditions and show how those conditions can be corrected. This purpose would lead to a thesis stating agreement with the findings of the inspectors but arguing that the unsafe conditions will be corrected. The elementary education major would attempt to show her audience whether the educator's theory would work if put into practice in a classroom. Her thesis would answer that question.

In college assignments, the professor often will give you a writing assignment along with assigned reading. Thus, you can begin to think about your purpose for writing as you read. Suppose in a communications course, the professor assigned Don Lago's "Symbols of Mankind" along with this topic:

> Write an essay showing how humans have communicated and still communicate using symbols other than letters and words. Refer to Lago's examples but also show examples that you see in your daily life.

Given such a specific topic, you would know what the purpose of your paper would be even before you wrote it: to show that people still communicate with symbols other than letters and words. And you would have a built-in thesis: People still use symbols other than letters and words to communicate. Your task would be to find examples of such symbols and show how they are similar to those of the primitive people mentioned in Lago's essay.

Sometimes an assignment may not be specific. Suppose you are taking an ecology course and the professor assigns you to read Krutch's essay and write a response to it. Whether you use a brainstorming list, clustering, freewriting, or the journalist's questions, you will have to go through the process of invention to find your purpose and thesis just as we did in the text following Krutch's essay.

Use one or more of the invention strategies to find a purpose and thesis for writing in response to one of the following sources.

> As a people we Americans greatly prize success. And in our eyes success all too often means simply outdoing other people by virtue of achievement judged by some single scale — income or honors or headlines or trophies — and coming out at "the top." Only one person, as we see it, can be the best — can get the highest grades, be voted the most attractive girl or the boy most likely to succeed. Though we often rejoice in the success of people far removed from ourselves — in another profession, another community, or endowed with talent we do not covet — we tend to regard the success of people close at hand, within our own small group, as a threat. We fail to recognize that there are many kinds of success, including the kind of success that lies within a person.
>
> Margaret Mead and Rhoda Metraux, *A Way of Seeing*

> New research on the physical and athletic differences between men and women shows that in some respects women may be at least as tough as men. Some evidence suggests that women's endurance may be equal or perhaps even superior to men's. Women's bodies are constructed so that certain crucial organs are better guarded from injury; ovaries, for instance, lie inside the pelvic cavity, far better placed for protection than testicles.
>
> P. S. Wood, "'Female Athletes: They've Come a Long Way, Baby"

> It is possible to stop most drug addiction in the United States within a very short time. Simply make all drugs available and sell them at cost. Label each drug with a precise description of what effect — good and bad — the drug will have on the taker. This will require heroic honesty. Don't say that marijuana is addictive or dangerous when it is neither — unlike "speed," which kills most unpleasantly, or heroin, which is addictive and difficult to kick.
>
> Gore Vidal, "Drugs"

■ Organizing and Drafting a Source Essay

If you have defined your purpose and stated a thesis, you are ready to begin organizing and drafting your essay. But remember that just as when you write from personal experience, your thesis and purpose can change as you are writing because your ideas can change while writing.

Beginning with a possible thesis (remember that it can change), you can look back over your brainstorming list (or other invention list) to pick out points to support your thesis. For example, consider the thesis for the essay in response to Krutch's essay:

Hunting purely for sport is wrong, but in most cases there is nothing wrong with hunting for food and profit.

Since the first part of the thesis agrees with Krutch, you can evaluate the list of points under possible agreement. Suppose that in evaluating these, you find that although you are against sport hunting, you do not consider it the "pure evil" Krutch does. You do, however, agree that there is no reason to kill for sport, so you decide that this point will be the topic of your first body paragraph (Don't worry about the introduction; you can write it later, even last). You also notice that the only reason Krutch sees for killing for sport is that the hunter feels a kind of power. With these two points in mind, you can brainstorm again:

Only reason for sport killing is feeling of power.
Hunter doesn't use animal for food.
Hunter hangs up heads or skins, trophies.
Brags to his friends.
Not too brave to shoot an animal with a powerful gun.
Hunter feels brave, though.

Once you have some notes for your first body paragraph, you can then decide what you will say in the following paragraphs and in what order you will arrange your ideas. To do so, you can examine the list of points to support the second part of your thesis: that there is nothing wrong with hunting for food and profit. As you look through the list, you can discard points that you cannot use to support the thesis: children killing insects, the possibility that hunting is an instinct (this would be impossible to support in a short essay). You are left with three issues to develop to oppose Krutch's argument and support your own: hunting for food, hunting for profit, hunting as a means of thinning deer herds.

At this point, you can decide on the order in which you will cover these points. For instance, after your first body paragraph agreeing with Krutch's criticism of sport hunting, you might arrange the paragraphs in which you disagree in this order:

Paragraph defending hunting for food.
Paragraph on how hunting can thin deer herds to reduce starvation among deer.
Paragraph on hunting for profit.

As you draft the essay, you might find that you need more than one paragraph to cover one of the points, or you might decide to change the order of the paragraphs. You could do either one while drafting the essay or later in revising it. However, if you are not quite sure what you want to say on each point, you should do some brainstorming before drafting. You might make a brainstorming list like the following.

Hunting for Food

Not endangered species, plentiful animals.
Meat in supermarkets comes from animals killed for food too, no difference.
Laws against how many animals you can kill, even for food.
One deer provides lots of meals.
Good to freeze deer meat.
People in rural areas hunt a lot.

Once you have this much information for each paragraph, either in your head or on a list, you are ready to begin drafting the essay. In drafting, you need to organize and develop each paragraph as much as possible.

■ Organizing and Developing Body Paragraphs

Like the paragraphs in an essay, the paragraphs in an essay responding to a source should focus on and develop a point that supports your thesis. As you gain experience in responding to sources, you will discover your own means of organization. The following sections discuss several ways to organize body paragraphs so that they draw on the source while allowing you to develop your ideas.

The Three-Step Method

Three-step method: A method used to develop paragraphs in response to a source. Step 1: state the source's point; step 2: give your reaction to the source; step 3: provide support for your reaction.

The **three-step method** of organizing a paragraph works like a conversation. First, you state one point from the source. Second, you state your opinion of that point. Third, you back up your opinion with examples. This method can take different forms. You can use one form when you agree with an idea in the source, another when you disagree, another when you have mixed feelings about the idea, and still another when you want to raise an issue not mentioned in the source.

Agreeing with the Source   To use the three-step method to agree, pose these three questions:

1. What is the idea from the source and who said it? (Start with a tag and then paraphrase, quote, or use a combination of paraphrase and quotation.)
2. Why do you agree with the source?
3. What are your agreements or examples to support your agreement?

As you answer the questions, you will generate the information you need to develop a body paragraph, as the following example shows.

Step 1: Krutch says that killing animals just for sport is "pure evil."

Step 2: I agree because, as Krutch says, there is no reason to kill for sport except to gain a feeling of power.

Step 3: For example, take a big-game hunter who displays the heads of the animals on the wall of a den. This is just a way for the hunter to show off to others that he is brave. But really he is not because even a lion is no match for a high-powered rifle. And since people do not eat lions, all the hunter gets is the skin and the head, which are just trophies to show off.

As you can see, step 3 requires that you develop examples to support the agreement with Krutch stated in step 2. At this point, it may be necessary to return to the brainstorming list to come up with ideas and examples. At other times, you may have the topic more clearly in mind, and you can develop step 3 just by writing down your response to the question. Whatever the case, if step 3 is not fully developed, the paragraph will not be very specific. But if you think carefully about all three steps, you will end up with a well-developed body paragraph. Consider the paragraph based on the preceding example:

> Krutch says that killing animals just for sport is "pure evil." I agree because, as Krutch says, there is no reason to kill for sport except to gain a feeling of power. For example, a big-game hunter who displays the heads of the animals on the wall of a den is just showing off to others that he is brave. But really he is not very brave because even a lion is no match for a high-powered rifle. And since people do not eat lions, all the hunter gets is the skin and the head, which are just trophies to feed his ego.

EXERCISE 8.3 Choose a point you agree with in one of the paragraphs in Exercise 8.2. Using the three-step method, write a paragraph in response to it. Make sure step 3 is fully developed; use invention strategies if needed.

Disagreeing with the Source Just as you can use the three-step method to agree with a point in the source, you can also use it to disagree. For instance, the second part of the thesis in response to Krutch's essay says that most of the time it is acceptable to hunt for food. Krutch does not consider the "hunter-for-food" as evil as the sport hunter but says he may be "wicked and . . . misguided." The response essay disagrees. To use the three-step method for disagreeing, pose these questions:

1. What is the idea from the source and who said it? (Start with a tag and then paraphrase, quote, or use a combination of paraphrase and quotation.)
2. Why do you disagree with the source?
3. What are your arguments or examples to support your disagreement?

Again you answer the questions to develop the paragraph. Here is a sample paragraph with each step marked:

> (Step 1) Krutch claims that people who hunt for food "may be as wicked and misguided as the vegetarians sometimes say" (35). (Step 2) Krutch overlooks the fact that many people in rural areas hunt to help feed their families. (Step 3) Butchered and frozen, a deer can provide many meals for a family, and eating the meat from an animal killed by a hunter is no different from eating supermarket meat. In both cases, the animal was killed for food. Game laws prevent senseless killing, but even if they did not exist, hunters should not kill more food than they or their families can eat. Also, they should never hunt endangered species, but there is nothing wrong with hunting to feed a family.

E X E R C I S E   8.4   Choose an idea that you disagree with in one of the paragraphs in Exercise 8.2. Using the three-step method, write a paragraph showing why you disagree.

Writing a Mixed Response   Sometimes you will find two closely related points in a source. You may agree with one but disagree with the other, yet because the points are closely related, you want to respond to them in the same paragraph. You can use the three-step method in two different ways when you have such mixed feelings.

To stress agreement, use these questions:

1. What are the conflicting points from the source? (Start with a tag and then paraphrase, quote, or use a combination of paraphrase and quotation to state both points.)
2. What point do you disagree with and why? Give examples.
3. What point do you agree with and why? Begin with a transition to show contrast (such as *but, however, on the other hand, nevertheless*) and then state the point you agree with and give reasons.

As you read the following sample paragraph with the steps marked, notice how step 2, unlike in the earlier forms, is further developed. That is; to stress your agreement with part of the idea, you have to first show the part you disagree with.

(Step 1) Krutch compares sport hunters to murderers, saying that the murderers' "deeds are not gratuitously evil" (35). (Step 2) With this comparison, Krutch is too extreme. Even though a murderer may have a motive, killing a person is worse than killing an animal because people, unlike animals, have hopes, dreams, and emotions that animals do not feel. (Step 3) Nevertheless, Krutch is right to show sport hunting as "gratuitously evil." The word "gratuitous" means "for no reason," and to kill without reason, even an animal, makes no sense. It is, as Krutch says, "killing for killing's sake" (35).

To stress disagreement, you merely reverse the order of steps 2 and 3. In other words, your paragraph puts material showing agreement in the middle and then ends on a note of disagreement.

(Step 1) Krutch compares sport hunters to murderers, saying that the murderers' "deeds are not gratuitously evil." (Step 2) Krutch is right to show sport hunting as "gratuitously evil." The word "gratuitous" means "for no reason," and to kill without reason, even an animal, makes no sense. It is, as Krutch says, "killing for killing's sake" (35). (Step 3) Nevertheless, with this comparison, Krutch is too extreme. Even though a murderer may have a motive, killing a person is worse than killing an animal because people, unlike animals, have hopes, dreams, and emotions that animals do not feel.

Now the disagreement is stressed because it comes last in the paragraph. When do you stress agreement? When do you stress disagreement? That depends on your thesis. The end of the paragraph serves as a "last word" on the point the whole paragraph develops. Thus, it should follow from the thesis of your whole essay. If you are using the thesis presented earlier in response to Krutch's essay, you will stress disagreement because that thesis generally disagrees with Krutch. The end of the paragraph should always agree with your position in your thesis. Otherwise, you will sound as if you are changing your opinion halfway through the essay, and your audience will become confused.

E X E R C I S E   8.5   From a paragraph in Exercise 8.2 choose a point that you have mixed feelings about. Using the three-step method, write a paragraph in response. Stress agreement or disagreement, depending on your feelings.

Raising a Point Not Mentioned in the Source   Sometimes you may read a source and find that the source does not cover some important points about the topic. The brainstorming list in response to Krutch contains a point about hunting for profit, something Krutch never talks about. You can, however, discuss the point, using the following questions.

1. What is the point that the source does not mention?
2. Why is this point important?
3. What examples support the importance of this point?

You might write the following paragraph after answering those questions.

> (Step 1) Krutch fails to mention that sometimes hunting can be a source of income for people in need. (Step 2) If the animals being hunted are not endangered species, a person should be allowed to earn a supplemental income by hunting. (Step 3) A friend of mine, Kurt Olson, traps raccoon and fox each winter and sells the pelts. Both animals are plentiful, and both are nuisances to farmers and rural residents because they prey on chickens and pets. So while Kurt is helping rid the area of pests, he is also earning money that he uses to help pay his college tuition. During the winter, other trappers in the area depend on the money they earn to help support their families.

E X E R C I S E   8.6   Choose an issue not raised in one of the paragraphs in Exercise 8.2. Develop a paragraph showing why that issue is important to the topic developed in the source.

The Three-Step Method Turned Upside Down

Three-step method upside down: A variation of the three-step method. Step 1: state your reaction to an issue; step 2: provide support for your reaction; step 3: refer to the source to help support your reaction or to show that the source is in error.

Sometimes you can put the idea from a source last in a paragraph, in a sense turning the **three-step method upside down.** This method works best when you agree with the source, but it also can work when you disagree or raise a point the source does not mention. It won't work, however, for handling mixed feelings about a point. Examine each of the following paragraphs and compare it with the related example of the three-step method.

Agreement

(Step 1, your point) There is no reason to kill for sport except to gain a feeling of power. (Step 2, support for your point) For example, a big-game hunter who displays the heads of the animals on the wall of a den is just showing off to others that he is brave. But really he is not very brave because even a lion is no match for a high-powered rifle. And since people do not eat lions, all the hunter gets is the skin and the head, which are just trophies to feed his ego. (Step 3, support for your point from the source) As Krutch says, killing animals just for the sport of it is ''pure evil'' (35).

Disagreement

(Step 1, your point) Many people in rural areas hunt to help feed their families. (Step 2, support for your point) Butchered and frozen, a deer can provide many meals for a family, and eating the meat from an animal killed by a hunter is no different from eating supermarket meat. In both cases, the animal was killed for food. Game laws prevent senseless killing, but even if they did not exist, hunters should not kill more food than they or their families can eat. Although hunters should never kill endangered species, even for food, there is nothing wrong with hunting to feed a family. (Step 3, your disagreement with Krutch) So Krutch is wrong to claim that people who hunt for food ''may be as wicked and misguided as the vegetarians sometimes say'' (35).

Issue Not Mentioned in Source

(Step 1, your point) If the animals being hunted are not endangered species, a person should be allowed to earn a supplemental income by hunting. (Step 2, support for your point) A friend of mine, Kurt Olson, traps raccoon and fox each winter and sells the pelts. Both animals are plentiful, and both are nuisances to farmers and rural residents because they prey on chickens and pets. So while Kurt is helping rid the area of pests, he is also earning money that he uses to help pay his college tuition. During the winter, other trappers in the area depend on the money they earn to help support their families. (Step 3, pointing out that Krutch ignores the issue) In criticizing hunting, Krutch doesn't mention that sometimes hunting can be a source of income for people in need.

Whether you use the regular three-step method or turn it upside down often depends on how you perceive the issue as you are drafting. Sometimes you may have the issue clearly focused, so you start with the source. And sometimes you may write your way into an idea and then find a point in the source that backs you up or that your paragraph shows to be in error.

E X E R C I S E   8.7   Turning the three-step method upside down, rewrite one of the paragraphs you wrote for a previous exercise.

**Paragraphs
Without Reference
to the Source**

Sometimes, even though the whole of your essay is responding to a source, you may write paragraphs that develop only your ideas. There is nothing wrong with such paragraphs as long as the whole of the essay deals with and mentions the source at some points. Paragraphs with only your ideas may come before or after paragraphs that deal directly with the source. The first of the following two paragraphs is the one disagreeing with Krutch's claims about the "hunter-for-food." The paragraph following it expands on the disagreement but without reference to Krutch.

> Krutch claims that people who hunt for food "may be as wicked and misguided as the vegetarians sometimes say" (35). Krutch overlooks the fact that many people in rural areas hunt to help feed their families. Butchered and frozen, a deer can provide many meals for a family, and eating the meat from an animal killed by a hunter is no different from eating supermarket meat. In both cases, the animal was killed for food. Game laws prevent senseless killing, but even if they did not exist, hunters should not kill more food than they or their families can eat. Also, they should never hunt endangered species, but there is nothing wrong with hunting to feed a family.
>
> Most people who hunt for food hunt legally, killing only their limit of plentiful species. Along with supplying themselves with food, these hunters prevent animals from starving to death. For instance, many deer would starve to death each winter because deer herds need more food than nature provides in a snow-covered forest. In this sense, nature is crueler than hunters.

The second paragraph does not refer to Krutch, yet it adds support for the argument against Krutch's claim that hunting for food may be wicked.

E X E R C I S E   8.8   Using only your ideas and without reference to the source, write a paragraph that could lead into or follow from one of the paragraphs you wrote in one of the earlier exercises.

■ Writing an Introduction to a Single-Source Essay

In Chapter 4, you learned various strategies for writing an introduction: raising a question, leading in with examples, quoting a famous person, referring to something you have read, and many others. You also learned that whether you write your introduction first or last does not matter, as long as it accomplishes the following:

1. Gets the reader's attention;
2. Introduces the topic;
3. Limits the topic;
4. States your thesis about the topic.

An introduction to a source essay, like any other introduction, should achieve these goals. However, it should also make clear that you are writing in response to a source. There are two common ways to write an introduction to an essay in response to a source.

Opening Summary and Thesis

One introductory strategy presented in Chapter 4 was the reference to something you read. In writing from personal experience and observation, you use that reference as a "jumping off point." An example in Chapter 4 started with a reference to Banesh Hoffman's essay on Albert Einstein and then led to a thesis arguing that students should not be afraid to visit teachers during office hours. The body of that essay went on to talk not about Einstein but about the benefits of individual conferences with teachers. In other words, the writer used the reference to Einstein only as a way into the topic.

In writing in response to a source, you refer to what you have read — the source — and then develop the essay in response. This reference to the source, instead of just serving as a way to approach a topic, should briefly summarize the source so that the reader knows what your thesis is responding to. You might write the following introduction to an essay on Krutch's work.

In *The Great Chain of Life,* Joseph Wood Krutch argues that hunters who kill animals just for sport are doing the worst kind of evil. Krutch says that they are worse than liars, thieves, and even murderers because their actions have no purpose other than to make them feel powerful. As for people who hunt for food, Krutch believes they at least have a purpose, but he also says they may be evil too. Hunting purely for sport is certainly wrong, but in most cases there is nothing wrong with hunting for food and profit.

This introduction presents a summary of Krutch's essay, starting with reference to the book it is from and a tag using Krutch's full name the first time it is mentioned. Then with short tags, the paragraph states how Krutch feels about people who hunt for sport and what he implies about those who hunt for food. The thesis of the response essay follows. Thus, the introduction clearly shows what source the essay will respond to, what the source has said on the topic, and what the essay will say in response.

E X E R C I S E   8.9   Write an introduction with a summary and thesis for an essay in response to one of the sources in Exercise 8.2. Your summary may be briefer than the summary of Krutch's essay because the sources are shorter. Be sure to use tags as needed.

Adding an Introductory Strategy to the Summary and Thesis

Any of the strategies for writing an introduction (discussed in Chapter 3) can be added to the summary and thesis to help get the reader's attention. The following discussion shows how some of them can work with the summary and thesis. Start with the introductory strategy, follow with the brief summary, and then state your thesis. You need to make a smooth transition from the introductory strategy to the summary; pay close attention to how the sample paragraphs move from the introduction to the first mention of Krutch's essay.

Selecting   This strategy starts with a straightforward statement about the broad subject area of which the topic is a part, gives brief but specific examples within that subject area, and then focuses on one example for the topic of the essay.

> Sports can be violent. To some people, boxing should be outlawed because the boxer's purpose is to injure his opponent. Other people wonder how something as dangerous as auto racing can be a sport. And others question even the violence of football. To Joseph Wood Krutch, the worse sport is hunting. In *The Great Chain of Life,* Krutch argues that hunters who kill animals just for sport are doing the worst kind of evil. Krutch says that they are worse than liars, thieves, and even murderers because their actions have no purpose other than to make them feel powerful. As for people who hunt for food, Krutch believes they at least have a purpose, but he also says they may be evil too. Hunting purely for sport is certainly wrong, but in most cases there is nothing wrong with hunting for food and profit.

This introduction begins with a broad subject area, violent sports, and then narrows the subject down to Krutch's topic on hunting. In other words, the writer selected hunting for sport from other violent sports.

Narrating   Setting up a scene with a brief narration can grab the reader's attention before moving to the summary.

> A tiger strides warily through the jungle, its muscles stretching its gold and black coat. It senses danger as it moves into a clearing to confront whatever is giving off a scent unlike any other in the jungle. It never finds its adversary, for in a moment it lies dead, streams of red blood mixing with its black and gold stripes. Three

men, feeling triumphant, pull up in a jeep, shoot it once more to be sure, and then cart it back to civilization where its head and skin will hang on a wall or cover a floor. In *The Great Chain of Life,* Joseph Wood Krutch argues that hunters who kill animals just for sport are doing the worst kind of evil. Krutch says that they are worse than liars, thieves, and even murderers because their actions have no purpose other than to make them feel powerful. As for people who hunt for food, Krutch believes they at least have a purpose, but he also says they may be evil too. Hunting purely for sport is certainly wrong, but in most cases there is nothing wrong with hunting for food.

The brief scene in the narration gives the reader an idea of the beauty of the tiger and of the uncaring nature of the hunter. Thus it supports Krutch's point about the brutality of hunting for sport. At the same time, this brutality is in contrast to the idea of hunting for food, which the essay will argue is acceptable.

Asking Questions   A question or two can often make the reader curious before you begin the discussion of the source.

> Is a man who kills his limit during deer season and then butchers and freezes the meat so his family has food the same as a man who shoots a lion on a safari, mounts the head in his office, uses the skin for a throw rug in front of his fireplace, but has no taste or use for the meat? This and other questions about hunting are implied in Joseph Wood Krutch's *The Great Chain of Life.* Krutch argues that hunters who kill animals just for sport are doing the worst kind of evil. He says that they are worse than liars, thieves, and even murderers because their actions have no purpose other than to make them feel powerful. As for people who hunt for food, Krutch believes they at least have a purpose, but he also says they may be evil too. Hunting purely for sport is certainly wrong, but in most cases there is nothing wrong with hunting for food and profit.

Here the question sets up the contrast between the hunter who kills for food and the hunter who kills for sport. After the summary, the thesis then answers the opening question.

Surprising the Reader   Any statement that surprises readers will usually get their attention.

> Killing an animal can be worse than killing a person. This is one point Joseph Wood Krutch makes in *The Great Chain of Life.* Krutch argues that hunters who kill animals just for sport are doing the worst kind of evil. He says that they are worse than liars, thieves, and even murderers because their actions have no purpose

other than to make them feel powerful. As for people who hunt for food, Krutch believes they at least have a purpose, but he also says they may be evil too. Hunting purely for sport is certainly wrong, but in most cases there is nothing wrong with hunting for food and profit.

The opening statement needs much explanation because few people would agree with it; thus readers would want to find out when killing an animal is worse than killing a person.

Using some kind of introductory strategy along with the summary and thesis can liven up the opening of your essay. There is one catch, though. Sometimes the introductory strategy, when added to the summary, will make the introduction seem rather long. If you feel your introduction is too long, you can cut it into two paragraphs, making the introductory strategy the first paragraph and the summary with thesis the second.

E X E R C I S E   8.10 Add an introductory strategy to the introduction you wrote in Exercise 8.9. Make sure you have a smooth transition from the strategy to the summary.

■ Writing a Conclusion to a Single-Source Essay

The conclusion of an essay in response to a source is not much different from the conclusion to a personal experience essay. Chapter 3 presented various strategies for conclusions: presenting a solution to a problem, challenging the reader, looking to the future, and posing a final question or questions (usually a question your essay has answered). It also discussed the purposes of a conclusion:

1. To stress the importance of your thesis;
2. To leave a lasting impression;
3. To give the essay a sense of completeness.

Given these purposes, a conclusion should restate the thesis in different words, be more general than the body paragraphs, and be short enough that it does not make the reader forget the body.

The conclusion of a source essay should have these same purposes and qualities. But, like the rest of the essay, the conclusion should refer to the source. The following paragraph is a possible conclusion, using the question strategy, for the essay in response to Krutch.

All hunters are not the same. Krutch is correct in condemning people who shoot animals merely for the thrill of it. And though he admits that people who hunt for food have a purpose, his suspicions that they may be wicked are misguided. The sport hunter is evil; the food hunter is practical. Most people can easily condemn the hunter who shoots an animal to hang its head on a wall, but how easy is it to condemn the hunter who shoots an animal to put food on the table?

The conclusion opens with a very general statement that recalls the thesis. The following reference to Krutch then restates his main arguments before moving to a fairly specific restatement of the thesis, which contrasts evil and practicality. The closing question furthers the contrast but places the responsibility on the reader to make a judgment.

Writing a conclusion to a source essay is no more difficult than writing a conclusion to any other essay. Just comment generally on the source and keep the purposes of conclusions in mind.

■ Revising and Editing Checklists

In Chapter 5 you learned a lot about revision, and you may have referred to Chapter 10 to answer your questions about editing. When you write in response to a source, you need to think about the same questions of revision and editing that concern you when writing an essay from personal experience. But the source essay presents additional concerns. These checklists should help you revise and edit.

Revising

1. Is the title of the source mentioned in your introduction?
2. Do you use the author's full name the first time you cite it with a tag?
3. Does the introduction briefly summarize the thesis of the source?
4. Does the essay refer to the source at various points so that it avoids drifting off into a personal essay?
5. Are the source's points clearly tagged so that the reader can tell them from your own?
6. Do you present the source's ideas accurately and clearly when you paraphrase them?
7. Do you use your own words and sentence structure when you paraphrase?
8. Do your responses logically follow or lead to the source's ideas? In other words, are you and the source talking about the same issue?
9. If you have used the three-step method, are all steps clear, and is step 3 fully developed?
10. Do your body paragraphs end in agreement with your thesis?
11. Does your conclusion mention the source as it reasserts your thesis?

Editing

1. If the source is a book, have you underlined the title?
2. If the source is an essay, have you placed the title in quotation marks?
3. If you quote the source, have you used its *exact* words in every instance?
4. If you have left words out of a quotation, have you used ellipsis points?
5. In integrating quotations, have you avoided sentence errors such as comma splices and run-on sentences?
6. When you have included ideas from the source, have you cited them in your paper with parenthetical citation (page numbers in parentheses)?
7. If required, at the end of the essay have you included a "works cited" entry for the source? If so, have you used the proper entry form?

Essays for Reading

No Job, But He Got His Money's Worth
Robert Ehrenmann

> Robert Ehrenmann, from Warsaw, Indiana, was a recent graduate of Indiana State University when he wrote this essay. The essay first appeared as a letter to the editor in the *Terre Haute Tribune-Star* in 1988.

Vocabulary Cues

tedious: boring, monotonous, tiresome
bowels: the lower interior of a building, deep in the basement
memorabilia: things worthy to be preserved and remembered
archivist: a person in charge of keeping historical records of an
     institution, organization, or geographical area
incoherent: disorganized, not making sense
technocrat: an unflattering term for a scientific technician

Questions to Guide Your Reading

1. What is a liberal arts education?
2. How did Ehrenmann discover the value of his education?
3. Why does he believe a liberal arts education is the best way to prepare for the future?

During the past four years, my family and I shelled out about $48,000 for an education. That education did not train me in any specific career; even if I wanted to, I could not get a job as a computer programmer, dental technician, air traffic controller, accountant, or zookeeper. I am a history major, so people always ask me where I plan to teach. I have no interest in teaching. With graduation upon me, I have thought a lot about education and what it did for me.

I'm not sure that my education can be measured by either the tuition bill or the starting salary. Why study literature and religion when they probably will not help me get a job? What defines an education anyway?

I am what is called in the education business a "liberal arts graduate" — sort of a catchall term for those students who learn a buffet of subjects like mathematics, economics, philosophy, history, literature, science, religion, political science, and sociology. Some call it the "old-fashioned" education. And it wasn't until the middle of my senior year that I started to realize why those subjects were even important.

I spent the month of January doing some fairly tedious work in the bowels of the library of the Indiana Historical Society. I worked on a survey that collected and sorted raw materials about the history of blacks in the state. I also organized unprocessed historical collections that were actually random newspaper clippings, receipts, letters, and other memorabilia that had been donated to the society. My job was to take these fragments of life, place them in a historical context, and then write an index for the collection.

The job was boring at times, but I learned to take the skills I had developed in college and apply them to a job I had never even considered before. In writing an index, I found I could be coldly objective, just as I had learned in studying history. But I was no longer just a history student — I had become an archivist. It was the job of others to interpret my collections.

Being so coldly objective was not easy after four years of education that taught me to have an opinion about virtually everything. But I was able to adapt my writing skills to this new style. My writing was clear, concise, organized, and technically well written. In writing an index, I was able to take my basic writing skills I had learned from studying history and transfer them to a new occupation.

Here's another example. One collection I organized was an utter mess. It consisted of newspaper clippings and old programs that had cluttered an attic. I did not know how to begin to organize this heap into history.

I had this same feeling in college when I organized a seemingly incoherent mass of information into a paper. As I had done then, I solved this problem by concentrating on a very small part of the material. I focused on the newspaper clippings. After I separated the clippings, I noticed different subjects: church, family, and business. I worked the mess into a cohesive collection with a theme. Voilà, a new skill!

My brief stay at the historical society taught me what an education should be: a process that encourages knowledge and creativity. In a world filled with technocrats, liberal arts colleges are training students to think and express themselves by exposing them to a broad range of subjects. Their education is composed of learning basic knowledge and applying it to develop creative solutions to new problems. It will be the well-rounded education that will lead us into the next century, and such an education cannot be measured in dollars and cents.

I think I received my money's worth. My education provided me with a wide variety of educational opportunities, and I was able to apply these to a new job situation. My education has allowed me the freedom of choosing many career opportunities, and now I can build on that foundation.

Questions for Study and Discussion
1. Why wouldn't Ehrenmann be qualified for any of the jobs he mentions in the first paragraph?
2. What does he mean when he says education can't be measured by the cost of tuition or a starting salary?
3. Why might Ehrenmann's liberal arts education be called an "old-fashioned" education?
4. How did writing indexes to collections show Ehrenmann that he had learned a lot from his education?

5. At one point, Ehrenmann compares writing an index with writing a paper in college. How is his organization of the "utter mess" of newspaper clippings part of the writing process?
6. Do you agree with Ehrenmann that a liberal arts education is the best preparation for the twenty-first century?
7. Why does Ehrenmann claim that his education will enable him to choose from many careers? Do you agree?
8. How would you compare Ehrenmann's education with the education you plan to pursue?

Writing Assignment

Write an essay of 500–700 words in response to Ehrenmann's claim that a liberal arts education is the best education for the future.

Drugs

Gore Vidal

Gore Vidal was born in 1925 and wrote his first novel, *Williwaw,* when he was nineteen years old. Since then, he has written many novels, including *Myra Breckenridge, Burr,* and *Kalki,* as well as hundreds of essays. Vidal is one of America's most controversial writers and commentators. "Drugs" was first published in the *New York Times.*

Vocabulary Cues

precise: exact
exhortation: strong advice, an urgent appeal
GNP: gross national product, an economic indicator of the nation's worth
Homer: a poet of ancient Greece
perennially: continually, year after year
Mafiosi: Mafia leaders
Dr. Spock: a doctor widely known for his books on raising children
Dr. Leary: a former Harvard professor who in the 1960s saw LSD as a means of self-discovery and urged young people to take the drug

Questions to Guide Your Reading

1. How does Vidal propose to stop most drug addiction?
2. What does the Bill of Rights have to do with drugs?
3. What does Vidal say America should have learned from the prohibition of alcohol?

It is possible to stop most drug addiction in the United States within a very short time. Simply make all drugs available and sell them at cost. Label each drug with a precise description of what effects — good and bad — the drug will have on the taker. This will require heroic honesty. Don't say that marijuana is addictive or dangerous when it is neither, as millions of people know — unlike ''speed,'' which kills most unpleasantly, or heroin, which is addictive and difficult to kick.

For the record, I have tried — once — almost every drug and liked none, disproving the popular Fu Manchu theory that a single whiff of opium will enslave the mind. Nevertheless many drugs are bad for certain people to take and they should be told why in a sensible way.

Along with exhortation and warning, it might be good for our citizens to recall (or learn for the first time) that the United States was the creation of men who believed that each man has the right to do what he wants with his own life as long as he does not interfere with his neighbor's pursuit of happiness (that his neighbor's idea of happiness is persecuting others does confuse matters a bit).

This is a startling notion to the current generation of Americans. They reflect a system of public education which has made the Bill of Rights, literally, unacceptable to a majority of high school graduates (see the annual Purdue reports) who now form the ''silent majority'' — a phrase which that underestimated wit Richard Nixon took from Homer who used it to describe the dead.

Now one can hear the warning rumble begin: if everyone is allowed to take drugs everyone will and the GNP will decrease, the Commies will stop us from making everyone free, and we shall end up a race of zombies, passively murmuring ''groovy'' to one another. Alarming thought. Yet it seems most unlikely that any reasonably sane person will become a drug addict if he knows in advance what addiction is going to be like.

Is everyone reasonably sane? No. Some people will always become drug addicts just as some people will always become alcoholics, and it is just too bad. Every man, however, has the power (and should have the legal right) to kill himself if he chooses. But since most men don't, they won't be mainliners either. Nevertheless, forbidding people things they like or think they might enjoy only makes them want those things all the more. This psychological insight is, for some mysterious reason, perennially denied our governors.

It is a lucky thing for the American moralist that our country has always existed in a kind of time-vacuum: we have no public memory of anything that happened before last Tuesday. No one in Washington today recalls what happened during the years alcohol was forbidden to the people by a Congress that thought it had a divine mission to stamp out Demon Rum — launching, in the process, the greatest crime wave in the country's history, causing thousands of deaths from bad alcohol, and creating a general (and persisting) contempt among the citizenry for the laws of the United States.

The same thing is happening today. But the government has learned nothing from past attempts at prohibition, not to mention repression.

Last year when the supply of Mexican marijuana was slightly curtailed by the Feds, the pushers got the kids hooked on heroin and deaths increased dramatically, particularly in New York. Whose fault? Evil men like the Mafiosi? Permissive Dr. Spock? Wild-eyed Dr. Leary? No.

The Government of the United States was responsible for those deaths. The bureaucratic machine has a vested interest in playing cops and robbers. Both the Bureau of Narcotics and the Mafia want strong laws against the sale and use of drugs because if drugs are sold at cost there would be no money in it for anyone.

If there was no money in it for the Mafia, there would be no friendly playground pushers, and addicts would not commit crimes to pay for the next fix. Finally, if there was no money in it, the Bureau of Narcotics would wither away, something they are not about to do without a struggle.

Will anything sensible be done? Of course not. The American people are as devoted to the idea of sin and its punishment as they are to making money — and fighting drugs is nearly as big a business as pushing them. Since the combination of sin and money is irresistible (particularly to the professional politician), the situation will only grow worse.

Questions for Study and Discussion

1. Why does Vidal say labeling drugs would require "heroic honesty"?
2. What differences does he see among different types of drugs?
3. Why does Vidal tell his audience he has tried almost every drug? Does this confession help or hurt his argument?
4. According to Vidal, what attitude do most Americans have toward the Bill of Rights?
5. What does Vidal say that most people think would happen if drugs were legal? How does he respond to this position?
6. What lesson does Vidal say America should have learned from history? Why hasn't the citizenry learned this lesson?
7. According to Vidal, who was responsible for the drug deaths he mentions? Explain how he came to his conclusion.
8. Why would organized crime want strong laws against drugs?
9. What does Vidal mean when he says "American people are as devoted to the idea of sin and punishment as they are to making money — and fighting drugs is nearly as big a business as pushing them"?

Writing Assignment

Write an essay of 500–700 words responding to Vidal's proposal to legalize drugs. Assume an audience of citizens and lawmakers.

CHAPTER 9

Writing the Multiple-Source Essay

Just as you may write in response to one source, you may sometimes compare and contrast two sources or you may draw on several sources. Like most writing, multiple-source writing occurs both on the job or at school. A sales manager, for example, would probably consult many market reports and economic sources before writing a plan for the company's yearly sales campaign. A scientist working on a particular experiment would read what other scientists found in similar experiments and refer to their writings when he wrote a report on the experiment. And any student writing a term paper is writing a multiple-source essay. This chapter will not ask you to write a term paper, but it will teach you the basics of writing a multiple-source essay so that you can write a term paper, or any other paper requiring sources, if one is assigned in another class.

■ Responding to Two Sources

A common type of multiple-source essay asks you to compare and contrast two sources. You have read Joseph Wood Krutch's essay from *The Great Chain of Life*, which generally condemned hunting; now read another opinion on the topic.

In Defense of Hunting
John C. Dunlap

Born in 1946, John C. Dunlap has written articles and essays in sporting magazines such as *Rod and Reel, Field and Stream,* and *Sports Afield.* In addition to writing, he teaches high school in Vermont. This essay first appeared in *Time* magazine.

"What are your moral justifications for hunting?"

The man who asked me this is my neighbor, a well-educated and thoughtful newcomer to our little valley in northeast Vermont. He and his partner have just built a small house across the way. We want to be friends; there are going to be difficulties.

My first reaction is to trot out all the standard, unconvincing arguments about game management, about hunting as a last vestige of our primitive selves. It's easy, after so many years of assault, to feel defensive about this subject. Instead, I have a Socratic inspiration.

"What are your justifications for *not* hunting?" I ask.

So I get to listen to *his* standard unconvincing arguments: the sacredness of life; the obligation not to interfere with its mechanisms; the storm of death; the suffering; the continuing evolution of man.

The hypocrisy of all this is staggering.

Vegetarians

The only opponents I'll listen to for long are vegetarians. I won't listen a minute to meat eaters who pay the butcher and supermarket to kill, package, and distribute their meals. But even the sophistic arguments of the vegetarians inevitably irritate me. It's funny, they think I'm kidding when I ask if plants feel pain. Plants can fill their lives with peace, and their stomachs with nourishment, plant life fashions dazzling displays of color and shape and even responds to classical music. But when the gardener approaches with pruning shears, suddenly plants are numb and indifferent.

I am not a theologian who can argue complicated precepts of morality. I am, I hope, a reasonably intelligent and sensitive man who tries to think clearly about what he does. And what I do is hunt, and sometimes kill.

So who doesn't? Does the power that orchestrates affairs in our universe accord a deer more importance than a fly quivering in a strip of sticky tape? Show me where. No sensible person will argue that significance is related to size — but there are few advocates of the small.

The universe shows no less enthusiasm in exterminating life than in creating it. What do all the opponents of hunting think the sweet-singing "feathered glories" are doing, carving graceful arcs in the evening air? They're killing, just as fast as they can. Even doves, man-made symbols of gentleness, pick through the farmer's silage bins down the road, looking for juicy bugs to snip in half and devour. And the jewel-like trout, darting among the mossy rocks — they're busy killing, too. The foxes and bobcats of our forests are predators as well, and it's fortunate for their prey that they are. As wise Theseus points out at the conclusion of Chaucer's "Knight's Tale," death is forever busy "Converting all things back into the source / From which they were derived, to which they course."

Good Intentions

Urban moralists so often seem to have an image of hunting seasons as bloody free-for-alls. They know virtually nothing about the fish and game departments' endless and difficult assessments of herd size and habitat quality. How many "friends of wildlife" have tramped through the deep snows of early April to count the many thousand deer carcasses strewn through the woods? Not many, I bet. Can this "natural" solution to excessive animal numbers be acceptable to them? We interfere everywhere to keep living things happy and healthy and call it progress — but not here. Just as surely as you can rob a man with a pen, so too can deer be killed with good intentions. If we were to outlaw hunting, millions of beasts would suffer and die each year as they competed for limited feed. In fact, social and economic developments have so altered the habitat that we must now assume increased responsibility to manage wildlife intelligently. Who pays for this management? The hunters pay, with their licenses; the opponents talk.

The intelligence and practicality of game management in the form of hunting seasons were proved to me long ago. Most state departments of fish and game have excellent literature explaining their policies and practices better than I am able to do here. I suggest this as beginning reading material for those who condemn hunting; I have yet to argue this issue with someone who was well informed.

Passions

Then again, it seems clear that opponents of hunting fashion their moral stance not on a cosmic model, as they so often say, but on a merely human one. Indeed, arguments on both sides usually come down to passions, and these interest me most. For just as the urban world has largely been stripped of its wildness and suburbs poisoned and thoroughly paved over, it is possible that, given enough time, our very instincts will suffer the same fate: our mysterious inner forests cut down, our spiritual waters polluted and dammed. Paradoxically, hunting — which deals in death — can intensify our understanding of life.

So, how *can* I do it? I go hunting because I cannot resist prowling out in the dark mornings and the umber dusks — the cracks, as I have heard them described, between the worlds. I go to have shadowy, sometimes violent encounters with my brother animals. I go to watch a silent, indifferent power fill the woods, and see the woods awed in its presence.

Contrasting the Essays for Invention

Before you can write an essay contrasting the Dunlap and Krutch sources, you should list the main points of each. The lists are like brainstorming lists but you do not put down anything that comes to mind. Rather, you limit yourself to the points from each essay. It helps to place the lists side by side to sort out each author's points.

Krutch	*Dunlap*
Hunting sets people apart from each other.	Dunlap and neighbor disagree on hunting.
Sport hunting true evil.	Hunting no different from eating meat killed for supermarkets.
No reason to kill for sport.	Plants have lives but are killed for food.
Sport hunters as bad as murderers.	Insects killed; does size make a difference?
Sport hunters are on a power trip, eliminate vitality in universe.	All animals in nature kill to survive.
Food hunters have reason but still might be wicked.	Hunting helps game management, and license fees pay for it.
Killing for sport shows "reality of evil."	Hunting brings us closer to inner passions, hunt "brother animals."

Once you have these lists, you can break the topic down into a list of issues — arguments that are important to the overall argument of whether people should hunt. Each author will not always deal with each issue, so you need to examine both lists to find all the issues. Also, you can raise and list issues of your own. As you list each issue, give one author's opinion on it, then the other's, and finally your own.

Hunting sets people apart.
Krutch: Can't understand how someone could "think an animal more interesting dead than alive."
Dunlap: Asks why people do *not* hunt.
Your opinion: People's ideas about hunting depend on their background.

Hunting for sport.
Krutch: Worst kind of evil, no reason, power trip to reduce vitality in the universe.
Dunlap: Does not comment.
Your opinion: Maybe not as bad as Krutch says, but definitely wrong.

Hunting for food.
Krutch: May be as wicked as vegetarians say.
Dunlap: No different than eating supermarket meat or eating plants because plants are killed, too, and all of nature is involved in killing for survival.

Your opinion: Nothing wrong with hunting for food as long as animals are not endangered species and hunters do not kill more than can be eaten.

Hunting and game management.
Krutch: Does not comment.
Dunlap: Hunting thins deer herds, which is necessary in winter, and license fees help pay for game management.
Your opinion: Hunting for food does help game management as long as hunters do not kill more animals than they are allowed.

Hunting and our relationship to nature.
Krutch: Sport hunters destroy nature
Dunlap: Hunters get close to their inner passions in confrontations with "brother animals."
Your opinion: Hunting for food is another way to use nature and must be done responsibly, but we should not enjoy killing animals or think of ourselves as animals.

Hunting for profit.
Krutch: Does not comment.
Dunlap: Does not comment.
Your opinion: Hunting or trapping to sell meat or skins is acceptable if animals are not endangered species.

Once you have a list of issues such as this one, you can begin to find your purpose and a possible thesis.

E X E R C I S E   9.1 Read the following two passages and make a list of issues, noting the author's opinions from each paragraph and your own opinions. For the purposes of the exercise, the authors are called Smith and Jones.

Smith: In Favor of Grading

The grading system is an element of the curriculum that colleges and universities could not do without. Grades allow professors to separate one student's work from another for the purpose of rewarding the student who works harder and displays a strong grasp of the subject matter. A simple system in which students received either a P for passing and an F for failing would not show any difference between the student who scrapes by with C work and the interested and talented student capable of excellence. Grades also motivate students to work harder and thus learn more. Though some students may be more concerned with the grade than learning about the subject, in striving for a good grade they can't help but learn. Students also find grades useful in measuring their strengths and weaknesses, just as employers use grades to distinguish between the potentially talented employee and the potentially average or mediocre.

Jones: Against Grading

The grading system may very well be the greatest block to learning in colleges and universities today. Many students place more emphasis on earning a grade than on mastering the course material. This emphasis leads to cramming, brownnosing, and, in extreme cases, cheating. All teachers have heard the notorious question: "Will this be on the test?" This obsession with grades is not the fault of the students but the fault of the system. Schools and society so admire the almighty A — the mark of "the winner" — that students see courses as just another footrace, rather than an opportunity to learn. A colleague of mine has joked that on the first day of class he would like to promise everyone an A, require no attendance, and then see who shows up for the sheer joy of learning. I doubt he would have enough students to hold a conversation, let alone a discussion. Grades serve no purpose other than to render learning unimportant and to foster unhealthy competition. The argument that grades help employers identify potential employees does not hold water either, for most employers must retrain college graduates for the specific tasks of the company.

Finding a Thesis and Organizing Your Draft

Like all the previous essays discussed in this text, the essay in response to two sources should have a clear thesis and pattern of organization. Also, as in previous essays, your thesis and pattern of organization can change if in drafting you discover ideas that you did not have when you began. If so, you may have to revise your thesis and your means of supporting it. If you examine your list of issues and can't come up with a thesis to cover all of them, you might begin writing on the one or two issues you feel reasonably certain about. However, often by examining the list, you can find a thesis and pattern of organization to guide you as you write your draft.

Finding a Possible Thesis   In the single-source essay in response to Krutch, you compared the issues on which you agreed with him and those on which you disagreed. The process of finding a thesis to respond to two sources is similar. You first review your list of issues and opinions to see where you agree (or partly agree) with one source, where you agree (or partly agree) with the other, and where you have raised issues not mentioned in either. Then make another list. (Sometimes if you have a strong grasp of the topic, you can do this in your head.)

Agreement with Krutch

1. Hunting sets people apart, but background is determining factor in whether a person hunts.
2. There is no reason to hunt for sport.

Agreement with Dunlap

1. Hunting sets people apart, but background is determining factor in whether a person hunts.
2. Hunting for food is acceptable.
3. Hunting for food helps game management.
4. Hunting helps define our relationship to nature, though we should not enjoy the violence, as Dunlap seems to.

Additional Issue

Earning supplemental income by hunting is acceptable. Dunlap would probably agree; Krutch would probably disagree, or at least partly disagree.

In examining this list, you can see that you agree with Krutch that there is no reason to hunt for sport. You also can see that you not only agree with some of Dunlap's reasons to hunt for food but have added another reason he does not mention. You can begin to try out a possible thesis:

> There is no reason to hunt merely for sport, but there are many good reasons to justify other kinds of hunting.

This thesis could give you a start. However, recall that Chapter 3 said that a thesis should not be vague. The phrase "many good reasons" might strike some readers as vague. You can briefly specify the reasons:

> There is no reason to hunt merely for sport, but other kinds of hunting can help define our relationship to nature, provide food, contribute to game management, and offer a means of supplementing income.

This thesis would work, but it may be a little too specific because it locks you into a pattern of organization that you might not find effective as you write the draft. So you might look for alternatives that are more specific than your first attempt but that allow more flexibility than the second.

> Hunting purely for sport is brutal, but not all hunting is a form of brutality.

This thesis allows you to show why you believe there is no good reason to hunt for sport but also to separate other kinds of hunting so that you can argue that they are acceptable.

Of course, refining and focusing the thesis can be done at any point in drafting and revising. If you can start with a focused thesis, fine, but even the first thesis, as vague as it is, would give you a start, although you might have to revise it later.

EXERCISE 9.2 Using the issues you listed in Exercise 9.1, find a possible thesis for an essay on grading in response to Smith and Jones.

Organizing Your Draft As always, you can write sections of your draft in any order you wish and arrange them later. Or you can list the issues in the order you want to discuss them and then follow the list as you draft. Just as in drafting the single-source essay, you probably want to discuss your agreement that sports hunting is brutal in the first body paragraph. That way, your readers will know you are not in favor of all hunting before you try to convince them why certain types are acceptable. You might try a list that follows Dunlap's pattern of organization and then add the issue he does not mention:

Hunting for food
Hunting and game management
Hunting and our relationship to nature
Hunting for profit

The advantage to this list is that in putting the issue on hunting for profit last, you would show that you have taken the topic further than both sources because neither Krutch nor Dunlap mentions the issue. However, if you find that this issue does not lead to your most convincing point, you can put it earlier in the essay. Or you might want it to follow the paragraph on hunting for food since both issues show how people use the game they hunt. Likewise, you might see that game management is a way of defining our relationship to nature and put your coverage of it after the more general discussion of hunting and nature. As a result, you would have the following list:

Hunting for food
Hunting for profit
Hunting and our relationship to nature
Hunting and game management

This order might work well because the last body paragraph now covers one of the strongest arguments for hunting. Also, the movement from hunting for personal gain — food and profit — to hunting and the larger questions of nature has a certain logic to it.

As you consider the order in which you will cover the issues, try out various lists. Not only will the lists provide possible patterns for your draft, but they will stimulate your thinking on the topic, causing you to see connections between one issue and another. If you don't find a possible order in which to discuss the issues, you can write about them one at a time and then think about how you will arrange the sections you have written. This method will also help you think about the relationship of issues to one another. Whether you decide on your order first, last, or somewhere in between, this part of the process requires much thought.

E X E R C I S E   9.3 Arrange the list of issues from Exercise 9.1 in two or three different ways. Then for each list, write a few sentences explaining its advantages and disadvantages.

■ Responding to Three or More Sources

Some writing you do in college and later will ask you to respond to a number of sources on one topic. In college writing, the term paper is the obvious example. You may also find that papers shorter and less formal than term papers can benefit from the use of sources. You have learned how to write in response to one or two sources. Responding to three or more is not much more difficult. The key is to pay careful attention to invention, as you find the sources' opinions and as you develop your own on the various issues. The following four essays first appeared in *USA Today* in 1987, and each deals with the cost of attending colleges. Read them carefully, taking notes as appropriate. Add annotations of your own if you like.

Colleges Must Cut Costs, Help Students
USA Today Editorial

If you were counting on lower inflation to ease the financial pain of sending your children to college, count again.

We may have conquered inflation during the past six years, but college tuitions still increased twice as fast as the cost of living — faster than new houses, health care, energy, food, and cars.

And although inflation has been less than 2 percent, tuition next fall is expected to be 6 percent to 8 percent higher than last September. It may rise 5 percent the year after.

You don't need a college degree to know something's wrong here.

A new study of college costs by the American Council on Education tries to put the tuition increases in the best light.

Tuitions haven't increased much more than inflation since 1970, the report says.

That may sound like good news. But it's not. What really counts is how much higher education costs today, and next year, and the next.

Why is tuition going up faster than other costs? "The simple answer," says the report, "is that nobody knows."

Well, it's time somebody found out.

Every time costs rise, college slips beyond the reach of more middle-class families. It's even worse for poor families. Since 1980, the percentage of students from families with less than $30,000 income has fallen from 68 percent to 37 percent.

Student borrowing is five times higher than it was a decade ago. Up to one-half the students leave college with a degree in one hand and a promissory note in the other. Many owe so much they can't afford low-paying public service jobs such as teaching or social work.

The colleges say they need to catch up on faculty and staff salaries, building programs, and maintenance that fell behind during the double-digit inflation days of the '70s.

But these excuses are wearing thin. Colleges have had plenty of time to catch up.

Administrators also point to increased costs for sophisticated equipment, science facilities, computers, books, and the need to compensate for declining federal aid.

But if they can't control these costs, somebody else will. Congress is already under pressure from parents worried that they won't be able to afford college for their children.

Education Secretary William Bennett argues that cutting federal aid will reduce costs. He's wrong.

Cutting student loan and financial aid programs is one of the worst possible ways to balance the federal budget. While tuition trailed inflation in the 1970s, federal student aid more than tripled. When student aid slowed down, college costs took off.

Government officials and educators must work together to increase educational opportunties, not limit them. That means liberal student loan programs, with strong payback provisions. It means restraining spending on campus.

Everybody doesn't want to go to college. But everybody who wants to deserves the chance.

Colleges Must Not Cut Quality to Curb Costs
Sheldon Hackney

Sheldon Hackney is president of the University of Pennsylvania.

Educational opportunities should be determined by a student's abilities and interests, not financial status. The individual student benefits, but so does the nation if students attend the schools that can challenge them.

At Penn, we admit students on their academic qualifications, then work with them to find the necessary financial support. We hold to that policy despite the rising costs and changes in federal student aid that have left most U.S. colleges in a financial crunch.

Higher education is a complex and expensive enterprise. It's labor intensive, and that labor is highly specialized. Top scholars are expensive to attract and retain, especially in fields such as business, law, medicine, science, and engineering, where we compete for employees with the for-profit sector.

The rapid increase in knowledge also has its costs. Major new disciplines are emerging, and simply keeping up with existing ones increases expenses yearly. Lab equipment is more sophisticated and more expensive now, and computers — Penn, for example, has 10,000 computer work stations — have become an integral part of teaching, research, and administration.

In recent years, colleges have assumed a greater burden in providing student financial aid, augmenting state and federal aid with their own funds. This year, more than 40 percent of Penn's students will receive financial aid, including more than $20 million from university resources.

In addition, universities are as large as small cities and require many of the same support services. Penn is the largest private employer in the Philadelphia region; our public safety force is larger than most of the state's 900 municipal police departments; our annual utility costs are upward of $18 million; and insurance costs have doubled in two years.

In response to mounting costs, universities have implemented cost-saving programs, ranging from purchasing stationery at bulk rate to generating their own electrical energy. They have more intelligently managed their endowment portfolios to provide a more secure economic base and better endowment income, and they have approached fund-raising more creatively.

Penn will spend $30 million in endowment income this year and raise more than $140 million in research funding, and more than $50 million from alumni and friends to augment tuition revenue, which covers less than one-half the cost of the education we provide.

Colleges must continue to hold down costs without sacrificing their educational missions. But federal aid is vital both to assist individuals in reaching their potential and to ensure that society will have an educated citizenry, a future generation of doctors, engineers, teachers, and other college-trained professionals, and the benefit of the kind of basic research that is best done by academic institutions.

Taxpayer Subsidies Help Fuel Tuition Hikes
William J. Bennett

A longtime educator, William Bennett wrote this essay when he was secretary of education in Ronald Reagan's administration.

As colleges and universities begin announcing next year's tuition increases, many parents once again find themselves pained and baffled by the skyrocketing cost of college education.

Many colleges have announced tuition increases for next year ranging from 4 percent to, in one case, 20 percent — even though inflation in 1986 was only 1.8 percent.

In fact, tuition has risen at twice the rate of inflation since 1980. No wonder that some 82 percent of the American people worry that college costs will soon be out of reach of most families.

For a while, the higher education establishment denied that much of a problem existed. Recently, though, they have switched gears. The American Council on Education is now encouraging the higher education community to "intensify its efforts to identify the causes of tuition inflation."

This is welcome. But it would be better still if the American Council on Education also urged the higher education community to act to keep tuition inflation down.

Such action is needed. As things now stand, tuition inflation threatens to cancel out the beneficial effects of federal college aid programs.

Instead of helping families meet the cost of a college education, the $14 billion per year federal subsidy seems to enable college administrators to raise prices ever higher.

While the current structure of federal student aid may not cause tuition inflation, there is little doubt that it helps make it possible — because when colleges raise prices, the taxpayers increase their subsidy to help families make up the differences, then colleges raise tuition again, and so on.

We have proposed reforms that would address this problem. But the primary responsibility for containing education costs cannot lie with the federal government. It lies with our colleges and universities.

No one doubts that there is a lot of fat in some areas of higher education — just as there has been in some areas of U.S. business.

The pressures of economic competition have forced a lot of businesses to slim down and become more cost-efficient. U.S. higher education needs to look to that example, rather than justifying whopping tuition increases by merely saying, as one university official recently said, that "new knowledge is inherently more expensive."

Americans have always been generous when it comes to providing funds for higher education. So we shall remain. But it's time for our colleges and universities to do better at living up to their end of the bargain.

It's Simply Classical Economics
Dennis O'Brien

Dennis O'Brien is president of the University of Rochester.

The most interesting aspect of Secretary of Education William J. Bennett's crusade for collegiate economy is his touching belief that he knows the proper form of the college curriculum.

Bennett's arguments against higher education are tightly connected:

First, colleges do not have the proper classical curriculum; second, they are wasteful, inefficient, and/or greedy. Certainty is the mother of efficiency; if you know the truth (the classical curriculum), the truth will make education free — or at least cheaper.

Bennett is one of the great educational theorists of the 19th century. His views are a tribute to his alma mater, Williams College, and its famous 19th-century president, Mark Hopkins. No less a person than James A. Garfield said that all you need for good education is "a student on one end of a log and Mark Hopkins on the other." Hopkins himself stated there was only one book needed in the library, the Bible.

Well, one book, one log, and one teacher make for pretty economical education. The 19th-century classical curriculum, fixed in content, direct in instruction, and sure in its moral assumptions, was a model of efficiency.

At the risk of being expelled from the University Presidents Mutual Protective Alliance, I have great sympathy with the secretary's urge to revive the classics, but the classical curriculum just won't do for the 20th — and 21st — century.

Somehow, Bennett has forgotten the rise of science, which played no role in the classical curriculum. If the classical curriculum delivered old truths, the scientific curriculum discovers new truths. Discovery is risky, uncertain, contentious, and "inefficient." Which line of research will discover the cure for cancer?

The modern college curriculum is not only scientific by addition, it is "scientific" throughout. We discover not only physical laws, but review our economic, political, artistic, and moral scholarship. Who knows, perhaps one day I may discover that Bill Bennett speaks great wisdom.

However, the secretary is correct: On the model of 19th-century collegiate education, modern universities are "inefficient."

The fundamental issue is, do we want an educational delivery service or an instrument of discovery?

Identifying the Issues

With four essays on the same topic, you certainly get a lot of information. To identify the issues important to the topic, you need to look over your notes and make a list. If one essay raises the same issue as another, there is no point in listing it twice on this list, though later you will compare the sources' opinions on each issue. An initial list might look something like this:

Tuition has increased faster than inflation since 1980.
Tuition has not increased much more than inflation since 1970.
Reasons for increases not clear.
Financial aid has been cut.
Scientific curriculum costs more.
Equipment costs more.
Skilled professors cost money.
Government needs to give schools more support.
Higher tuition hurts students without money.
Schools have high costs for utilities, insurance, and so on.
More government support can lead to higher tuition.
Schools need to conserve on costs.

E X E R C I S E   9.4   Read the essays at the end of this chapter on spanking in the schools. Make notes on them and then make a list of issues.

When you first list the issues, many of them will overlap because more than one source discusses the same issue. So you need to condense your list by grouping related items. For example, the first two issues deal with tuition increases compared with increases in the cost of living and inflation. Thus, you can define the more general issue as tuition versus inflation. Likewise, you can group all the reasons for higher tuition together under the more general issue of reasons. Other items show that financial aid is an important issue, and still others deal with funding — where money comes from to run universities. Grouping related issues into general topics, you might come up with a list like this:

Tuition versus inflation
Reasons for higher tuition
Financial aid
Funding

With a list this size you can begin to sort out how the author of each source feels about each issue. Each author will not necessarily comment on each issue, particularly if you are using many sources. Some authors may discuss only one or two of the issues. But by breaking down the issues, you can begin to see what your opinions are in contrast to the opinions of the authors. Here is one list you might create:

Tuition Versus Inflation
USA Today: Tuition has gone up only a little more than inflation since 1970.

Bennett: Tuition has gone up twice as much as inflation since 1980.

Your opinion: Tuition seems to have caught up with inflation since 1970. Now it should not go up more than inflation does.

Reasons for Higher Tuition
USA Today: Nobody seems to know, but catching up with inflation on salaries and building costs caused higher tuition and more expensive equipment such as computers.

Bennett: High financial aid lets colleges charge a lot; colleges need to "trim fat" from programs.

Hackney: In many fields professors have to get high salaries or they will work in industry rather than teach; universities have tried to cut costs, but operating costs, such as utilities and insurance, are up; also scientific equipment is expensive.

O'Brien: New scientific curriculum costs more than older classical curriculum, which he says Bennett favors.

Your opinion: Colleges should cut waste, but it is true that professors have to be paid well to stay in teaching, and new equipment raises costs.

Financial Aid
USA Today: Since 1980 there has been a large drop (68 to 37 percent) of students from families making less than $30,000, and students borrow more; financial aid cuts hurt students; they need to be increased.

Bennett: Higher financial aid contributes to higher tuition.

Hackney: Financial aid cuts have hurt students; students' opportunities should not be closed because of lack of money; colleges have had to provide more financial aid themselves.

Your opinion: Students who are needy and are willing to work hard in college deserve financial aid such as Pell grants. Also, they should not be denied loans as long as they will pay them back.

Funding
USA Today: Government and colleges need to work together on funding; government should not cut aid and colleges should avoid wasteful spending.

Bennett: Colleges and universities need to do more to hold up "their end of the bargain."

Hackney: Colleges are following "cost-saving programs" and raising more money themselves; however, "federal aid is vital."

Your opinion: Colleges and government have to work together, maybe in some kind of program where the government helps schools by need but also gives a certain amount of money to a school that raises its own money.

E X E R C I S E 9.5 Group the issues you listed in Exercise 9.4 into a more general list, and then make notes on your opinions and the opinions of each source.

Finding Your Thesis and Organizing Your Draft

Just as when you write in response to one or two sources, when writing a multiple-source essay you may find that your thesis and pattern of organization can change. Still, it is helpful to write a possible thesis and determine a pattern of organization to guide you as you draft.

Finding Your Thesis   With a list of issues and notes on the sources' opinions and your own, you can begin to find where you stand on the topic. Look over the list and compare your opinions on each issue with the opinions of the sources. If necessary, go back and reread the sources if you are not clear about your opinion on an issue. Then go over the list of your opinions and try to write a sentence that expresses them generally. Remember that the thesis cannot mention each issue specifically, so try to develop a general but clear expression of your opinion. For example, the notes for your essay on college costs might lead to the following thesis:

> The government must work together with colleges and universities so all students who have the desire and ability to seek higher education can afford it.

This thesis, of course, cannot cover every opinion you expressed in your notes, but it allows you to get into the specifics of the issues in the body of the paper. There, you will expand on it, covering specific details about the need for working together to provide more financial aid, cutting wasteful spending, and meeting costs for new equipment and faculty salaries.

E X E R C I S E 9.6 Using your notes from Exercise 9.5, write a thesis for an essay on spanking in the schools.

Organizing Your Draft   As with any essay, you can write sections of your draft in any order you wish and arrange them later or you can list the issues in the order you want to discuss them and then write the draft following that order. Remember that as you draft, you may discover a different purpose and thesis from the one you started with. Suppose you began drafting with the list of issues in the order presented earlier:

Tuition versus inflation
Reasons for higher tuition
Financial aid
Funding

This list would fit the thesis in the previous section because it suggests that you are defining a problem in the first three issues and then examining a solution in the last: how schools should be funded to minimize costs. However, if in writing you found that you were more interested in the hardships caused to students by cuts in financial aid, you could move that section to the end and discuss tuition versus inflation, reasons for high tuition, and funding problems as causes that create an undesirable effect on students. Thus, your purpose would change, and you would need to write a new thesis.

As you write your draft, remember to be flexible. If you start with a thesis and an arrangement of the issues, you might be able to follow it through. Remember, though, that the steps of the writing process overlap, so while drafting you may discover a thesis and a purpose that replace the ones you came up with in your original invention process. This can be frustrating, of course, but the writing process can be messy, as you learned in Chapter 1, and often our best ideas come as a result of writing.

■■■■■■■■■■■■■■

E X E R C I S E   9.7   Arrange the issues from Exercise 9.5 in an order that would develop the thesis you wrote in Exercise 9.6. Then rearrange the list to see if you can discover another purpose and thesis.

■ Organizing Body Paragraphs in the Multiple-Source Essay

When you are writing about multiple sources, you are dealing with many issues and opinions. Thus, you need to take care that your paragraphs are focused and coherent. You can use any form of the three-step method in the multiple-source essay, discussing one source in one paragraph and another source in another paragraph. However, at times you may want to discuss more than one source in a paragraph. Different versions of the three-step method can help.

Responding to Two Sources: The Three-Step Method

In the essay on hunting, you would probably want to make some direct comparisons of what Dunlap says and what Krutch says. You can use the three-step method from Chapter 8 by changing the questions a little.

1. What does the first source say?
2. What does the second source say?
3. What are your comments on the sources and why? Do you agree with both? disagree with both? agree with one and not the other? have mixed feelings on one? on both?

Answering the questions, in most cases, will enable you to write a coherent paragraph on a particular issue. Here are some examples.

(Step 1) Krutch argues that sport hunters destroy nature for no other reason than to "bring terror and agony" (35). (Step 2) Dunlap says that hunting — "which deals in death — can intensify our understanding of life," and he sees himself as a "brother animal" in a sometimes violent struggle with nature (13). (Step 3) Krutch may be exaggerating somewhat. Most sport hunters probably do not think of themselves the way he does. But they probably enjoy the power they feel in shooting an animal, and that is wrong. Dunlap sees hunting as more of a contest that helps us understand the idea of survival of the fittest and brings us closer to nature. But do we have to kill animals to understand nature? Can't hiking and camping bring us close to nature? Most hunters probably enjoy the thrill of the chase, but they should not glory in the idea of the violence as Dunlap does. Hunting for food is another way to use nature and must be done responsibly, but we should not enjoy killing animals or think of ourselves as animals.

This paragraph expresses mixed feelings on both Krutch's and Dunlap's opinions of how hunters relate to nature. It then asserts the writer's opinion. By following the three steps, it sticks to and examines one issue in the debate on hunting.

At other times you can discuss two sources that you agree with, expanding on their arguments.

(Step 1) The *USA Today* editorial points out that the percentage of students attending college from poor and lower-middle-class families dropped to 37 percent from 68 percent in 1980 (8a). (Step 2) Sheldon Hackney argues that "a student's abilities and interests, not financial status," should enable him or her to attend college (8a). (Step 3) These comments are right, for if the lower-income students can't afford to go to college, how can they advance in society? If college costs are beyond them, they will not have social mobility, which is one of the greatest promises of America. Without it, people lose hope and confidence in themselves and in their country.

Using the agreement between the sources as a starting point, the paragraph develops the issue of educational opportunities for students from low-income families.

At other times the sources might strongly disagree with each other, and you can follow with a discussion of your opinion on the issue.

> (Step 1) Bennett claims that when the government raises financial aid, colleges and universities raise tuition because students with more aid can pay more (8a). (Step 2) In contrast, the *USA Today* editorial points out that student aid tripled in the 1970s when tuition costs were low compared with inflation, and as tuition costs have gone higher in the 1980s financial aid has been cut (8a). (Step 3) Bennett seems to be accusing schools of taking advantage of the government, but the figures from *USA Today* show that this is a false accusation. Some schools might do what Bennett says, but it would be foolish for schools to raise prices when aid is high because they could make tuition too expensive even for students who get financial aid. A school that tried to take advantage of the government and students this way would not be in business for long because students would go to schools where they can get their money's worth.

EXERCISE 9.8 Using the three-step method, write a paragraph responding to two sources on one issue regarding spanking in the schools.

Responding to Three Sources: The Four-Step Method

This method is similar to the three-step method except that an additional question deals with the third source.

1. What does the first source say?
2. What does the second source say?
3. What does the third source say?
4. What are your comments on the sources and why? Do you agree with all three? disagree with all? agree with one and not the others? agree with two and not one? have mixed feelings on one? on two? on all?

Four-step method: A strategy for organizing a body paragraph that extends the three-step method to respond to three sources. The first three steps tell what the sources said, and the fourth step develops the writer's response.

Just as with the three-step method, your response to each source may vary. Thus, this method can produce many different kinds of paragraphs. Here is one example of how the four steps work.

> (Step 1) Sheldon Hackney argues that "federal aid is vital" to help students reach their potential (8a). (Step 2) Similarly, the *USA Today* editorial calls for "liberal student loan programs, with strong payback provisions" (8a). (Step 3) William Bennett,

however, says increased financial aid is not the answer to the high cost of education (8a). (Step 4) With lower financial aid, how does Bennett expect students to pay for college? Many already work part time, and the time spent working takes time from studying. Students can work and go to school, but if they work too many hours they cannot fulfill their potential, as Hackney says. I don't see anything wrong with increasing loans because if the program is run right to make sure people pay the loan back, the government actually makes money. It would not be hard to keep track of the loans by using a computer to identify borrowers when they file their income tax. If they have not paid that year, they could be forced to pay the loan along with their taxes. While loans should be increased, grants should continue for the needy and talented so that they do not spend the rest of their lives paying for college. Whatever the program, students need financial aid from the federal government.

This paragraph agrees with two of the sources, Hackney and *USA Today,* while disagreeing with Bennett. The four steps enable the writer to address the issue of financial aid in response to all three sources. The paragraph is a bit long, however. If you use the four-step method and find that the paragraph is too long to follow, you can break for a new paragraph as you begin step 4.

EXERCISE 9.9 Using three sources and the four-step method, write a paragraph on one issue regarding spanking in the schools.

The Source Sandwich

Despite its odd name, the **source sandwich** can be an effective way to organize a body paragraph. Paragraphs using this method start with reference to a source, follow with the writer's comments, and end with reference to another source. Each source is like a piece of bread, and the writer's comments are the meat in the middle, as the following paragraph shows.

Source sandwich: A method for developing a body paragraph in a multiple-source essay. The paragraph begins and ends with statements from the sources, "sandwiching" the writer's comments — "the meat" — in between.

(Bread) Bennett claims that when the government raises financial aid, colleges and universities raise tuition prices because students with more aid can pay more (8a). (Meat) Bennett seems to be accusing schools of taking advantage of the government, but this is a false accusation. Some schools might do what Bennett says, but it would be foolish for schools to raise prices when aid is high because they could make tuition too expensive even for students who get financial aid. A school that tried to take advantage of the government and students this way would not be in business for long because students would go to schools where they can get their money's worth. (Bread) As the *USA Today* editorial points out, student aid tripled in the 1970s when tuition costs were low compared with inflation, and as tuition costs have gone higher in the 1980s financial aid has been cut (8a).

You probably recognize much of the information in this paragraph because it is similar to the version illustrating the three-step method. In this paragraph, however, the second source has been moved to the end of the paragraph where it still denies Bennett's claim and backs up the writer's. You can also use the source sandwich with three sources, putting two first and one last, or vice versa, depending on your purpose.

(Bread) Dennis O'Brien, president of the University of Rochester, points out that increases in scientific education have contributed to the high cost of education (8a). Likewise, Sheldon Hackney mentions the costs of technological equipment and salaries for professors in fields where they could earn a great deal in private industry (8a). (Meat) Education certainly costs more these days. Just a few years ago, a school did not have to worry about budgeting money for computers. But today, most schools have computer labs for everything from physics to writing. Also, as other equipment becomes more advanced, it costs more, but without it students can't learn the most current knowledge. (Bread) Thus, William Bennett is wrong to say that schools should not point to the increased cost of knowledge to justify higher tuition (8a).

EXERCISE 9.10 Use the source sandwich to write a paragraph on one issue regarding spanking in the schools.

All of the methods for organizing body paragraphs allow you to discuss two or three sources. Until you gain more experience writing source essays, you probably should not try to deal with more than three sources in a paragraph. And even experienced writers rarely discuss more than two or three because too many sources in a paragraph can cause the reader to get confused and will not leave much room for the writer's comments. Your comments are the most important part of the essay.

As you gain experience, you will find additional ways to organize according to your purpose and depending on the sources. Remember that even in a multiple-source essay, you can use the simple three-step method dealing with one source at a time if that seems the best way to organize the essay. You can also raise issues not mentioned in the sources, so that some of your paragraphs might not refer to the sources at all. The methods considered here may not cover every situation or solve all your organizational problems, but they can help make your paragraphs more coherent if you use them in planning, writing, and revising your drafts.

■ Writing an Introduction to a Multiple-Source Essay

Like any introduction, the introduction to the multiple-source essay should get the reader's attention, introduce and limit the topic, and state your thesis. Chapter 8 presented two types of introductions for single-source essays: opening summary, and introductory strategy and summary. These two can work for some multiple-source essays. A third type draws on some of the strategies you learned in Chapter 3.

Opening Summary   In the single-source essay, this method includes a summary of the source's essay and a statement of your thesis. You can use the same technique in writing about two or three or even four sources, as long as you keep the summaries brief.

In *The Great Chain of Life,* Joseph Wood Krutch argues that hunters who kill animals just for sport are doing the worst kind of evil. He also questions the morality of people who hunt for food, though he admits they have a purpose. John C. Dunlap, author of "In Defense of Hunting," asks why people do not hunt, and he goes on to argue that hunting is no different from eating food from a supermarket, that it contributes to game management, and that it helps people understand nature. Hunting purely for sport is brutal, but not all hunting is a form of brutality.

A recent issue of *USA Today* printed an editorial and three guest columns debating the causes and effects of increases in college tuition. The editorial criticized colleges for higher costs but also recommended that the government increase financial aid. Sheldon Hackney, president of the University of Pennsylvania, defended colleges, arguing that they are trying to save money but that higher costs for teachers and equipment lead to higher tuition. He also contended that federal aid should be increased. Dennis O'Brien, University of Rochester president, said higher costs were the result of scientific education. In contrast, Secretary of Education William Bennett said colleges waste money and raise tuition whenever financial aid goes up. Education is crucial to America. Instead of arguing about tuition costs, the government should work together with colleges and universities so that all students who have the desire and ability to seek higher education can afford it.

In both introductions, the summaries are short, in some cases only one sentence stating the author's thesis. Sometimes you may have to reduce a whole book to one sentence. The summary introduction works best only if you have a small number of sources.

Introductory Strategy and Opening Summary

All the strategies you learned in Chapter 3 can be used to get the reader's attention and define the topic before you move to your summary and thesis. Depending on the length of the strategy and the summary, however, you may need to extend the introduction to two paragraphs. Compare the following introductions.

Opening Question: One Paragraph

Is a man who kills his limit during deer season and then butchers and freezes the meat so his family has food the same as a man who shoots a lion on a safari, mounts the head in his office, uses the skin for a throw rug in front of a fireplace, but has no taste or use for the meat? In his essay about killing for sport, Joseph Wood Krutch argues that hunters who kill animals just for sport are doing the worst kind of evil. He also questions the morality of people who hunt for food, though he admits they have a purpose. John C. Dunlap, author of "In Defense of Hunting," asks why people do not hunt, and he goes on to argue that hunting is no different from eating food from a supermarket, that it contributes to game management, and that it helps people understand nature. Hunting purely for sport is brutal, but not all hunting is a form of brutality.

Narrating: Two Paragraphs

Anthony Washburn entered a prestigious eastern university last fall, quite an accomplishment for a young black man from a single-parent home in Nashville, Tennessee. With a private scholarship, a government Pell grant, earnings from a part-time job, and what little his mother could contribute, he managed to pay his tuition, buy his books, and have a little pocket change. Anthony is back in Nashville this fall. No, he didn't flunk out. But when tuition increased $1500 and the government decided his private scholarships disqualified him from the Pell grant, Anthony had to defer his dream. Now he is working full time, taking evening classes at a local state university, and hoping to earn enough money to return east next year. These days, we hear about students like Anthony all too often.

A recent issue of *USA Today* printed an editorial and three guest columns debating the causes and effects of increases in college tuition. The editorial criticized colleges for higher costs but also recommended that the government increase financial aid. Sheldon Hackney, president of the University of Pennsylvania, defended colleges, arguing that colleges are trying to save money but that higher costs for teachers and equipment lead to higher tuition. He also contended that federal aid should be increased. Dennis O'Brien, University of Rochester president, said higher costs were the result of scientific education. In contrast, Secretary of Education William Bennett said colleges waste money and raise tuition whenever financial aid goes up. Education is crucial to America. Instead of arguing about tuition costs, the government should work together with colleges and universities so that all students who have the desire and ability to seek higher education can afford it.

The first of these introductions is very much like the example in the last chapter: it adds the question strategy, but now there is a summary of Dunlap's essay along with the summary of Krutch's. The second uses narration to involve the reader, to add human interest before getting to the topic. Because of the length of the narration, the summary and thesis must follow in a second paragraph. An introduction of this sort is more appropriate to a longer paper. You wouldn't want an introduction of two paragraphs if the whole essay is only five or six paragraphs.

Introductory Strategy Without Direct Reference to the Sources

If you are writing on a topic and read five, six, or more sources, you cannot summarize all of them in the introduction because by the time you get to your thesis, you will have lost the reader's attention. When you have many sources, it is best just to use one of the introductory strategies to define and limit the topic and state your thesis. Any of the strategies studied in Chapter 3 would work. For instance, you could add the thesis on the cost of education to the narration about Anthony and use that paragraph as an introduction. Then you could discuss the sources only in the body paragraphs. Using the sources only in the body is fine as long as the introduction has done the job of introducing your topic and stating your thesis.

Another way to handle several sources in the introduction is to write one or two sentences saying that several authors have been concerned with the topic and have written on it. Note the italicized sentence in the following introduction:

A popular slogan of people who support increased funds for education reads, "If you think education is expensive, try the cost of ignorance." Any student or parent today knows the cost of higher education. Tuition, which has risen dramatically in the last few years, is only one part of the cost of pursuing a degree. Books, supplies, incidentals, and, for many students, living costs can double the price. *Several educators and authorities have attempted to find the causes and propose solutions to the rising costs of higher education, but no one has the answer.* With many students facing the cost of ignorance, the government should work together with colleges and universities so that all students who have the desire and ability to seek higher education can afford it.

Using the opening quotation, this is a standard introduction, but the italicized sentence lets the reader know that you have been reading about the topic and that the essay will more than likely refer to some of the educators and authorities for support. Thus, the reader is prepared for the body paragraphs that follow.

E X E R C I S E   9.11 Using strategies of your choice, write two different introductions to set up the thesis on spanking in the schools that you wrote in Exercise 9.6.

■ Writing a Conclusion to a Multiple-Source Essay

Just as in any essay, the conclusion for a multiple-source essay has the following purposes: to stress the thesis, to leave an impression, and to give the essay a sense of completeness. You can use any of the strategies you learned in Chapter 3. As in the single-source essay, you should try to refer to the sources in the conclusion if you are writing about two or three sources.

> Krutch is right to say that "killing for killing's sake is a terrifying phenomenon" (35). However, Dunlap's arguments about the laws of nature and the purpose of game management show that not all hunters kill for the sake of killing. People have hunted since the beginning of time, and though hunting is associated with uncivilized societies, hunters can be civilized if, along with their guns, they take responsibility and respect for nature into the woods.

Working the sources into such a conclusion is not difficult because there are only two. However, when you have many sources, you cannot refer to all of them in the conclusion. You can either use a concluding strategy without reference to the sources or pick a particularly strong quote from one source and work it in, as in the following examples.

No Reference to the Sources

University administrators and government officials must find a way to keep college affordable without sacrificing the quality of education. Money should not stand between students and their desire to develop themselves to their fullest potential. Ask Anthony Washburn.

You may recognize this strategy from Chapter 3, where it was called "echoing the introduction." While the thesis is echoed in the first two sentences, the reference to Anthony returns the reader to the human interest element that began the essay. While this conclusion is effective, a quotation from one source could work as well:

University administrators and government officials must find a way to keep college affordable without sacrificing the quality of education. Money should not stand between students and their desire to develop themselves to their fullest potential. As the *USA Today* editorial put it, "You don't need a college degree to know something's wrong here" (8a).

E X E R C I S E   9.12 Write two different conclusions for an essay on the topic of spanking in the schools.

■ Revising and Editing Checklists for the Multiple-Source Essay

Many of the concerns you will have in revising and editing the multiple-source essay are similar to those that apply to the single-source essay and, for that matter, to all essays. The following checklists can guide your revision and editing.

Revising

1. Does your introduction make it clear that you will be drawing on multiple sources?
2. Each time you cite a source for the first time, do you use the author's full name?
3. Are the source's points clearly tagged so that the reader can tell them from your own?
4. Does the essay refer to the sources at various points so that it avoids drifting off into a personal essay?
5. Do you present the sources' ideas accurately and clearly when you paraphrase them?
6. Do you use your own words and sentence structure when you paraphrase?
7. Do your responses logically follow from or lead to the sources' ideas? In other words, are you and the sources talking about the same issue?
8. When you are discussing more than one source at a time, is the position of each source clear?
9. If you use the three-step method, are all steps clear and is step 3 fully developed?
10. Do your body paragraphs end in agreement with your thesis?
11. Does your conclusion reassert your thesis?

Editing

1. If a source is a book, have you underlined the title?
2. If a source is an essay, have you placed the title in quotation marks?
3. If you have quoted the sources, have you used their *exact* words?

4. If you have left words out of a quotation, have you used ellipsis points?
5. In integrating quotations, have you avoided sentence errors such as comma splices and run-on sentences?
6. Have you cited sources with parenthetical citation (page numbers in parentheses)?
7. Have you used the proper forms for entering the sources on your list of works cited?

Essays for Reading

Unlike the Essays for Reading in earlier chapters, the first two essays here form a pair that addresses the same topic: whether children, particularly gifted children, should be grouped in classes according to their ability. The Vocabulary Cues, Questions to Guide Your Reading, Questions for Study and Discussion, and Writing Assignments apply to both essays.

Vocabulary Cues

thwarted: blocked, stopped

psychoanalytic: having to do with psychoanalysis, an approach to psychology based on the theories of Freud

repress: to push out of the conscious mind into the subconscious

neurotic: having to do with a mental disorder

defense mechanism: a mental trick that is used to avoid facing painful feelings or thoughts

spontaneously: without planning, suddenly

assailed: challenged

impoverished: made poor

innate: possessing since birth, born with

heterogeneous: unseparated, all types mixed together

caste: a social class

dividends: benefits

Questions to Guide Your Reading

1. Why is Bettelheim against grouping gifted students together in the same classes?
2. What does he say about gifted students becoming bored?
3. What does he say happens to average and below-average students when they are grouped in classes by themselves?
4. What does he say happens when all students, regardless of ability, are together in the same class?
5. How does Mott defend against the idea that grouping gifted students creates "a caste of intellectual snobs"?
6. According to Mott, who or what should decide how students are placed in groups?
7. What does Mott say happens to the learning rate when students are grouped by ability?

Grouping the Gifted

Bruno Bettelheim

Bruno Bettelheim is a psychiatrist who has written numerous books on psychological development, education, and other topics. He has been a principal, a professor of education, and a professor of psychology and psychiatry. This essay first appeared in the *National Education Association Journal* in 1964, but the topic still concerns educators today.

An argument often advanced on behalf of special classes for gifted children is that in regular classrooms these children are held back and possibly thwarted in their intellectual growth by learning situations that are designed for the average child. There can be little doubt that special classes for the gifted can help them to graduate earlier and take their place in life sooner. On the other hand, to take these children out of the regular classroom may create serious problems for them and for society.

For example, in regular classrooms, we are told, the gifted child becomes bored and loses interest in learning. This complaint, incidentally, is heard more often from adults, parents, or educators than from students. Nevertheless, on the strength of these complaints, some parents and educators conclude that special classes should be set up for the gifted.

Although some children at the top of their class do complain of being bored in school, the issue of why they are bored goes far beyond the work they have in school. If the findings of psychoanalytic investigation of feelings have any validity, feelings of boredom arise as a defense against deep feelings of anxiety. To be bored, therefore, is to be anxious.

The student who is bored by his studies is the student who can take few constructive measures of his own to manage his anxieties. Consequently, he represses or denies them; he must ask others, specifically his teachers, to keep him frantically busy, studying and competing intellectually so that he will not feel anxiety.

The gifted child who is bored is an anxious child. To feed his neurotic defense mechanism may serve some needs of society, but to nourish his neurosis certainly does not help him as a human being.

Psychology, like nature, does not permit a vacuum. If study material does not hold the student's attention because of his easy mastery of it, the result is not necessarily boredom. Other intellectual interests can fill the unscheduled time. Is it reasonable to assume that gifted children learn only when pressed by the curriculum?

Several years ago I observed what happened to a number of gifted children who were taken out of a highly accelerated, highly competitive private school and placed in a public high school of good academic standing where, by comparison, the work was so easy as to be "boring."

Close inspection revealed an interesting and worthwhile development in most of the transplanted youngsters. In the special school for the gifted, these children had shown little ability to use their own critical judgment. Instead, they had relied heavily on their teachers' direction. In the slower-paced school, no longer having to worry about keeping up, these students began to reflect spontaneously on many problems, some of which were not in the school program.

The students acquired on their own a much deeper appreciation of life, art, literature, and other human beings. No longer exhausted by meeting assigned learning tasks, these youngsters had energy to branch out, broaden their interests, and understand far more deeply.

Prolonged, rarely assailed security may be the best preparation for tackling difficult intellectual problems. Because the gifted child learns easily, he acquires a feeling of security in a regular class. On the other hand, if such a child is put into a special class where learning is not easy for him, where he is only average among a group of extremely gifted youngsters, he may, as often happens, come to feel that he has only average abilities which are not up to coping with difficult challenges.

Another argument advanced for special classes for the gifted is that removing highly capable students from the regular classroom lessens anxiety among the slower learners. Possibly so. But how do anxieties become manageable except through a friendly working relationship with someone felt to be superior — in this case the faster learners in the classroom?

In many of our big cities today, the students left behind in the noncollegiate programs are marked as a lower breed. Instead, most of them come from poor, lower-class homes. Surrounded by students who have little interest in acquiring an education, lacking companionship with students who want to learn, and receiving no encouragement at home, these children apply themselves even less than they would if there were good students in class with whom to identify.

In order to achieve educationally, many children from economically impoverished homes need to be challenged and motivated by example. Grouping deprives these children of such stimulation. They are left behind as second-class students, a situation which is more likely to create hopelessness than to lessen anxiety. Should some of them display outstanding leadership or ability, they are sent away to join their intellectual peers, leaving the nongifted group even more impoverished.

Grouping children intelligently has much in common with mountain climbing. In mountain climbing, the guides usually distribute themselves ahead of and behind beginners or less skilled climbers. Placed in the center of the group with people who have learned both the skill and the teamwork required in mountain climbing, the beginner is likely to learn quickly and well.

If, however, all of the good climbers are put into one party, and all of the poor ones in another, the second group is likely to fail miserably or perish altogether.

When the debate over what is the "best" education for the child reaches an impasse, the argument is frequently switched to what is best for society. Today we are told that we need more scientists and more engineers to "survive." Therefore, we must speed the growth of young people who have the necessary talent.

Does anyone really know what the needs of society will be thirty years hence? Can science guarantee survival? Might society not have a greater need for fresh, imaginative ideas on how to organize a worldwide society? Might we not have a greater need for men of broad social vision than for scientists? And since ideas mature slowly, maybe what we need is not a speeding up but a slowing down of our all-too-fast pace.

I am not suggesting that we dismiss our concern for the gifted, that we leave well enough alone. On the contrary, our schools can and must improve. I am simply saying that arguments for the special education of gifted children do not yet rest on scientifically solid ground. What we need now is not quick remedies but carefully balanced and controlled experiments, based on hard thinking and planning.

Grouping the Gifted Is the Best Way
Kenneth Mott

> Kenneth Mott has many years of experience as a teacher, principal, and education administrator. When he wrote this essay, he was supervisor of social studies for the Louisiana Department of Education. Mott's essay followed Bettelheim's in the *National Education Association Journal*.

I regard gifted children as those who possess some quality or innate ability which has been recognized and identified by any number of testing and observation devices and who manifest interest and success in either physical, intellectual, or artistic pursuits.

These might be children who are gifted athletes but who have real trouble mastering academic subject matter, or students who are poor athletes but are highly intellectual "quiz kids" who knock the top off all measuring devices. "Gifted" may describe pupils of average intelligence who have exceptional ability in art or music, or it may refer to the child with an IQ of 135 who excels in everything.

How can we deal with these gifted? I firmly believe that we should group them as nearly as possible according to interest and ability (giftedness) and challenge them with a type of program that will help them to grow to the fullest extent of their abilities and capacities.

This grouping could take the form of special subject arrangements in the elementary grades, a situation in which a class is heterogeneously grouped most of the day but is divided at times into special interest or ability class groups for special instruction. In high school, it may take the form of grouping students in regular classes according to any number of criteria but basically those of interest and proficiency (or lack of proficiency) in various subject areas.

One of the basic arguments against grouping the gifted is the fear of creating a caste of intellectual snobs. Similarly, some educators fear that the average and slow students would come to regard themselves as inferior.

If my definition of gifted is accepted, then these fears are groundless. After all, the schools have grouped gifted athletes for years. Yet how many regard themselves as part of an elite? Do varsity athletes look down upon other pupils as inferior? The vast majority apparently do not.

Consider also the amount of "gifted grouping" in speech, music, art, and journalism. Schools have readily grouped the gifted in these areas without any apparent ill effect. To the extent of my observation, encouraging gifted debaters, musicians, artists, and writers to develop their special talents does not create envy or feelings of inferiority among less talented students.

If educators sincerely desire to promote individual growth and self-respect, they have no grounds, as far as I can see, to fear any kind of grouping. The teacher, not the manner in which a class is organized, determines students' attitudes toward individual differences. Before he can hope to instill the proper attitude, however, the teacher needs to make a critical analysis of his own attitudes toward such differences.

If a group of gifted or nongifted students form the wrong concept about themselves, the fault probably lies with the teachers, parents, or administrators. I have confidence that if teachers accept and respect individual worth, that if they challenge and spark interests in young people, the individual student will mature and grow successfully along the lines of his interests and abilities. I say, let those with similar "gifts" associate, plan, and enjoy being together.

Many educators disagree with the idea of gifted grouping because they believe that it does not affect achievement significantly. They cite pilot studies which indicate that no significant change in achievement results when children are separated into slow and accelerated classes.

The fact is, however, that in a vast majority of pilot studies the children have been grouped only according to IQ scores, which are far from reliable, and the conclusions have been based on achievement scores which measure only mastery of factual detail.

Unfortunately, there are no reliable devices for measuring growth in such areas as creativity, attitudes, personal adjustment, latent interest and talent, and innate capacity.

My opinion, which is based on more than a decade in the classroom, is that learning skyrockets when individuals are grouped according to interest and ability and are motivated, challenged, and inspired by a type of school work that will yield some measure of success to them.

Heterogeneous classrooms frequently produce frustration in children who are persistently unable to do the same work that most of the other children do. Frustration is also produced when bright children are not properly challenged by their school work, as is too often the case in heterogeneous classrooms.

I have little fear of gifted students' being pushed beyond their endurance, for I have faith in the ability of most teachers to recognize the limits to which any student should be pushed. On the other hand, I don't believe giftedness should be wasted away simply because a bright or talented student is content to proceed at what is — for him — a snail's pace or to stand at the top of a class of students with less ability.

Several schools with which I am familiar have experimented with grouping the gifted in a reading program. (The regular procedure had been to have three or four reading groups in one classroom under one teacher. The teacher's time was divided among several small groups.)

The experiment involved putting slow readers from different classrooms in one classroom, average readers from different classrooms in another class, and fast readers in still another class. Each classroom still had one teacher, but he no longer had to divide his time among several different groups. The control group consisted of a class organized and taught under the regular procedure mentioned above.

After two years, the researchers found greater overall progress at all reading levels in the experimental group. In fact, some slower readers joined the average ones and some average ones moved up to the fast group. In this case, special ability grouping paid dividends all around.

I believe the same results could have been achieved in science, social studies, mathematics, or English. By decreasing the range of interest and/or ability levels, the teacher is able to do more toward helping individual growth.

While I do not believe that children should be regarded as resources to be molded to the needs of society, I do believe that as individuals they are endowed with certain characteristics and attributes — "gifted" of nature — which represent their potential success in life. Where children have certain "gifts" in common, they should be allowed to work and study together.

Questions for Study and Discussion

1. Mott says IQ tests are not a reliable way to place students into groups and then argues that teachers should identify the gifted students. Compare his argument with Bettelheim's claim that there is no reliable way to place students into groups.
2. Compare each author's arguments on the issue of boredom. According to Bettelheim, why do students get bored?
3. How does Mott support his claim that grouping gifted students will not create snobbery or make less talented students inferior? What does Bettelheim say on this issue?
4. Why, according to Mott, have studies of grouped classes not shown that students in them learn faster? What evidence does he offer that grouping can speed up learning?
5. What do you think of Bettelheim's claim that students in a mixed class are like a mountain climbing team where the experienced climbers help the inexperienced?
6. What is Mott's position on molding students to fit the future needs of society? What does Bettelheim say about society's future needs? What do you think?

7. In elementary, high school, or college, if you have ever been placed in a class because of your ability, or lack of ability, how did you feel? Did you learn more, less, or about the same amount as you would have learned in a mixed class?

Writing Assignments

1. Write an essay of 600–800 words that compares and contrasts Mott's and Bettelheim's essays while developing a thesis of your own. You can limit the topic to cover just elementary students or just high school students. Also you can consider the benefits or drawbacks of grouping for all students — the average and below average — as well as the gifted.

2. Mott and Bettelheim are concerned with students in elementary and high school, but some college classes group students by ability — for example, there are English and math classes for students who need to catch up in those subjects, and some schools have honors courses for students who are advanced in a particular subject. Write an essay of 600–800 words in which you argue the value, or lack of value, of grouping students by ability in college. During the invention process, consider these questions: Should there be more of such classes? fewer? How do the issues Mott and Bettelheim discuss apply to college students?

More Essays for Reading

The next five essays appeared in *USA Today* in 1988 and form a set. Each discusses the issue of whether teachers and principals should be allowed to spank students in elementary and high schools. The Vocabulary Cues, Questions to Guide Your Reading, Questions for Study and Discussion, and Writing Assignment apply to all five essays.

Vocabulary Cues
corporal: physical, having to do with the body
flogged: whipped with a heavy strap or rod
neurosurgeon: a surgeon who operates on the nervous system
horrific: horrible, terrifying
octave: a group of eight
percussion: having to do with drums and drumming
beget: cause to exist
barbarians: people who are uncivilized and violent
acknowledge: recognize with respect
unscathed: unharmed physically or mentally
unalienable: unchangeable, unquestionable, not to be doubted
deter: discourage, prevent
rampant: uncontrollable, widespread
rigorous: severe, strict
abhorrent: disgusting, completely unacceptable
Pandora's box: a set of problems (In Greek myth, Pandora was the
     first woman. She was given a box by the gods and told not to
     open it because it contained all the problems and illness that
     could happen in the world. But being curious, she opened it,
     turning loose all the problems that humans have faced ever
     since.)

Questions to Guide Your Reading
1. Does spanking prevent bad behavior?
2. What message does spanking send to students?
3. What effects, good or bad, could spanking have on students?
4. Who should decide if children should be spanked in schools?
5. What are possible alternatives to spanking?

Teachers Must Stop Hitting Our Children
USA *Today* Editorial

Vicki Elmore got so mad at an assistant principal who spanked her 7-year-old son that she whacked him over the head with a wooden paddle.

It got her a six-month jail sentence. The Pell City, Ala., mother, who's appealing her sentence, is one of a growing number of parents fighting back against school officials who hit their children.

They belong to groups like People Opposed to Paddling Students (POPS) in Houston; Schools Without Abuse Toward Students (SWATS) in Peoria, Ill.; and End Violence Against the Next Generation (EVANG) in Berkeley, Calif.

And they're forming a national network to work together to ban corporal punishment.

Students, they say, are the only people today subject to physical punishment. Sailors aren't flogged at sea anymore. Guards can't hit prisoners. And spouse abuse is illegal.

But schoolchildren in most states aren't protected by law from such punishment. More than 1 million are spanked annually, according to the U.S. Department of Education.

It has to be that way, some say, so teachers can keep control of their classrooms. But it doesn't have to be that way.

Spanking doesn't work. It doesn't deter disruptive behavior; it encourages it. It may make teachers feel better. But it sends students the wrong message. It creates resentment and anger. It hurts learning.

And it can hurt its victims.

Jamie Logan's dream of a military career has ended. She was spanked twice with a board for leaving her Portsmouth, Ohio, school cafeteria, without permission, to call her orthodontist when her braces broke. A neurosurgeon and other physicians say they can't cure her limp.

Jamie's case may be the extreme. But hers, and others like hers, wouldn't happen if we outlawed spanking.

That's why the American Medical Association is against corporal punishment. And the National Congress of Parents and Teachers. The American Bar Association. The National Education Association. The American Academy of Pediatrics. The American Public Health Association. The American Psychological Association.

Nine states won't allow spanking: California, Hawaii, Maine, Massachusetts, Vermont, New Hampshire, Rhode Island, New York, and New Jersey.

Spanking has been banned by many big-city school districts. And parents are trying to get it outlawed in the 41 states that still permit it.

No one is trying to deny teachers the authority they need to maintain discipline. The point is that hitting students is not an acceptable way to do it.

Resourceful educators know they can accomplish more by restricting the privileges of unruly students, by separating them from their audiences, by meting out in-school suspensions and extra academic work, by counseling students and consulting their parents.

Good teachers know hitting isn't discipline. And hurting isn't teaching.

Taming the Classroom ''Pit Bulls''
Steve Marmel

Steve Marmel is a humorist and comedian, as is evident in his comic approach to this serious topic.

It's a well-known law: Every school has its troublemaker. It's as though, when construction is done, the architect looks at his building and says, ''Wait! What this place needs is a real jerk!''

You know the kid. The one who shot spitballs at the girls he liked, took lunch money from the kids he hated, had a comment for everything the teacher said, and went to his parents and whined about how unfair the world was. Every school had a kid who deserved to get smacked.

Those who object to corporal punishment are the same ones who believe this ''no bad dog'' stuff. But every species has a pit bull, and you can't discipline a killer instinct with a tender scratch behind the ears.

One problem: The educator who makes the disciplinary decision is usually the one who has a short fuse and a long day. It's judge, jury and executioner, all rolled up in an English teacher. Not a bad job if you can get it. But a kid hit too hard will be too sore to ever sit back down at his desk.

Like any great social cause, this one has its hypocritical segments: the parents who are selfish about corporal punishment. ''Nobody hits my child but me,'' they say. That may be true, but then they're not locked in a crowded classroom with the horrific little lunatics.

The choir director at my junior high school once suggested lining eight troublemakers up — forming an octave — and ''smacking'' the Beach Boys' classic *Be True to Your School.* But none of the kids wanted to be percussion and the idea was scrapped.

The true master of horror at my school was the teacher who took a small group of volunteers into a ''tunnel'' that allegedly ran between two buildings. He told us there were only a few minutes of air, turned the corner in the pitch-black hallway, ''broke'' his flashlight, and the fun began! Compared to that, I'd take a sore backside any day of the week.

True corporal punishment exists among fellow students in a game called ''bombardment.'' Played in gym class, the object is to hurl semi-inflated balls at your best friend's face — for fun. Maybe if aggravated teachers whipped a Teflon-coated beach ball at the kid, this controversy would be over.

Barbarians Beget More Barbarians
Sherry Roberts

Sherry Roberts is a writer and editor of *Carolina Piedmont Magazine.* As her essay indicates, she is also a concerned parent.

I drop off my children daily at what has got to be the ugliest school in the world. It is the most unimaginative structure, a flat-topped concrete box.

I pay an outrageous sum for my children to attend classes in that box because inside are several lovely ideas, one of which is posted on the wall, a law, a bill of rights: All children in the box have "the right to be without fear of being hurt."

I consider that document to be as important as any in the National Archives. It acknowledges that children have basic human rights, which will be respected in school — a revolutionary idea for a North Carolina school, even a private one.

In most public and some private schools, not only in North Carolina but in 40 other states, corporal punishment is a way of life. We, as a society, say it is all right to beat, spank, hit, slap, strike, and assault our children. We are barbaric and we are raising barbarians.

We live in daring (or desperate) times, when more and more children are using violence against themselves, their friends, their parents. This generation needs no more lessons in violence. Instead, it needs to learn the course of compromise, compassion, and control.

Schools insist they need corporal punishment to maintain order. It is distressing that academicians and teachers aren't smart enough to find alternatives to spanking. Schools that forbid spanking and practice innovative techniques in discipline show their respect for the rights of children, thus teach children to respect the rights of others. They report virtually no discipline problems.

But administrators and teachers will not learn those techniques as long as they have the crutch of the states' corporal punishment laws. It takes time and energy to work creatively with a child's discipline problems. It requires not one brain cell to beat him.

And laws will not change until parents change them. Parents who spank at home and see nothing wrong with school officials doing it at school justify themselves and the schools by saying: "I was spanked as a kid and I turned out all right."

But did they? Did those people really emerge unscathed? I think not. Part of human destiny is to grow and develop, to break the pattern, to change the world for the better. It is not good enough to justify life; we must improve it.

Children are humans. They have certain unalienable rights. Rights keep the jungle of ugliness at bay, so that we can find beauty in the most unlikely places.

Schools Must Be Able to Spank Their Students

Dennis L. Cuddy

Dennis L. Cuddy is a former public school teacher.

With the beginning of the new academic year, there's a growing debate over whether corporal punishment, as now allowed in 39 states, should be prohibited by the government.

Polls consistently show parental concern over school discipline, and in the schools where I taught, corporal punishment seemed a deterrent to student misbehavior.

Some advocates of "students' rights" consider spanking barbaric. However, it was the permissive "students' rights" movement of the 1960s which was partly responsible for the increased chaos and student violence in schools since that time.

Since there's obviously no rampant child abuse on the part of America's teachers, one must assume those wishing to prohibit teachers the use of corporal punishment object to this form of discipline per se.

Will they next want the government to prohibit parents from spanking their children?

Parents have a right to use corporal punishment, and teachers have a responsibility to reinforce parental authority. Many children have been taught the biblical commandment, "Honor thy father and thy mother."

If parents who've spanked their children for serious infractions at home instruct teachers to do likewise for similar behavior at school, then for government to prohibit teachers from doing so might undermine parental authority.

Teachers should use corporal punishment only with parental permission because some parents prefer to spank their own children, and some would prefer their children to be suspended from school for a day instead of being spanked.

That should be their right.

Teachers should never use corporal punishment in anger, and there should always be a witness present to ensure that it isn't administered abusively. Furthermore, it should be used only after lesser disciplinary actions have failed.

It's most desirable, if possible, to use positive alternatives to corporal punishment, suspensions and expulsions.

I conducted an experiment demonstrating that when students are introduced to a successful teaching method previously unfamiliar to them, discipline problems decreased by over 25%.

Thus, if American school systems would compile their teachers' successful instructional methods and distribute them for other teachers to use voluntarily, not only would teaching improve, but student discipline would as well.

However, for government to prohibit completely parentally approved corporal punishment would be going too far.

Most of America's teachers are responsible adults and should not have the disciplinary option taken away from them.

Maintaining Discipline Is a Two-Way Street
Albert Shanker

Albert Shanker taught in the New York City school system for many years. When he wrote this essay, he was president of the American Federation of Teachers, the largest teachers' union in the country.

''It's nothing a little old-fashioned discipline wouldn't cure . . .'' How many times have strong discipline codes been offered as panaceas for all that ails U.S. public schools?

It is easy to make this argument. Districts and schools should, of course, have rigorous (and fair) discipline codes and procedures and ensure that especially destructive students don't disrupt everyone else's educational opportunities. But when it comes to the issue of corporal punishment — whether or not teachers or administrators can strike students — the argument becomes much trickier.

Suppose a school district decides corporal punishment is an acceptable disciplinary tool. What would the offenses be? Chewing gum? Smoking a cigarette in the bathroom? Talking back to a teacher? Hitting a classmate? Torturing the class hamster?

And what method of punishment should be used by school personnel? Hand spankings? A paddle? How much force is enough? What if the punishment doesn't work?

Where would the punishment be doled out? In the privacy of the principal's office? In front of the whole class? During a school assembly?

Parents undoubtedly have some thoughts on the subject. Some parents approve of giving schools the authority to physically discipline their students while others find the very idea of corporal punishment abhorrent. If schools then listened to the wishes of parents, would a teacher be able to spank one-half of the class and not the other?

What if a student is bigger than a teacher? He or she could then hit back. It is much easier to imagine giving a light spanking to a first-grader than striking an 18-year-old high school senior who happens to be on the football team!

And let's not forget the legal and insurance problems that are involved with corporal punishment, especially if there is an injury. And corporal punishment becomes a Pandora's box in such cases as when the teacher is white and the student is black, the teacher is male and the student is female, etc.

Of course, there are those students who are truly violent and don't belong in school to begin with. Muggers, drug dealers, and those kids who feel compelled to carry a knife or a pistol have no business being in school.

But while the debate on corporal punishment goes on, we should explore ways of organizing schools, teaching and learning that reduce the incidence of bad behavior.

We demand that students sit still and keep quiet for five or six hours at a time — something most adults can't do — then punish those students who can't comply. Discipline is a two-way street.

We need to demand good behavior from students — that is part of learning to be good citizens. But we also need to make sure that the schools don't provoke the very behavior we don't want.

Questions for Study and Discussion

1. The *USA Today* editorial gives an example of a girl who was permanently injured because of a spanking. Do you think this example is typical? If not, is it still a good example?
2. Nearly all the authors mention alternative punishments to spanking. What are these? Do you think they would be more or less effective than spanking?
3. Dennis Cuddy is in favor of spanking, but he also specifies exactly when and how it should be done. Why is he so specific and what do you think of the method of spanking he suggests?
4. Cuddy, Marmel, and Shanker all raise the question of how hard a student could be spanked, and we know that some kinds of spanking would not cause injury. Should light spankings be allowed? Who would determine what a light spanking is?
5. Shanker says that it would not be as easy to spank a high school football player as it would a first grader. Should the age, grade level, or size of the student determine how he or she is punished?
6. Shanker also says it would be difficult to decide what offenses a student should be spanked for. Can you think of any kind of misbehavior that would deserve a spanking, or should spanking be banned completely?
7. Parents should have some say in whether their children are spanked. Since some parents want teachers to spank their kids, and others are strongly against spanking, how can schools satisfy both groups?
8. Roberts calls spanking barbaric. Do you agree that all spanking, even by parents, is barbaric?
9. Roberts also doubts people who say that being spanked as children did not affect them as adults. Do you agree with her that such people have been injured in some way they do not recognize?
10. Several times the question of children's rights was raised in these essays. To what extent do children have rights in our society? To what extent should they be denied rights granted to adults?

Writing Assignment

In response to these essays, write an essay of 700–800 words arguing that children who misbehave in school should or should not be spanked. Make sure your essay includes ideas from the sources as well as your own.

Editing Your Writing

I n editing your writing, you probably have looked into this chapter earlier, either at your teacher's request or on your own. Editing is the last step in the writing process. When you are editing your writing, your goal is to make sure all the language follows standard English forms. Before we consider what standard English is, we will look at forms of English that are not standard.

The English language is spoken in many different ways around the world. Even here in America, groups of people speak the language somewhat differently. A person from New York does not pronounce words the same way a person from Georgia does. Similarly, some of the forms used by different groups vary. For example, someone from a rural area of the Midwest might say, "The workers *was* tired at the end of the day." A young urban person might say, "The workers *be* tired at the end of the day." In contrast, other people would say, "The workers *were* tired." Similarly, working-class people might say, "He *don't* seem to be a good candidate for mayor" or "It *don't* look like the sun is going to come out today," while other people would say, "He doesn't seem" or "It doesn't look."

The way a group of people talks is called a **dialect,** and groups of people who speak the same dialect make up a **speech community** (see Paul Roberts's essay at the end of this chapter). Dialects can be determined by various factors: class, geography, race, nationality. Since America has many groups of people, there are many American dialects of English. The pronunciations and forms in these dialects are not so different that people from different groups cannot understand one another. It is wrong to think that other people's dialect, or your own, is just a form of bad grammar and that people who speak it are inferior. If you are

Dialect: A version of a language spoken by a particular group within a larger society. Dialects vary from the standad version of the language and may be determined by class, geography, nationality, or race.

Speech community: A group of people who share the same dialect.

aware that you speak a dialect, your goal should not be to change the way you speak, for when you are around your family and the people you have grown up with, you will need the dialect to remain part of the group. Rather, you should keep the dialect for situations when you need it, but you should also learn to speak and write the standard English you will need in college and on the job.

Standard English: The version of English spoken and written in business, schools, government, and media.

Standard English is the language used in government, business, school, and the media. It is also the language of power. Some linguists argue that standard English allows for better communication and that it is capable of expressing more complex ideas. Other linguists say that all dialects communicate equally, that all are just as capable of expressing complex ideas, and that standard English became the standard form of the language because it is the version of English used by the upper-middle and upper classes. Whatever the case, the rules of standard English are not written in stone by some supreme being running the universe, but standard English is still very powerful because it is used by the people with the best jobs and the most influence in the country. It would be nice if we could all use our own dialects, but unfortunately, if we want careers and affluence, we have to use standard English.

The discussions of editing in this chapter consider not so much errors as nonstandard forms. Errors are errors only when you are trying to use one dialect and you mistakenly use a form of another. For example, in the neighborhood in New Jersey where I grew up, it is common to address a group of people with the pronoun *yous*. In standard English, the pronoun form for addressing a group is *you*. If I were writing a report to other professors at my university, I would be in error if I addressed them as *yous* because I would be using a nonstandard form in a piece of writing that should be written in standard English, the language of colleges and universities.

As a beginning writer, particularly if you have grown up using a nonstandard dialect, you may find editing one of the most bothersome parts of writing. You finish an essay, you believe it develops a thesis, you feel it is thoughtful and interesting, but you worry that you have used nonstandard forms that could distract the reader from getting your point. While organizing and presenting interesting ideas are the most important elements of writing, a piece of writing that is full of nonstandard forms will not be very effective.

You need not be a grammar whiz to edit out nonstandard forms. First, you probably do not use as many as you think you do. Most beginning writers have trouble with two or three forms, but because they use each one over and over, they feel as if they have many errors, when actually they are making one error many times. This chapter covers common lapses from standard English and gives you enough background in grammar so that you can learn to reduce, if not eliminate, nonstandard forms. Remember that learning to write standard English takes time, but if you keep an error log, as suggested in Chapter 1, and if you review the appropriate sections of this chapter each time you identify nonstandard forms in your writing, you will gradually eliminate them.

■ Standard English Sentences and Nonstandard Forms

To understand the most common sentence errors, you should review how standard English sentences work.

Subjects and Verbs The basic parts of a sentence are its *subject* and its *verb*. The following exercises and discussion will help you become skillful at identifying subjects and verbs.

E X E R C I S E   10.1 Complete the following sentences with any word or words that fit. Don't worry about having the correct answers; just find words that make sense.

1. _____ cost $18,000 with all the options.

2. _____ is considered the father of our country.

3. In the 1960s _____ helped lead the civil rights movement for black people in America.

4. _____ declared war on Japan after the bombing of Pearl Harbor.

5. _____ was one of the best athletes in my high school.

6. _____ won the last election for president, and _____ lost.

7. Because _____ turn orange, brown, and gold, _____ is my favorite season of the year.

8. _____ won the TV ratings poll last week, but _____ think that _____ is a better show.

9. _____ celebrate the Fourth of July each year, and in many towns across the country _____ fill the sky with bright colors and loud noise.

10. _____ will never replace human beings because _____ are machines, and _____ can't do anything without human beings to operate them.

11. _____ and _____ are my best friends.

12. _____ and _____ play the meanest guitars in rock.

Subject: The subject of a sentence or clause is the person or thing that does something (performs an action) or the person or thing which something is said about.

This was not a quiz to see if you knew the answers but an exercise to teach you about subjects in sentences. The **subject** of a sentence is the person or thing that *does* something (performs an action) or the person or thing that something is said about (for example, *John is a doctor* tells about John the subject).

Every word that you added to the sentences in the exercise was a subject. For instance, if you started sentence number 9 with *Americans*, you named a group that does something. It celebrates the Fourth of July. If you added the word *fireworks* later in the sentence, you named a thing that does something — fills the sky. In number 2, when you answered *George Washington*, you named a person about whom something was said — that he is the father of our country. Identifying subjects is fairly easy, and knowing how to do it can help you correct sentence errors, as you will see.

E X E R C I S E   10.2   Copy the following paragraph and underline each subject in each sentence. (Some sentences have more than one subject.)

When you go down a coal mine, it is important to try and get to the coal face when the miners are at work. This is not easy because when the mine is working, visitors are a nuisance and are not encouraged. But if you go at any other time, it is possible to come away with the wrong impression. On a Sunday, for instance, a mine seems almost peaceful. The time to go there is when the machines are roaring and the air is black with coal dust, and when you can actually see what the miners have to do.

George Orwell

E X E R C I S E   10.3   As in Exercise 10.1, add words that make sense in the following sentences.

1. The boy scout _____ the child across the street.

2. Neil Armstrong _____ the first human on the moon.

3. A Porsche Targa _____ over $25,000 dollars, but it _____ speeds of over 130 miles per hour.

4. Christopher Columbus _____ America in 1942.

5. Thomas Edison _____ the light bulb.

6. The Beatles _____ the hottest tunes on the charts in the 1960s.

7. I _____ my teeth and _____ my hands before I _____ to bed.

8. To make money, some kids _____ lawns in the summer, _____ leaves in the fall, and _____ snow in the winter.

9. Back home, before I _____ to college, my mother always _____ my clothes, _____ my room, and _____ my dinner.

10. I _____ to get married someday, but I _____ to get an education and _____ different people before I _____ down with a family.

Verb: The verb of a sentence or clause is the word which shows what the subject does or what the subject is, was, or will be.

This time you have filled in the verbs in each sentence. A **verb** is the word in a sentence that shows either action — what the subject is doing — or a state of being — what the subject is or was. Note the difference in the following examples. The verb is italicized.

Action: Robert Oppenheimer *supervised* hundreds of other scientists in the construction of the first atomic bomb.
Being: Robert Oppenheimer *was* a professor at Princeton University in the 1950s and 1960s.

In the first sentence, Oppenheimer does something — supervises. The second sentence identifies what he was after his work on the bomb — a professor at Princeton. Like subjects, verbs are a necessary part of each sentence. In fact, each sentence must have at least one subject and at least one verb, even though many sentences have more. Knowing how to identify subjects and verbs will help you write complete sentences and avoid sentence errors.

For practice in identifying verbs, go back to the paragraph in Exercise 10.2 and put two lines under verbs that go with the subjects you marked.

Editing Sentence Fragments.

Sentence fragment: A fragment is a phrase or dependent clause which is punctuated as a complete sentence.

Once you can identify subjects and verbs, it is not too difficult to eliminate sentence fragments. A **sentence fragment** is a group of words punctuated with a period as if it were a complete sentence when in fact it is only part — a fragment — of a sentence. A fragment may have a subject and a verb, but it cannot stand alone as a complete thought. We often speak in fragments, even when using standard English, but in most kinds of writing, fragments distract from your meaning.

EXERCISE 10.4 The following are groups of words punctuated as sentences. Some of the groups have subjects and verbs and could therefore be sentences. Others are missing either a subject or a verb or do not express a complete statement, so they are fragments. Identify each as either a sentence or a fragment.

1. Jogging in urban neighborhoods.
2. Harry Truman, a former president from Missouri.
3. Computer word processing can help beginning writers produce better essays.
4. A tragic automobile accident with six people, four children and two adults, dead.
5. Jogging in urban neighborhoods is a test of survival skills.
6. Governor Phalen's new tax plan places an unfair burden on low-income taxpayers.
7. Using the writing process makes writing less difficult.
8. To write an essay without first making notes.
9. To shop in Greeley's Corner Market is to take a step back in time.
10. Tricia Edwards, star of the North College women's field hockey team.

If you identified the fragments correctly, you identified groups of words that do not have both a subject and a verb *and* that do not express a complete statement that makes sense by itself.

Consider sentence number 10, for example. A reader would want to ask, "What about Tricia Edwards?" Adding a few words will answer the question and make a complete sentence:

Tricia Edwards, star of North College's women's field hockey team, dominates her sport more than any other athlete in the state, male or female.

Now *Tricia Edwards* is the subject, and *dominates* is the verb, which says something about her, making a complete sentence. Another way to change the fragment into a sentence is to simply add the verb *is* after the subject *Tricia Edwards:*

Tricia Edwards is the star of North College's women's field hockey team.

That statement of fact is a complete sentence.

A sentence, then, must have at least one subject and one verb and must be a statement that makes sense by itself. One type of fragment is a **phrase.** A phrase is any group of words that does not have a subject or a verb or both.

Phrase: A group of words that does not contain a subject or a verb or both.

EXERCISE 10.5 The following groups of words have at least one subject and one verb, but some of them are not sentences because they do not make sense by themselves. Identify each group of words that makes sense as a sentence and each group that causes you to want more information as a fragment.

1. Although earning a college degree can mean a higher-paying job and more enriched life.
2. Swimming regularly can strengthen the lungs and the heart.
3. When the meal was over, no one wanted to clean up and do the dishes.
4. Cooking can be fun.
5. While the band played "Auld Lang Syne."
6. Because no one wanted to do the dishes.
7. If space travel becomes a reality for the average person.
8. A book that occupied most young children for hours.
9. Which means I cannot go out to dinner Saturday night.
10. A coloring book can occupy most young children for hours.

Clause: A group of words that contains at least one subject and one verb.

Independent clause: A clause with at least one subject and one verb that can stand alone as a sentence.

Dependent clause: A clause with at least one subject and one verb that cannot stand alone as a sentence because it depends on an independent clause to complete its meaning.

If you were able to separate the sentences from the fragments, you also were able to tell the difference between independent clauses and dependent clauses. A **clause** is any group of words that contains at least one subject and one verb. There are two types of clauses: independent and dependent.

An **independent clause** has at least one subject and one verb, and it also makes sense by itself. For instance, "I missed my bus this morning" has the subject *I* and the verb *missed*, and it expresses a complete piece of information. An independent clause is always a complete sentence. Understand this rule and you will avoid fragments: *To be a sentence a group of words must have at least one independent clause.*

A **dependent clause** also has at least one subject and one verb, but it does not make sense by itself. For instance, "Because I missed my bus this morning" has the subject *I* and the verb *missed,* but it is not a complete statement because it does not express the complete thought of what happened as a result of missing the bus. A dependent clause is never a complete sentence by itself; it *depends* on an independent clause to complete its meaning. "Because I missed my bus this morning, I was late for work" joins the dependent clause to the independent clause "I was late for work," and so it is a complete sentence.

We have seen two types of fragments: *phrases,* which are groups of words without a subject or verb, and *dependent* clauses which do have a subject and verb but do not make sense by themselves.

You probably did pretty well in telling the difference between the sentences and the fragments in the exercise, but to make your knowledge pay off you need to be able to identify fragments when they appear in your own writing. This can be more difficult; sometimes the fragments make sense because of the sentences before or after them. Still, they will distract a reader and thus hinder you from getting your meaning across.

EXERCISE 10.6 In the following paragraph, underline any fragments you find. Then correct each fragment by joining it to the sentence before or after it.

> Working and going to college can take a lot out of a person. Because there is not always enough time to work and study. If people have to work the night before a test, they will not have a chance to study. Or to even review their notes. Also, the next morning when the time comes for the test. They will be tired. Causing them to not do well. But determined people find a way to hold a job and go to college at the same time. They plan their work schedules and their study schedules carefully, and eventually they earn that degree. If they have the determination.

EXERCISE 10.7 Examine a piece of writing you have done for another class. See if you find any fragments, whether your teacher has marked them or not. Correct the fragments by joining them to the sentence before or after.

EXERCISE 10.8 As fast as you can, freewrite a paragraph of 50–75 words on anything you like. When you are finished, see if you can find any fragments. If you do, correct them by joining them to the sentence before or after.

Editing Run-on Sentences and Comma Splices

Like fragments, run-on sentences and comma splices are distracting. Thus, they can prevent a reader from getting your point. These two errors are very similar.

Run-on sentence: Two independent clauses joined without punctuation or a connecting word.

Run-on Sentences   A **run-on sentence** occurs when two independent clauses are joined together with *no* punctuation at all. Some instructors refer to run-on sentences as fused sentences or run-together sentences. The error results when two strings of words capable of standing alone as sentences are joined together without punctuation. Remember that the term run-on has nothing to do with the length of the sentence (a common misconception). Here are some examples of run-on sentences to illustrate the definition.

1. Jill was sad her sister was not. (Two short independent clauses.)
2. We went to a movie it was a Disney film. (Two short independent clauses, but this time the second has the pronoun *it* as the subject. Beginning writers often have trouble realizing that small words such as *it* can serve as subjects.)
3. The china Susannah had picked out cost more than most of the wedding guests were willing to spend therefore she received very few pieces. (The independent clause "she received very few pieces" is tacked on with *therefore* but without punctuation, a common error.)
4. The students wrote first drafts of their essays then they began the revision process. (Two sentences joined with *then* and no punctuation.)

There are four ways to fix run-ons.

1. Make two sentences:

   The students wrote first drafts of their essays. Then they began the revision process.

This type of correction solves the grammatical problem, but it can lead to choppy style unless the sentences being separated are long.

2. Join the independent clauses with a semicolon:

   The students wrote first drafts of their essays; then they began the revision process.

This method works if either the two clauses are short and closely related ("Mary loves pizza; John hates it") or the sentence contains a connecting word that cannot take a comma. Such connectors are *consequently, furthermore, however, moreover, nevertheless, thus, then,* and *therefore*. These can join independent clauses only if you use a semicolon. For instance, "The children were tired; consequently, they were acting cranky."

Coordinating conjunction: The seven words *but, and, for, nor, or, so,* and *yet* (BAFNOSY). They are the only words that can join independent clauses with only a comma.

3. Join the independent clauses with a **coordinating conjunction.** These seven words are coordinating conjunctions: *but, and, for, nor, or, so,* and *yet*. The first letters of the conjunctions can spell out BAFNOSY. BAFNOSY does not mean anything; it is a nonsense word, but remembering it can help you remember the coordinating conjunctions. Coordinating conjunctions are powerful little words because they are the only words in the English language that allow you to join two sentences with only a comma:

   The students wrote first drafts of their essays, and then they began the revision process.

Using a coordinating conjunction with a comma is probably the most common method of correcting run-on sentences. It often leads to nicely balanced sentences that show a relationship between one independent clause and another.

4. Change one of the independent clauses in the run-on sentence to a dependent clause:

After the students wrote first drafts of their essays, they began the revision process.

Making one clause dependent is a good way to correct a run-on sentence because the relationship between the clauses tends to produce mature style by drawing tighter relationships (of time, of cause, of contrast, of condition) between clauses.

Comma splice: Two independent clauses joined with only a comma but no coordinating conjunction.

Comma Splices Like run-ons, **comma splices** join two independent clauses improperly. In the comma splice, the writer tries to link two independent clauses with only a comma or with a comma and a word that is not a coordinating conjunction. Commas are not powerful enough by themselves to join two independent clauses. Here are some examples of comma splices:

1. Jill was sad, her sister was not. (Two short independent clauses connected with only a comma.)
2. We went to a movie, it was a Disney film. (Two short independent clauses. As in the run-on, the pronoun subject *it* may confuse you.)
3. The china Susannah had picked out cost more than most of the wedding guests were willing to spend, therefore she received very few pieces. (An independent clause tacked on with *therefore* and a comma. Since *therefore* is not a coordinating conjunction, it requires a semicolon to join independent clauses. Only a coordinating conjunction can join independent clauses with a comma.)
4. The students wrote first drafts of their essays, then they began the revision process. (Two sentences joined with a comma and a word that is not a coordinating conjunction. *Then* is commonly mistaken for a coordinating conjunction; remember that there is no *T* in BAFNOSY.)

▪▪▪▪▪▪▪▪▪▪▪▪

E X E R C I S E   10.9 Identify the following sentences as complete sentences, run-on sentences, or comma splices. Correct any run-on sentences or comma splices.

1. Fast food is cheap it is more nutritious than people think.
2. The Zanger family moved into a new house, then they bought all new furniture.
3. Vermont is a beautiful place to live it gets a lot of snow in the winter.
4. After the Iran-Contra hearings, many voters distrusted the Reagan administration.
5. It was raining the game was canceled.
6. During the Vietnam War, young people were more politically active than they are today.
7. In May, thousands of students will be graduating from state colleges and universities, however, many will leave their states to seek employment in other parts of the nation.
8. During the energy crisis of the 1970s, U.S. auto manufacturers began to market small cars; then they returned to making large cars when gasoline became more plentiful.
9. More students seem to be seeking help in the Writing Center thus they have been improving their writing.
10. The university lecture series often presents interesting and prestigious speakers, for example, former British Prime Minister Harold Wilson spoke last month, and this week former President Gerald Ford delivered two lectures.

E X E R C I S E   10.10 Correct any run-on sentences or comma splices that you find in these paragraphs:

The individual inventor was a hero of the nineteenth century however, we rarely hear about individual inventors anymore. We use computers all the time, who invented them? Though we may associate the television with Dumont, there is no single person credited with its invention. Similarly, we associate names such as Goddard and Von Braun with rocketry, still we don't think of someone inventing the first rocket the way we think of Edison inventing the light bulb or Bell inventing the telephone.

Younger students often mature more in their first semester of college than they have in all their years of high school. They have so many additional responsibilities to take on, college requires that they have to discipline themselves. If they don't, no one else will help them. Many students enjoy taking on new responsibility, it makes them feel good about themselves. They gain new self-respect, they realize they can face the difficult tasks of life on their own.

E X E R C I S E   10.11 Freewrite for about ten minutes on a topic of your choice. Edit your freewriting to eliminate any run-on sentences or comma splices.

■ Editing Verb Forms

As a speaker of English, you use verbs hundreds, even thousands, of times each day. Most of the time you probably use the standard English forms. In fact, most speakers use standard English verbs without really knowing how the verb system works. Yet from hearing others speak, they know which verb form to use. At times, however, people use verb forms that are part of a dialect and thus not standard English.

English has a very complex system of verbs, but you can use standard English verb forms without knowing all there is to know about the system. To edit problems with verbs, however, you should know the differences among infinitives, main verbs, and helping verbs, along with the difference beween regular and irregular verbs.

Infinitives, Main Verbs, and Helping Verbs

Infinitive: An infinitive is the basic form of a verb before it is used to show action, time, or relationships.

Infinitives   **Infinitives** are the basic form of every verb before it is used to show action, show relationships, or mark the time when something happened. Infinitives are easy to identify because they are usually preceded by the word *to:* to be, to cry, to die, to eat, to fall, to have, to love, to make, to pull, to sing, to succeed, to try, to win, and so on. (Note, however, that not every word preceded by *to* is an infinitive form of the verb. Nouns can follow *to* in phrases such as *to church, to town, to California.*)

Although infinitives are the basic form of the verb, they can never serve as the verb in a sentence when they are preceded by *to*. There is *only one good reason* to know what an infinitive is — so you won't mistake it for the verb when you are trying to tell if a group of words is a complete sentence. Consider the following group of words:

To live in a very nice neighborhood someday.

A student might mistake this group of words as a sentence, thinking that the verb is "To live." Although the word *live is* a verb because it indicates some action, when it's preceded by *to* it can't be the main verb in a sentence. Thus it can't be part of the subject-verb construction needed to make a complete sentence. Editing the sentence, you could write:

I want to live in a very nice neighborhood someday.

Now this sentence still has the infinitive *to live,* but it also has the main verb *want* and the subject *I* and is a complete sentence. If you know what an infinitive is, you won't mistake it for the verb in a sentence, and you will reduce the possibility of writing fragments.

E X E R C I S E   10.12   Indicate the infinitives in the following sentences.

1. Elliot asked Chris to close the window.
2. To try for success is to succeed.
3. Alicia wanted to return to college when her daughter started school.
4. General Rommel ordered his men to attack.
5. Rommel's army moved on when the enemy had to retreat.
6. Many doctors are trying to discover a cure for AIDS.
7. Nowadays, airlines do not allow passengers to smoke on short flights.
8. The president planned to veto the bill from Congress.
9. Bullfighters face great danger to entertain the crowd.
10. Anthony began to cut school when his parents were divorced.

E X E R C I S E   10.13   Now underline the infinitives in this paragraph.

In the past ten years, many colleges and universities have opened writing centers. These centers are places where students can go to improve their writing. Students work with tutors to think of ideas for writing, to work on rough drafts, to revise drafts, and to edit their writing to eliminate nonstandard forms. Any students who want to be better writers should check to see if their college or university has a writing center.

Main verb: In a sentence or clause, the word that shows the action or links the subject to the rest of the clause or sentence.

Main Verbs   The word in the sentence that shows the action or links the subject to the rest of the sentence is the **main verb.** Main verbs also show **tense** — the time something takes place. The main verb and the subject form a complete sentence; every sentence must have at least one main verb. Thus, it is important to be able to identify the main verb in a sentence. Examine the main verbs in these sentences:

Tense: A verb form that marks the time of the action in a sentence. Tense is indicated by the endings of regular verbs, by the forms of irregular verbs, or by helping verbs.

Japan *exports* more cars than any other country.
During our vacation, we *visited* Colorado, Arizona, and California.
By evening, the temperature had *dropped* twenty degrees.
Marcia will *work* Wednesday evening.
Elio *has* a new sweater.
After working for a year, Wilma will *have* enough money to take a cruise.
Janice *is* a medical student specializing in surgery.
Janice is *studying* to be a surgeon.

Mr. and Mrs. Del Colletti are *moving* to Florida next month.
John F. Kennedy *was* the youngest person ever elected president.
Kennedy had *been* president three years when he was *assassinated*.

Each of the italicized verbs in these sentences serves as a main verb. As you can see, main verbs can take many forms. Some show action. Others show action and have *-ed* or *-ing* on the end. Others are verbs of being, such as *is* and *was*. But in each case, the main verb either shows action or links the subject to the part of the sentence that says something about the subject.

E X E R C I S E   10.14   Return to Exercise 10.13, but this time place two lines under each main verb.

Helping verb: A verb form used with the main verb of a clause to show tense.

Helping Verbs   Sometimes a main verb has one or more verb forms before it, such as *can, do, am, are, is, was, were, has, have, had, will, could, would, should,* and so on. These verbs are called **helping verbs** because they help readers understand sentences by marking tense — the time the action took place or the time something is said about the subject. There are many tenses in the system of English verbs, but you do not need to learn the names of them. As a speaker of English, you know how most tenses work from hearing and using them. But knowing how to identify helping verbs will help you separate them from the main verb. When you are editing to find fragments, comma splices, and run-on sentences, it is very important to be able to locate main verbs. Compare the following pairs of sentences. In each pair, the main verb is marked in the first sentence, and any helping verbs are marked in the second.

Main verb:	Shavonda had *left* the party early.
Helping verb:	Shavonda *had* left the party early.
Main verb:	The car was *stolen* this morning.
Helping verb:	The car *was* stolen this morning.
Main verb:	Rick should have *been* in class today.
Helping verb:	Rick *should have* been in class today.
Main verb:	If we had *known* that the restaurant served bad food, we would have *eaten* somewhere else.
Helping verb:	If we *had* known that the restaurant served bad food, we *would have* eaten somewhere else.
Main verb:	The Vietnam War will *go* down in history as a national tragedy.

Helping verb:	The Vietnam War *will* go down in history as a national tragedy.	
Main verb:	Lionel Johnson is *running* for mayor.	
Helping verb:	Lionel Johnson *is* running for mayor.	
Main verb:	With some luck, our team can *win* the conference championship.	
Helping verb:	With some luck, our team *can* win the conference championship.	

With a little study and practice, you can tell the difference between main verbs and helping verbs. Some verbs, however, can be tricky because sometimes they are used as main verbs and sometimes they are used as helping verbs. Examine the following list and examples:

am	*Main verb:*	I *am* from New Jersey.
	Helping verb:	I *am* writing an essay. (Main verb is *writing*.)
are	*Main verb:*	Many of the freshmen *are* business majors.
	Helping verb:	Many of the freshmen *are* majoring in business. (Main verb is *majoring*.)
do	*Main verb:*	You *do* well on exams.
	Helping verb:	But you *do* need to study. (Main verb is *need*.)
had	*Main verb:*	Lucinda *had* her paycheck in her purse.
	Helping verb:	Lucinda *had* returned from work. (Main verb is *returned*.)
has	*Main verb:*	Jeff *has* five hundred dollars in the bank.
	Helping verb:	Since last summer, Jeff *has* saved five hundred dollars. (Main verb is *saved*.)
have	*Main verb:*	Most beginning writers *have* a strong desire to learn standard English.
	Helping verb:	Many beginning writers *have* learned to use standard English. (Main verb is *learned*.)
is	*Main verb:*	Mrs. Lynch *is* a police officer.
	Helping verb:	She *is* trying to become a detective (Main verb is *trying*.)
was	*Main verb:*	The winning dog *was* a greyhound.
	Helping verb:	The greyhound *was* running fast. (Main verb is *running*.)
were	*Main verb:*	The DiMaggio brothers *were* great baseball players.
	Helping verb:	We *were* sleeping during the storm. (Main verb is *sleeping*.)

The verbs in the examples can be either main verbs or helping verbs. As you look for verbs when you are editing your essays for sentence errors, make sure each sentence has at least one main verb to go with the subject.

E X E R C I S E   10.15   Return to Exercise 10.13 and circle all helping verbs.

E X E R C I S E   10.16   Examine a paragraph or two of some writing you have done. Underline the helping verbs and put two lines under the main verbs.

Regular Versus Irregular Verbs

Regular verbs: The group of verbs that take -*ed* to show past tense and -*s* when used with third-person subjects.

Regular Verbs   **Regular verbs** are the group of English verbs that take the same endings when used a certain way. For example, when preceded by the subjects *he, she,* and *it,* a regular verb in present tense has an -*s* added to the end:

He talks. She looks. It crawls.

Also regular verbs have -*ed* added to show that something happened in the past. This is true whether the verb is in simple past tense or whether it is in a past form that takes one or more helping verbs. Compare these forms of regular verbs:

Present	*Simple Past*	*Past Forms with Helping Verbs*
I talk.	I talked.	I have talked.
You laugh.	You laughed.	You had laughed.
He jumps.	He jumped.	He would have jumped.
She calls.	She called.	She had called.
It cooks.	It cooked.	It has cooked.
We walk.	We walked.	We could have walked.
You smile.	You smiled.	You have smiled.
They travel.	They traveled.	They will have traveled.

Though each verb is different, each has -*ed* on the end to show both the simple past tense and various forms of the past tense using helping verbs. In other words, there is a *regular* way — adding -*ed* — to show the past forms of these verbs.

Nonstandard forms of regular verbs usually occur either from leaving the -*s* off the present form that follows *he, she,* or *it,* or leaving the -*ed* off the past or other forms. Compare the following sentences.

Present Tense

Nonstandard: She walk to school every day.
Standard: She walks to school every day.

Nonstandard: He cook dinner when his wife work late.
Standard: He cooks dinner when his wife works late.

Nonstandard: It snow heavily each winter.
Standard: It snows heavily each winter.

Simple Past Tense

Nonstandard: She talk to the police officer about the burglary.
Standard: She talked to the police officer about the burglary.

Nonstandard: He ask his parents if he could borrow the family car.
Standard: He asked his parents if he could borrow the family car.

Nonstandard: It rain last night.
Standard: It rained last night.

Past Forms with Helping Verbs

Nonstandard: She has change her mind.
Standard: She has changed her mind.

Nonstandard: He would have play in the outfield if his foot was not injure.
Standard: He would have played in the outfield if his foot was not injured.

Nonstandard: It had cool off by evening.
Standard: It had cooled off by evening.

If you have a problem using -s and -ed endings in your writing, you need to edit very carefully because probably in speaking you do not use the endings or hear them in the speech of others. Thus, you must edit by sight because you won't hear the nonstandard form when you read aloud. Look at the regular verbs in your sentence, and try to make sure that you add -s if you are using *he, she,* or *it* in present tense and -ed if the verb is in past tense or in a past form that uses one or more helping verbs.

EXERCISE 10.17 Before each sentence is an infinitive form of the form in parentheses. Use the correct main verb in each sentence.

1. (to walk) Despite yesterday's snow storm, Jim _____ all the way across town.

2. (to use) Every year, the university _____ tons of paper.

3. (to use) Every year, universities across the nation _____ tons of paper.

4. (to enter, to bomb) America _____ World War II when Japan _____ Pearl Harbor.

5. (to answer) You always _____ the questions correctly.

6. (to play) We _____ poker every Thursday night.

7. (to call) Andrea _____ you last night.

8. (to describe, to listen) The victim _____ the mugger to the police officer, who _____ carefully.

9. (to type, to edit) Lester _____ the second draft of his essay; later he _____ it to make sure he used standard verb forms.

10. (to swerve, to crash) A large truck _____ off the road and _____ into a telephone pole.

E X E R C I S E   10.18   Change nonstandard verbs to standard forms in the following paragraph.

Old television shows run daily on cable television stations throughout the country. Thus, generations of young people sees programs their parents watch as children. Most of these programs are situation comedies such as *Leave It to Beaver, Father Knows Best,* and *Mr. Ed.* Others are Westerns, which enjoy much popularity back in the fifties and are now making a comeback through the cable reruns. These programs are shown in black and white, but to a generation raise on color TV, they are still as entertaining as they were thirty years ago.

Irregular Verbs

Irregular verbs:
Irregular verbs do not follow a particular form when marking past tense or when used with a helping verb.

Unfortunately for people trying to use standard English, many verbs in the language are irregular. **Irregular verbs** are verbs that do not follow a particular pattern in their past forms and in the form used with a helping verb. Some irregular verbs have similar patterns, but overall there are no hard and fast rules for these verbs. Here is a comparison of some regular and irregular verbs.

Infinitive	*Present Forms*	*Simple Past*	*Past Forms with Helping Verbs*
to be	am/are/is	was/were	have been/ has been
to break	break/breaks	broke	is broken
to have	have/has	had	was had

Infinitive	Present Forms	Simple Past	Past Forms with Helping Verbs
to jog	jog/jogs	jogged	had jogged
to live	live/lives	lived	have lived/ has lived
to own	own/owns	owned	has bccn owned
to ruin	ruin/ruins	ruined	was ruined
to run	run/runs	ran	has run
to type	type/types	typed	were typed
to write	write/writes	wrote	had written

As you can see from these comparisons, the irregular verbs are tricky. Sometimes for the present forms you can add an -s to make the form used with *he, she,* and *it,* but at other times even the present tense takes different forms, as with the verb *be.* Also, to form the simple past or past forms used with helping verbs, you can't just add -ed. The following is a list of many irregular verbs.

Infinitive Form	Present	Simple Past	Past Forms with Helping Verbs
to be	am/is/are	was/were	have been
to beat	beat/beats	beat	has beaten
to begin	begin/begins	began	have begun
to bite	bite/bites	bit	was bitten
to blow	blow/blows	blew	has blown
to break	break/breaks	broke	is broken
to bring	bring/brings	brought	were brought
to build	build/builds	built	will be built
to catch	catch/catches	caught	is caught
to choose	choose/chooses	chose	are chosen
to come	come/comes	came	had come
to cost	cost/costs	cost	have cost
to deal	deal/deals	dealt	has dealt
to dig	dig/digs	dug	will be dug
to do	do/does	did	has done
to draw	draw/draws	drew	were drawn
to drink	drink/drinks	drank	has drunk
to drive	drive/drives	drove	had driven
to eat	eat/eats	ate	have eaten
to fall	fall/falls	fell	have fallen
to fight	fight/fights	fought	has fought
to find	find/finds	found	was found
to fly	fly/flies	flew	has flown
to forget	forget/forgets	forgot	was forgotten
to freeze	freeze/freezes	froze	have frozen

Infinitive Form	Present	Simple Past	Past Forms with Helping Verbs
to get	get/gets	got	has got/gotten
to give	give/gives	gave	have given
to go	go/goes	went	has gone
to have	have/has	had	has had
to know	know/knows	knew	had known
to lead	lead/leads	led	have led
to lend	lend/lends	lent	will be lent
to make	make/makes	made	has made
to ride	ride/rides	rode	was ridden
to ring	ring/rings	rang	has rung
to run	run/runs	ran	had run
to say	say/says	said	were said
to see	see/sees	saw	have seen
to set (put)	set/sets	sat	had sat
to shake	shake/shakes	shook	has shaken
to sing	sing/sings	sang	was sung
to sink	sink/sinks	sank	has sunk
to sit (chair)	sit/sits	sit	have sit
to speak	speak/speaks	spoke	was spoken
to spring	spring/springs	sprang	has sprung
to steal	steal/steals	stole	has stolen
to swim	swim/swims	swam	have swum
to swing	swing/swings	swung	has swung
to take	take/takes	took	was taken
to tear	tear/tears	tore	is torn
to throw	throw/throws	threw	had thrown
to wear	wear/wears	wore	had worn
to write	write/writes	wrote	have written

This list is certainly long, and there are still more irregular verbs in English! It probably would be impossible to memorize all the forms. Fortunately, there is no need to. More than likely, you know most of these forms already because you use many of them every day. However, you need to find out which irregular verbs give you trouble. The following sections discuss some common problems that beginning writers have with irregular verbs.

Confused Forms of Be   There are so many different forms of the verb *be* that it is very easy to confuse them. The following are some common errors. Read through them and note which forms give you trouble.

Nonstandard Forms Present Tense	Standard Forms
I is, I be	I am
you is, you be	you are

Nonstandard Forms	Standard Forms
Present Tense	
he/she/it be	he/she/it is
we is, we be	we are
they is, they be	they are
Simple Past Tense	
I were, I be	I was
you was, you be	you were
he/she/it be/were	he/she/it was
we was, we be	we were
they is, they be	they were
Past Forms with Helping Verbs	
I been	I have/had been
you been	you have/had been
he/she/it been	he/she/it has/had been
we been	we have/had been
they been	they have/had been

Confusing Forms of Do   The verb *do* is used in many different nonstandard forms by speakers from different parts of the country. One particularly troublesome use is the difference between the simple past form, *did,* and the form used with a helping verb, *done.* Be very careful not to confuse these. As the following examples show, *did* should always be used alone, while *done* should always be used with a helping verb.

Nonstandard Forms	Standard Forms
Present Tense	
I does	I do
you does	you do
he/she/it do	he/she/it does
we does	we do
they does	they do
Simple Past Tense	
I done	I did
you done	you did
he/she/it done	he/she/it did
we done	we did
they done	they did
Past Forms with Helping Verbs	
I have/had did	I have/had done
you have/had did	you have/had done
he/she/it has/had did	he/she/it has/had done
we have/had did	we have/had done
they have/had did	they have/had done

Confused Forms of Go Very few people confuse present forms of the verb *go,* but the simple past form, *went,* and the form used with helping verbs, *gone,* often cause problems. Particularly, many people use *went* with a helping verb. *Went,* as the simple past form, should not be used with a helping verb, just as *gone* must always have a helping verb. Compare the uses of these forms:

Nonstandard:	Many students *have went* to Florida for spring break.
	Some *had went* before the break began.
Standard:	Many students *have gone* to Florida for spring break.
	Some *had gone* before the break began.
	Some *went* before the break began.

Confused Forms of See The most common nonstandard use of the verb *see* happens when people confuse the form used with a helping verb, *seen,* for the simple past form, *saw.* Compare the differences in these sentences:

Nonstandard:	I *seen* Phil on his way to work.
Standard:	I *saw* Phil on his way to work.
	I *have seen* Phil on his way to work.
	I *had seen* Phil on his way to work.

Confusion of Forms Ending in -en For many irregular verbs, the form used with a helping verb ends in *-en: broken, chosen, driven, frozen, spoken, stolen, taken,* among others. But students often leave the *n* off and use the simple past with the helping verb, thus creating a nonstandard form. Compare the nonstandard with the standard forms:

Nonstandard:	The boy cried when he found that his bicycle *was broke.*
Standard:	The boy cried when he found that his bicycle *was broken.*
Nonstandard:	We *had drove* four hundred miles in one day.
Standard:	We *had driven* four hundred miles in one day.
Nonstandard:	The lake *will have froze* by next week.
Standard:	The lake *will have frozen* by next week.
Nonstandard:	Jim's book *has been stole.*
Standard:	Jim's book *has been stolen.*
Nonstandard:	Mr. Axelrod *had took* his daughter to the doctor last Tuesday.
Standard:	Mr. Axelrod *had taken* his daughter to the doctor last Tuesday.

E X E R C I S E   10.19 Replace the nonstandard forms of irregular verbs with standard forms in the following sentences.

1. We seen Angel at the carnival last night.
2. The car was stole sometime last night after we had went out to the movies.
3. We had knew car thefts was on the rise in our city.
4. The students who have did their assignments on time will earn better grades.
5. I always done my assignments on time.
6. We brang some hot dogs to the picnic.
7. After we have ate our lunch, we will meet you to go swimming.
8. Beverly Sills sung at the Metropolitan Opera House many times before she had sang in Europe.
9. The geese have flew south for the winter.
10. I wish they had not went so soon.
11. After Gooden had threw three wild pitches, the manager thought he should have took him out of the game.

E X E R C I S E   10.20 Edit the following paragraph so that all irregular verbs are in the standard forms.

I never gone to a water park until last summer when I was visiting California. It were a very large place with ten different water slides and three different swimming pools. One even have waves. One of the water slides were over five stories high, and it was very steep. I want to go down it, but I was afraid at first. After I seen little kids going down this slide, I feel foolish, so I done it myself. Well, when I hit the pool at the bottom, I thought my back was broke. After that, I decide to stick to the smaller slides and the pool.

E X E R C I S E   10.21 Review papers you have written. Pick a page or two and circle irregular verbs you have used in the standard forms. This will show you how much you know about them. Then look for any nonstandard forms and change them to standard forms.

■ Editing Pronoun Problems

As discussed in Chapter 4, the repetition and variation of key words help give a paragraph cohesion. Study the following paragraph on former

President Jimmy Carter, noticing the connections of the varied references to the "new President."

> The new President . . . was an ambitious and intelligent politician. *He* had a rare gift for sensing what people wanted and appearing to give it to them. Liberals thought *he* clearly stood with them; conservatives were equally convinced that *he* was on their side. *He* was especially adept at using symbols. *He* emerged from airplanes carrying *his* own garment bag; after *his* inauguration *he* walked up Pennsylvania Avenue hand-in-hand with *his* wife Rosalyn and *his* daughter Amy.
>
> Robert A. Divine et al., *America, Past and Present*

Noun: A noun is any word that refers to a person, place, thing, quality, or condition. Nouns have singular, plural, and possessive forms.

The words *he* and *him* are pronouns that refer back to the **noun** *President*. Recall the definitions of nouns and pronouns from grammar school and high school:

Noun: A noun refers to a person, place, thing, feeling, or condition. Nouns can be singular, plural, or possessive: (*president, presidents, president's*).

Pronoun: Word that takes the place of a noun. Pronouns also have singular, plural, and possessive forms and show gender: masculine, feminine, or neuter.

Pronoun: A **pronoun** is a word that takes the place of a noun. Pronouns can be singular, plural, or possessive. They also show whether the noun is masculine, feminine, or neuter (having no gender). Pronouns also show the concept of **person.** *I* and *we* are first-person pronouns because they refer to ourselves. *You,* which is both singular and plural, is the second-person pronoun because it addresses a second person. *He, she, it,* and *they* are third-person pronouns because they refer to a third party.

Person: The form of a pronoun that indicates the speaker (first person: *I, we*), someone spoken to (second person: *you,* both singular and plural), or someone spoken about (third person: *he, she, it, they*).

Without pronouns, writing would become so repetitious that readers would quickly become bored. Consider the paragraph on President Carter rewritten without any pronouns, including those referring to other nouns besides *President.*

> The new President . . . was an ambitious and intelligent politician. The President had a rare gift for sensing what people wanted and appearing to give what people wanted to people. Liberals thought the President clearly stood with liberals; conservatives were equally convinced that the President was on the conservatives' side. The President was especially adept at using symbols. The President emerged from airplanes carrying the President's own garment bag; after the President's inauguration the President walked up Pennsylvania Avenue hand-in-hand with the President's wife Rosalyn and the President's daughter Amy.

Without the pronouns this paragraph not only sounds ridiculous but is also confusing to read.

E X E R C I S E   10.22   In the following paragraph, all the pronouns are used correctly. Write down each pronoun and the noun it refers to.

> Writing is necessary for many jobs. It is particularly important in business. Executives have to write letters even if they have secretaries to do the typing. Memos are the lifeblood of office communications. They are written to people above and below the executive. When a memo is well written, it will get the executive's point across no matter who the audience is.

In a good paragraph, pronouns help create cohesion, but if you don't use them correctly, they can destroy cohesion. Four problems can arise with pronouns: faulty reference, faulty agreement, shifts of person, and misused pronoun case.

Faulty Reference

Faulty reference: A pronoun error that occurs when a pronoun does not have a noun to refer to, or when readers cannot tell which noun the pronoun refers to.

Because a pronoun takes the place of a noun, it must have a noun to take the place of, or refer to. In the sentence "Jim knew he passed the exam," the pronoun *he* refers to Jim.

When writers use pronouns without having a noun to refer to, readers can get confused. Read the following sentences and pay close attention to the italicized pronouns:

> Tuition costs are getting too high, but *they* are always raising tuition anyway. *They* need to find a better way of raising money to keep *it* going.

Who are *they?* University officials? State legislators? And what is *it* that they are trying to keep going? Compare a rewritten version:

> Tuition costs are getting too high, but the state legislators are always raising tuition anyway. They need to find a better way to keep the university going.

In the rewritten version, the pronoun *they* now refers back to the noun *state legislators,* making clear whom the writer means. Also, replacing the pronoun *it* with the noun *university* lets readers know what the writer is referring to.

E X E R C I S E   10.23   The following short paragaraphs contain faulty pronoun references. To make the paragraphs more cohesive, correct any faulty reference by adding a noun where needed. Then indicate which remaining pronouns refer to the nouns you added.

The Concorde is a supersonic jetliner built by France and England. It takes them across the Atlantic Ocean to America in only three hours. I would like to do it, but it is around $1500.

Jeopardy is my favorite TV game show. It takes intelligence on *Jeopardy*. They have to answer some tough questions, but they win a lot of money. They are on all different subjects, and they cannot always answer them.

I enjoy boats. My father bought it used, but it is good for fishing, water skiing, or just cruising. We go out in it on weekends and enjoy the sunshine, fresh air, and water. Dad usually lets me drive it.

Faulty Agreement

Faulty agreement: A pronoun error that occurs when the pronoun differs in number or gender from the noun it refers to.

When a pronoun refers back to a noun, the pronoun must agree with the noun in number (singular or plural) and gender (masculine, feminine, or neuter). Almost no one has a problem with gender agreement. You would not write or say, for instance, "*Sally* went to bed because *it* was tired."

However, faulty agreement in number is a common error. Examine the underlined words in these sentences:

When a father has to punish their children, they feel as bad as the kids do.

When fathers have to punish their children, they feel as bad as the kids do.

When a father has to punish his children, he feels as bad as the kids do.

In the first sentence, the noun *father* is singular, referring to *one* father, yet the pronouns *their* and *they,* which replace the noun *father,* are plural, referring to more than one father. As a result, the sentence contains faulty agreement because the noun is singular and the pronouns are plural. In the second sentence, the noun *father* has been made plural by adding an -s (note that the verb has been changed to its plural form too). Now both the noun and the pronouns are plural. They agree in number, and the sentence is correct. In the third sentence, the noun *father* is singular, but the pronouns have been changed to singular, so the sentence is correct.

The most common pronoun agreement error occurs in the type of sentences just examined. Notice in the first sentence that *a father* means any father, an example of one that refers to all fathers. Compare this sentence:

A student can usually get financial aid if eligible.

One student is eligible for financial aid. You use this form often in speech, and very few people notice an error if you say, "A student can get financial aid if they are eligible." In writing, however, this usage can confuse readers because the beginning of the sentence refers to one person, but the end of the sentence refers to more than one person. The best way to correct this type of error is to change the noun to the plural form so that it matches the plural pronoun:

Students can get financial aid if *they* are eligible.

If you keep the singular noun, you have to write, "A student can get financial aid if he or she is eligible." This sounds a bit awkward, so in referring to a group, use plural forms for the noun and pronouns whenever possible.

EXERCISE 10.24 The following short paragraphs have pronoun agreement problems. Make all pronouns agree with nouns to add to the cohesion of the paragraphs.

Most police officers carry guns. It is usually a .38-caliber pistol. Each time a police officer shoots their gun, they must file a report telling why and how the weapon was used.

American automobiles look more like foreign cars these days. It is usually small and square. The engine has four cylinders, and they get good gas mileage and need little service.

A counter worker in a fast food restaurant has a difficult job. They have to deal with a customer and put up with all their complaints. Even if the customers are pleasant, the counter workers have to write down the order correctly, but most of all he or she is responsible for all the money in the cash register.

Unnecessary Shifts of Person

Shift of person: A pronoun error that occurs when a writer, without purpose, shifts from using a pronoun in one person (often third person, *he/she/it/they*) to using a pronoun in another person (often the second person, *you*).

Pronouns can be classified as first, second, or third person:

	Singular	*Plural*
First person	I	we
Second person	you	you
Third person	he, she, it	they

When you are writing, you need to be as consistent as possible in using first-, second-, and third-person pronouns. Read this short paragraph in which the subject pronouns are underlined:

Many people do not vote because <u>they</u> do not believe that their vote makes a difference. <u>They</u> think all politicians are the same and it does not matter who wins, so <u>you</u> just don't bother to vote.

You probably noticed that the first two pronouns are in the third-person form, *they.* This form is the best choice because the writer is speaking about a third party — people who do not vote. But with the last pronoun, the writer shifts to the second-person form, *you.* Thus, the writer has switched from speaking about others to speaking directly to the reader.

You should use the second-person form, *you,* only when you mean the reader specifically. For example, in this book I often use *you* because I am talking to you as an individual student reading the book. At other times, I might use the third person, *they,* when talking about beginning writers as a whole group of people, of which you are one member.

Most problems in shift of person come about when writers switch to the second person but are not addressing readers directly. For instance, if you were writing to other college students about English requirements in your high school, you should not say, "In my high school, you had to take senior English." The second-person *you* does not work because very few, if any, members of your audience went to your high school. As you edit your papers, be sure to use second-person forms only when you are addressing your audience directly.

E X E R C I S E   10.25   In the following sentences, change any pronoun forms that create an unnecessary shift of person. If a sentence uses *you* correctly, indicate that the sentence is correct.

1. Sally really likes her boyfriend because you have a lot of fun with him.
2. Before astronauts can travel in outer space, you need to have years of training.
3. To cook spaghetti, you must have a large pot.
4. Many people exercise to improve their health, but you should check with your doctor before beginning an exercise routine.
5. Home repairs are expensive, but you can save money by doing them yourself if you purchase a good book on home repair.
6. We were playing well against the best team in the conference, but you never knew when they would get hot and crush you.
7. Would you like to win $10,000?
8. Plumbing is a good trade because most plumbers work for themselves and you earn high wages.
9. When class began, you had to be in your seat and ready to begin.
10. Recycling aluminum products can help you earn extra money.

Pronoun Case

Pronoun case is the form of a pronoun that indicates its use in a sentence. A pronoun used as a subject is a subject pronoun (in the subjective case); a pronoun used as an object is an object pronoun (in the objective case); a pronoun used to show possession is a possessive pronoun (in the possessive case). We concentrate here on common errors with subject and object pronouns.

Subject Pronouns	*Object Pronouns*	*Possessive Pronouns*
I, we	me, us	my, mine, our, ours
you	you	your, yours
he, she, it, they	him, her, it, them	his, her, hers, its, their, theirs

When you write sentences, it is sometimes easy to confuse these pronouns and use a subject pronoun when you need an object pronoun or vice versa. The following italicized pronouns are used in nonstandard forms. They are all object pronouns used as subjects.

Her and her husband are planning a trip to Europe.
Jim and *me* study math every Thursday.
Us and the Jones family went on a picnic.
Me wants some candy.

In the last sentence, you probably recognize the kind of language a very young child would speak. Here the error is obvious; as an adult you would never use *me* in this way. In the other sentences, the errors are not so clear, because each sentence has two subjects: *her* and *her husband, Jim* and *me, us* and *the Jones family*. When there is only one subject, you probably have very little trouble choosing the right pronoun. For instance, you would not say, "*Her* is planning a trip to Europe" or "*Us* went on a picnic." But the second subject can easily confuse you because often the two together do not sound too bad. Corrected, the preceding sentences should read:

She and her husband are planning a trip to Europe.
Jim and *I* study math every Thursday.
We and the Jones family went on a picnic.
I want some candy.

Some of these sentences may sound a little strange to you if you are not accustomed to using the correct pronouns in speech, but these pronouns are the forms used for subjects in standard English.

E X E R C I S E   10.26 Indicate any pronoun that does not follow the standard English form for subject pronouns. Then replace the incorrect pronoun with the subject form.

1. Leo, Hector, and me are taking a computer class.
2. Bill and me met some new friends who have a boat, and next week them and us are going fishing.
3. Kim, Linda, and me earned the highest marks on the test.
4. When the bus arrived, us and them got on.
5. Ellen loves to smoke cigarettes, but she knows them are not good for her health.
6. Her and her kids wash the family car once a week to keep it looking new.
7. The children decorated the Christmas tree with their father, and him and their mother put presents under it after the children went to bed.
8. Her and I have been friends for eleven years.
9. Because him and his brother were good at fixing cars, them and another fellow opened up a repair shop.
10. Erica, Jill, and me hate Brussels sprouts, but it seems as if them and carrots are on the cafeteria menu almost every day.

Sometimes subject pronouns are used incorrectly in place of object pronouns. Consider the following incorrect uses of subject pronouns.

The teacher gave *we* students a difficult assignment.
Between you and *I,* Alice's son is a little brat.
We bought presents for *she* and her children.
You shouldn't let *he* or his brother borrow money from you.

None of the italicized pronouns are subjects. In the first sentence, *teacher* is the subject, not *we.* In the second sentence, *son* is the subject; *we* and *you* are the subjects in the third and fourth sentences. Because the italicized pronouns are not subjects and also do not show possession, they should be object pronouns:

The teacher gave *us* students a difficult assignment.
Between you and *me,* Alice's son is a little brat.
We bought presents for *her* and her children.
You shouldn't let *him* or his brother borrow money from you.

EXERCISE 10.27 Replace incorrectly used subject pronouns with object pronouns in the following sentences.

1. Elaine bought concert tickets for she and I.
2. Classical music can be appreciated by we teenagers.
3. I don't like the new boss, but let's keep my feelings between you and I.

4. George and Dawn went to a party at the Jordans' house, but they did not like either they or their friends.
5. Grammar is difficult for other students and I, but we are catching on.
6. The company gave we secretaries a party because we had completed all our work on time.
7. Please do not leave because of Sheila and I.
8. Between we two, Mark needs to learn some table manners.
9. Because Lois is a good singer, Reverend Walls asked she and her husband to join the church choir.
10. Who is the better singer between her husband and she?

As you draft, revise, and edit your papers, pay close attention to the pronouns. They add cohesion to paragraphs, but when used incorrectly, they can confuse your readers.

■ Easily Confused Words

Easily confused words: Words that sound the same when spoken but are spelled differently and have different meanings.

In English, many words sound the same as other words when spoken. However, many words that sound the same, or almost the same, are spelled differently and have different meanings. When you write, it is easy to confuse such words. In a draft, you might write, "A four-bedroom house is probably to large for a single person." If you noticed that the word *to* does not seem right, you have caught the confusion between *to* and *too*. Although there are many such confusing words, you probably have trouble with only a few of them. The following list explains the meanings and differences between words that can easily be confused. If you find yourself having trouble with any of these words, consult the list as you edit your drafts and after your teacher has returned your paper. Confused words take time and patience to eliminate, but if you find out which words give you the most trouble, the list will help you eliminate your errors.

a/an When we are referring to most things in English, we use the article *a*: *a* boat, *a* boy, *a* school, *a* computer, *a* house. *A* is used before words beginning with most consonants. *An* is used with words that start with the vowels *a, e, i, o,* and *u,* if the *u* is pronounced like "uh." For example: *an* umbrella, *an* ulcer, *an* uncle, *an* upset, *an* unfortunate person, *an* unforeseen circumstance. If a word begins, with a *u* or any sound that is pronounced "you," use *a.* For example, *a* unicorn, *a* university, *a* useful tool, *a* eulogy, *a* European. To simplify the rules, remember that *an* is used before all vowel sounds except those that sound like "you"; otherwise, use *a.* Study the following lists:

a	*an*
a bus	an apple
a eunuch	an envelope
a home run	an honor (Silent *h* creates the vowel
a kite	sound *o*.)
a miracle	an improvement
a useless plan	an octopus
	an urgent message

are/our   When you confuse these two words, you are mixing up a verb, *are,* with a pronoun that shows possession, *our.* Compare the words in the following sentences:

Jim and Mike *are* coming to *our* house tonight.
Our tomato plants *are* growing tall.
They *are* rooting against *our* team.
Are you coming to *our* party this weekend?
Where *are our* books?

do/due   *Do* is a verb: "I *do* my homework late in the evening." *Due* means required to be done by a certain time: "My car payment is *due* the first week of each month." *Due* can also be used in place of *because:* "The picnic was canceled *due* to the rain." Compare these words in the following sentences:

Do you know when our term papers are *due?*
Due to the holiday, your paper will not be *due* until next week. Thus, you will have time to *do* other assignments.
We always *do* our income taxes the day before they are *due.*

feel/fill   You *feel* good or bad, or you *feel* something with your hands. You *fill* a glass, a bowl, or any other container.

I always *feel* better when I *fill* my gas tank.
The boss *feels* that we should *fill* the large storage room with the old merchandise.
If you *fill* your stomach with junk food, you won't *feel* hungry for dinner.

have/of   Rarely does anyone confuse *have* with *of,* but often people use *of* for *have* as part of a verb form. A common error is to mistakenly write: "I should *of* done better on the test." Using *of* as a verb is nonstandard. It happens because when we speak we often make contractions of verb forms. *Could have* becomes *could've, would have* becomes *would've,* and *should have* becomes *should've.* When we hear these contractions, we do not hear *could've* but *could of,* which is not a standard English form. Compare the following sentences. Which ones use standard forms?

We *could have* danced all night.
We *could've* danced all night.
We *could of* danced all night.

hear/here   *Hear* is what you do with your ear. This meaning is not hard to remember because the word *ear* is in *hear*. *Here* refers to a place:

Come *here* so that I can *hear* you better.
Did I *hear* you say you won't be *here* tomorrow?
When he gets *here,* we will have to *hear* all about his trip.

it's/its   *It's* is a contraction of *it is:* "It's raining today." *Its* is the possessive form of the pronoun *it:* "We liked the car because of *its* shiny paint job." You would never say or write "We liked the car because of *it is* shiny paint job," but it is easy to write "*it's* paint job" because we associate apostrophes with possession and often think all words with apostrophes are possessive (see discussion of apostrophes in the next section). However, the apostrophe is not used with pronouns to show possession. *It* is a pronoun and thus never uses an apostrophe for the possessive. Compare *it's* and *its* in these sentences:

Our dog hides when *it's* time for *its* bath.
It's too bad *it's* cloudy today.
We assumed the computer was broken when *its* screen went blank, but
   it's working now.

knew/new   *Knew,* like the word *know,* comes from the word *knowledge.* Notice that all three start with *kn. New* means fresh, unused:

Jim bought *new* shoes. Ellen has a *new* book.
Mike *knew* that soon he would have to make *new* friends.
The *new* teacher *knew* she would have to win her students' confidence.
The experienced soldiers *knew* that the *new* recruits were not ready for
   combat.

know/no   Like *knew, know* comes from *knowledge. No* is a negative answer or a word used to mean none.

No, we can't go with you to the park; we *know* you will forgive us.
I *know* I will have *no* chance to pass Chemistry I unless I study.
Linda *knows* the course will pose *no* problems for her because she took
   advanced chemistry in high school and earned an A.
Did you *know* that *no* one failed chemistry last semester?

passed/past   *Passed* is the past form of the verb *pass:*

Driving through Washington D.C., we *passed* the White House.
I *passed* her the ketchup.
Anna *passed* the test.

In contrast, *past* can be a noun, adjective, or adverb, but it is never a verb:

The *past* can come back to haunt us.
She is *past* president of the city council.
We walked *past* the ice cream shop.

Compare the use of these words:

In *past* seasons, the Bears' quarterback *passed* much more effectively
   than he did this year.
The word *passed* is the *past* tense of the verb *pass.*
She was not a good student in the *past,* but this semester she has *passed*
   all her tests and is earning high grades.

right/write   When you *write,* you do what this book has been trying
to teach you to do. When you are *right,* you are not wrong. Also you
have a *right* to vote, and you know *right* from *left.* Note the differences
in the use of these words:

All American citizens have the *right* to speak or *write* their opinions
   freely.
Next time I will *write* down the directions to your house, for I got lost
   when I made a *right* instead of a left at the corner.
Your plan for increasing sales seems *right,* but *write* a report so the sales
   force will know what are you trying to do.

than/then   These words are very confusing in writing because many
people pronounce them the same way when speaking. *Than* is used in
comparisons: "Her chili is spicier *than* mine." *Then* marks time, signi-
fying that one thing came after another: "Keith set the table; *then* we all
sat down for dinner." If you confuse these words, be careful to edit them
by sight as you read your draft. Compare their use in these sentences:

If you would rather buy a Japanese car *than* an American car, *then* you
   will need to spend more money.
Then José said that the Dodgers are a better team *than* the Mets.
Typewriters made writing easier *than* it had been when writers used only
   pen and paper; *then* computers came along, making writing even easier.

their/they're/there   These words may be confused more often than any others, so you need to edit carefully if you have trouble using them. *Their* is a pronoun that shows possession: "All the farmers are harvesting *their* crops." *They're* is a contraction for *they are:* "*They're* harvesting their crops." *There* refers to a place or is used with a verb to point to something: "I like New York, but I have not been *there* in years. *There* is the Statue of Liberty." Compare the way the words are used in these sentences:

They're going to Disneyland for *their* vacation even though they have been *there* six times before.
In the Rocky Mountains, *there* are some of the tallest peaks in the world. *They're* as much as 14,000 feet above sea level.

threw/through   *Threw* is the past form of the verb *throw:* "The pitcher *threw* his fastball." *Through* is not a verb: "Are you *through* watching television? I would not want to sit *through* that movie again." Note the differences:

Merle was galloping *through* the woods when her horse *threw* her.
After making a crucial error, Lenny *threw* down his mitt and decided he was *through* with baseball.
When Michelle was *through* reading the newspaper, she *threw* it away.

to/too/two   *Two* is the word for the number 2. It is rarely confused with the others, but *to* and *too* are not as easy to keep straight. *To* is a preposition used to indicate motion toward: "*to* the store." It is also used with the dictionary form of a verb to make the infinitive form: *to have, to be, to run. Too* is a word indicating degree. Students don't often use *too* when they mean *to,* but very often when they mean *too*—as in "*too* large," "*too* small," "*too* tired" — they leave off the second *o.* To remember when to use *too,* think of it as having *too* many *o*'s. Compare the usages in these sentences:

We stayed up late *to* watch a Dracula film festival on cable, but after seeing *two* movies, we were *too* tired to see any more.
Too many students want *to* major in business without knowing *too* much about it.
Two drinks can be *too* much if you are driving.

weather/whether   *Weather* refers to climate conditions: rain, snow, wind, sunshine, and so on: "The *weather* should be clear today." *Whether* can substitute for *if:* "Phil does not know *whether* he wants to major in aviation." Note the different uses of these words:

The team did not know *whether* the game would be canceled because of bad *weather.*
The *weather* report was unclear about *whether* it would rain.

Whether you live in a warm or cold climate, there will always be days when the *weather* is not to your liking.

who's/whose   *Who's* is a contraction of *who is:* "*Who's* at the door?" *Whose* is a possessive pronoun, and as such it never uses apostrophes to show possession. Comparing *who's* and *whose* in these sentences should help you see the difference:

Who's the person *whose* car is parked in the driveway?
Who's having a party at *whose* house?

you're/your   *You're* is a contraction of *you are. Your* is a possessive pronoun, and therefore has no apostrophe: "*your* parents," "*your* children," "*your* book," "*your* grades." Compare *you're* and *your* in the following sentences:

You're doing well in this course, and *your* grades reflect *your* effort.
Your friends and relatives are proud that *you're* attending college.
If *you're* working hard, *you're* getting closer to attaining *your* goals.

E X E R C I S E   10.28   Indicate which form of the words in parentheses should be used in each sentence.

1. How (do/due) you (feel/fill) about this cold (whether/weather)?
2. (Its/it's) supposed to warm up tomorrow, but I'm not (to/too/two) sure it will.
3. I (know/no) that the (whether/weather) reports can't always be trusted.
4. In the (past/passed), my grades were low, but now that I have learned to (write/right), I am improving in all of my work.
5. I (should've/should of) done better last semester, but (its/it's) (too/to) late (to/too) worry about that now.
6. I (knew/new) I wasn't a good student (then/than), but this semester I am studying more effectively, and I (know/no) I will earn higher grades (than/then) I did last semester.
7. (Who's/Whose) writing course are you taking?
8. Excuse me, I didn't (here/hear) you?
9. (Who's/Whose) (your/you're) writing teacher?
10. Dr. Gaston. She is (knew/new) (here/hear) this year.
11. I (should've/should of) signed up for her class (too/to/two) because I need to get (through/threw) my English requirements.
12. Writing courses are not something you should just get (through/threw).
13. I (know/no), but at times (their/they're/there) really tough for me; I barely (passed/past) my first one.

14. Maybe you (should've/should of) given your teacher (a/an) apple. Ha! Ha! Or better yet, you (should've/should of) handed in (you're/your) papers when they were (do/due).

15. (Write/right)!

Correct any words that are misused in the following sentences.

1. Many of the varsity athletes our doing well academically.
2. But their are some people who believe athletes are not serious about there education.
3. These people don't know how hard athletes have too work during the season.
4. Their expected to practice four hours a day and do not have to much time to study.
5. A athlete also must miss some classes when he or she goes on road trips with the team.
6. Some of the athletes try to due there homework while riding on the team bus.
7. Still, its common to here some students and teachers stereotype athletes as dumb jocks.
8. There not aware that at many schools the GPA of the athletes is higher then the GPA of the student body as an whole.
9. Granted some athletes do not have good grades, but then their are many nonathletes who's grades aren't to good either.
10. Weather there athletes or not, all students are do respect, and know one has the write to stereotype them.

Correct misused words in the following paragraphs.

Its sometimes common to believe that large cities such as New York and Los Angeles are the best places to live for people who enjoy a urban lifestyle. But smaller midwestern cities have much too offer. St. Louis, for example, with it's renovated waterfront and numerous restaurants and theaters, is a charming city. Indianapolis, do to much recent development, will soon be known for more then the Indy 500. Cincinnati boasts major league sports teams, some excellent restaurants, and a wonderful music hall, while maintaining the fill of a small town in it's ethnic neighborhoods. Even Minneapolis, despite the cold whether, is more cosmopolitan then most people no. So if your looking to settle in a city, don't overlook the cities of the Midwest.

Their has been much controversy about "colorized" films. Ted Turner, owner of Atlanta cable station WTBS, has purchased the rights too many of the great black and white film classics of the passed. Turner has had many of these films colorized, much too the displeasure of many directors, actors, producers, and fans. They argue that its wrong to change the way the original filmmakers conceived these films. A adventure film, such as *Captain Blood* with Errol Flynn, almost seems to benefit from colorization, but theirs something lost when *The Maltese Falcon,* with it's shadowy scenes and dark plot, is made to look as bright as any situation comedy. Legally, Turner has the write to due what he wants with the films, but weather colorization is morally or artistically ethical is not to easy to say.

E X E R C I S E   10.31   Read over a short piece of your writing. Circle easily confused words that you have used correctly. Change any that you have used incorrectly.

■ Punctuation

As you have been developing your writing skills, you probably have had questions about punctuation. Punctuation can be troublesome. Do you need a comma or not? Should you use a semicolon or a comma? Many teachers have heard the story about the student who always left commas out. He became so frustrated that he put a line full of them at the end of his paper and then wrote his teacher a note saying she could put them in anywhere she wanted. This story may or may not be true, but it shows the frustration writers sometimes feel when they do not have control of their punctuation. Punctuation can be tricky, but when it comes right down to it, there are not as many rules as you think.

Using the Comma   The comma is the mark of punctuation used most often. Some people say they can punctuate with commas by listening for pauses when they read sentences aloud. This method works sometimes but not always, and sometimes it can cause you to add unnecessary commas. While it is good to use your ear as you punctuate, you cannot rely only on it. There are five rules that can help you use commas effectively.

Rule 1: Commas and Coordinating Conjunctions   Earlier in this chapter, you learned to use coordinating conjunctions as a way to fix comma splices and run-on sentences. There are seven coordinating conjunctions: *but, and, for, nor, or, so,* and *yet* (BAFNOSY). The following is the rule governing commas used with coordinating conjunctions (or BAFNOSY words).

Put a comma before the conjunction when the conjunction joins two complete sentences. That is, if there is a sentence before and a sentence after the conjunction, use a comma. Remember that a sentence must have at least one subject and one verb.

Note the examples:

Keith hated steak, **but** he loved hamburgers.
subject   verb   subject   verb

TV sportscasters must know a lot about sports, **and** they must
subject   verb   subject
be able to speak clearly.
verb

Jill could not quit her job, **for** she needed money badly.
subject   verb   subject   verb

Aunt Victoria never drank, **nor** did she go into bars.
subject   verb   subject verb

You should buy snow tires while they are on sale, **or** in the
subject   verb
middle of a snowstorm you will have to pay a lot for them.
subject   verb

Ed was rushing to get to the hospital, **so** ignoring the traffic light,
subject   verb
he sped through the intersection.
subject verb

I love to see plays, **yet** I do not like to read them.
subject verb   subject   verb

Using commas with coordinating conjunctions is not too difficult if you remember that before you add the comma, you need a complete sentence before the conjunction and a complete sentence after. Sometimes beginning writers learn half the rule, thinking that every time they use a conjunction, they should place a comma before it. This notion leads to a lot of unnecessary commas. For example:

Vito is poor, **but** proud.
I must save money now because in the summer I am buying new dining
room funiture, **and** in the fall a new sofa for the living room.

The first sentence is short. Thus, the comma seems out of place. But length has nothing to do with the punctuation. The comma should not be there because there is no subject and verb after the conjunction *but*. In contrast, the second sentence is quite long — twenty-seven words, in fact. When beginning writers see a sentence this long, they think it must need a comma somewhere. But if you look at the ten words following the conjunction *and,* you will not find a subject and verb. Thus, the comma is not correct.

E X E R C I S E   10.32   Add any commas needed before conjunctions, and indicate any that are not needed. Note the sentences in which a comma is used correctly with a conjunction.

1. Vince is an excellent swimmer but he is afraid to try scuba diving, or water skiing.
2. After becoming the first person to fly across the Atlantic, Charles Lindbergh became an international hero, and he was invited to many different countries.
3. Calvert Country Club has a short, but difficult golf course.
4. Last year's president of the student government ran again this year, but she lost by four hundred votes.
5. The movie was, so long and boring.
6. The novel *Mutiny on the Bounty* has been made into a film many times yet no version is as good as the one with Clark Gable and Charles Laughton.
7. Would you rather paint the house this summer, or wait for the cool weather in the fall?
8. Louise enjoys living in the city because she can go downtown to shop and see films or out to the parks to go jogging.
9. Angelo eats neither pork chops, nor veal cutlets yet he claims to love meat.
10. The university planned a reception, for the new freshmen from Japan.

E X E R C I S E   10.33   Add and cross out commas to correct the punctuation of this paragraph. Circle any commas used correctly.

Charles Darwin's theory of evolution shocked the world in the nineteenth century, and still causes controversy today. Through the study of plants, and animals Darwin theorized that humans had evolved from animals. Scientists were fascinated by Darwin's work yet they worried that it questioned the teachings of the Bible. Thus, Darwin had many enemies in the scientific community but also many friends who defended him. The British philosopher Thomas Huxley believed strongly in Darwin's theory, so he wrote essays, and gave speeches in Darwin's defense. Today most scientists accept Darwin's theory of evolution but many religious people question it. People can believe in Darwin's theory, or in the biblical story of creation, but the origin of the human race remains a controversial topic.

Sentence openers: Any
word, phrase, or
dependent clause that
comes before the first
independent clause in a
sentence. A comma is
usually placed after a
sentence opener.

Rule 2: Commas and Sentence Openers   All sentences must have at
least one independent clause, a clause with a subject and a verb that can
stand on its own. Very often, however, sentences do not start with an
independent clause. Instead, a sentence may open with a word or a phrase
or a dependent clause.

Word	*Yesterday,* the Electro Power Company announced that it may build two nuclear power plants. *However,* the plants will be much smaller than those now operating in the United States.
Phrase	*In 1979,* a near meltdown in the nuclear reactor at Three Mile Island in Pennsylvania led to new safety regulations for nuclear power plants. *Despite the near tragedy at Three Mile Island,* the Electro Power Company believes that nculear plants are safe.
Dependent Clause	*Before Electro builds the reactors,* its plans must be approved by the federal government. *After the construction begins next May,* federal inspectors will visit the plants periodically to ensure that regulations are followed.

Rule 2 is not as difficult to remember as some others. In most cases,
you can trust your ear to help you punctuate; usually you pause after
reading the sentence beginning and before you read the independent
clause. This is not always true for the one-word beginnings, but for the
others listening for the pause can help you hear where to put the comma.

E X E R C I S E   10.34   Put commas where needed after sentence openers.

1. On the fourteenth of July the French celebrate Bastille Day.
2. Just as the Fourth of July celebrates America's freedom Bastille Day
   celebrates freedom for the French.
3. In many countries one national holiday is as significant to the
   people as July Fourth is to Americans.
4. For example the English celebrate Guy Fawkes day.
5. Despite its name this holiday does not honor Fawkes.
6. As a member of a revolutionary group Fawkes devised a plan to
   blow up Parliament, the building that houses British lawmakers.
7. Before Fawkes could carry out his plan he was caught.
8. As a result he was hanged for treason.
9. On the first day of May Russia celebrates the anniversary of the
   Communist Revolution of 1917.

10. Though many Americans do not think that communism is something to celebrate the first of May is the most important holiday in Russia.

E X E R C I S E 10.35 Add commas after sentence openers in this paragraph.

Although workers today take medical insurance for granted it is only in the last fifty years that companies began to provide benefits for workers who fall ill or are injured on the job. In nineteenth-century industrial America medical benefits were unheard of. If workers were hospitalized they had to pay their own bills. Even when injured on the job a worker would not receive any compensation from his or her company. In contrast, nowadays, a worker injured in a job-related accident would have all bills paid by the company and might even receive an additional sum if the injury occurred as a result of the company's negligence.

E X E R C I S E 10.36 Review a paper you have written, and circle the commas you have used after sentence beginnings. If you find any commas missing, add them.

Items in a series: Three or more words, phrases, or clauses that occur one after the other. Commas separate items in a series.

Rule 3: Commas in a Series When you have a series of three or more words, phrases, or clauses, separate them with commas:

Words Ricardo bought *a hat, a sweater,* and *a coat.*

Phrases Brian takes a walk *in the morning, just after lunch,* and *early in the evening.*
Althea has won awards for *singing in a church choir, working with disadvantaged children,* and *protecting the rights of animals.*

Clauses Now is not a good time to apply for a mortgage because *not much property is available, prices are high,* and *interest rates are rising.*

E X E R C I S E 10.37 Add commas to separate items in a series.

1. The prisoner's dinner consisted of a piece of stale bread a bowl of soup and a cup of water.
2. He tore at the bread with his teeth gulped up the soup and washed them down with the water.

3. Bananas mangos coconuts and pineapples are all tropical fruits.
4. Washington Jefferson Lincoln Roosevelt Truman and Kennedy are very famous presidents, but who remembers Fillmore Pierce Hayes Taft or Cleveland?
5. To become a good carpenter, you must learn to use tools to identify different types of wood and to make careful measurements.
6. The band stopped playing the dancers stopped dancing and the lights dimmed.
7. When you go to the store, pick up milk bread and eggs.
8. John Mike and Sarah are all baseball fans, but John likes the Red Sox Mike likes the Yankees and Sarah likes the Mets.
9. Looking straight ahead balancing herself gracefully and stepping carefully forward, the tightrope walker began her performance.
10. The Studebaker the De Soto and the Nash were once popular cars, but they are no longer manufactured.

Sentence interrupter: A word, phrase, or dependent clause that interrupts the flow of a sentence. Interrupters are punctuated with commas before and after them.

Rule 4: Commas and Sentence Interrupters Sometimes a word or phrase interrupts the flow of a sentence. This does not mean that there is something wrong with the sentence. The interrupter adds something to the sentence, although the sentence usually can be understood without it. Interrupters can be one word, a phrase, or even a clause. Use a comma before and after an interrupter.

Word	The drinks are expensive. The food, *however,* is priced reasonably and very tasty.
	The restaurant, *consequently,* attracts customers who care more about food than drinks.
Phrase	We will, *of course,* come to the wedding.
	Almost everyone, *at one time or another,* falls in love.
Clauses	Writing an essay, *as you know,* takes planning and time.
	Siamese cats, *though they can be mean,* are very popular pets.

Sentence interrupters, like sentence openers, can often be punctuated by ear. If you read the example sentences aloud, you will notice a pause before and after the interrupter. Put commas where you pause. Most beginning writers have little trouble with the comma before the interrupter, but they sometimes forget the comma after it. Remember to put commas both *before* and *after* sentence interrupters.

E X E R C I S E 10.38   Add commas where needed with sentence interrupters. Indicate commas that are correctly used.

1. Walt Whitman, according to F. O. Mathiessen is America's greatest poet.
2. Other American poets of course have written great poems.
3. Emily Dickinson along with Whitman is considered one of the greatest American poets of the nineteenth century.
4. In the twentieth century, T. S. Eliot wrote *The Waste Land,* and it, of course, ranks among the best poems ever written.
5. Eliot as a result earned respect and fame worldwide.
6. Eliot's poems however are difficult to read.
7. Many Americans, consequently, have not read *The Waste Land* or any other Eliot poems.
8. Poetry, as we know has never been very popular in America.
9. Eliot unlike Dickinson, wrote poems that only highly educated people can understand.

E X E R C I S E 10.39   Add commas where needed to set off sentence interrupters. Indicate any commas used correctly to punctuate interrupters.

Painting a room is not too difficult if you follow the right procedures. You will, however have to have the proper equipment: paint rollers, a roller pan, drop cloths, a brush for the trim, masking tape, and of course enough paint. Before painting, you must prepare the walls by filling in all cracks and holes with spackling compound and by washing the walls thoroughly. The preparation though time-consuming will ensure a good paint job. Once you have prepared the walls, place masking tape on the edges of the woodwork. Then spread your drop cloths on the floor. Next, using the brush, paint about a two-inch border around the woodwork. Now fill the roller pan with paint. Using the roller begin painting the walls. Painting with a roller unlike painting with a brush, takes very little time. Use even strokes to cover the walls thoroughly. Before you know it, your room will look fresh and clean. And as a result of doing the job yourself, you will save money.

Nonessential phrases and clauses: Phrases and clauses that occur after or in the middle of a sentence. They are set off from the rest of the sentence with commas.

Rule 5: Commas and Nonessential Phrases and Clauses   Nonessential phrases and clauses add information to a sentence, but without them the sentence would still make its main point. Nonessential phrases and clauses often appear in the middle of sentences, as in these examples:

Phrases	Enrico Fermi, *a University of Chicago professor,* was a pioneer in the development of nuclear power.

Phrases	Enrico Fermi, *a University of Chicago professor,* was a pioneer in the development of nuclear power. The furnace, *installed in 1970,* no longer works efficiently. Isaiah Williams, *running at his best,* won the marathon.
Clauses	Enrico Fermi, *who was a University of Chicago professor,* was a pioneer in the development of nuclear power. Sicilian pizza, *because it has a thick crust,* is more filling than other types of pizza.

Nonessential phrases and clauses also can appear at the end of a sentence. When they do, a comma comes before them and a period after.

Phrases	The boy fell off his tricycle, *scraping his knee.* Mrs. Phelps wanted a Pekingese, *a dog originally bred in China.*
Clauses	The workers at the nursing home were doing a wonderful job, *though no one except the patients knew it.* Sabina rode a Vincent's Black Shadow, *which is a rare motorcycle no longer manufactured.*

In all of these sentences, you could take out the words between the commas or after the comma and before the period, and you would still understand the main point of the sentence. You would not have as much information, but the main point would not change. Like sentence interrupters, nonessential phrases and clauses can sometimes be punctuated by ear. Remember that if the nonessential part is in the middle of the sentence, put the comma *before* and *after* it.

E X E R C I S E   10.40   Add commas needed to punctuate nonessential phrases and clauses. Indicate commas used correctly with nonessential phrases or clauses.

1. Alejandro Varges a doctor from Brazil recently moved to California and opened a clinic.
2. Mexico which is the name of a country, is the name of a small town in Missouri.
3. We are reading *Billy Budd* Herman Melville's last book.
4. The draft of *Billy Budd,* which was unfinished when Melville died, was edited by scholars and published in the 1920s, nearly forty years after it was written.
5. Buzz Aldrin who was one of the first humans on the moon had a difficult life in the years immediately after he retired from NASA, but he overcame his problems including depression.

6. Willi Kwong a senior from Malaysia was offered a job by the bank of Hong Kong which is one of the most prestigious banks in the world.
7. A Rolls-Royce Silver Cloud which costs over $100,000 is guaranteed for life.
8. The Silver Cloud once had a sealed hood, which prevented anyone but a certified Rolls-Royce mechanic from working on the car.
9. Boston Celtics star Larry Bird played college basketball at Indiana State University which is often mistaken for Indiana University known for its great teams coached by Bobby Knight.
10. Bird who was a freshman at Indiana University transferred to Indiana State wanting to play at a smaller school.

EXERCISE 10.41 In the following paragraph, add commas needed to punctuate nonessential phrases and clauses. Indicate commas used correctly with nonessential phrases or clauses.

Shopping at home which was unheard of just a few years ago is now a billion-dollar business. With cable TV reaching millions of homes, TV has become a live catalog, and buyers with major credit cards can pick up the phone and make a purchase choosing items from jewelry to barbecue grills. The various items, which are supposedly priced low appear on the screen for about five minutes with price and phone number. An enthusiastic announcer describes the item making it sound like the bargain of a lifetime. Though TV shopping is growing, most people because they like to see exactly what they are buying still shop in stores.

Using the Semicolon

The **semicolon** has two uses. One is very rare; the other is very common. The rare use requires a semicolon between items in a series when there are commas within each item. This sounds confusing, but the following paragraph will give you an example:

Semicolon: A mark of punctuation used to connect items in a series that already have commas within them and, more commonly, to join independent clauses without a coordinating conjunction or with connecting words such as *consequently, however, nevertheless, thus, then,* and *therefore.*

The favorites to win the state basketball tournament are the Greenville Tigers, whose star players are Hall, Marx, and O'Keefe; the West Park Braves, who rely on Palmero, Van Bibber, and Cruz; and the South Central Titans, who boast the strongest front line in the league with McGee, Washington, and Nix.

The main series in this sentence consists of three teams: the Tigers, the Braves, and the Titans. But for each team a list of players is mentioned. Each list forms a series itself, and thus the players' names must be set off with commas. To avoid confusion, the main items in the sentence — the names of the teams — are separated by semicolons. This kind of sentence is rare. Although it is good to know the rule in case you write or read such a sentence, you should not concern yourself too much with this use of the semicolon. If you want to know more about it, consult a handbook of grammar.

The second use of the semicolon is very common, and it is important to know because semicolons can help you fix comma splices and run-on sentences. Simply stated, the rule is as follows:

Use a semicolon to join two sentences without a coordinating conjunction.

The sun was going down; people were leaving the beach.
My new suit fit well; my new shoes were too tight.
Writing is fun; however, grammar can be boring.
Some people think studying grammar is fun; others hate it.
Although the Corvair was a poorly engineered car, it is now a classic; consequently, collectors will pay a high price for a Corvair in good condition.

Notice that each pair of sentences could also be joined with a coordinating conjunction and a comma. Notice also that some sentences use connectors such as *however* and *consequently*. But because these connectors are not coordinating conjunctions, you need to use the semicolon with them. Compare the preceding sentences with these, which use a comma and a coordinating conjunction:

The sun was going down, *and* people were leaving the beach.
My new suit fit well, *but* my new shoes were too tight.
Writing is fun, *yet* grammar can be boring.
Some people think studying grammar is fun, *but* others hate it.
Although the Corvair was a poorly engineered car, it is now a classic, *so* collectors will pay a high price for a Corvair in good condition.

Whether you choose to join sentences with a comma and coordinating conjunction or with a semicolon depends on the effect you want to create. A semicolon usually draws a tighter relationship between the sentences and can be especially effective if both sentences are short: "Edmond moved to Chicago; he stayed there all his life." You should vary the way you connect sentences to create variety.

The semicolon is an easy way to join two sentences, but be sure that when you use it, both sentences you join are complete sentences. A common error is to begin a sentence with a dependent clause (not a complete sentence), follow it with a semicolon, and then end with an independent clause. That is not correct because the dependent clause should be followed by a comma. Compare these sentences:

Incorrect   Because many people rent movies to watch at home on a VCR; attendance is down at cinemas.

Correct	Because many people rent movies to watch at home on a VCR, attendance is down at cinemas.

Another common error is to join two sentences with a comma and a connector that is *not* a coordinating conjunction (*consequently, however, moreover, nevertheless, then, thus, therefore,* and so on).

Incorrect	The lights in the theater dimmed, then the curtain went up.
Correct	The lights in the theater dimmed; then the curtain went up.

EXERCISE 10.42 Add semicolons where needed in the following sentences. Replace incorrectly used semicolons with commas. Indicate sentences that are punctuated correctly with a C.

1. Orange juice is sweet grapefruit juice is sour.
2. When the orange crop is threatened by an early frost; the price of oranges rises.
3. The winter will be over soon then the weather will get warmer.
4. Although we were tired, we went to the opera; after all, we had paid a lot of money for the tickets, so we couldn't waste them.
5. Your paper was excellent it earned an A.
6. Because knights wore heavy armor; they were not very agile in a fight, but they were well protected.
7. Disposable lighters first became popular in the late 1960s now they are more common than matches.
8. Broken bones were once set in casts made of plaster today casts are made of fiberglass.
9. Because fiberglass casts are lighter; patients on crutches have an easier time getting around.
10. Beginning writers often confuse semicolons and commas, therefore, it is good to know the rules for using them.

EXERCISE 10.43 In the following paragraph, correct any punctuation errors in the use of semicolons and commas.

We take plastic bags for granted, however, the process by which they are made is interesting and complex. Plastic pellets are put into a machine called an extruder. The extruder melts the pellets and forces them through a long, steel tube, then a plastic film comes out of the other end in a bubble. The machine, in other words, works like a child's bubble pipe. The plastic bubble is then blown full of air until it is the right size for the bags being made. This bubble is then stretched into a tube and inserted into a set of rollers. The plastic tube passes through the rollers, and it is flattened and cooled. At the end of the rollers is a cutting and sealing device it cuts a certain length of the tube and seals the bottom end to make a bag. Though this process is complex; an extruder is capable of producing thousands of bags a day.

Using the Apostrophe

You are probably very familiar with **apostrophes** used in contractions: *couldn't, don't, doesn't, he'll, I'm, I'll, she'd, we're, they're,* and so on. You may also know that apostrophes are used to show possession, but beginning writers often have trouble with the rules for using apostrophes to show possession. Before we discuss the rules, try the following exercise.

E X E R C I S E   10.44   Underline the name of the author of each source mentioned. Remember that titles of sources are either in quotation marks or in italics.

Apostrophe: A mark of punctuation that indicates where letters have been taken out of two words forming a contraction (*they're, he's, couldn't*), or that is used with an *-s* to show possession (*Milt's gloves, Elaine's children*). If a plural word already ends in *-s*, the apostrophe follows it (*the Tigers' coach, the students' favorite hangout*).

1. The stories in Doris Lessing's *The Grass Is Singing* are based on her experiences as a young British woman living in Africa.
2. Ken Purdy's essay ''The Honest Repairman — a Vanishing American'' is unfair to those repairmen who do honest work.
3. Don Lago's ''Symbols of Mankind'' contains many instances of striking or catchy language.
4. ''Letter from Birmingham Jail'' is one of Martin Luther King's most powerful essays.
5. I like Shakespeare's plays more than modern plays; for example, I find Eugene O'Neill's plays depressing.
6. Shakespeare's *As You Like It* is my favorite comedy, but I think *King Lear,* which is one of Shakespeare's tragedies, is my favorite play of all.
7. In our political science class, we are reading Niccolò Machiavelli's *The Prince,* a book written in the Renaissance but relevant to politics today.

8. Kurt Vonnegut's novels have been very popular with college students over the last twenty years, but many literary critics believe that only Vonnegut's *Slaughterhouse Five* is a truly accomplished novel.
9. In the last ten years, Mina Shaughnessy's *Errors and Expectations* has had an impact on methods of teaching beginners to write.
10. Richard Altick's *Victorian People and Ideas* offers valuable historical background for the student of Victorian literature.

Now that you have underlined the names of each author, compare them. What do they all have in common? If you answered that each has an **apostrophe** and the letter *-s* added to the end, you are right. The apostrophe and *-s* added to each name show that the author is the owner of the source that follows: Shakespeare's *King Lear,* Lessing's *The Grass Is Singing,* O'Neill's plays, King's most powerful essays.

You use the apostrophe and *-s* to show possession when you are writing about sources. But you also need to show possession when you are writing about other types of ownership. If you were writing about a car belonging to your father, you would write, "my *father's* car." Here are some additional examples: Professor *Klein's* class, *Wally's* sister, *Lisa's* grades, *Washington's* victories, the *car's* engine, Monday *night's* television schedule, the *book's* pages.

The last two examples may seem a bit confusing. You may wonder how a night of the week can own anything. But if you think about it, the television schedule *belongs* to Monday night rather than to another night of the week, just as the pages belong to the book you are talking about rather than to some other book. Here are some additional examples: *today's* world, *yesterday's* news, the *machine's* controls, the *rocket's* flight, the *essay's* thesis. In each of these examples, the word following the apostrophe and *-s* belongs to the word that has the apostrophe and *-s* on the end of it.

■■■■■■■■■■■■■■

E X E R C I S E   10.45   In the following paragraphs, add apostrophes where needed. The ownership words already have the *-s* added, so all you need to do is put the apostrophe before the *-s*.

England's theatrical tradition may be the greatest in the world. While some plays were written before the English Renaissance, the Renaissance represents the beginning of greatness on the British stage. Thomas Kyd's *The Spanish Tragedy* is one of the important plays of this period because it probably influenced Shakespeare's *Hamlet.* Christopher Marlowe's *Edward II* and *Dr. Faustus* certainly rank among the great plays of the English Renaissance, and Shakespeare's *Hamlet, King Lear,* and *Macbeth* may be the most powerful tragedies ever written.

Last weekend, my friend Bill's car broke down in the middle of the night as he was driving back to campus after attending his former high school's homecoming game. So he called me at 3:00 A.M. to come out to help him. He told me he had his tools with him, but Bill's mechanical ability leaves much to be desired, so he needed my help. When I got there, the car's trunk was stuck, so we couldn't get to Bill's tools. He ended up calling a tow truck, which he could have done in the first place. Needless to say, I wasn't too happy.

In Exercises 10.43 and 10.44, the ownership words were singular. Shakespeare is one man, Bill is one friend, and his car is one car. To show possession when a word is plural, follow two rules:

1. If the plural ends in *s,* just add an apostrophe: the birds' flight south, the Smiths' home, the Yankees' position in the standings, the companies' hiring policies, the three boys' parents.
2. If the word is plural but does not already end in s, then add the apostrophe and *-s:* the women's opinions, the men's opinions, the children's favorite stories.

EXERCISE 10.46 Add apostrophes where needed in the following sentences. Be careful to consider both singular and plural words.

1. The presidents speech praised the six northeastern states success in reducing unemployment.
2. The childrens school clothes cost more than their parents new coats.
3. Three cars tires were slashed yesterday on Ninth Street.
4. Outside the deans office, marchers and signs proclaimed the unfairness of the tuition hikes, but the students protest turned out to be futile when tuition was raised for the next semester.
5. The doctors fee for setting Peters broken leg was more than reasonable.
6. Did you receive this months *Time* magazine in todays mail?
7. Carlos worked so quickly that he earned two days pay in half a days time.
8. Kenny got a job selling womens shoes.
9. The child ruined the tables finish when he tried to clean it with cleanser.
10. The Larsons new home is located on Poplar Street.

By twelve o'clock, nearly a hundred men lined up outside the city's only soup kitchen. When the doors opened, they filed in. Tables lined the long hall. The men's lunch was a bowl of soup, slice of buttered bread, and cup of coffee. Tired and hungry, they were thankful for anything to eat. When they finished the meal, they knew they would be back on the streets, facing unemployment and people's indifference

Essays for Reading

What's Wrong with Black English
Rachel L. Jones

Rachel Jones wrote this essay during her sophomore year at Southern Illinois University. The essay was first published in *Newsweek* and has been reprinted many times since.

Vocabulary Cues

patois: dialect or slang of a particular group
deduced: figured out
doggedly: with great determination
rabid: having rabies
articulate: well spoken
flourish: something that shows style
assimilating: making similar, fitting in with

Questions to Guide Your Reading

1. What kind of home did Jones grow up in?
2. Why does Jones speak as she does?
3. What advantages does she see in speaking standard English?

William Labov, a noted linguist, once said about the use of black English, "It is the goal of most black Americans to acquire full control of the standard language without giving up their own culture." He also suggested that there are certain advantages to having two ways to express one's feelings. I wonder if the good doctor might also consider the goals of those black Americans who have full control of standard English but who are every now and then troubled by that colorful, grammar-to-the-winds patois that is black English. Case in point — me.

I'm a 21-year-old black born to a family that would probably be considered lower-middle class — which in my mind is a polite way of describing a condition only slightly better than poverty. Let's just say we rarely if ever did the winter-vacation thing in the Caribbean. I've often had to defend my humble beginnings to a most unlikely group of people for an even less likely reason. Because of the way I talk, some of my black peers look at me sideways and ask, "Why do you talk like you're white?"

The first time it happened I was nine years old. Cornered in the school bathroom by the class bully and her sidekick, I was offered the opportunity to swallow a few of my teeth unless I satisfactorily explained why I always got good grades, why I talked "proper" or "white." I had no ready answer for her, save the fact that my mother had from the time I was old enough to talk stressed the importance of reading and learning, or that L. Frank Baum and Ray Bradbury were my closest companions. I read all my older brothers' and sisters' literature textbooks more faithfully than they did, and even lightweights like the Bobbsey Twins and Trixie Belden were allowed into my bookish inner circle. I don't remember exactly what I told those girls, but I somehow talked my way out of a beating.

"White pipes." I was reminded once again of my "white pipes" problem while apartment hunting in Evanston, Ill., last winter. I doggedly made out lists of available places and called all around. I would immediately be invited over — and immediately turned down. The thinly concealed looks of shock when the front door opened clued me in, along with the flustered instances of "just getting off the phone with the girl who was ahead of you and she wants the rooms." When I finally found a place to live, my roommate stirred up old memories when she remarked a few months later, "You know, I was surprised when I first saw you. You sounded white over the phone." Tell me another one, sister.

I should've asked her a question I've wanted an answer to for years: how does one "talk white"? The silly side of me pictures a rabid white foam spewing forth when I speak. I don't use Valley Girl jargon, so that's not what's meant in my case. Actually, I've pretty much deduced what people mean when they say that to me, and the implications are really frightening.

It means that I'm articulate and well versed. It means that I can talk as freely about John Steinbeck as I can about Rick James. It means that "ain't" and "he be" are not staples of my vocabulary and are only used around family and friends. (It is almost Jekyll and Hyde-ish the way I can slip out of academic abstractions into a long, lean, double-negative-filled dialogue, but I've come to terms with that aspect of my personality.) As a child, I found it hard to believe that's what people meant by "talking proper"; that would've meant that good grades and standard English were equated with white skin, and that went against everything I'd ever been taught. Running into the same type of mentality as an adult has confirmed the depressing reality that for many blacks, standard English is not only unfamiliar, it is socially unacceptable.

James Baldwin once defended black English by saying it had added "vitality to the language," and even went so far as to label it a language in its own right, saying, "Language [i.e., black English] is a political instrument" and a "vivid and crucial key to identity." But did Malcolm X urge blacks to take power in this country "any way y'all can"? Did Martin Luther King Jr. say to blacks, "I has been to the mountaintop, and I done seed the Promised Land"? Toni Morrison, Alice Walker, and James Baldwin did not achieve their eloquence, grace, and stature by using only black English in their writing. Andrew Young, Tom Bradley, and Barbara Jordan did not acquire political power by saying, "Y'all crazy if you ain't gon vote for me." They all have full command of standard English, and I don't think that knowledge takes away from their blackness or commitment to black people.

Soulful. I know from experience that it's important for black people, stripped of culture and heritage, to have something they can point to and say, "This is ours, *we* can comprehend it, *we* alone can speak it with a soulful flourish.'' I'd be lying if I said that the rhythms of my people caught up in ''some serious rap'' don't sound natural and right to me sometimes. But how heartwarming is it for those same brothers when they hit the pavement searching for employment? Studies have proven that the use of ethnic dialects decreases power in the marketplace. ''I be'' is acceptable on the corner but not with the boss.

Am I letting capitalistic, European-oriented thinking fog the issue? Am I selling out blacks to an ideal or assimilating, being as much like white as possible? I have not formed a personal political ideology, but I do know this: it hurts me to hear black children use black English, knowing that they will be at yet another disadvantage in an educational system already full of stumbling blocks. It hurts me to sit in lecture halls and hear fellow black students complain that the professor ''be tripping dem out using big words dey can't understand.'' And what hurts most is to be stripped of my own blackness because I know my way around the English language.

I would have to disagree with Labov in one respect. My goal is not so much to acquire full control of both standard and black English, but to one day see more black people less dependent on a dialect that excludes them from full participation in the world we live in. I don't think I talk white, I think I talk right.

Questions for Study and Discussion
1. According to William Labov, what is the goal of most black Americans regarding language?
2. How did Jones learn to speak standard English?
3. Why did Jones have trouble with bullies in school?
4. What other problems did she have as a result of her speech?
5. Why does Jones think it is dangerous to believe that speaking in standard English is talking white?
6. Jones quotes James Baldwin, a well-known black writer. What did Baldwin mean when he said, ''Language is a political instrument'' and ''a key to identity''?
7. What examples does Jones give that show language as a political instrument?
8. Jones mentions several black politicians and writers, arguing that they used standard English to gain power. Can you think of times these people might use black English?
9. Jones seems to contradict herself when she says she often enjoys speaking black English with friends and family but then says she talks ''right'' when speaking standard English. Is one language right and the other wrong? Are there times when black English would be right?

Writing Assignments
1. Interview three or four people from different groups such as minorities, blue-collar workers, white-collar workers, people from a particular region. Ask them about the way their group speaks and list

examples of nonstandard words or phrases used by each person. Write a short essay showing how the language of each person's group differs from standard English.

2. Rachel Jones says her "goal is not so much to acquire full control of both standard and black English, but to one day see more black people less dependent on a dialect that excludes them from full participation in the world we live in." Do you think it is better for people from a group to forget its dialect and concentrate on learning standard English, or do you think it is better to know both? Write a short essay explaining your position.

Speech Communities
Paul Roberts

Paul Roberts was a professor at San Jose State College in California and Cornell University in New York. He is the author of many books on language. This essay is part of Roberts's most famous book, *Understanding English,* written in 1959.

Vocabulary Cues

Dannemora: a prison in upstate New York
oddities: odd things
ennobling: to make noble
hypothesis: a theory, an unproved argument
conversely: in contrast
obscurity: a condition of being unknown or unclear
connote: to carry emotional meaning
evokes: calls forth, brings to mind
disdain: strong disapproval, scorn

Questions to Guide Your Reading

1. What is a speech community?
2. Which speech community does Roberts say is best?
3. According to Roberts, if we admire a certain way of speaking, what are we really admiring?

Speech communities . . . are formed by many features: age, geography, education, occupation, social position. Young people speak differently from old people, Kansans differently from Virginians, Yale graduates differently from Dannemora graduates. Now let us pose a delicate question: aren't some of these speech communities better than others? That is, isn't better language heard in some than in others?

Well, yes, of course. One speech community is always better than all the rest. This is the group in which one happens to find oneself. The writer would answer unhesitatingly that the noblest, loveliest, purest English is that heard in the Men's Faculty Club of San Jose State College, San Jose, California. He would admit, of course, that the speech of some of the younger members leaves something to be desired; that certain recent immigrants from Harvard, Michigan, and other foreign parts need to work on the laughable oddities lingering in their speech; and that members of certain departments tend to introduce a lot of queer terms that can only be described as jargon. But in general the English of the Faculty Club is ennobling and sweet.

As a practical matter, good English is whatever English is spoken by the group in which one moves contentedly and at ease. To the bum on Main Street in Los Angeles, good English is the language of other L.A. bums. Should he wander onto the campus of UCLA, he would find the walk there unpleasant, confusing, and comical. He might agree, if pressed, that the college man speaks "correctly" and he doesn't. But in his heart he knows better. He wouldn't talk like them college jerks if you paid him.

If you admire the language of other speech communities more than you do your own, the reasonable hypothesis is that you are dissatisfied with the community itself. It is not precisely other speech that attracts you but the people who use the speech. Conversely, if some language strikes you as unpleasant or foolish or rough, it is presumably because the speakers themselves seem so.

To many people, the sentence "Where is he at?" sounds bad. It is bad, they would say, in and of itself. The sounds are bad. But this is very hard to prove. If "Where is he at?" is bad because it has bad sound combinations, then presumably "Where is the cat?" or "Where is my hat?" are just as bad, yet no one thinks them so. Well, then, "Where is he at?" is bad because it uses too many words. One gets the same meaning from "Where is he?" so why add the *at?* True. Then "He going with us?" is a better sentence than "Is he going with us?" You don't really need the *is,* so why put it in?

Certainly there are some features of language to which we can apply the terms *good* and *bad, better* and *worse.* Clarity is usually better than obscurity; precision is better than vagueness. But these are not often what we have in mind when we speak of good and bad English. If we like the speech of upperclass Englishmen, the presumption is that we admire upperclass Englishmen — their characters, culture, habits of mind. Their sounds and words simply come to connote the people themselves and become admirable therefore. If we knew the same sounds and words from people who were distasteful to us, we would find the speech ugly.

This is not to say that correctness and incorrectness do not exist in speech. They obviously do, but they are relative to the speech community — or communities — in which one operates. As a practical matter, correct speech is that which sounds normal or natural to one's comrades. Incorrect speech is that which evokes in them discomfort or hostility or disdain.

Questions for Study and Discussion

1. What does Roberts mean when he says the best speech community "is the group in which one happens to find onself"?
2. How serious is Roberts when he says that the best English is found in the Men's Faculty Club of San Jose State College?
3. Why wouldn't a bum "talk like them college jerks if you paid him"?
4. Why do people, according to Roberts, admire some versions of English more than others? Does his argument apply to Rachel Jones's admiration of standard English?
5. What point is Roberts trying to make in the paragraph where he says that "'He going with us?' is a better sentence than 'Is he going with us?'"
6. What are the "features of language to which we can apply the terms *good* and *bad, better* and *worse*"?
7. Do you agree with Roberts's point that language connotes the people who speak it? Why or why not?
8. Roberts says that most people see speech as incorrect when it makes them feel uncomfortable or hostile toward the speaker. Relate this argument to Jones's problems with her peers.

Writing Assignment

Rachel Jones argues that standard English is "right." Roberts argues that correctness is "relative to the speech community." Drawing on these two essays, write an essay giving your opinion on the idea of correctness in language.

Acknowledgments

Chapter 1: Page 28, "Writing: The Agony and the Ecstasy" by Pamala Gasway. Reprinted by permission of Pamala Gasway. **Chapter 2:** Page 44, Excerpted with permission from "Unforgettable Albert Einstein" by Banesh Hoffman in the *Reader's Digest*, January 1968. Copyright © 1967 by The Reader's Digest Assn., Inc. **Chapter 4:** Page 114, "Black and Well-to-Do" by Andrea Lee from *The New York Times*, February 17, 1982. Copyright © 1982 by The New York Times Company. Reprinted by permission. **Chapter 5:** Page 143, From "Full Time Mom to Re-Entry Woman" by Elaine Pies. Reprinted by permission of Elaine Pies. Page 152, From "The Maker's Eye: Revising Your Own Manuscripts," by Donald M. Murray from *The Writer*, October 1973. Copyright 1973 by Donald M. Murray. Reprinted by permission of the author and Roberta Pryor, Inc. **Chapter 6:** Pages 167 and 183, From *Psychology and Life* by Phillip G. Zimbardo, 11th ed. Glenview, Illinois: Scott, Foresman and Company, 1985. Pages 168 and 180, From *Biology: The World of Life* by Robert A. Wallace, 4th ed. Glenview, Illinois: Scott, Foresman and Company, 1987. Page 172, Definition of *effective*. Copyright © 1981 by Houghton Mifflin Company. Reprinted by permission from THE AMERICAN HERITAGE DICTIONARY OF THE ENGLISH LANGUAGE. Page 185, From *America, Past and Present* by Robert Divine, T. H. Breen, George M. Frederickson, and R. Hal Williams, 2nd ed. Glenview, Illinois: Scott, Foresman and Company, 1987. Page 186, From "How to Read Faster" by Bill Cosby in *Power of the Printed Word Program*. Copyright © 1979 by International Paper Company. Reprinted by permission of International Paper. Page 190, From "Achievement of Desire" in *Hunger of Memory* by Richard Rodriguez. Boston: David R. Godine, 1982. Copyright © 1982 by Richard Rodriguez. Reprinted by permission of David R. Godine, Publisher. **Chapter 7:** Page 216, From Don Lago, "Symbols of Mankind," in *Science Digest*. March 1981, p. 16. © by The Hearst Corporation. **Chapter 8:** Page 222, From *The Great Chain of Life* by Joseph Wood Krutch. Copyright © 1956 by Joseph Wood Krutch. Copyright © renewed 1984 by Marcelle L. Krutch. Reprinted by permission of Houghton Mifflin Company. Page 226, Copyright © 1970 by Gore Vidal. Reprinted from *Homage to Daniel Shays: Collected Essays 1952–1972,* by Gore Vidal, by permission of Random House, Inc. Page 241, "No Job, But He Got His Money's Worth" by Robert Eherenman in the *Terre Haute Tribune Star*, June 4, 1988, p. 8. Reprinted with permission of Robert Eherenman. **Chapter 9:** Page 246, "In Defense of Hunting," by John C. Dunlap, in *Newsweek,* March 7, 1983. Copyright 1983 John C. Dunlap. Used by permission. Page 254, "Colleges Must Cut Costs, Help Students," *USA Today* Editorial in *USA Today,* March 3, 1987. Copyright 1987, USA TODAY. Reprinted with permission. Page 255, "Colleges Must Not Cut Quality to Curb Costs," by Sheldon Hackney in *USA Today,* March 3, 1987. Reprinted by permission of Dr. Sheldon Hackney, President, University of Pennsylvania. Page 257, "Taxpayer Subsidies Help Fuel Tuition Hikes," by William J. Bennett from *USA Today,* March 3, 1987. Page 258, "It's Simply Classical Economics," by Dennis O'Brien from *USA Today,* March 3, 1987. Reprinted by permission of Dennis O'Brien, President, University of Rochester. Page 274, "Grouping the Gifted," by Bruno Bettelheim from *NEA Journal,* Vol. 54, No. 3, March 1965. Copyright © 1965 NEA. Reprinted by permission. Page 276, "Grouping the Gifted is the Best Way," by Kenneth Mott from *NEA Journal,* Vol. 54, No. 3, March 1965. Copyright © 1965 NEA. Reprinted by permission. Page 280, "Teachers Must Stop Hitting Our Children," *USA Today,* Editorial in *USA Today,* March 11, 1988. Copyright 1988, USA TODAY. Reprinted with permission. Page 282, "Taming the Classroom 'Pit Bulls' " by Steve Marmel from *USA Today,* March 11, 1988. Copyright © 1988, Steve Marmel. Reprinted by permission. Page 282, "Barbarians Beget More Barbarians," by Sherry Roberts from *USA Today,* March 11, 1988. Copyright © 1988, Sherry Roberts. Reprinted with permission. Page 283, "Schools Must Be Able to Spank Their Students," by Dennis L. Cuddy from *USA Today,* August 30, 1988. Reprinted with permission of Dennis L. Cuddy, Ph.D. Page 285, "Maintaining Discipline Is a Two-Way Street," by Albert Shanker from *USA Today,* March 11, 1988. Reprinted with permission of Albert Shanker. **Chapter 10:** Page 339, "What's Wrong with Black English," by Rachel L. Jones in *Newsweek,* December 27, 1982. Copyright 1982 Rachel L. Jones. Used by permission. Page 342, Excerpt from pages 315–317 of *Understanding English* by Paul Roberts. Copyright © 1958 by Paul Roberts. Reprinted by permission of Harper & Row, Publishers, Inc.

Index

write, 305, 306, 320
Writer, 2–10
  purpose of, 5–6
    essays and, 49
  role of, 4–5
Writing. *See also* Writing as process;
    Writing process
  audience for, 6–8
    attitude of, 7
  environment for, 20
  of essays. *See* Writing essays
  general versus specific, 32–47. *See
    also* General versus specific
    writing
  reshaping in, 24–25
  specific. *See* Specific writing
  timed
    anxiety and, 82
    essay examination and, 81
  "Writing: The Agony and the Ecs-
    tasy," 28–29

Writing as process, 1–31
  computers in, 26–27
  drafting in, 19–22
  editing in, 25–26
  invention strategies in, 10–19
  revision in, 23–25
  writers in, 2–10
Writing essays
  examinations and, 78–82
  process of, 52–65
    audience in, 60
    drafting in, 61–63
    finding topic in, 52
    invention strategies to find topic
    in, 53–56
    organizing invention notes in, 61
    revising drafts in, 63–65
    thesis sentence in, 56–60
  product in, 48–51
  strategy of, 65–75
    analyzing causes in, 68–69

    analyzing process in, 66–68
    classifying in, 71–72
    comparing and contrasting in,
    69–71
    defining in, 73–74
    mixing in, 74–75
  in timed situations, 75–82
Writing process. *See also* Writing;
    Writing essays
  definition of, 1–2
  drafting and, 21–22
Writing situation, 4–5
  process analysis and, 67
  revision and, 119–123
5 W's plus H method, 17–19, 40–42

Yes/no note in margin of text, 179
yet, 101, 136, 295, 324, 325, 332
you, 288, 313, 314
your, 322
you're/your, 322
yous, 288